Understanding and Managing Strategic Governance

Understanding and Managing Strategic Governance

WEI SHI
ROBERT E. HOSKISSON

WILEY

Published by John Wiley & Sons, Inc., Hoboken, New Jersey.
Published simultaneously in Canada.

For general information on our other products and services or for technical support, please contact our Customer Care Department within the United States at (800) 762-2974, outside the United States at (317) 572-3993 or fax (317) 572-4002.

Wiley also publishes its books in a variety of electronic formats. Some content that appears in print may not be available in electronic formats. For more information about Wiley products, visit our website at www.wiley.com.

Library of Congress Cataloging-in-Publication Data is Available:

Names: Shi, Wei, 1981- author. | Hoskisson, Robert E., 1948-author.
Title: Understanding and managing strategic governance / Wei Shi, Robert
   Edwin Hoskisson.
Description: First edition. | Hoboken, New Jersey : Wiley, 2021. | Includes
   index.
Identifiers: LCCN 2021022872 (print) | LCCN 2021022873 (ebook) | ISBN
   9781119798255 (cloth) | ISBN 9781119798309 (adobe pdf) | ISBN
   9781119798286 (epub)
Subjects: LCSH: Corporate governance. | Decision making. | Strategic
   planning. | Information technology—Management.
Classification: LCC HD2741 .S4985 2021 (print) | LCC HD2741 (ebook) | DDC
   658.4—dc23
LC record available at https://lccn.loc.gov/2021022872
LC ebook record available at https://lccn.loc.gov/2021022873

Cover Design: Wiley
Cover Image: © Sergey Mironov\shutterstock

SKY10027859_070121

*The book is dedicated to our parents, Xiangsheng Shi,
Shimei Hui, Claude W. Hoskisson, and Carol B. Hoskisson,
for their constant love and support.*

Contents

Preface

Corporate executives are responsible for making a myriad of strategic decisions that shape a firm's competitiveness and performance. Yet, executives' strategic choices are constrained by governance actors, such as the board of directors or institutional investors, who can directly or indirectly influence corporate decisions. Although much has been written about corporate governance, there is no systematic analysis of how governance actors can influence strategic decisions. A company's strategic decisions such as R&D investment and business expansion determine its competitive position and ability to care for its stakeholders. Meanwhile, governance actors can influence these important decisions through deliberate involvement but also through unintentional means. Thus, understanding and managing how governance actors shape strategic decisions is crucial to both corporate executives and governance actors.

This book explains the impact of governance actors on strategic decisions, which is referred to as *strategic governance*, and provides suggestions on how corporate executives can leverage governance actors to make effective strategic decisions. To facilitate our discussion, we classify governance actors into internal and external governance actors and analyze their respective influences on a myriad of strategic decisions, including corporate strategy, competitive strategy, global strategy, innovation strategy, stakeholder strategy, and corporate political strategy. Internal governance actors refer to governance actors who have direct employment relationships with a firm and include the board of directors, peer executives, and employees. In contrast, external governance actors are those who do not have direct employment relationships with a firm and consist of investors, customers, suppliers, and external information intermediaries, such as financial analysts, rating agencies, and government regulators.

HOW TO USE THIS BOOK

The book is organized as follows. Chapters 1 and 2 introduce internal governance actors and external governance actors and discuss the channels through which they can play a governance role and influence executive decisions. From Chapters 3 to 8, we explain the influence of internal and external governance actors on a given specific strategy. We also provide our recommendations on how corporate executives can manage their relationships with governance actors to design effective strategies. In Chapter 9, we offer our evaluation of new trends in the governance landscape and our recommendations on how corporate executives and governance actors can work together to navigate these trends successfully.

In formulating each chapter, we carefully studied the most recent academic research to ensure that the content about strategic governance is up to date and accurate, as evidenced by the detailed endnotes for each chapter. In addition, we continuously read articles appearing in many different business publications (e.g., *Wall Street Journal, Bloomberg Businessweek, Fortune, Financial Times, Fast Company, Forbes,* and *Harvard Business Review,* to name a few). By studying a wide array of sources, we have identified valuable examples of how companies across the world are affected by governance actors and their consequences on managerial strategic decisions.

Each chapter begins with a boxed example labeled *Strategic Governance Challenge,* and there are breakout examples within the body of each chapter (labeled *Strategic Governance Highlight*) to illustrate critical governance issues of concern or provide more in-depth understanding of critical strategic issues resulting from governance activities in each chapter.

Although the book is written so that it can be read from cover to cover, each chapter also stands on its own. Readers can select and read the chapters most relevant to their interests (corporate strategy, competitive strategy, innovation strategy, global strategy, and so on).

AUDIENCE AND APPROACH

The book will be suitable for three groups of readers. First, corporate executives who directly get involved in making strategic decisions may find it interesting to learn how governance actors can affect their decisions. Managerial guidance provided by the book can help them capitalize on governance actors to make effective, viable strategic decisions. Second, governance actors such as board members and institutional investors may find the book valuable. This book will devote much attention to revealing some unintended consequences of governance actors on strategic choices, which is critical for governance actors to avoid or alleviate their negative implications. Third, this book covers a comprehensive list of topics at the interface of strategy and corporate governance. In this sense, it can benefit a general audience that seeks to understand the role of corporate governance in critical strategic decisions. Likewise, it might be useful as a textbook for strategic management or corporate governance courses. In particular, the book is apropos for board of director training, graduate university courses, and executive education programs.

To maximize your opportunities to understand as you read and think about how actual companies are managing the strategic governance challenges, we emphasize a lively and user-friendly writing style. Collectively, no other book on corporate governance presents you with the understanding of how salient current corporate governance trends are affecting major strategic decisions using a *combination* of useful and insightful *research* and *applications* in a variety of local and global companies as does this book. We provide managerial guidance on leveraging governance actors and managing conflicting interests to achieve sustainable competitive advantages. The interests of governance actors are often not aligned with each other in the short term, and governance actors may impose conflicting demands on corporate executives. Therefore, it is important for executives to understand and manage such conflicting demands and avoid strategic pitfalls that can harm a firm's long-term competitiveness. Thus, no other book provides managerial suggestions to facilitate ways of dealing with the salient governance issues of the day for both top managers as well as involved governance actors.

We believe that this book not only helps corporate executives and governance practitioners better understand their roles in shaping firm strategic decisions and how they can leverage governance actors to make more effective strategic decisions but it also offers an overview for a general audience to understand the current trends in corporate governance and how they influence key strategic decisions on which corporate executives and governance actors must accommodate each other to implement such decisions.

ACKNOWLEDGMENTS

We would like to thank Sheck Cho of Wiley for his belief in our work, and we appreciate the financial support of Miami Hebert Business School, University of Miami, and Jones Graduate School of Business, Rice University. In addition, we would like to thank Haicao Zhu and Kim Kijong for their research assistance and Cibeles Duran for her careful copyediting of the entire book. We would also like to thank Claudia Kolker for her feedback on the book's introduction.

We would like to acknowledge the many collaborators and colleagues who have made this book possible. Although many other sources are cited in the book, our direct collaborators whose work is described or reflected in the book include: Ruth Aguilera, Jay Barney, Berry Baysinger, Juan Bu, Lowell Busentiz, Bert Cannella, Guoli Chen, Tao Chen, Shih-Chi (Sana) Chiu, Kubilay Cirik, Brian Connelly, Marie Dasborough, Parthiban David, Mark DesJardine, Fabrizio Ferri, Igor Filatotchev, Eni Gambeta, Orhun Guldiken,

Abhinav Gupta, Cheng Gao, Javier Gimeno, Colby Green, Wayne Grossman, Jeff Harrison, Matt Hersel, Charles Hill, Mike Hitt, Duane Ireland, Fuxiu Jiang, Jing Jin, Richard Johnson, Dave Ketchen, Heechun Kim, Hicheon Kim, Dave King, Balaji Koka, Kang Lee, Haiyang Li, Jiangyan Li, Qiang (John) Li, Toby Li, Yu Li, Yadong Luo, Gerry McNamara, Philipp Meyer-Doyle, Doug Moesel, Herman Ndofor, Seemantini Pathak, Gerry Sanders, Doug Schuler, Laszlo Tihanyi, Tom Turk, Kevin Veenstra, Jack Walker, Bill Wan, Kai Wang, Jim Westphal, Mike Wright, Chongwu Xia, Xiwei Yi, Daphne Yiu, Anthea Zhang, Xiaojia Zheng, Zhihui Sun, and Daniel Zyung among others.

Wei Shi is an associate professor of management and Cesarano Faculty Scholar at Miami Herbert Business School, University of Miami. He obtained his MBA from Tulane University and PhD in business administration from Rice University. His primary research interest focuses on the influence of corporate governance actors and upper echelons on strategic decisions. He has taught courses in strategic management, corporate governance and organization, and corporate governance. His research has been published at outlets such as *Academy of Management Journal, Strategic Management Journal, Organization Science, Journal of Management,* and *Journal of Corporate Finance,* and covered by *Harvard Business Review* and the *Wall Street Journal.* He is a senior editor of *Corporate Governance: An International Review* and sits on the editorial boards of multiple journals, including *Strategic Management Journal, Organization Science, Journal of Management,* and *Global Strategy Journal.* He currently serves as a board member of International Corporate Governance Society and a representative-at-large for Strategic Leadership and Governance Interest Group of Strategic Management Society.

Robert E. Hoskisson is the George R. Brown Emeritus Chair of Strategic Management at the Jesse H. Jones Graduate School of Business, Rice University. He received his PhD from the University of California–Irvine. His research topics focus on corporate governance, acquisitions and divestitures, corporate and international diversification, and cooperative strategy. He has taught courses in corporate and international strategic management, cooperative strategy, and strategy consulting. He has co-authored over 30 books, including recent books on business strategy and competitive advantage. Dr. Hoskisson has served on several editorial boards for such publications as the *Strategic Management Journal* (associate editor), *Academy of Management Journal* (consulting editor), *Journal of International Business Studies* (consulting editor), *Journal of Management* (associate editor), and *Organization Science.* His research has appeared in over 130 publications, including the *Strategic Management Journal, Academy of Management Journal, Academy of Management Review, Organization Science, Journal of Management, Academy of Management Perspective, Academy of Management Executive, Journal of Management Studies, Journal of International Business Studies, Journal of Business Venturing, Entrepreneurship Theory and*

Practice, California Management Review, and *Journal of World Business.* Dr. Hoskisson is a fellow of the Academy of Management and also a fellow of the Strategic Management Society. He was a representative-at-large on the board of governors of the Academy of Management for three years. He also served as president of the Strategic Management Society and served on its executive committee for 6 years and on its board of directors for a total of 12 years.

CHAPTER 1

Introduction to Strategic Governance and Internal Governance Actors

---

BOX 1.1   Strategic Governance Challenge: Chaos in the Board Room

---

According to a recent survey of 341 chief marketing officers, chief marketing officers (CMOs) spend 68.5 percent of their time "managing the present" and only 31.5 percent "preparing for the future." The survey took place before the COVID-19 pandemic, making it especially telling since strategic marketing is meant to focus on developing initiatives that help build future competitiveness. This type of short-termism, research suggests, has been a rising trend among top management teams for decades. Executives, after all, must increasingly contend with pressures from performance-oriented governance actors such as activist shareholders when making strategic decisions. Some researchers, however, do not consider this trend problematic, asserting that company executives must manage firms for long-term value creation and short-term performance. Under this view, corporate leaders who avoid these twin imperatives do so at their peril.

While boards of directors are duly bound to act with care and loyalty and without conflicting interests for the benefit of shareholders, activist owners among the shareholders pursue returns without necessarily regarding long-term strategic visions, often playing a powerful role in short-termism.

One recommendation for short-termism includes "reward long-term investors" by creating more tiers for tax breaks for long-term investors because the current taxing system rewards trading securities rather than owning companies for the long term. Board members may also align executive compensation with long-term results to motivate them to carry out visions for the long run. These proposals typically try to address governance challenges due to activist shareholders steadily gaining influence on corporate strategic decisions, often forcing election of their board candidates to provide direct inputs into major strategic decisions.

In March 2020, for example, activist hedge fund Impala Asset Management LLC filed documents nominating two directors to Harley-Davidson's board. Impala investors also called for replacing then-CEO Matthew Levatich, who had shifted the firm's marketing focus to a more diverse customer base with Harley's "More Roads" campaign, away from its traditional base of 35- to 60-year-old Americans who buy expensive motorcycles. While Harley holds approximately 50 percent of the US market share in this segment, in recent years the company had been losing sales to bikes produced by BMW, Ducati, and Triumph. According to Impala, the management change was "needed because the current board wasn't proactive enough to address the poor performance," noting that, in 2019, Harley Davidson underperformed its peers and missed its unit shipping guidance for a fifth year in a row, even while Levatich's pay had been raised to more than $11 million, a figure higher than any he had been paid since taking over in 2015. In February 2020, a new CEO, Jochen Zeitz, was abruptly put in place due in part to the pressure of Impala as Levatich stepped down, and Zeitz is refocusing Harley on its traditional business.

In addition to pressuring for reshuffled management, activist shareholders may also use what are known as "wolf pack" strategies. Hedge fund activists team up to foster a common agenda, often forcing firm leaders to boost short-term performance at the expense of the interests of long-term investors and other stakeholders. Such pressures have a compounding effect. One director notes: "From dealing with multiple crises, to being sued, to orchestrating spinoffs, buyouts, and mergers, to dealing with activists, these all bring their own set of challenges." The director makes the point that tough issues, once outlier events, have become commonplace as company leaders come under an increasingly "hot spotlight" from multiple stakeholders, forcing directors to answer more quickly and proactively.

We have written this book to enable practitioners to navigate the new, ever-more challenging governance environment. Managers and board members urgently need up-to-date, sophisticated comprehension on what we call strategic governance: the tools and orientation to fully understand and then manage the increasingly chaotic world of corporate governance and strategic decision-making.

Sources: Campbell, P. (2020). Managing tough issues in the boardroom. https://boardmember.com/managing-tough-issues-in-the-boardroom/, accessed July 13, 2020; Coppola, G., & Weiss, R. (2020). Harley-Davidson gets an unlikely rider. *Bloomberg Businessweek*, July 27, 8–10; Sampson, R. C., & Shi, Y. (2020). Are US firms becoming more short-term oriented? Evidence of shifting firm time horizons from implied discount rates, 1980–2013, *Strategic Management Journal*, forthcoming; Welch, D., Deveau, S., & Coppola, G. (2020). Activist battling Harley's board urges focus on core riders. *Bloomberg*, www.bloomberg.com, March 20; Christie, A. L. (2019). The new hedge fund activism: Activist directors and the market for corporate quasi-control. *Journal of Corporate Law Studies* 19 (1): 1–41; Moorman, C., & Kirby, L. (2019). How marketers can overcome short-termism. *Harvard Business Review Digital Articles*, www.hbs.com, 2–5; Thomas, L. (2019). Stop panicking about corporate short-termism. *Harvard Business Review Digital Articles*, www.hbs.com, 2–4; Porter, M.E. (1992). Capital disadvantage: America's failing capital investment system. *Harvard Business Review* 70 (5): 65–82.

How many corporate governance teams are equipped to face the strategic challenges spurred by the cross currents within the contemporary activist environment? Authentic strategic governance must go beyond simply making a set of decisions in response to a specific issue, and move toward a comprehensive approach for dealing with activist governance actors. Although activists are mostly found outside the firm, more are working from the inside upon the election of activist representative board members. As activist governance players proliferate and refine new techniques (as those described in the Strategic Governance Challenge Box 1.1), top executives and boards of directors must make critical strategic decisions, often under conflicting pressures. Top managers face the difficulty of needing to move the company forward while managing the challenges to their leadership from outside stakeholders, many of whom hold leverage over firm ownership voting rights, wield power to marshal governance advocates, and exert influence over the views of journalists and analysts.

The Harley-Davidson case that opens this chapter stands as a powerful example of how activist shareholders, the primary initiators of activist campaigns, often try to gain control of a company or replace management. But the activist may force major corporate change through other ways, such as by demanding divestitures and selloffs.[1] Announcements to sway the strategic decision-making of a board and CEO have significant influence on stock prices.[2] Activist announcements often impact stock market analysts' views, prompting changes in analysts' buy or sell recommendations, which may influence a firm to change its strategy.[3]

Generally, hedge funds and activist pension funds originate this kind of activism. But, as we will see in our book, other corporations also engage in external governance campaigns through hostile takeover attempts for corporate control or by buying noncontrolling block ownership. Even shareholder governance watchdogs, such as the Institutional Shareholder Services (ISS) and Glass Lewis, as well as government regulators such as the Securities and Exchange Commission, may take actions that demand a strategic response. To manage these types of external governance actors, a firm's internal governance team needs to understand how to best interact with these actors and how to make strategic decisions that will respond to or counteract their targeting, while at the same time capitalizing on the expertise and experiences that these external influencers provide. Boards and managers must also prepare to handle legal interventions, as activist shareholders increasingly turn to the courts in efforts to maintain shareholder rights and value. Responding to these actions is proving expensive; the price of director and officer (D&O) insurance, for example, rose by 104 percent in the United States in the first quarter of 2020 compared with the same period a year earlier. The price rose by 255 percent for the same timeframe in Australia.[4]

The board of directors serves as a firm's central internal governance mechanism. Directors monitor management, provide advice on major strategic decisions, and direct employment relationships especially by selecting top executives and establishing executive compensation structures. Meanwhile, owners, especially institutional owners, are the main external governance mechanism for publicly traded firms. Historically, top executives have largely held control over major strategic decisions as boards only symbolically monitor, providing merely a "rubber stamp" on the critical strategic decisions.[5] Although this tendency continues, especially in countries with large family-controlled diversified business groups like in India and many Asian (South Korea, Japan, Taiwan) and Latin American countries,[6] change is occurring quite drastically in Western countries, especially in the United States and United Kingdom. Activist investors, who exercise their voice about strategic decisions and executive compensation, drive the change. Their central approach consists of buying significant stakes of shares to seek control of firms or to use the proxy voting system to place activist investor representatives on boards of directors of targeted firms. Activists lobby corporations for corporate governance changes along with proxy intermediaries and governance watchdogs such as ISS and Glass Lewis. Government policy and associated agencies have also fostered more shareholder power and transparency through increased regulation as with the Sarbanes-Oxley (SOX) and Dodd-Frank Acts. These combined forces have increased the potency of shareholder activism, especially when other institutional investors (even index focused institutional investors) follow the lead of the activists.[7]

Although the activism noted above has caused turmoil among firms' board members and top management teams, the practice has created more intense governance and has given more voice to shareholders on strategy issues. For instance, activists have pursued more long-term compensation packages, which has created pressure for improved performance. Yet the greatly added pressure to perform has led some firm leaders to "cook the books," contributing to more financial fraud.[8] Another indirect effect of activism impacts areas such as supply chains and market power, such as when a firm targeted by activists causes pressure on suppliers, especially those heavily dependent on the target for a large portion of their sales, to reduce costs.[9]

These increasing and sometimes severe impacts of shareholder activism explain the burgeoning number of academic treatises on corporate governance, usually defined as a set of mechanisms used to manage stakeholder relationships, establish rules to determine and control enterprise strategic decision-making, and distribute the returns from investments.[10] At its core, corporate governance seeks to help ensure effective strategic decisions, facilitate the firm's strategic goals, and foster stakeholders' cooperation to achieve those goals. However, though the goals may be straightforward, the practice can prove difficult because of the many potentially conflicting interests of the various stakeholders.

Although substantial research examines the impact of these influences on governance outcomes, such as executive compensation,[11] less focus occurs on the effects that governance actors have on the various areas of organizational development, including corporate strategy (such as acquisitions and divestitures), competitive strategy, global expansion, and stakeholder policies like more socially responsible and nonmarket investments. We aim to provide strategic governance recommendations and direction for executives as well as board members to understand antecedents that trigger interaction between firm executives and activist governance actors, what the consequences of responses might be, and possible strategic actions that firm executives and governance actors might take under specific strategic governance situations. Such guidance might become particularly important when conflicting influences arise among executives, board members, and outside governance stakeholders during key strategic decisions. We lay out the organization of our book in Figure 1.1. Our discussion of internal governance mechanisms in this chapter will proceed to an exploration of external governance mechanisms in Chapter 2, followed by an examination of the direct effects of governance actors in the following chapters on specific strategies and strategic decision-making and the indirect effects on other stakeholders, including competitors, suppliers, and customers, while tracking the impact on focal firm performance and shareholder returns.

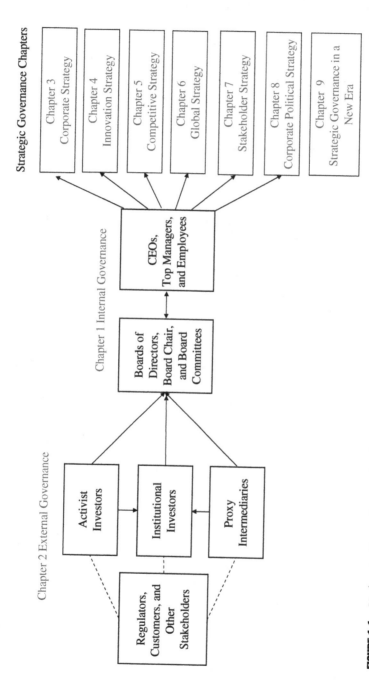

Strategic Governance Chapters

Chapter 3
Corporate Strategy

Chapter 4
Innovation Strategy

Chapter 5
Competitive Strategy

Chapter 6
Global Strategy

Chapter 7
Stakeholder Strategy

Chapter 8
Corporate Political Strategy

Chapter 9
Strategic Governance in a New Era

Chapter 1 Internal Governance

CEOs, Top Managers, and Employees

Boards of Directors, Board Chair, and Board Committees

Chapter 2 External Governance

Activist Investors

Institutional Investors

Proxy Intermediaries

Regulators, Customers, and Other Stakeholders

FIGURE 1.1 Understanding and managing the strategic governance challenge.

INTERNAL GOVERNANCE

Although corporate executives are responsible for making a myriad of strategic decisions that contribute to a firm's competitiveness and performance, their choices are constrained by internal corporate governance actors such as the board of directors and employees. While much has been written about internal governance, especially about boards, no systematic analysis exists on how internal governance actors influence strategic decisions. We examine relatively unchartered territory by examining the actors' impacts on decision-making, beginning with an analysis of the different board attributes and tools that directors use to govern firm executives and shape decisions. Our discussion will include a look at how employees, as another important internal stakeholder, can also shape corporate governance and strategic decisions.

Corporate governance, though more challenging than in the past, is critical to firm success. Under its scope, directors make the vital decision of selecting an appropriate CEO to guide the strategic direction of the firm. If the board makes an unwise choice, not only in selecting but also in setting the compensation of the strategic leader, shareholders and stakeholders all suffer. As such, effective leadership succession plans and appropriate monitoring and direction-setting efforts by the board of directors contribute positively to a firm's performance. Boards face unforeseen circumstances, as in the need to replace a CEO due to financial misconduct. In this case, research shows that directors tend to choose a successor with a degree from a religious university, since such a choice has been shown to reduce the likelihood of misconduct.[12] Similarly, when KPMG, one of the big four accounting firms, was questioned by the Internal Revenue Service and found culpable of engaging in inappropriate tax shelters for years in the late 1990s and early 2000s, the directors of the company hired a new CEO, appointed a former judge onto its board, and established board committees focused on fostering better professional ethics and risk compliance norms through its operations committee. Likewise, they pursued vigorous ethics and risk training for all employees.[13] Their efforts saved KPMG from suffering a fate similar to Arthur Andersen, a former "Big Five" accounting firm that ceased to operate due to the Enron fiasco.

In addition, choosing an outside versus an inside CEO (one who is currently employed at the firm) can lead to more strategic risk taking for the organization, but such increased risk taking can result in performance extremeness.[14] Increased strategic risk taking is analogous to swinging for the fence in baseball (trying to hit a home run). Although Babe Ruth set home run records, he also set record strikeouts at the plate. Appropriate executive compensation also influences risk taking. Too much emphasis on CEO stock options leads to excessive strategic risk taking and can lead to some good performance, though poor performance (striking out) is more likely.[15]

PURPOSES FOR BOARDS OF DIRECTORS

A board of directors is a group of individuals elected by shareholders whose primary responsibility is to act in the best interests of stakeholders, particularly owners, by formally monitoring and controlling the firm's top-level managers. Board members reach their expected objectives by using their powers to set strategies and policies for the organization and reward and discipline top managers. The work of boards, though important to all shareholders, becomes especially important to a firm's individual shareholders with small ownership percentages since they depend heavily on the directors to represent their interests.

Unfortunately, evidence suggests that boards have not been highly effective in monitoring and controlling top-level managers' decisions and subsequent actions.[16] This problematic conclusion may be even more prevalent in emerging-market countries. However, large differences exist in the arrangement of governance systems between developed and emerging markets around the world. The Strategic Governance Highlight (Box 1.2) provides an illustration of how boards conduct strategic governance in Europe, Japan, and China. Although insider-dominated boards still prevail in much of the world, the trend is changing, especially in developed countries like Germany and Japan, but also in emerging market countries like China.

As noted earlier, among emerging countries and historically in the United States, inside managers dominate boards of directors. Yet, we concur with the widely accepted view that a board with a significant percentage of its membership composed of the firm's top-level managers provides relatively weak monitoring and control of managerial decisions. Under such a board, managers sometimes use their power to select and compensate directors and exploit their personal ties to implement strategies that favor executive interests. In 1984, in response to this concern, the New York Stock Exchange (NYSE) implemented a rule requiring outside directors to head the audit committee. Subsequently, after the SOX Act was passed in 2002, other new rules required that independent outside directors lead important committees, such as the audit, compensation, and nominating and governance committees. Policies of the NYSE now require companies to maintain boards of directors that are composed of a majority of outside independent directors, as well as to maintain fully independent audit committees.

But while the additional scrutiny of corporate governance practices has led boards to devote significant attention to recruiting quality independent directors,[17] the emphasis on outside directors has led to 40 percent of boards having only one inside manager on the board: the CEO. This scenario produces another less-than-ideal dynamic that leads to less monitoring of executive

BOX 1.2　Strategic Governance Highlight: Boards in Europe, Japan, and China

Corporate governance is of concern to individual firms as well as nations. Although corporate governance reflects company standards, it also collectively reflects the societal standards of countries. Standards are changing, even in emerging economies, such as in the level of independence of board members to enact practices for effective oversight of a firm's internal control efforts. Since firm leaders seek to invest in countries with national governance standards that are acceptable to them, especially when expanding geographically into emerging markets, national governments pay attention to corporate governance.

German firms with more than 2,000 employees are required to have a two-tiered board structure that places the responsibility of monitoring and controlling managerial (or supervisory) decisions and actions in the hands of a separate group. All the functions of strategy and management are the responsibility of the management board. However, appointment to management falls under the responsibility of the supervisory tier, while employees, union members, and shareholders appoint members to this supervisory tier. Proponents of the German structure suggest that it helps prevent corporate wrongdoing and rash decisions by "dictatorial CEOs," making the board more stakeholder- versus shareholder-dominant. However, critics maintain that the structure slows decision-making and often ties a CEO's hands during strategy development and implementation. The corporate governance practices in Germany makes it difficult to restructure companies as quickly as in the US. Also, because of the role of local government (through the board structure) and the power of banks in Germany's corporate governance structure, private shareholders rarely have major ownership positions in German firms.

As in Germany, banks in Japan have an important role in financing and monitoring large public firms. Because the main bank in a *keiretsu* (a group of firms tied together by cross-shareholdings) owns a large share position and holds a large amount of corporate debt, it has the closest relationship with a firm's top-level managers. The main bank managers provide financial advice to firm leaders and also closely monitor managers, although they have become less significant in fostering corporate restructuring. Japanese firms are also concerned with a broader set of stakeholders than are firms in the US, including employees, suppliers, and customers, because of their group ties. Moreover, a *keiretsu* is more than an economic concept—it, too, is a family-like network. Some believe, though, that extensive cross-shareholdings impede the type of structural change that is needed to improve the nation's corporate governance practices. However, recent changes in the governance code in Japan have been fostering better opportunities for improved shareholder monitoring.

China has a unique and large economy, mixed with both socialist and market-oriented traits. Over time, the government has done much to improve the corporate governance of listed companies, particularly in light of increasing privatization of businesses and the development of equity markets. However, the stock markets in China remain young and in development. In their early years, these markets were weak because of significant insider trading, but with stronger governance, they have improved. There has been a gradual decline in the equity held in state-owned enterprises while the number and percentage of private firms have grown, but the state still relies on direct and/or indirect controls to influence the strategies that firms employ. Even private firms try to develop political ties with government officials because of their role in providing access to resources and to the economy. Political governance—control mechanisms used by political actors to achieve their political objectives—permeates listed firms in China. In fact, oftentimes political governance supersedes corporate governance. At times, executives and boards must satisfy government-mandated social goals above maximizing shareholder returns. Such a model sets up potential conflicts between the owners, particularly between the state owner and the private equity owners of such enterprises.

Along with changes in the governance systems of specific countries, multinational companies' boards and managers also evolve (see Chapter 6). For example, firms that have entered more international markets are likely to have more top executives with greater international experience and to have a larger proportion of foreign owners and foreign directors on their boards. These encounters tend to shift governance systems toward more stakeholder-oriented systems in the United States and more shareholder-oriented systems in Europe and China and other emerging market countries.

Sources: Shi, W., Aguilera, R., & Wang. K. (2020). State ownership and securities fraud: A political governance perspective. *Corporate Governance: An International Review* 28 (2): 157–176; Aguilera, R. V., Valentina, M., & Ilir, H. (2019). International corporate governance: A review and opportunities for future research. *Journal of International Business Studies* 50 (4): 457–498; Oehmichen, J. (2018). East meets West—corporate governance in Asian emerging markets:

A literature review and research agenda, *International Business Review* 27: 465–480; Foley, S. (2017). The battle of the US corporate governance codes, *Financial Times*, www.ft.com, February 5; Soltani, B., & Maupetit, C. (2015). Importance of core values of ethics, integrity and accountability in the European corporate governance codes, *Journal of Management & Governance* 19: 259–284; Aguilera, R. V., Judge, W. Q., & Terjesen, S. A. (2018). Corporate governance deviance, *Academy of Management Review* 43: 87–109; Chie, A., & Giovanni, G. (2017). Unstash the cash! Corporate governance reform in Japan, *Journal of Banking & Financial Economics* 37: 51–69; Lai, L., & Tam, H. (2017). Corporate governance, ownership structure and managing earnings to meet critical thresholds among Chinese listed firms, *Review of Quantitative Finance & Accounting* 48: 789–818; Du, X., Jian, W., & Lai, S. (2017). Do foreign directors mitigate earnings management? Evidence from China, *International Journal of Accounting* 52: 142–177; Lincoln, J. R., Guillot, D., & Sargent, M. (2017). Business groups, networks, and embeddedness: Innovation and implementation alliances in Japanese electronics, 1985–1998, *Industrial & Corporate Change* 26: 357–378; Schuler, D., Shi, W., Hoskisson, R. E., & Chen, T. (2016). 'Windfalls of emperors' sojourns: Stock market reactions to Chinese firms hosting high ranking government officials. *Strategic Management Journal* 38 (8): 1668–1687; Berkman, H., Cole, R. A., & Fu, L. J. (2014). Improving corporate governance where the state is the controlling block holder: Evidence from China, *European Journal of Finance* 20: 752–777; Kosaku, N. (2014). Japan seeks to lure investors with improved corporate governance, *Wall Street Journal*, www.wsj.com, June 28; Li, J., & Qian, C. (2013). Principal-principal conflicts under weak institutions: A study of corporate takeovers in China, *Strategic Management Journal* 34: 498–508; Fiss, C., & Zajac, E.J. (2004). The diffusion of ideas over contested terrain: The (non)adoption of a shareholder value orientation among German firms, *Administrative Science Quarterly* 49: 501–534.

decisions by the board,[18] since monitoring becomes more focused on financial control rather than strategic control, especially without sufficient insider managers to properly inform the outside members about the intricacies of long-term strategic decisions and how they are implemented.[19] In fact, such boards (with the CEO as the only insider) pay the chief executive excessively, have more instances of financial misconduct, and have lower performance than boards with more than one insider.[20] Boards should seek balance to be sufficiently knowledgeable and achieve the most effective approach to fulfilling their purpose over time in representing stakeholder interests. Next, we take a closer look at board characteristics, monitoring, and setting executive compensation to further understand strategic governance.

BOARD STRUCTURE AND PROCESS: EFFECTIVE BOARD STRATEGIC CONTROL AND MONITORING

Mainly driven by the argument under agency theory that top managers have too much power and thereby use the firm for better perquisites (such as compensation), board members abide by an institutional norm holding that governance should be focused on control and overcoming potential managerial malfeasance, which is often labeled as the *audit culture*.[21] Too focused on auditing, board members may not sufficiently emphasize the need for stewardship and providing strategic advice. As boards are primarily formed to oversee the decision-making processes of corporations, while CEOs and the top management teams are in charge of decision management,[22] strategic governance should center on better use of the human and social capital of board members to improve, and not just watch over, strategic decision-making.[23]

Because of the audit culture found on many boards, outside directors have not been used fully to contribute to strategic decision-making. However, outside board members can help shape the content, context, and conduct of strategy formulation.[24] According to a survey by Russell Reynolds Associates,[25] boards of companies that exceeded total shareholder return (TSR) compared to relevant benchmarks for two or more years in a row spend more time on forward-looking, value-creating activities such as strategic planning and review and oversight on major strategic transactions, and less time on audit or compliance activities than their fellow directors on other boards. As a result, "the emphasis on board independence and control may hinder the board contribution to the strategic decision-making."[26]

Board Chair

To facilitate better strategic governance, we examine the relationship between the board chair and the chief executive officer. As mentioned, the audit culture prompted by agency theory[27] creates a relationship between a CEO and a control-oriented chair marked by distance and authority. This relationship does not always need to be solely control-oriented and can have a collaborative approach in which the board chair provides strategic advice. For example, when Hewlett-Packard split into two companies, Meg Whitman became CEO of Hewlett-Packard, Inc., and at the same time board chair of Hewlett-Packard Enterprise. She said in a CNBC interview: "I know the role of the chairman, and I know how it is different than the role of the CEO. The chairman is not there to run the company. The chairman [role] is to help the board be productive, help the CEO be successful." As Whitman suggests, the chairman may play a supportive role to the CEO, providing a close source of advice and guidance.[28] Also, separating the CEO and chair roles (as opposed to cases in which the CEO is also the chair), as Whitman did, may enhance CEO–board collaboration by reducing the demands on the chief executive's time, allowing the CEO to specialize in managing the firm's strategy and operations.

Although many firms still assign the chairman position to the CEO to provide a unitary authority structure,[29] some scholars under the agency theory advocate for separate roles to provide better control of management.[30] Having the positions as separate roles with a collaborative board chair can provide both improved strategy and better board leadership. Research supports this conclusion, finding that board chairs can provide significant value (up to 9 percent improved firm performance) through advice and counsel, legitimacy, information linkages, and preferential access to external commitments and support.[31] This approach proves particularly beneficial when firms face fast-changing external environments such as in high technology firms. In essence, by providing improved strategic governance, board chairs can add significantly to firm value.

Board Committees

Board members who chair key board committees can also add to firm value through their approach to strategic governance.[32] In fact, the importance of board committees has grown over time due to increased legal requirements and the growing complexity of the business environment.[33] Research tells us about the overall board structure or board member demographics, such as functional backgrounds and ages, but not so much about the detailed work of directors that mostly occurs in committees. In particular, all boards, especially in Western cultures, have committees that identify new board members and facilitate CEO search processes (nominating and governance committees), set executive compensation (compensation committee), and oversee financial reporting (audit committee). These three dominant committees are today required by public stock exchanges and the SOX Act. The SOX Act additionally requires that they be headed by independent outside directors—those that are not inside managers and have no stakeholder affiliation (such as legal representation or customer or supplier relationship). The three committees, part of the audit culture, function to protect shareholders and other stakeholders from managerial malfeasance. Managers should not have the power to nominate board members that supervise their decisions, set their own compensation, or make aggressive or fraudulent accounting decisions.

In theory, shareholders appoint directors. In practice, however, shareholders simply ratify director candidates selected by the board's nominating committee, although the proxy voting process has become increasingly complex due to activist discontent.[34] As described in more detail in the Strategic Governance Highlight (Box 1.3), activist board members are elected to targeted boards and often represent *wolf pack* hedge funds who have teamed together. These board members push for share price increases and other activist agenda items, which may come at the expense of other stakeholders. The nomination process is hence critical in making appropriate director appointments, as the

BOX 1.3   Strategic Governance Highlight: How Did Boards Become More Activist-Oriented?

The 1980s was known for hostile takeovers and the use of junk bonds to facilitate large takeovers by corporate raiders. This period inspired a book and movie titled *Barbarians at the Gate*, which chronicles the takeover by Kolberg, Kravis, and Roberts (KKR) of RJR Nabisco in a stunning $24 billion deal. However, in the early 1990s, the market for corporate control became dampened after the collapse of the junk bond market and the jailing of Michael Milken and the failure of his firm, Drexel Burnham Lambert.

In the late 1990s, institutional investors, such as pension funds and mutual funds, became more active. Although institutional investor activism rose in this period, the market for corporate control declined because of defensive actions by boards that largely insulated firms from pressure. But activist hedge funds stepped in with more offensive actions. In the 2000s, activist hedge funds began to nominate unaffiliated board members and influence their election to boards. One legal observer called this approach *quasi-control* because it uses board power rather than just ownership voice, as pension fund holders had used in the 1990s, although it falls short of actual corporate control. When activist fund representatives fill one or more board seats, their influence often leads to the replacement of significant corporate managers, such as the CEO or CFO, and the replacements often favor the strategic decisions preferred by the activists.

In *wolf-pack activism,* funds ready for aggressive campaigns team together with other activist investors. This tactic may include securing minority board representation (especially by way of negotiated settlement), which represents a much cheaper alternative to engaging in a proxy contest or pursuing a hostile takeover. In this manner, activist hedge funds can pursue a number of different companies compared to focusing their efforts entirely on one or two targets. As such, the amount of capital that they need to invest in specific target companies has gone down over time.

What regulatory and other changes occurred to allow for an atmosphere of wolf-pack activism? Changes in Securities and Exchange Commission regulations and the entrance of shareholder proxy advisory intermediaries facilitated the changes. The SEC enacted a proxy access rule in 2010, though it was later vacated by the US Court of Appeals for the District of Columbia Circuit in 2011. However, in recent years, many S&P 500 companies have adopted proxy access bylaws, which usually allow shareholders who hold 3 percent of the shares of a company for at least three years the ability to nominate directors without going through a proxy contest. Rather than risk a proxy contest, firms have allowed more access to the nomination process. In fact, 88 percent of the board seats won in 2016 were achieved through settlement agreements rather than proxy contests, compared to 70 percent in 2013 and 66 percent in 2014.

Proxy advisory intermediaries, such as Institutional Shareholder Services (ISS) and Glass Lewis, have enabled the power of other institutional investors, often in support of the activist shareholders. Because institutional investors are significant shareholders, often having shares over the SEC 3 percent rule, they hold power to nominate directors directly during the proxy voting process. And because institutional investors frequently follow large proxy advisor voting recommendations, activist investors team with these intermediaries to get their board members elected. Under SEC rule changes and proxy advisor power, firm leaders are more likely to settle with activist shareholders and support a campaign for minority board representation rather than risk a negative vote in a proxy contest.

Sources: Benoit, D., & Grant, K. (2015). Activists' secret ally: Big mutual funds – large investors quietly back campaigns to force changes at US companies. *Wall Street Journal*, www.wsj.com, August 10 www.wsj.com/articles/activist-investors-secret-ally-big-mutual-funds-1439173910; Coffee J. C., & Palia, D. (2016). The wolf at the door: The impact of hedge fund activism on corporate governance. *Journal of Corporation Law* 41(3): 545–607; Baigorri, M., & Kumar, N. (2017). Black swans, wolves at the door: The rise of activist investors. *Bloomberg*, www.bloomberg.com, July 12; Christie, A. L. (2019). The new hedge fund activism: Activist directors and the market for corporate quasi-control. *Journal of Corporate Law Studies* 19(1): 1–41; Wong, Y.T.F. (2020). Wolves at the door: A closer look at hedge fund activism. *Management Science* 66(6): 2347–2371.

effectiveness of the board with regard to its monitoring role depends on the quality of the board members selected.[35]

For board members to affect strategic governance, the same standard applies. Corporations often replace one or more directors each year. Each replacement represents a chance to shape the board to meet the corporation's strategic needs. An unexpected death of one director can shape corporate acquisitions strategy, which indirectly shows the impact on strategy that even one director can have.[36] Not surprisingly, nominating committees increasingly seek board members with specific functional expertise, such as

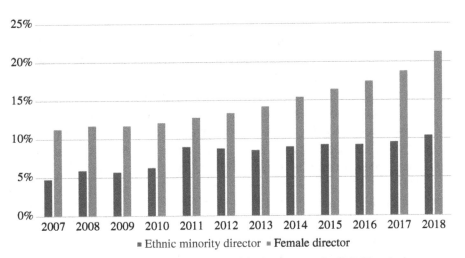

Note: Data taken from the ISS Director database and calculation based on a sample of 1,814 firms that have
belonged to the S&P 1500 index. Ethnic minority director refers to the percentage of African American,
Hispanic, and Asian directors and female director refers to the percentage of female directors.

FIGURE 1.2   Board diversity of S&P 1500 firms.

in labor, environmental, compensation, or public policy. For example, when
a firm is experiencing operational problems, appointing a chief operating
officer (COO) or CEO with operational experience from another firm helps
the appointing firm to improve its performance.[37]

Nomination committees may also seek directors to match diversity
characteristics of customers or to extend operations into global markets. Diversity
may improve board effectiveness. Growing evidence suggests that board
gender diversity is associated with a number of desirable organizational outcomes,
such as avoidance of securities fraud,[38] more vigilant monitoring of the
top management teams,[39] more ethical firm behavior,[40] and higher accounting-
based performance and stock market returns.[41] As Figure 1.2 shows, boards
have become more diverse over time in regard to appointing more females and
ethnic minority members. But these positives are stymied if, for example, solely
one woman is placed on a board as a token to create institutional legitimacy.[42]
Recognizing the positive effects of diverse membership on boards, institutional
investors are using their power to push companies to appoint more women
and minorities. For instance, BlackRock, a large mutual fund manager, suggested
that diverse boards "make better decisions" and that it planned to focus
on the issue in discussions with company leaders ahead of annual meetings.[43]
Yet we note that diverse demographic characteristics do not always mean that
the new "diverse" members will have diverse opinions as current board members.
For example, directors are inclined to select a demographically different

new director who can be recategorized as an in-group member based on his or her similarities to them on other shared demographic characteristics, and such recategorization also increases demographically different directors' tenures and likelihood of becoming board committee members.[44] We also note that board demographic diversity can be detrimental to unity among members, making firms become attractive targets for hostile stakeholders; interestingly, as a result, firms with a more demographically diverse board are more likely to be targeted by activist investors, presumably because boards are unable to form an effective coalition against activist investors.[45]

The nominating and governance committees—sometimes held as a single, combined committee—carry out important functions. The governance committee can conduct a management audit, assessing the capabilities and potential of the company's board and management team, and suggest training to sensitize the directors to environmental, regulatory, or diversity issues that affect strategy. Such an audit focuses board attention on human assets and helps plan changes in leadership. In fact, succession planning forms another crucial issue under the purview of the governance committee. When a CEO is dismissed or moves to another firm, a board of directors without a strong succession plan may scramble for a replacement, which may lead to serious strategic consequences. Many boards have authorized their nominating committees to seek out potential executive talent to avoid shocks upon surprise departures. Some boards hold an annual joint session of the compensation committee, the nominating and governance committees, and the executive committee to discuss succession planning and executive resource development. Another important issue lies in appointing qualified board committee chairs. When highly qualified chairs are passed over and less qualified members receive chair appointments, the selections can lead to a negative board climate,[46] which also may affect strategic governance. To avoid pitfalls from inadequate chair appointments or succession shocks, directors should formalize succession processes that can improve their information collecting and processing abilities and give rise to a greater quantity and quality of qualified chairs and CEO candidates.[47] The following example demonstrates the hazard in not having a succession plan in place.

In mid-2020, leaders of Cerberus Capital Management, a private equity firm holding more than 5 percent ownership of Commerzbank, the second largest German bank, sent a letter to the board chair that the bank "has not presented a coherent strategy and has failed to implement even its own progressively less-ambitious plans." Cerberus heads wanted to name two new supervisory board members to encourage significant changes to Commerzbank's supervisory board, management board, and the strategic plan. One month later, over disagreements with Cerberus (the bank's second largest shareholder), Commerzbank CEO Martin Zielke announced unexpectedly that he would step down from his position. The abrupt announcement came as a surprise and reduced the value of the firm, while the departure left a governance void at the bank.[48] Compared to German competitor Deutsche Bank's 1 percent loss, Coomerzbank shares fell 26 percent, when a new CEO was appointed in September 2020.[49]

Although board committees supervise managerial incentives and behavior, the relationship between committee chairs and top managers does not have to be adversarial. In fact, the compensation committee sets appropriate incentives so that the top managers, especially the CEO, will work on behalf of shareholders and stakeholders to create a strategy and make strategic decisions that will build both firm growth and stakeholder wealth. Pay structure for the top management team by the compensation committee creates a definite strategic governance issue.[50] A large pay differential among top management team members can give rise to problematic social comparison, since a smaller number of officers may get large pay packages, whereas others receive less.[51] Large pay dispersions can generate less cooperative teamwork and less effective overall strategy implementation, ultimately leading to lower firm performance. For instance, a large pay gap between CEOs and non-CEO top executives provides strong incentives for the latter to resort to misconduct as a means of outperforming others.[52] Relatedly, high pay dispersion among employees in R&D groups leads to less innovation,[53] which is especially detrimental to firms in the pharmaceutical industry or other industries that depend on innovation for continued profitability. Collective incentives focused on the top management team can also influence how much the whole firm will focus on corporate social responsibility issues.[54] Also, by setting the pay culture for the firm, not only for top managers but for employees overall, the compensation committee influences strategic implementation throughout the organization.

Audit committees may likewise influence strategy, albeit at times indirectly. As noted earlier, boards with a majority of outside directors depend on financial outcomes to judge firm performance, or what is labeled *financial control*.[55] Comparatively, a strategic control emphasis allows for the evaluation of strategic situations subjectively, based on the quality of board member strategic comprehension during decision-making. If no one on the audit committee can help inform outside board members to understand the strategic contingencies involved, their sole dependence on their accounting and financial orientation will likely affect the firm's strategy, since managers will take actions that involve less risk, such as more unrelated diversification.[56] That is, if managers feel that they are judged on financial outcomes alone rather than on the upfront agreement of the board (or committee) on the quality of their decisions using strategic controls, they are likely to seek to diversify the firm to reduce their employment risk (see Chapter 3).[57]

Business-level strategy (strategic positioning within the same industry) is also affected by these control systems. In a classic strategy book titled *Organizational Strategy, Structure, and Process*,[58] two polar business-level strategies are defined: defenders and prospectors. Defender strategies target stable and defensible market domains, seeking to solve the engineering problem by focusing efforts on producing and distributing goods and services in the most efficient and cost-effective manner possible. Alternatively, prospectors pursue strategies that tend to compete by continually finding and exploiting new product and market opportunities, seeking to establish strong product reputation and market dominance through product innovation and market development. Prospectors take risks, which enable them to quickly respond to new opportunities and changing competitive landscapes. When a firm pursues a less aggressive, more predictable, and stable strategy (such as those generally pursued by defenders), the audit committee can rely more on financial control, judging executives based on their achievement of financial objectives[59] and an appropriate tax strategy.[60] However, a prospector firm audit committee may need to allow executives to take on more risk. Directors should therefore make sure that the audit committee is structured with the right members to fit the business-level strategic approach that the firm pursues to enable proper strategy execution (see Chapter 4).

The most beneficial background for audit committee members and the optimal committee practices may differ between industries and even with the board as a whole; firms in high-technology industries with rapid change will need to have more emphasis on strategic control than more stable industries.[61] In addition to industry, the stage of the firm in its lifecycle or its strategic focus may also affect optimum governance characteristics and processes.[62] A small, young, rapidly growing firm with high institutional ownership, for example, may benefit more from directors with industry expertise and from a greater focus on serving, as in an advisory source to management. Conversely, a large, established firm in a declining industry, with a widely dispersed shareholder base, may benefit more from directors with financial expertise and a board more focused on its monitoring role.

EMPLOYEES AS INTERNAL GOVERNANCE ACTORS

Employees constitute an important group of internal stakeholders for firms. Employees not only provide human capital critical to sustain a firm's daily operations, but also play an essential role in maintaining and expanding customer bases. The impact of employees on corporate governance varies significantly

across the world. In the United States, the key channel for employees to participate in governance occurs through employee stock ownership plans (ESOPs).[63]
ESOPs are investment vehicles through which employers make tax-deductible
contributions of cash or stock into a trust, whose assets are allocated in a pre-
determined manner to employee plan participants.[64] By 2016, around 6,624
ESOPs and ESOP-like plans were active in the US, holding total assets of nearly
$1.4 trillion, according to the National Center for Employee Ownership.[65]

By making employees owners, such ownership can lead to a convergence
of interests between employees and shareholders.[66] Ownership gives employees a voice in corporate governance through their voting power, which can
prevent firms from maximizing the interests of shareholders at the expense
of those of the workers.[67] Yet in the United States, although employees can
influence corporate governance through their ownership, they typically do
not have board representation,[68] leaving employees with little say in boardroom discussions. As a result, directors often compromise employee interests
to satisfy the interests of shareholders in firm decision-making.[69] To address
this issue, several pieces of federal legislation have been introduced to grant
employees the right to sit on corporate boards. For example, the Reward
Work Act introduced by US senator Tammy Baldwin would empower workers by requiring public companies to directly elect one-third of their company's board of directors and reduce open-market stock buybacks.[70]

As shown in the Strategic Governance Highlight (Box 1.2), Germany and
other Western European countries have a two-tier board consisting of a board of
directors and a supervisory board. In this system, the law guarantees employee
representation on corporate boards of directors as a recognized fundamental
worker right. Employees can vote for representatives in supervisory boards
under corporate law, which is often referred to as *co-determination*. Like many
Western European countries, China requires publicly traded companies to have
a supervisory committee. Such a committee must include employee representatives elected by personnel through an assembly of some or all employees, or by
other means. Although employee representation on boards does not necessarily lead to higher profits and faster growth, it can inevitably change the power
dynamics of corporate boards,[71] leading directors to pay closer attention to
worker interests when making strategic decisions.

CHAPTER OVERVIEWS

As illustrated in Figure 1.1, we provide an overview of the book's organization, focused on introducing strategic challenges that boards of directors
face and how to overcome them. In this beginning chapter, we presented the

concept of strategic governance, seeking to illustrate that boards of directors and the top management team are confronting a more intense governance situation in which prominent stakeholders pursue goals beyond board monitoring, seeking to affect corporate and business level strategies. Reinforcing this idea, a recent survey of board of director members by PwC, a large accounting advisory firm, rated strategic oversight as the most important aspect of a board member when that member engages in direct communications with shareholders.[72] In the following chapters, we will clarify how boards and other governance actors affect a range of strategies.

Chapter 2, a companion chapter to internal governance (Chapter 1), overviews external governance actors in the United States and other countries. External governance actors consist of institutional investors, activist investors, financial analysts, business media, short sellers, suppliers, customers, rating agencies, and regulators. We go more in depth on how these actors influence changes in strategic governance, not only through the board of directors but also through their advocacy and direct intervention.

Chapter 3 investigates the role of governance actors in corporate strategies including diversification strategy, mergers and acquisitions, alliances, and divestitures. We also provide guidance on how corporate executives can manage conflicting governance actor demands when making corporate strategic decisions.

Chapter 4 examines how governance actors affect internal innovation investment and corporate entrepreneurship with a focus on entering new product markets through internal innovation, corporate venture capital, joint ventures, and direct acquisitions. Here, we likewise discuss how to leverage governance actors to best foster innovation and enter a new product market.

Chapter 5 focuses on the influence of governance actors on competitive strategies, such as the pursuit of differentiation versus cost leadership strategy, competitive aggressiveness, and competitive complexity. We introduced some of the influence on competitive strategies in regard to the audit committee's prospector- versus defender-oriented strategies. We will go more in depth and explore how company leaders can leverage governance actors to create better competitive strategy.

The global business environment has dramatically changed in the new competitive era. In Chapter 6, we provide an overview of the role that governance actors play in shaping firms' strategic choices for global expansion. Directors and top managers may also find ways to manage the governance influencers to increase the success of global strategies.

In Chapter 7, we discuss how governance actors shape firms' management of key stakeholder relationships, such as customers and suppliers, besides shareholders. We provide our guidance on leveraging internal and external governance actors to design successful stakeholder relationship strategies.

Corporate political strategy pertains to managing relationships with government actors. Firms can invest in lobbying, make political campaign contributions, and appoint directors with political ties to foster relationships with government actors. In Chapter 8, we explain the role of governance actors in corporate political strategy and how these actors can best be managed to facilitate an effective corporate political strategy.

In our final chapter, Chapter 9, we conclude with a summary of the strategic challenges that boards of directors face and provide additional recommendations for dealing with these challenges. We emphasize the growing governance issue under disruptive innovation associated with platform strategy such as that of Amazon, Apple, Uber, and many others, as well as digitalization. We also discuss policy implications and emerging trends at the interface of governance and strategic decisions.

NOTES

1. Boyson, N. M., Gantchev, N., & Shivdasani, A. (2017). Activism mergers. *Journal of Financial Economics* 126(1): 54–73; Shi, W., Connelly, B. L., Hoskisson, R., & Ketchen, D. (2020). Portfolio spillover of institutional investor activism: An awareness-motivation-capability perspective. *Academy of Management Journal* 63(6): 1865–1892.
2. Welch, D., Deveau, S., & Coppola, G. (2020). Activist battling Harley's board urges focus on core riders. *Bloomberg.com,* www.bloomberg.com, March 20.
3. Benner, M. J., & Zenger, T. (2016). The lemons problem in markets for strategy. *Strategy Science* 1(2): 71–89. Zenger, T. (2013). Strategy: The uniqueness challenge. *Harvard Business Review* 91(11): 52–58.
4. Uribe, A., & Scism, L. (2020). Companies are paying a lot more to insure their directors and officers. *Wall Street Journal,* www.wsj.com, June 21.
5. Chandler, A. D. (1977). *The visible hand –The managerial revolution in American business.* Cambridge: Harvard University Press; Herman, E. (1981). *Corporate control, corporate power.* New York: Cambridge University Press.
6. Boyd, B. K., & Hoskisson, R. E. (2010). Corporate governance of business groups, In A. M. Coplan, H. Takashi, & J. Lincoln (Eds.), *The Oxford Handbook of Business Groups.* New York: Oxford University Press.
7. Aiken, A. L., & Lee, C. (2020). Let's talk sooner rather than later: The strategic communication decisions of activist blockholders. *Journal of Corporate Finance* 62; Jahnke, P. (2019). Ownership concentration and institutional investors' governance through voice and exit. *Business & Politics* 21(3): 327–350.
8. Shi, W., Connelly, B. L., & Hoskisson, R. E. (2017). External corporate governance and financial fraud: Cognitive evaluation theory insights on agency theory prescriptions. *Strategic Management Journal* 38(6): 1268–1286.
9. Aslan, H. (2020). Shareholders versus stakeholders in investor activism: Value for whom? *Journal of Corporate Finance* 60.

10. Klein, P. G., Mahoney, J. T., McGahan, A. M., & Pitelis, C. N. (2019). Organizational governance adaptation: Who is in, who is out, and who gets what. *Academy of Management Review* 44(1): 6–27.

11. Lozano-Reina, G., & Sánchez-Marín, G. (2020). Say on pay and executive compensation: A systematic review and suggestions for developing the field. *Human Resource Management Review* 30(2).

12. Connelly, B. L., Shi, W., Walker, H. J., & Hersel, M. C. (in press). Searching for a sign: CEO successor selection in the wake of corporate misconduct. *Journal of Management*.

13. Sherman, E., & Eccles, R. G. (2007). KPMG(A): A near-death experience. *Harvard Business School Cases*.

14. Quigley, T. J., Hambrick, D. C., Misangyi, V. F., & Rizzi, G. A. (2019). CEO selection as risk-taking: A new vantage on the debate about the consequences of insiders versus outsiders. *Strategic Management Journal* 40(9): 1453–1470.

15. Sanders, W. G., & Hambrick, D. C. (2007). Swinging for the fences: The effects of CEO stock options on company risk-taking and performance. *Academy of Management Journal* 50(5): 1055–1078.

16. Kim, E. H., & Yao, L. (2018), Executive suite independence: Is it related to board independence? *Management Science*, 64, 1015–1033. Semadeni, M., & Krause, R. (2020). Innovation in the boardroom. *Academy of Management Perspectives* 34(2): 240–251.

17. Khanna, P., Jones, C. D., & Boivie, S. (2014). Director human capital, information processing demands, and board effectiveness, *Journal of Management* 40: 557–585.

18. Joseph, J., Ocasio, W., & McDonnell, M. (2014). The structural elaboration of board independence: Executive power, institutional logics, and the adoption of CEO-only board structures in US corporate governance, *Academy of Management Journal* 57: 1834–1858.

19. Baysinger, B., & Hoskisson, R. (1990). The composition of boards of directors and strategic control. *Academy of Management Review* 15: 72–87.

20. Zorn, M. L., Shropshire, C., Martin, J. A., Combs, J. G., & Ketchen, D. J. (2017). Home alone: The effects of lone-insider boards on CEO pay, financial misconduct, and firm performance. *Strategic Management Journal* 38(13): 2623–2646.

21. Power, M. (2000). The audit society–second thoughts. *International Journal of Auditing* 4(1): 111–119.

22. Fama, E. F., & Jensen, M. C. (1983). Separation of ownership and control, *Journal of Law and Economics* 26: 301–325.

23. Haynes, K. T., & Hillman, A. (2010). The effect of board capital and CEO power on strategic change. *Strategic Management Journal* 31(11): 1145–1163.

24. McNulty, T., & Pettigrew, A. (1999). Strategists on the board. *Organization Studies* 20(1): 47–74.

25. O'Kelley, J. R., Jones, A.-L., & Neal, P. 2019. Going for gold: The 2019 global board culture and director behaviors survey: Russell Reynolds Associates.

26. Pugliese, A., Bezemer, P.-J., Zattoni, A., Huse, M., van den Bosch, F. A. J., & Volberda, H. W. (2009). Boards of directors' contribution to strategy: A literature

review and research agenda. *Corporate Governance: An International Review* 17(3): 292.

27. Finkelstein, S., Hambrick, D. C., Cannella, A. A. (2009). *Strategic leadership: Theory and research on executives, top management teams, and boards.* New York: Oxford University Press.

28. Krause, R. (2017). Being the CEO's boss: An examination of board chair orientations. *Strategic Management Journal* 38: 698.

29. Finkelstein S., & D'Aveni, R. A. (1994). CEO duality as a double-edged sword: how boards of directors balance entrenchment avoidance and unity of command. *Academy of Management Journal* 37(5): 1079–1108.

30. Sundaramurthy, C., & Lewis, M. (2003). Control and collaboration: Paradoxes of governance. *Academy of Management Review* 28(3): 397–415.

31. Withers, M. C., & Fitza, M. A. (2017). Do board chairs matter? The influence of board chairs on firm performance. *Strategic Management Journal* 38: 1343–1355.

32. Harrison, J. R. (1987). The strategic use of corporate board committees. *California Management Review* 30(1): 109–125.

33. Kolev, K. D., Wangrow, D. B., Barker, V. L., & Schepker, D. J. (2019). Board committees in corporate governance: A cross-disciplinary review and agenda for the future. *Journal of Management Studies* 56(6): 1138–1193.

34. Hillman, A. J., Shropshire, C., Certo, S. T., Dalton, D. R., & Dalton, C. M. (2011). What I like about you: A multilevel study of shareholder discontent with director monitoring. *Organization Science* 22(3): 675–687.

35. Withers, M. C., Hillman, A. J. & Cannella, A. A. Jr. (2012). A multidisciplinary review of the director selection literature. *Journal of Management* 38: 243–277.

36. Shi, W., Hoskisson, R. E., & Zhang, Y. A. (2017). Independent director death and CEO acquisitiveness: Build an empire or pursue a quiet life? *Strategic Management Journal* 38: 780–792.

37. Krause, R., Semadeni, M., & Cannella, A. A. Jr. (2013). External COO/presidents as expert directors: A new look at the service role of boards. *Strategic Management Journal* 34: 1628–1641.

38. Cumming, D., Leung, T. Y., & Rui, O. (2015). Gender diversity and securities fraud. *Academy of Management Journal* 58(5): 1572–1593.

39. Adams, R. B., & Ferreira, D. (2009). Women in the boardroom and their impact on governance and performance. *Journal of Financial Economics* 94(2): 291–309.

40. Nekhili, M., & Gatfaoui, H. (2013). Are demographic attributes and firm characteristics drivers of gender diversity? Investigating women's positions on French boards of directors. *Journal of Business Ethics* 118(2): 227–249.

41. Abdullah, S. N., Ismail, K. N. I. K., & Nachum, L. (2016). Does having women on boards create value? The impact of societal perceptions and corporate governance in emerging markets. *Strategic Management Journal* 37(3), 466–476. Post, C., & Byron, K. (2015). Women on boards and firm financial performance: A meta-analysis. *Academy of Management Journal* 58(5): 1546–1571.

42. Guldiken, O., Mallon, M. R., Fainshmidt, S., Judge, W. Q., & Clark, C. E. (2019). Beyond tokenism: How strategic leaders influence more meaningful gender diversity on boards of directors. *Strategic Management Journal* 40(12): 2024–2046.

43. Chasan, E. (2017). BlackRock puts its votes behind proposals to get women on boards. Bloomberg.com, July 14.

44. Zhu, D. H., Shen, W., & Hillman, A. J. (2014). Recategorization into the in-group: The appointment of demographically different new directors and their subsequent positions on corporate boards. *Administrative Science Quarterly* 59(2): 240–270.

45. DesJardine, M. R., Shi, W., & Marti, E. (2020). Board demographic diversity as an opportunity for shareholder activism. Working paper, University of Miami.

46. Garg, S., Li, Q. (John), & Shaw, J. D. (2018). Undervaluation of directors in the board hierarchy: Impact on turnover of directors (and CEOs) in newly public firms. *Strategic Management Journal* 39(2): 429–457.

47. Schepker, D. J., Nyberg, A. J., Ulrich, M. D., & Wright, P. M. (2018). Planning for future leadership: Procedural rationality, formalized succession processes, and CEO influence in CEO succession planning. *Academy of Management Journal* 61(2): 523–552.

48. Kowsmann, P. (2020). Commerzbank's CEO and chairman to resign amid pressure from activist Cerberus. *Wall Street Journal*, www.wsj.com, July 3.

49. Arons, S. (2020). Commerzbank names Deutsche Bank's Knof CEO to lead cost cuts. *Bloomberg Businessweek*, www.bloomberg.com, September 26.

50. Chen, K. D., & Wu, A. (2016). *The structure of board committees*. Boston: Harvard Business School.

51. Fredrickson, J. W., Davis-Blake, A., & Sanders, W. G. (2010). Sharing the wealth: Social comparisons and pay dispersion in the CEO's top team. *Strategic Management Journal* 31(10): 1031–1053.

52. Shi, W., Connelly, B. L., & Sanders, W. G. 2016. Buying bad behavior: Tournament incentives and securities class action lawsuits. *Strategic Management Journal* 37(7): 1354–1378.

53. Yanadori, Y., & Cui, V. (2013). Creating incentives for innovation? The relationship between pay dispersion in R&D groups and firm innovation performance. *Strategic Management Journal* 34(12): 1502–1511.

54. Derchi, G.-B., Zoni, L., & Dossi, D. (2020). Corporate social responsibility performance, incentives, and learning effects. *Journal of Business Ethics*, forthcoming.

55. Baysinger, B., & Hoskisson, R. E. The composition of boards of directors and strategic control, 72–87.

56. Hoskisson, R. E., & Hitt, M. A. (1988). Strategic control systems and relative R&D investment in large multiproduct firms. *Strategic Management Journal* 9(6): 506–621.

57. Baysinger & Hoskisson. The composition of boards of directors and strategic control, 72–87.

58. Miles, R. E., & Snow, C. C. (1978). *Organizational strategy, structure and process.* New York: McGraw-Hill.

59. Hsu, P., Moore, J. A., & Neubaum, D. O. (2018). Tax avoidance, financial experts on the audit committee, and business strategy. *Journal of Business Finance & Accounting* 45(9/10): 1293–1321.

60. Higgins, D., Omer, T., & Phillips, J. (2015). The influence of a firm's business strategy on its tax aggressiveness. *Contemporary Accounting Research* 32(2): 674–702.

61. Carcello, J. V., Hermanson, D. R., & Zhongxia Ye. (2011). Corporate governance research in accounting and auditing: Insights, practice implications, and future research directions. *Auditing: A Journal of Practice & Theory* 30(3): 1–31.

62. Lynall, M. D., Golden, B. R., & Hillman, A. J. (2003). Board composition from adolescence to maturity: A multitheoretic view. *Academy of Management Review* 28: 416–431.

63. Blasi, J., Conte, M., & Kruse, D. (1996). Employee stock ownership and corporate performance among public companies. *ILR Review* 50(1): 60–79.

64. Hart, M. A. (2001). ESOPs in corporate acquisitions: What every buyer should know about the target company's ESOP. *Benefits Law Journal* 14(1): 9–31.

65. NCEO. (2018). A statistical profile of employee ownership. *National Center for Employee Ownership.* Retrieved from http://www.nceo.org/articles/statistical-profile-employee-ownership.

66. Li, J., Shi, W., & Dasborough, M. (in press). CEO positive framing and employee ownership. *Human Resource Management.*

67. Faleye, O., Mehrotra, V., & Morck, R. (2006). When labor has a voice in corporate governance. *Journal of Financial and Quantitative Analysis* 41(3): 489–510.

68. Palladino, L. (2019). *Worker representation on US corporate boards.* Working paper, University of Massachusetts at Amherst.

69. Cobb, J. A. (2015). Risky business: The decline of defined benefit pensions and firms' shifting of risk. *Organization Science* 26(5): 1332–1350.

70. Baldwin, T. (2019). Text -S.915 – 116th Congress (2019–2020): Reward Work Act.

71. Holmberg, S. R. (2019). Workers on corporate boards? Germany's had them for decades. *New York Times.* Retrieved from www.nytimes.com/2019/01/06/opinion/warren-workers-boards.html.

72. PwC's 2019 Annual Corporate Directors Survey. (2019). The collegiality conundrum: Finding balance in the boardroom. www.pwc.com/acds19.

CHAPTER 2

Introduction to External Governance Actors

BOX 2.1   Strategic Governance Challenge: Shareholders' Heterogeneous Goals

---

"While we don't run the company worrying about the stock price in the short run, in the long run our stock price is a measure of the progress we have made over the years."

– J.P. Morgan, the second largest shareholder of Royal Dutch Shell

"The Company [shall] exercise the rights and perform the obligations as an investor of the state-owned major financial enterprises on behalf of the State in accordance with applicable law."

– Central Huijin Investment Co., Ltd., the largest shareholder of Industrial & Commercial Bank of China

Shareholders have differing priorities and goals. As reflected in the quotes above, goals may vary by country and type of company, such as privately owned versus state-owned. Many other varied aims occur as well. While some shareholders focus on garnering short-term financial returns, others more invested in social issues may attempt to push portfolio firms to adopt socially responsible practices. In other cases, family owners focus on sustaining the controlling family's legacy whereas state shareholders attempt to achieve their social and political agendas.

Even the same type of shareholder may pursue different investment strategies. For example, institutional investors can be broadly classified into three types based on their trading strategies: dedicated institutional investors (high ownership stability and large-sized stake), transient

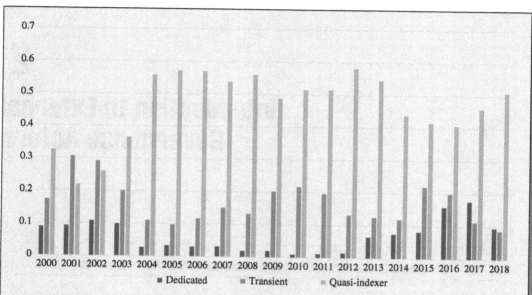

FIGURE 2.1   Institutional ownership for S&P 1500 firms (2000–2018).
Source: Thomson Reuters 13F.

institutional investors (low ownership stability and small-sized stake), and quasi-indexer institutional investors (high ownership stability and small-sized stake). In Figure 2.1, we calculate the average of dedicated, transient, and quasi-indexer institutional investor ownership for Standard & Poor 1500 companies from 2000 to 2018. Although the figure does not show a clear pattern in terms of ownership growth, it does suggest that quasi-indexer investors account for the largest percentage of institutional ownership in most years.

Because these three types of institutional investors pursue different investment strategies, they impose conflicting demands and pressures on managers. Transient institutional investors often push company leaders to focus on generating short-term financial returns, whereas dedicated ones often enable them to devote attention to long-term investment projects. Faced with conflicting demands, managers need to evaluate not only the power of each type of institutional investor reflected by their ownership level but also their ability to form a coalition. For example, although ownership by dedicated institutional investors may be low, these investors can obtain the support from quasi-indexer institutional shareholders, prompting managers to prioritize their preferences. To handle the various pressures, and despite the presence of less-committed investors like transient ones, a firm's investor relations team carries out the key task of frequently communicating with the investors to encourage support for top managers' long-term investment projects.

Sources: Connelly, B., Shi, W. Hoskisson, R. F. & Koka, B. (2019). Shareholder influence on joint venture exploration. *Journal of Management* 45(8): 3178–3203; Crespi, R., Renneboog, L. (2010). Is (institutional) shareholder activism new? Evidence from UK shareholder coalitions in the pre-Cadbury Era. *Corporate Governance: An International Review* 18(4): 274–295; Hoskisson, R. E., Hitt, M.A., Johnson, R. A., & Grossman, W. (2002). Conflicting voices: The effects of ownership heterogeneity and internal governance on corporate strategy. *Academy of Management Journal* 45: 697–716; Bushee, B. J. (1998). The influence of institutional investors on myopic R&D investment behavior. *Accounting Review* 73(3): 305–333.

In Chapter 1, we saw the impact of internal governance actors, referring to authority by parties residing within the boundaries of the firm, on corporate decision-making. Employees have a strong voice in corporate governance in Western European countries, but the board of directors remains the key internal governance actor around the world. Meanwhile, external governance pertains to control emanating from actors outside the nucleus of the company,[1] including *regulators, institutional investors* that have invested in the firm, *activist investors* that have targeted the firm for change, investors that have shorted its stocks (*short sellers*), *creditors, customers, rating agencies,* and *competitors.* These external stakeholders likewise influence firm governance and key strategic decisions.

As illustrated in Figure 2.2, external governance actors can be broadly classified into four types based on two dimensions. The first refers to whether an external governance actor affects governance and strategic decisions directly or indirectly. Direct influence occurs if the external influencer can appoint its own board representatives or decide rules through enacting laws and regulations. In contrast, actors can play an indirect governance role if impact on governance and strategic decisions takes place through influencing a firm's stock price (as do financial analysts) and shaping a firm's reputation (as does the media). The second dimension reflects whether the interests of an external governance actor align or not with those of the firm. For example, despite varying investment horizons among institutional investors, as discussed in the introductory Strategic Governance Challenge Box 2.1, they all expect firms to perform well financially. Similarly, activist investors also depend on a firm's ability to deliver desirable financial performance for successful returns.

	I	II
Direct influence	• Institutional investors • Activist investors • Creditors	• Regulators
Indirect influence	III • Customers • Suppliers	IV • Short sellers • Competitors • Rating agencies • Media • Social activists
	Aligned interests	**Different interests**

FIGURE 2.2   Classification of external governance actors.

However, some external governance actors may not have a direct interest in the firm's increased financial performance. Short sellers, for instance, have irreconcilable interest conflicts with firms because these investors can only make profits from declining stock prices and, based on their analysis, expect firm strategies to flounder. Competitors as external governance actors obviously have different interests from the focal firm. In addition, financial analysts and credit rating agencies attempt to provide independent, third-party evaluations of the firms they follow, and are generally impartial to firms' actual financial performance.

As noted in the introductory Strategic Governance Challenge, dedicated institutional investors may want a firm to allocate resources to developing new products and building new factories that can advance long-term competitiveness. By contrast, activist hedge funds may want the firm to return cash to shareholders through issuing dividends or to boost its stock price through share repurchases.[2] In the extreme, short sellers are motivated to find and spread negative news to drive a firm's stock price lower, a tactic that infuriated Elon Musk, CEO of electric vehicle automaker Tesla, when short sellers attempted to depreciate Tesla's stock value in 2018. When the effort failed, as Tesla stock climbed toward the end of 2019 and into 2020, Musk sent a box of short shorts, and offered to send more, to hedge fund manager David Einhorn, one of the short investors who lost money in the unsuccessful scheme.[3] Top managers must maneuver amidst the conflicting demands and pressures when making key strategic decisions. We will look closer at main external governance actors and discuss the specific mechanisms through which they play an influential role. We will then offer our guidance on how to cope with the multiplicity and complexity of these governance players.

EXTERNAL GOVERNANCE ACTORS WITH DIRECT INFLUENCE AND ALIGNED INTERESTS

Quadrant I of Figure 2.2 shows the influence of external actors. Institutional investors, activist investors, and creditors have aligned interests with those of their portfolio firms, and may exert a direct impact on firm decisions.

Institutional Investors

Institutional investors refer to entities that invest money on behalf of other people. Examples include mutual funds, pension funds, hedge funds, and insurance companies. These investors have become an important participant in equity markets around the globe (see Box 2.2, Strategic Governance Highlight). As of July 28, 2020, over 72 percent of Tesla's floating shares was held by institutional investors, with dominant investors as follows: 6.5 percent owned by Baillie Gifford and Company, 5.78 percent owned by Capital World Investors, and 4.67 percent owned by Vanguard Group. For Apple, 62 percent of floating shares were owned by institutional investors with the following dominant ones: 7.77 percent owned by Vanguard, 6.34 percent owned by BlackRock, and 5.66 percent owned by Berkshire Hathaway. Increasing institutional shareholding has challenged the separation of ownership and control underpinning corporate governance in the last three decades.[4] Because institutional investors now hold over 70 percent of the entire US capital market and a small number of them hold significant stakes in public companies,[5] they "stand today as empowered as ever, having gained the ability to influence a firm's business and investment policy in a substantial manner."[6]

As explained in Chapter 1, institutional investors have aligned interests with their portfolio firms and direct channels to influence governance through participation in voting for board members. This type of investor can influence strategic decisions through "voice" and "exit" tactics.[7] Because of their substantial collective equity positions, the investors can and will monitor top managers and constrain their value-destroying behavior through direct discussions, voting against managerial proposals, or appointing their own board members. In other words, they will "voice" their positions.[8] When top managers fail to make decisions in the interest of shareholders, institutional investors may threaten to sell their holdings, or "exit," which can depress stock prices. Reduced stock prices in turn can hurt top managers' personal wealth and job security.[9] Through participation in voting and sometimes appointing board representatives, in addition to exit strategies, institutional investors can influence both compensation[10] and dismissal of a CEO.[11]

BOX 2.2   Strategic Governance Highlight: Institutional Investor Ownership around the Globe

Institutional investors have become an important player in the global equity market. In 2019, total assets under management by institutional investors grew to $52 trillion. These investors are considered domestic if they reside in the same country as the portfolio firm, and foreign if residing outside of the firm's home country. Using a sample of 53,303 firms from 46 countries included in the MSCI ACWI index, we calculate the mean of domestic institutional ownership and foreign institutional ownership from 2000 to 2017. We find that firms in the United States have the highest level of domestic institutional ownership (38.8 percent) and firms in Ireland have the highest level of foreign institutional ownership (32.8 percent). Across all the firms, domestic institutional ownership stands at 13 percent, whereas foreign institutional ownership is 4.3 percent. Figure 2.3 suggests that foreign institutional ownership has been increasing, rising from 2 percent in 2000 to over 5 percent in 2017.

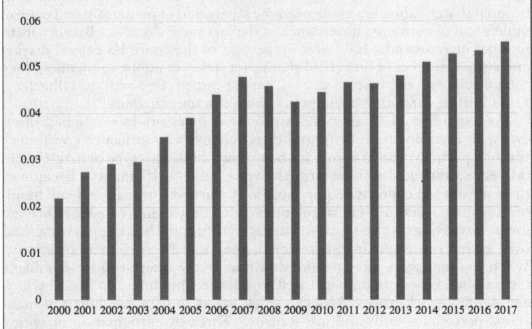

FIGURE 2.3   Foreign institutional ownership, 2000–2017.
Source: FactSet

Yet, blockholder stakes by foreign institutional investors has become a concern for national security. In recent years, market players and regulators show unease about foreign investment in US companies with advanced technologies. The Foreign Investment Risk Review Modernization Act of 2018 overhauled procedures, allowing the US government to review any deals involving foreign buyers that take a noncontrolling stake in an American company if involving critical infrastructure, technology, or sensitive personal data. As a result, firms with blockholder stakes by foreign institutional investors can be investigated for national security reasons.

Meanwhile, foreign institutional investors not only provide capital to firms but also play a significant role in facilitating international expansion through cross-border mergers and acquisitions, since these investors serve as important channels of information about countries and industries in which they have accumulated investment experience. These foreign investors may also help firms adapt to different country and cultural governance practices and thereby improve a firm's governance quality.

Given both liabilities and advantages of foreign institutional investors, firms need to take actions to mitigate the liabilities and capitalize on the advantages.

Sources: Shi, W., Gao, C., & Aguilera, R. (2021). The liabilities of foreign institutional ownership: Managing political dependence through corporate political spending. *Strategic Management Journal* 42(1): 84–113; Boston Consulting Group. (2020). Global Asset Management 2020: Protect, adapt, and innovate; Bu, J., & Shi, W. (2020). Foreign institutional investors and location choice of cross-border mergers and acquisitions. Working paper, University of Miami; Ferreira, Miguel A., & Matos, P. (2008). The colors of investors' money: The role of institutional investors around the world. *Journal of Financial Economics* 88(3): 499–533.

Institutional investors exhibit substantial differences among themselves.[12] Based on their legal types, the investors can be classified into public pension funds, private pension funds, mutual funds, insurance companies, and banks. Their observed investment and trading behavior (see Strategic Governance Challenge Box 2.1) further separates them into the categories of (1) dedicated institutional investors associated with high ownership stability and large stake size, such as Berkshire Hathaway, (2) transient institution investors that have low ownership stability and small stakes, like Numeric Investors L.P., and (3) quasi-indexer institutional investors that have high ownership stability and small ownership stakes, such as CalPERS.[13] For all institutional investors that filed form 13(F) with the Securities and Exchange Commission in the period of 2000 to 2018, 2.68 percent acted as dedicated, 30.96 percent acted as transient, 52.99 percent acted as quasi-index, and the rest (13.38 percent) cannot be classified into any of the three.

Institutional investors may also be categorized based on their incentives, as (1) market-driven institutions that are motivated principally by financial gains, such as hedge funds and mutual funds, (2) politically driven institutions that are insulated from market forces, such as sovereign wealth funds and public pension funds, (3) socially driven institutions that consider both financial return and social/environmental good to bring about social change, such as socially responsible investment funds, and (4) multilateral investors that have a variety of financial relationships with the firm, like private pension funds and bank funds.[14]

The various institutional investors exert distinct influences on corporate governance. Dedicated institutional investors, given their large stakes and high ownership stability, monitor and seek to hold direct dialogue with top managers, as well as pressure them to pursue long-term strategic decisions. In contrast, due to their low ownership stability, transient institutional investors often lack direct channels to communicate with and monitor top managers. However, the threat of exit by these transient investors can lead top managers to make decisions that align with their interests.[15]

The ability of institutional investors to exert their influence on governance and strategic decisions hinges on two factors: their level of ownership and their capacity for collective action. As the overall ownership of institutional investors increases, their ability to shape firm decisions strengthens.[16] Specifically, institutional investors with substantial stakes possess strong voting power and their exit can have a profound influence on stock prices; therefore, top managers are more inclined to make strategic decisions that reflect their interests. Institutional investors that engage in collective action create another persuasive force on company decision makers. This approach becomes particularly important for institutional investors without substantial ownership in companies, as a lack of large stakes in portfolio firms leads to the need for collective action to impose pressure on managers and influence firm decisions.[17] For example, institutional investors connected through the network of holdings have been shown to coordinate votes on proxy items.[18]

Yet many factors can create hurdles for a unified front. Geographic distance, for example, can complicate planning and coordination. Because institutional investors that are geographically close to one another tend to have strong social networks and find it easier to coordinate their actions, geographic concentration enhances their ability to play a more compelling governance role.[19] But collective action may also be limited by the investors' distinct investment horizons. For instance, dedicated institutional owners may expect firms to engage in long-term investment projects, which can be opposed by transient institutional investors with a focus on garnering short-term financial returns.[20]

Activist Investors

No recent governance development has affected firms' strategic decisions as profoundly as the growth in shareholder activism after the global financial crisis in 2008. Unlike passive investors that only buy and sell stocks, activist investors attempt to intervene in vital decisions. Between 1942 and the 1970s, individual shareholders (corporate raiders) were the key players on the shareholder activism stage.[21] The establishment of the Interfaith Center on Corporate Responsibility in 1971 and the Investor Responsibility Research Center in 1972 triggered a significant increase in social shareholder proposals,[22] sponsored by foundations, religious and environmental organizations, and religious and socially responsible investment funds.[23] Then, in 1985, since the founding of Institutional Shareholder Services and the Council of Institutional Investors, institutional investors have become primary players in shareholder activism.[24] Public pension funds and labor union funds were early sponsors of governance proposals.[25] Mutual funds soon joined the activism bandwagon with a focus on corporate governance issues.[26] Hedge funds entered the stage of activism in the 1990s and have attained prominence rapidly[27] (see the Strategic Governance Highlight Box 1.3 for more background information).

In contrast to activism with a focus on improving firms' governance deficiencies, which we will discuss shortly, hedge fund activists concentrate their attention on financial performance and attempt to seek immediate financial outcomes from their investments.[28] These activists focus on pressuring firms to take measures that can create shareholder value in the short run. Although firms targeted by hedge funds experience an improvement in financial performance and operational efficiency in the short run,[29] the benefits can come at the expense of nonshareholder stakeholders' interests.[30] For example, suppliers might get pressured to lower their pricing or customers might have health concerns as firms may bring unsafe products to the marketplace with the goal of achieving short-term financial performance.

Activist investors can be nonfinancial corporations with strategic motivations, known as *corporate shareholder activists*.[31] Corporations sometimes purchase minority stakes in a company with the goal of intervening in the targeted firm's strategic decisions.[32] Unlike institutional investor activists (including hedge funds) that focus on attaining financial returns, corporate shareholder activists concentrate on achieving strategic goals such as gaining access to targeted firms' complementary resources and capabilities or

BOX 2.3 Strategic Governance Highlight: Increasing Shareholder Activism around the Globe

Shareholder activism is not unique to the United States and has spread to other parts of the world. For example, during the first half of 2019, non-US targets accounted for 45 percent of global capital deployed to shareholder activism campaigns. Europe and the Asia-Pacific region (including Asia, Australia, and New Zealand) experienced an upsurge in shareholder activist activity in this year, accounting for over one-third of the total capital deployed in activism worldwide. Activist shareholders are also pursuing deals in countries perceived to be either unfriendly or challenging to their strategies. In Japan, for example, Oasis Management—an activist investor that has taken on Nintendo, Panasonic, and Toshiba—targeted Tokyo Dome, an 84-year-old Japanese stadium operator, because of its sluggish performance in 2020. BHP, an Australian multinational in mining, metals, and petroleum, faced a revolt during its 2019 annual meetings by shareholders demanding that the company cut ties with groups that lobby for the fossil fuel industry. More recently, under pressure from activist shareholder Cerberus Capital Management, the board of Germany's second-largest lender Commerzbank AG dismissed the CEO and chairman due to persistent poor performance.

Data from Activist Insights suggest that 1,878 foreign shareholder activism campaigns occurred from 2010 to 2018. These campaigns refer to activist actions taken by investors not from the same country as the targeted firm. Canada received the largest number of foreign shareholder activism campaigns (275) and the US activist shareholders initiated the largest number of foreign campaigns (745).

Several factors drove the rise of global shareholder activism. First, as activism opportunities in the United States shrink, activist shareholders seek opportunities in other countries. Second, as institutional investors are important allies of activist investors, the increase of foreign institutional ownership around the world empowers activist shareholders to launch campaigns in foreign countries. Third, governance reforms in many countries create a better-functioning market with the free flow of capital and investments and allow corporate law systems internationally to keep converging. Such reforms also afford greater minority rights to shareholders and empower activists with additional legal tools to launch activist campaigns.

Sources: Kowsmann, P. (2020). Commerzbank's CEO and chairman to resign amid pressure from activist Cerberus. *Wall Street Journal.* July 3. https://www.wsj.com/articles/commerzbanks-ceo-and-chairman-to-resign-amid-pressure-from-activist-cerberus-11593802828; Lewis, L., & Inagaki, K. (2020). How Japan Inc. became a target for activist investors. *Financial Times.* 3 February. https://www.ft.com/content/4a36f3b0-4419-11ea-a43a-c4b328d9061c; Hume, N. (2019). BHP hit by shareholder revolt over membership in industry lobby groups. *Financial Times.* 7 November. https://www.ft.com/content/cb456e50-0134-11ea-b7bc-f3fa4e77dd47; Weinstein, G., de Wied, W. S., & Richter, P. (2019). The road ahead for shareholder activism. *Harvard Law School Forum on Corporate Governance.* https://corpgov.law.harvard.edu/.

supporting strategic initiatives. For example, in 2016, GE acted as a corporate shareholder activist when its Medical Systems Information Technologies business became the largest shareholder in genetics-testing firm NeoGenomics by acquiring an 11.5 percent stake. After being notified of GE's intent to alter the strategic trajectory of the firm, NeoGenomics top decision makers added significant new lab capacity, expanded from the United States to Europe, and strengthened its product development.

Investors differ in the intensity of their activism.[33] Some investors, like Trian Fund Management and Pershing Square Capital Management, specialize exclusively on activist campaigns. Other multi-strategy hedge funds pursue a diversified strategy including activism to beat the market returns. Some private equity funds (such as T. Rowe Price) do not use activism as their regular investment strategies but engage in occasional activist plays. Private equity firms like KKR, Golden Gate Capital, and Sycamore Partners, for instance, have in the past acquired minority stakes in public companies (typically under the 5 percent public reporting threshold) to approach management and initiate a dialogue regarding a buyout. Lastly, some mutual funds, like BlackRock and Vanguard, and individual investors who tend to pursue a passive investment strategy also occasionally engage in activism to influence firm strategic decisions. In 2018, Laurence Fink, CEO of BlackRock, in his annual letter to chief executives in which BlackRock invests, called on these executives to articulate long-term plans and how their organizations contribute to society.[34]

Activist investors use multiple tactics to achieve their goals. Most investors privately discuss their proposals and demands with top managers of firms or request board seats.[35] Others release publicly disclosed letters to criticize management and board performance and request changes. For instance, in February 2020, Carl Icahn penned an open letter to shareholders of Occidental Petroleum Corporation, criticizing management's failure to "maintain a prudent balance sheet" and for making unwise acquisition decisions. In March 2020, he boosted his Occidental stake to almost 10 percent and

Occidental changed board members so that Icahn's representatives were on Occidental's board in response.[36]

The most hostile tactic is a proxy contest. A proxy contest takes place when shareholders join forces and attempt to gather enough shareholder proxy votes to win a corporate vote. In 2017, hedge fund Trian Fund Management launched a high-profile proxy contest with consumer products giant Procter & Gamble. The fight ended with P&G conceding to adding Nelson Peltz to its board,[37] but not before spending around $100 million on the fight, as compared to Trian's $25 million spent.[38] Research suggests that activist campaigns ending in a proxy fight have average costs of $10.71 million for the activist shareholder.[39] Not surprisingly, parties increasingly move to settle. Data from FactSet SharkRepellent suggest that the percentage of proxy contests settled instead of fought increased from 17.5 percent in 2001 to 45 percent in 2016.

As noted in Box 2.3, shareholder activism is no longer constrained to the United States and has become widespread across global markets to bring about change. As companies in the US reduce their vulnerabilities to shareholder activism by improving their corporate governance practices, activist shareholders will seek new opportunities in markets where poor corporate governance practices may be used as a lever with shareholders.

Creditors

Most corporate governance discussions center around the ability of shareholders to monitor top executives. Creditors, such as banks and other lenders, are often perceived only as bystanders until firms become unable to make payments and end up in debt default.[40] Yet debt financing is much more common than equity financing. Data from the Thomas Reuters Loan Pricing Corporation indicates that, in 2016, the amount of syndicated loans issued ($2 trillion) was much higher than the amount of net equity ($250 billion). Although lenders cannot directly benefit from appreciating stock prices, their financial interests lie directly tied to borrowing firms. When borrowing firms cannot pay back principal and interest payments and fall into default status, lenders may be adversely impacted. In this sense, creditors have the incentive to monitor firms and their portfolios.

Companies can fall into default not only when top managers do not meet payments but also when they violate financial covenants,[41] or agreement promises such as upholding a specified financial ratio. Financial covenants place accounting-based risk and performance limits on borrowing firms and can include restrictions on a company's leverage, interest coverage, total fixed charges, and net worth. Unlike payment defaults, financial covenant violations are quite common. More than 40 percent of the firms were in violation of financial covenants at some point from 1997 to 2008.[42] Because a violation of a financial covenant can be considered a default event, the lender has the right to call for immediate repayment of, or expedite, the entire loan balance. But lenders rarely expedite the loan and often use the acceleration right to usher in a renegotiation of the credit agreement. Through these renegotiations, the lending firms shape the governance and decisions of borrowers not only by potentially changing the terms of the loan but also by taking opportunities to monitor and influence decision-making.[43]

This influence may occur in beneficial ways for the borrowing firm. As recent research[44] suggests, large creditors may exert governance impact outside of covenant violations or payment default status. After syndicated loan origination, corporate borrowers decrease capital inefficiencies, increase investments in productive assets, and improve operating performance relative to nonissuers, attesting to the monitoring role of creditors on the borrowers. In this sense, creditors act as external governance actors that have aligned interests with firm stakeholders and direct influence over decisions.

EXTERNAL GOVERNANCE ACTORS WITH DIRECT INFLUENCE AND DIFFERING INTERESTS

As illustrated in Quadrant II of Figure 2.2, we focus our discussion in this section on regulators; they are external governance actors with direct influence but have unaligned governance interests. Regulators, broadly defined as government organizations, such as the Securities and Exchange Commission in the United States or the Securities Regulatory Commission in China, as well as stock exchange commissions, can directly shape external governance environments through enacting and implementing laws and regulations by which firms must abide. The laws and regulations establish the legal system in which firms are embedded and provide a framework for the definition and protection of property rights.

Even when regulators do not directly get involved in enacting laws, they are responsible for implementing them. Regulators shape a country's legal system, which delineates and enforces the rights and responsibilities of different stakeholders within and around the firm,[45] and hence affect a company's governance and decisions. Common law countries, where case law in the form of published judicial opinions is of primary importance, give better legal protection to minority shareholders than civil law countries, where codified statutes predominate.[46] Research suggests that firms located in countries under common law are more inclined to prioritize the interests of shareholders than those located in countries under civil law.[47]

Regulators can mandate direct changes in governance practices. The Sarbanes-Oxley (SOX) Act, for example, led the New York Stock Exchange (NYSE) and NASDAQ to require that independent directors make up a majority of a listed firm's board of directors. Yet, firms often appoint independent directors who tend to be sympathetic to management,[48] showing how managers "fight back" against the regulation. Relatedly, after the SOX Act, the NYSE required its listed firms to appoint a nonmanagement director, or lead director, to preside at executive sessions and to disclose the name of that lead director on its website or in its proxy statement. In contrast, the NASDAQ did not enact any specific guidance about lead director appointments. Given the power that the NYSE wields, listed firms engage in ceremonial adoption of lead director positions and actually do not experience an improvement in governance and firm performance.[49] In other words, faced with coercive pressures from regulators, firms may adopt certain governance practices symbolically and decouple practice adoptions from implementation.[50]

In some countries, regulators can hold direct ownership in firms. For example, in China, the State-owned Assets Supervision and Administration Commission (SASAC), a ministerial-level governmental organization, directly owns and controls 96 central state-owned enterprises (SOEs) as of June 29, 2020. Although SOEs controlled by SASAC are structured as corporations legally separate from the government, establishing their own boards of directors, SASAC appoints and removes top executives of the supervised SOEs and evaluates their performance.[51] Similarly, in Brazil, government agencies control large corporations such as Banco do Brasil and Petrobras. Interestingly, at least in Brazil, minority state ownership might help alleviate some of the political control problems associated with controlling state ownership. Research suggests that a minority state ownership position improves performance and business investment in Brazil, but this positive impact is lessened when the minority position is in a firm affiliated with a large diversified business group.[52]

Despite differences in political systems around the world, regulators as external governance actors often do not share aligned interests with firms. The role of the SEC in the United States lies in protecting investors, maintaining transparent, fair, orderly, and efficient markets, and facilitating capital formation. The key mission of SASAC of China is to exercise the government's ownership power and achieve strategic government objectives.[53] In other words, unlike companies with a focus on delivering value to shareholders and other stakeholders, regulators have distinct priorities.

EXTERNAL GOVERNANCE ACTORS WITH INDIRECT INFLUENCE AND ALIGNED INTERESTS

As shown in Quadrant III of Figure 2.2, in contrast to investors and regulators that can directly influence a firm's corporate governance, customer firms in a supplier–customer relationship are a type of external governance actor that often lacks direct channels to affect the supplier's decisions, unless the customer has representatives in their suppliers' boardrooms or holds ownership stakes in the supplier firm. Meanwhile, unlike regulators, customer firms typically have aligned interests with their suppliers because supplier firms can benefit from customer firms' expansion and growing sales. The ties in the supplier–customer relationship extend to reputation. A customer firm's reputation may be tarnished, and performance adversely impacted, when their suppliers engage in socially irresponsible activity. For example, in 2010, 18 employees of Taiwan-based Foxconn that makes iPhones and iPads for Apple attempted suicide. Although people paid little attention to attributing the problem to Foxconn, the media and the public devoted more focus on blaming Apple, Foxconn's customer,[54] which was detrimental to Apple's reputation.

In the customer–supplier relationship, the influence that customers can exert on suppliers is often stronger than that which suppliers can have on the customer, particularly in cases of large buyers,[55] since suppliers often depend on them for revenues, profits, and survival. In other words, when suppliers depend highly on customers for revenues, these customers can influence suppliers' decision-making. Given Walmart's strong purchasing power, more than 1,300 Walmart suppliers have a presence in Northwest Arkansas, most within 30 miles of Walmart's home office located in Bentonville, according to the Arkansans Economic Development Commission.

Customers can influence suppliers' decision-making through several channels. First, customers can take partial ownership in supplier firms and use their ownership power to influence governance. Yet in the United States, this scenario occurs relatively rarely.[56] Data shows that equity stakes in customer–supplier relationships were present in only 3.31 percent of customer–supplier relationships between 1988 and 2001. But supplier–customer ownership is more common in Japan. Here, large companies are often structured as *keiretsu*, or a network of different companies, including banks, manufacturers, distributors, and supply chain partners, steeped in relationships. Automobile giant Toyota is operated as a keiretsu, in which suppliers and manufacturers belong to the same holding company. Common ownership between suppliers and customers can align their interests and reduce contracting costs.[57] Customer direct ownership stakes in suppliers enable the buyer to monitor the managerial behaviors of providers and influence their decision-making; usually the decision-making is more relationship-based versus transaction based where bidding can be adversarial.

Second, customers can exert a direct influence on supplier governance and strategic decisions by sitting on the boards of directors of supplier firms. A customer on the board—that is, an executive or director from a buyer firm also serving on the board of the supplier firm—can offer valuable resources, including market knowledge and customer orientation, thereby increasing the provider firm's performance compared with that of firms with no customer on the board.[58] Although customer board members are common in Japan, they have been decreasing in the United States,[59] due primarily to the SOX Act that called for an increase in the percentage of independent directors, whereas customer board members classify as linked directors.

Third, even customers without direct ownership or access to suppliers' boardrooms can play a governance role and influence suppliers' decisions via voting through their purchases. This mechanism is akin to the threat of exit by institutional investors. When a supplier depends heavily on a customer for revenues and profits, company leaders will avoid making decisions that go against the customer's preferences and choose strategic options that can satisfy their requests. As a result, suppliers will direct their investment in corporate social responsibility to choices that are similar to their customers, especially when these have strong bargaining power over the suppliers.[60]

Lastly, customers can influence suppliers' governance through interorganizational spillover. As noted in Box 2.4, the interorganizational spillover effect refers to the impact that seemingly unrelated events in a focal firm can have on the decisions and evaluations of other firms.[61] Due to the interorganizational spillover effect, cross-border acquisitions can improve the governance of nontarget firms when the acquirer country has stronger investor protection than the target country.[62] By the same token, suppliers may adjust their decision-making in response to changes in customers' governance practices. For example, when customers grant more short-term equity incentives to CEOs, suppliers have a tendency to reduce long-term oriented investment as a response because such incentives can lead customer CEOs to make short-term investment.[63]

Although we have focused on discussing the external governance role of customers on suppliers, we do not imply that suppliers cannot likewise shape customers' governance and strategic decisions. When small customers depend heavily on large suppliers for raw materials and input factors, these buyers will have high resource dependence on their providers.[64] Under such a scenario, suppliers exert a strong influence on customers' governance. In some companies, unions consolidate labor into a forceful bloc, wielding large

BOX 2.4   Strategic Governance Highlight: Interorganizational Spillover

David Quammen, author of *Spillover: Animal Infections and the Next Human Pandemic*, commented, "Make no mistake, they are connected, these disease outbreaks coming one after another. And they are not simply happening to us; they represent the unintended results of things we are doing." This interconnectedness occurs not only in pandemic outbreaks but also in the business environment. Firms are embedded in ecosystems. An event at a focal firm can impact the decisions and evaluations of peer companies that belong to the same category (such as the same industry). This occurrence is called *interorganizational spillover*.

Anecdotal evidence suggests that events in one firm can have some important consequences for other firms. For instance, the *E. coli* outbreak in 2015 at Chipotle restaurants in Seattle had consequential repercussions for other Mexican restaurants in the city. Similarly, the exposure of sexual abuse scandals within a film production company gave rise to the Me Too movement that affected the Hollywood industry as a whole. In 2020, the chief operating officer of Luckin Coffee, the largest domestic coffee chain in China, was accused of fabricating much of its reported sales in 2019. Extending the effect beyond borders, Carson Block, founder of Muddy Waters Research, a short-selling research firm, said, "This is again a wake-up call for US policymakers, regulators, and investors about the extreme fraud risk China-based companies pose to our markets."

Interorganizational spillover also explains the convergence of governance practices around the world. Countries such as Japan and Germany have gradually adopted governance practices that prioritize the interests of shareholders. Also, interlocked directors provide an important channel in facilitating interorganizational spillover. For example, interlocked directors enable the adoption of stock option plans among Germany companies.

Given the growing interconnectedness among firms, a key task for top managers these days entails mitigating negative spillover effects and capitalizing on the positive ones. Specifically, top managers need to constantly scan and monitor events that have occurred in peer firms; identify stakeholders that are most likely to change their assessment of focal firms due to spillover effects; and engage in targeted communication with targeted stakeholders.

Sources: Shi, W., Wajda, D., & Aguilera, R. (2021). Interorganizational spillover: A review and a proposal for future research. Working paper. Pisani, B. (2020). Luckin coffee is a painful reminder of "the extreme fraud risk" of some China-based companies. CNBC. April 3. https://www.cnbc.com/2020/04/03/luckin-coffee-debacle-is-a-painful-reminder-of-fraud-risk.html; Jargon, J. (2015). Chipotle grapples with *E. coli* outbreak. *Wall Street Journal.* November 3. https://www.wsj.com/articles/chipotle-grapples-with-e-coli-outbreak-1446506975; Yoshikawa, T., & Rasheed, A. A., (2009). Convergence of corporate governance: Critical review and future directions. *Corporate Governance: An International Review* 17(3), 388–404; Yu, T., Sengul, M., & Lester, R. H., (2008). Misery loves company: The spread of negative impacts resulting from an organizational crisis. *Academy of Management Review* 3(2), 452–472; Sanders, W. G., & Tuschke, A. (2007). The adoption of institutionally contested organizational practices: The emergence of stock option pay in Germany. *Academy of Management Journal* 50(1), 33–56; Pearson, Christine M., & Mitroff, Ian I. (1993). From crisis prone to crisis prepared: A framework for crisis management. *Academy of Management Perspectives* 7(1), 48–59.

negotiating power with employers. As a result, the employer firm's top managers must form governance practices and strategic decisions that reflect the preferences and interests of human capital suppliers—employees.

EXTERNAL GOVERNANCE ACTORS WITH INDIRECT INFLUENCE AND DIFFERING INTERESTS

Quadrant IV of Figure 2.2 lists governance actors whose interests are not aligned with focal firms and can influence governance and strategic decisions through indirect channels. For example, the interests of short sellers and competitors may oppose focal firm priorities. Meanwhile, rating agencies serve as independent, third-party information intermediaries, indifferent to the interests of firms. In addition, short sellers, competitors, and rating agencies are unlikely to have board representatives in focal firms and therefore influence governance and decisions indirectly.

Short Sellers

Short sellers borrow the firm's stock from others with an obligation to sell it back at an agreed-upon price.[65] They are motivated by the belief that the security's price will drop before they must return the security and thus differ from investors who hold a long position.[66] Short selling poses high risk because the sellers not only need to pay daily fees to the owner of the stock but also are subject to the risk of short squeezes. A short squeeze refers to an increase in an equity's price, forcing many short sellers to close their positions (as the price increases, short sellers' value decreases). In effect, this can push the price higher because it floods the market with buy orders to close short positions and leads the price to rise even more. Recently, retail investors built up stakes in GameStop—a video game, consumer electronics, and gaming merchandise retailer—in a short period of time with the help of Reddit—an information sharing platform, resulting in a jump in GameStop's stock price. The sharp rise in GameStop's stock price forced short sellers to buy back shares to limit their losses, leading to a short squeeze.[67]

Short sales have increased dramatically in recent years, today reflecting about a quarter of daily stock market volume.[68] Elon Musk made news in 2018 by tweeting disapprovingly about short sellers, which led to a settlement with the SEC about distributing misleading information.[69] Mike Pearson, CEO of Valeant, commented about one short seller that "his motivation is the same as one who runs into a crowded theater and falsely yells fire. He wanted people to run . . . so he could make money for his short-selling."[70] Patrick Byrne, CEO of Overstock.com, made headlines for referring to a "Sith Lord" conspiracy by short sellers to drive down the firm's stock price. Although CEOs often wage wars against short sellers and publicly denounce them, short-selling activities continue to rise even among firms belonging to the S&P 1500 index. Figure 2.4 shows that short interest—that is, the percentage of stocks shorted—stood at around 1 percent in 1995, but increased to about 5 percent in 2018. The highest level of short interest took place during the 2007–2008 financial crisis.

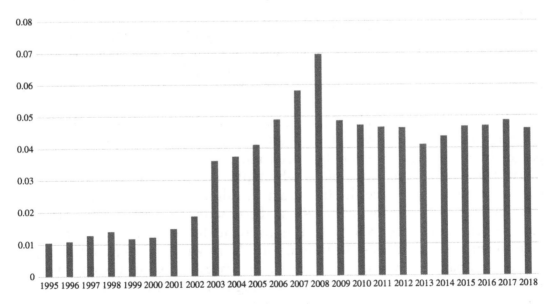

FIGURE 2.4 Average short interest of S&P 1500 firms (1995–2018).
Data source: Compustat Short Interest Supplemental

Because short sellers can benefit only from declining stock prices, these investors are motivated to dampen a firm's stock price. Meanwhile, top managers' employment and financial interests hinge on healthy stock prices. Short sellers hence play a governance role,[71] mainly in two ways. First, short sellers move to identify and disseminate negative information about shorted firms. These investors have a strong ability to analyze public information as well as reveal and trade on private information prior to becoming publicly available.[72] Some scholars even contend that short sellers are more informed and sophisticated than financial analysts.[73] Through disclosing negative information, these short-term investors can exert a downward pressure on stock prices.

Short sellers can also spread rumors, a tactic known as *short and distort*. For example, Lemelson Capital Management took a short position in Ligand, a pharmaceutical company, in May 2014, and then engaged in a short and distort campaign against the company. According to an SEC press release, Lemelson spread false claims through written reports, interviews, and social media, including that Ligand was "teetering on the brink of bankruptcy" and that Ligand's flagship Hepatitis C drug was going to become obsolete. Faced with the threat of rumors and the amplification of negative information, top managers exhibit high caution in making strategic decisions. Given these two reasons, short sellers have the effect of constraining financial misconduct[74] and value-destroying acquisitions,[75] as well as influencing CEO compensation design.[76] Yet, firms tend to complete an announced acquisition if there is an increase in the percentage of shares shorted after the announcement. This is because increasing short selling activity creates an egoistic threat to managers and can trigger escalation of commitment to the acquisition, given the adversarial relationship between managers and short sellers.[77] Although short sellers can generate some benefits for society, these investors have irreconcilably different objectives than the company's in which they open a short interest position.

Though most short sellers take a passive position in shorted firms and refrain from disclosing their short positions, a surge in the number of campaigns by activist short sellers has occurred in recent years, reaching 168 in 2019.[78] Unlike passive short sellers who build a company's short interest but do not publicly denounce the firms, activist short sellers publicly criticize a company and its management. Often, these activist investors will disseminate information about shorted firms to align the opinions of the broader investment community and the public with their own. They may, for example, call out managerial wrongdoing, such as in cases of executives engaging in accounting or major business fraud or having conflicts of interest. Such a case took place on January 8, 2018, when activist short seller Copperfield Research warned investors that managers at Tucows, an internet services company, were misrepresenting financials, before also noting that the company was acting as the domain registrar for numerous websites that supported racism and the abuse of children. Activist short sellers may likewise publicly denounce firms' lackluster performance. In late 2019, activist short seller Mako targeted Akoustis Technologies, claiming the company had "repeatedly undelivered over the last three years due to its old technology, tough competition, and mismanagement" and "is bound to succumb to competitive pressures" according to Activist Insight, which provides comprehensive information on activist investing worldwide.

Competitors

As they compete for market share, competitors represent one of the most important external stakeholders to firms.[79] A firm and its competitors mostly do not share the same interests; nevertheless, they indirectly influence each other. One such way involves keeping top managers focused on reducing slack, increasing efficiency, and maximizing profits to navigate strong product market competition and avoid bankruptcy.[80] Sir John Hicks once stated that top managers in less competitive industries tend to have more slack resources and therefore choose to enjoy the "quiet life."[81] In contrast, company leaders in competitive industries face constant pressure to reduce slack and enhance efficiency. Product market competition, by mitigating managerial slack, can prevent managers from pursuing a quiet life or extracting private benefits using slack resources. Yet intensive competition, though enabling a disciplining effect on managerial behaviors,[82] may sow the seed of misconduct as managers may undertake unethical or illegal means to survive rivalry. Increased competition in the car service industry, for instance, is associated with greater inspection leniency in vehicle emissions tests, a service quality attribute that customers appreciate but can include illegality and be socially costly.[83]

Competitors may also affect governance and strategic decisions through the interorganizational spillover effect (see Chapter 5 for more ideas). Company leaders stay highly keen on their competitors' moves and achievements,[84] taking note of events and responding to them under spillover influence. For example, chief executives will scale back strategic risk taking after a dismissal of a competitor CEO because the event triggers job security concerns among the observing executives.[85] Also, because firms and their competitors compete in the managerial labor market, a board's choice of corporate governance affects, and is affected by, the choices of governance by its competitors.[86] In another spillover scenario, more generous incentive compensations at one firm may induce its competitors to overpay their managers. By the same token, when a firm pumps up its stock price by using aggressive accounting practices to inflate earnings, competitors, faced with increased pressure, may also inflate earnings to avoid negative inferences about their strategic approach.[87]

Rating Agencies

Rating agencies, such as financial analysts and proxy advisory firms, serve an important role as "independent" third-party information intermediaries and play a crucial role in diffusing important information to a firm's external constituents, especially shareholders. Our discussion focuses on three types of rating agencies. First, *financial analysts* often employed by investment banks and brokerage firms read company financial statements carefully and question top executives in earnings conference calls with the goal of collecting information about covered companies and issuing recommendations to investors.[88] Second, *proxy advisory firms* such as Institutional Shareholder Services (ISS) and Glass Lewis & Co provide services to shareholders (oftentimes institutional investors) as to how they should vote their shares about information disclosed on proxy statements before shareholder meetings of listed companies. The third type of rating agencies pertains to *credit rating agencies* such as S&P Global Ratings, Moody's, and Fitch Group, which rate companies on their ability to make timely principal and interest payments and the likelihood of default.

Given their independence from the companies that they rate, rating agencies prove indifferent to firm performance. Yet, although the three types of rating agencies focus on different forms of assessments and serve varied constituents, they all play a governance role and influence rated firms' strategic decisions.[89] Rating agencies reduce information asymmetry between firms and external constituents, as they collect information about rated firms from various sources including financial statements, earnings conference calls, and direct communication with top executives. Through their function as information collectors, rating agencies play a monitoring role and, more importantly, influence the behavior of capital providers. Recommendations made by financial analysts, for example, may profoundly influence investors' trading actions[90]: positive recommendations can increase the demand for a company's stocks, whereas negative recommendations can give rise to selloffs. Likewise, recommendations by proxy advisory firms may profoundly sway shareholders' voting behavior.[91] And ratings by credit rating agencies, such as Standard & Poor's, can directly influence a firm's future borrowing costs. Although these rating agencies have indirect influence, capital providers, including equity holders and debt holders who follow their ratings, may exert direct influence on company governance and strategic decisions.

Given the role of financial analysts in influencing investors' trading behaviors, CEOs face a high likelihood of dismissal when firm performance falls short of analyst earnings forecasts[92] or when analyst recommendations are unfavorable.[93] Analyst coverage can also rein in excess CEO compensation[94] and prevent earning management.[95] However, the profound influence that analysts wield on investors creates strong pressure for top managers, which may induce managerial myopic behavior,[96] leading them to refrain from long-term investment[97] and even resort to financial misconduct.[98]

The growing power of proxy advisory firms is a direct outcome of the enactment of the Dodd-Frank Act in 2010, which gave shareholders an advisory vote in the compensation plans offered to executives, a procedure known as "say-on-pay." A survey conducted in 2012 suggests that around 72 percent of publicly traded companies review the policies of proxy advisory firms or engage with these firms for guidance on executive compensation designs. Not surprisingly, boards of directors design executive compensations in order to satisfy proxy advisory firms' expectations.[99] However, shareholders actually respond negatively to announcements of compensation redesigns that follow proxy advisory firms' guidelines,[100] implying that proxy advisory firm recommendations may not be value creating for shareholders. Beyond proxy advisory recommendations on compensation-related voting, in the context of uncontested director elections, directors who do not receive a positive recommendation from the advisory firms receive 19 percent fewer shareholder votes,[101] attesting to the significance of proxy advisory firms in influencing voting outcomes.

Shareholders and policy makers become growingly concerned about potential conflicts of interest inherent in proxy advisors' business models. The leading advisory firm, the ISS, sells both proxy voting services to investors and consulting services to companies seeking assistance with proposals to be voted by shareholders.[102] Others have criticized proxy advisory firms for their rigid and arbitrary standards.[103] Exxon Mobil's vice president for investor relations commented on the controversial role: "[Proxy advisors] are effectively our largest shareholders, despite having no direct stake in Exxon Mobil's success."[104] As a result, in 2020, the SEC introduced new requirements that make proxy advisors show their voting recommendations to public companies at the same time or before sending them to investors using their service.

As noted, another intermediary are credit rating agencies. The three big credit rating agencies—Moody's, Standard and Poor's, and Fitch Group—collectively control over 95 percent of the rating business. These agencies provide opinions on the creditworthiness of entities and financial obligations, as well as assess the credit risk of specific debt securities and the borrowing entities. Credit rating affects not only a firm's borrowing costs but also investors' behaviors.[105] Debt rating agencies certify the ability of a firm to pay the debt encumbered. This certification forms a critical element to firms' supply and cost of debt financing.[106] Many institutional investors are barred from investing in low credit rating firms or below a certain threshold (investment grade) due to concerns about client investors' wealth protection. Board directors should understand the importance of raising the firm's credit rating, a critical factor in the view of most stakeholders.[107] Companies with high credit ratings can overcome regulatory constraints and gain access to a wider "investor base" when seeking to borrow funds to finance specific investment projects. Meanwhile, investors may rely on the ratings to decide whether to buy a company's securities, since credit rating reflects a company's risk. Hence, firms with high credit ratings will face fewer financial constraints and managers enjoy more flexibility in their decision-making.[108]

Credit rating agencies are not without criticism. Because the company pays the credit rating agency to determine its rating, the agency will be inclined to give the company a more favorable assessment to retain its business, possibly biasing the fairness and objectivity of the rating process.

The Media

The media, including newspapers, television, and social media, can exert influence and control on managerial decisions through distribution of information to a broad spectrum of stakeholders.[109] Media companies focus on satisfying their audiences' demand for information and entertainment to maximize revenues by increasing readership and advertising income.[110] Therefore, the interests of the media often diverge from those of covered firms. The media can play a governance role not only by reducing information asymmetry between firms and external constituents[111] but also by acting as a social arbiter[112] that informs stakeholders and hence helps keep management accountable. Managers attempt to avoid actions that can trigger negative media coverage, which can adversely affect a firm's reputation and support from stakeholders.[113] Company leaders likewise make changes in response to instances of negative coverage. *Businessweek*, for instance, identifies "the worst" boards. Directors of firms that land on the unflattering list likely take substantial steps to make improvements, like increasing the number of outside directors or establishing more board diversity among outside members.[114]

Positive media coverage can also affect executive compensation, not necessarily by increasing the level of executives' total compensation,[115] but by reducing the share of CEO's compensation tied to firm financial performance.[116] Additionally, although positive media coverage can bring important resources, it comes at a cost for firms. For example, CEOs with more positive media coverage tend to possess stronger bargaining power; therefore, they will demand a higher level of compensation than those that derive less positive news stories.[117] Yet positive media coverage can also give rise to CEO overconfidence, increasing excessive firm risk-taking.[118] Research also suggests that the media's perspective of CEO compensation can be influenced by corporate philanthropic activities: firms engaged in philanthropy receive more media disapproval when they overcompensate their CEOs, but they are also more likely to decrease CEO overcompensation as a response.[119]

As social media has gained tremendous significance in society, its role in governance and strategic decisions has also increased. Compared with traditional media with a more targeted audience, social media can reach a maximum audience. Although information posted on social media often comes from nonexpert individuals and is less accurate, the medium provides a platform for timely and two-way communication. More importantly, users of social media may have unique connections through friends or families to attain and disburse information that may otherwise remain private.[120] Given the growing role of social media in swaying people's judgments and opinions, engaging in and managing social media becomes increasingly important not only for investor relations teams but also for top managers themselves. For example, on December 25, 2016, Brian Chesky, CEO of Airbnb, posted, "If @ Airbnb could launch anything in 2017, what would it be?" Chesky received more than 1,000 ideas in less than 24 hours.[121]

Social Activists

Social activists attempt to influence firms to make changes related to social issues. They often target companies whose practices encroach on the interests of stakeholders and society at large.[122] Unlike activist shareholders, social activists usually focus on nonfinancial goals. Although employee social activists can exert direct pressures on their top managers and the board of directors, these activists still need the support from outside social campaigners to be effective. In this sense, social activists are unable to exert a direct influence on firm governance and decisions.

Examples of the influence of social activism on firms abound. In 2014, the CEO of Mozilla, Brendon Eich, was forced to step down after his prior financial support for California's Proposition 8, banning same-sex marriage, inspired protests inside and outside of the company.[123] In 2018, Google employees staged walkout protests around the world over the company's handling of sexual harassment.[124] Due to pressures from social activists over environmental concerns, large banks such as Citibank, Goldman Sachs, JPMorgan Chase, and Wells Fargo are reported to have cut off liquidity and capital to many firms in the energy sector.[125] As social media provides a powerful platform for social activists to organize and reach a larger audience, the role of this form of activism in governance and strategic decisions is likely to grow.

Interactions among External Governance Actors

Our discussion has so far suggested that external governance actors exhibit varying interests, goals, and priorities. Yet, their influence on firm decisions does not take place independently. Instead, external governance actors interact with one another to shape corporate determinations. These interactions can be both collaborative and competitive.

Collaborative interactions take place when the influence of some external governance actors hinges on the support from counterparts. Activist shareholders can wield profound influence on firm governance because of support from institutional investors. ValueAct Capital Management LP was able to gain a board seat in Microsoft with less than 1 percent of ownership because large mutual funds—Franklin Templeton Investments and Capital Research & Management Co., with a combined ownership of more than 6 percent—stood behind the endeavor.[126] Similarly, shareholder and stakeholder activists depend on the media to broadcast their requests and demands and to seek other stakeholders' support. The need for media might explain why institutional investors are buying up newspapers to influence the tone of news coverage of their portfolio firms.[127] For example, after controlling newspapers such as *The Denver Post, The Boston Herald,* and the *St. Paul Pioneer Press,* Alden Global Capital acquired a 32 percent stake in shares of Tribune Publishing Company, owner of the Chicago Tribune, in 2019.[128] In 2020, hedge fund manager Chatham Asset Management LLC emerged as the winner in a bankruptcy auction for McClatchy Co., which publishes some 30 daily papers, including the *Miami Herald, the Sacramento Bee,* and the *Kansas City Star.*[129]

Collaborative influence also occurs through proxy advisory firms. As we previously noted, firms like ISS and Glass Lewis can affect firm governance and strategic decisions through their influence on shareholder voting choices. This influence includes institutional investors, who, compared with retail investors, own a higher percentage of US public firms' equities and are more likely to participate in shareholder voting.[130] While large institutional investors such as BlackRock have substantial resources needed to develop proprietary proxy voting guidelines and research company-specific issues, most small and mid-sized funds do not have the same level of resources. As such, they tend to rely more on the ISS's and Glass Lewis's guidelines in proxy voting and augmenting the advisory firms' influence over governance issues.[131]

But interactions among external governance actors can also be competitive and even adversarial. Hedge fund activists target firms for financial gains, whereas social activists push for social causes. Meanwhile, the media tends to focus on negative news stories due to the negativity bias—things of a more negative nature but of equal intensity have a greater effect on one's attention[132]—which can depress firm stock prices and thereby go against the interests of institutional investors. And since short sellers may engage in a short and distort strategy to drive down a firm's stock price, the relationship between short sellers and institutional investors may turn adversarial. The epic fight over global nutritional supplements company Herbalife between activist short seller, Bill Ackman, and activist long investor, Carl Icahn, is a case in point. In 2013, Ackman accused Herbalife of being a "pyramid scheme" and took a short position in the company, whereas Icahn took the other side of the short. Given their different positions, the two investors created a public media battle, inspiring the book, *When the Wolves Bite: Two Billionaires, One Company, and an Epic Wall Street Battle.*[133]

COPING WITH EXTERNAL GOVERNANCE ACTORS

As we have seen, company leaders face a multiplicity of external governance actors, each differing in terms of their influence channels and interest alignment with firms. But strategies exist for top managers to cope with external governance actors. We identify five types of coping strategies: acquiescence, compromise, avoidance, defense, and cooptation. Under *acquiescence*, executives may find that the best outcome lies in accepting the desired choices of an external governance actor. In a *compromise*, adopting only some of the anticipated choices by the external influencer may suffice. In an *avoidance* approach, executives may attempt to preclude the necessity to conform to the demands of the actor. *Defense* represents a form of active resistance to the external pressures. *Cooptation*, the most active response, refers to attempts to win over or assimilate the external governance actor's agenda as one's own. Figure 2.5 shows our suggested response strategies.

For external governance actors with direct influences and aligned interests (Quadrant I of Figure 2.2), top managers may use strategies of acquiescence and compromise. The interests of some external governance actors, such as activist investors, may not be consistent with those of a firm's internal stakeholders in the short run. However, these actors may possess industry expertise and insights and other types of knowledge. In this manner, when external governance actors' demands are valuable to firms' long-term competitiveness and performance, managers may conform to such demands (acquiescence).

Aligned Interests	Direct Influence	Example	Strategy
Aligned	Yes	Activist investors	Acquiescence and compromise
Different interests	Yes	Regulators	Acquiescence and cooptation
Aligned	No	Customers	Compromise and avoidance
Different interests	No	Rating agencies	Avoidance and defense

FIGURE 2.5   Response strategies to different external governance actors.

Yet, when the demands are misaligned with the firm's long-term interests or can trigger strong resistance from other stakeholders, managers may instead choose to compromise. For example, two activist shareholders, Marcellum Advisors GP and Ancora Advisors LLC, were contesting for board seats at Big Lots, a large retailer, after jointly buying over 10 percent of the firm's stock. Big Lots leaders reacted by adding board seat representation for both firms in a compromise to avoid a proxy battle, which would have been costly for all parties.[134] We may also see compromise in instances when institutional investors call for the directors to separate the CEO and board chair positions. If the board finds it critical to combine these two positions to ensure fast decision-making in a dynamic environment, the directors may resort to a compromise strategy by appointing a lead director position,[135] which can alleviate institutional investors' concerns that the CEO simultaneously serves as the board chair.

Acquiescence and cooption can be strategies used to cope with external governance actors who have different interests but direct influence on firms (Quadrant II of Figure 2.2). Given the coercive power possessed by regulators, who enforce laws and regulations, executives inevitably need to conform to or abide by guidelines enacted by the regulating officials (acquiescence). After the enactment of the SOX Act, the NYSE and NASDAQ passed provisions requiring firms to have mostly independent directors that meet a highly specific definition of this independence, and boards must comply to continue to be listed. However, company leaders can shape laws and regulations by engaging in corporate political activities (cooptation). In the United States, for example, executives may choose to allocate firm resources to lobbying or political campaign contributions to shape the policy making process.[136] In China, top managers of Chinese firms can directly influence public policies after being elected as members of the National People's Congress or the Chinese People's Political Consultative Conference.

For external governance actors that have aligned interests but no direct influence, including customers and suppliers (Quadrant III of Figure 2.2), compromise and avoidance become viable coping strategies. Although most customers do not have representatives in suppliers' boards or substantial stakes in the firms, they may represent an important source of revenues. Top managers of the supplier firms may need to compromise, even if customers' demands may not be in their interest in the short run, since failure to do so can result in losing important buyers. These managers may also consider pacifying customers by symbolically conforming to their demands (avoidance). As an exception to this quadrant and extending back to Quadrant I, avoidance may also be used to manage institutional investors. Executives that hold direct discussions with institutional owners about their concerns may pacify these owners through such communication without having to make significant changes, hence avoidance.[137]

Top managers may use avoidance and defense strategies to cope with external governance actors that have different interests and lack direct influence (Quadrant IV of Figure 2.2). Faced with pressure from the ISS, top managers can make changes that meet the proxy advisory firm's guidelines to attain sufficient shareholder support but decouple implementation from adoption. Relatedly, executives can undertake social influence tactics toward journalists to affect the favorability of media coverage[138] or symbolically adopt practices favored by the media. But when demands by external governance actors are fundamentally against a firm's interests, executives may consider publicly challenging external governance actors with a strong defensive move. Elon Musk, for example, has been engaged for some time in a digital cat-and-mouse fight with Tesla short sellers. His extraordinary use of Twitter to battle short sellers has often resulted a jump in Tesla's stock price, hurting the interests of the short sellers in the process.

Coping with external governance actors signifies a challenging task for top managers and boards of directors. Faced with conflicting demands, top managers need to assess an external governance actor's *power* to influence the firm, the *legitimacy* of its relationship with the firm, and the *urgency* of its claim on the firm.[139] After identifying the most critical external governance actor, top managers can then consider strategies proposed in Figure 2.5.

NOTES

1. Aguilera, R., Desender, K., Bednar, M. K., & Lee, J. H. (2015). Connecting the dots: Bringing external corporate governance into the corporate governance puzzle. *Academy of Management Annals* 9(1): 483–573.

2. DesJardine, M. R., & Durand, R. (2020). Disentangling the effects of hedge fund activism on firm financial and social performance. *Strategic Management Journal* 41(6): 1054–1082.
3. Garber, J. (2020). Tesla taunts short-sellers by selling 'short shorts.' *Fox Business*, July 6. www.foxbusiness. com/markets/tesla-red-satin-short-shorts.
4. Bebchuk, L. A., Cohen, A., & Hirst, S. (2017). The agency problems of institutional investors. *Journal of Economic Perspectives* 31(3): 89–102.
5. Ibid., 89–102.
6. Cremers, K. J. M., & Sepe, S. M. (2018). Institutional investors, corporate governance, and firm value. *Seattle University Law Review* 41: 388.
7. Hirschman, A. O. (1970). *Exit, Voice, and Loyalty: Responses to Decline in Firms*. Cambridge, MA: Harvard University Press.
8. Black, B. S. (1992). Agents watching agents: The promise of institutional investor voice. *UCLA Law Review* 39(4): 811–893; Gillan, S. L., & Starks, L. T. (2003). Corporate governance, corporate ownership, and the role of institutional investors: A global perspective. *Journal of Applied Finance* 13(2): 4–22.
9. Bharath, S. T., Jayaraman, S., & Nagar, V. (2013). Exit as governance: An empirical analysis. *Journal of Finance* 68(6): 2515–2547.
10. David, P., Kochhar, R., & Levitas, E. (1998). The effect of institutional investors on the level and mix of CEO compensation. *Academy of Management Journal* 41(2): 200–208.
11. Parrino, R., Sias, R. W., & Starks, L. T. (2003). Voting with their feet: Institutional ownership changes around forced CEO turnover. *Journal of Financial Economics* 68(1): 3–46.
12. Hoskisson, R. E., Hitt, M. A., Johnson, R. A., & Grossman, W. (2002). Conflicting voices: The effects of institutional ownership heterogeneity and internal governance on corporate innovation strategies. *Academy of Management Journal* 45(4): 697–716.
13. Bushee, B. J. (2004). Identifying and attracting the "right" investors: Evidence on the behavior of institutional investors. *Journal of Applied Corporate Finance* 16(4): 28–35.
14. Camara, K. A. D. (2004). Classifying institutional investors. *Journal of Corporation Law* 30(2): 219–254.
15. Bushee, B. J. (1998). The influence of institutional investors on myopic R&D investment behavior. *Accounting Review* 73(3): 305–333. Connelly, B. L., Tihanyi, L., Certo, S. T., & Hitt, M. A. (2010). Marching to the beat of different drummers: The influence of institutional owners on competitive actions. *Academy of Management Journal* 53(4): 723–742.
16. Hirschman, A. O. (1970). *Exit, voice, and loyalty: Responses to decline in firms, organizations, and states.* Cambridge, MA: Harvard University Press.
17. Gillan, S. L., & Starks, L. T. (2000). Corporate governance proposals and shareholder activism: The role of institutional investors. *Journal of Financial Economics* 57(2): 275–305.

18. Crane, A. D., Koch, A., & Michenaud, S. (2019). Institutional investor cliques and governance. *Journal of Financial Economics* 133(1): 175–197.
19. Huang, X., & Kang, J.-K. (2017). Geographic concentration of institutions, corporate governance, and firm value. *Journal of Corporate Finance* 47: 191–218.
20. Hoskisson, Hitt, Johnson, & Grossman. Conflicting voices.
21. Gillan, S. L., & Starks, L. T. (2007). The evolution of shareholder activism in the United States. *Journal of Applied Corporate Finance* 19(1): 55–73.
22. Proffitt, W. T., & Spicer, A. (2006). Shaping the shareholder activism agenda: Institutional investors and global social issues. *Strategic Organization* 4(2): 165–190.
23. Briscoe, F., & Gupta, A. (2016). Social activism in and around organizations. *Academy of Management Annals* 10(1): 671–727.
24. Gillan & Starks. The evolution of shareholder activism in the United States.
25. Romano, R. (2001). Less is more: making institutional investor activism a valuable mechanism of corporate governance. *Yale Journal on Regulation* 18: 174–252.
26. Brandes, P., Goranova, M., & Hall, S. (2008). Navigating shareholder influence: Compensation plans and the shareholder approval process. *Academy of Management Perspectives* 22(1): 41–57.
27. Greenwood, R., & Schor, M. (2009). Investor activism and takeovers. *Journal of Financial Economics* 92(3): 362–375.
28. DesJardine & Durand. Disentangling the effects of hedge fund activism on firm financial and social performance.
29. Brav, A., Jiang, W., Partnoy, F., & Thomas, R. (2008). Hedge fund activism, corporate governance, and firm performance. *Journal of Finance* 63(4): 1729–1775.
30. DesJardine & Durand. Disentangling the effects of hedge fund activism on firm financial and social performance.
31. Ibid.
32. Holderness, C. G., & Sheehan, D. P. (1988). The role of majority shareholders in publicly held corporations: An exploratory analysis. *Journal of Financial Economics* 20: 317–346.
33. Harvey, N., & Pearson, C. (2018). Exploring the impacts of shareholder activism on sustainability. *Sustainability*.
34. Krouse, S. (2018). BlackRock CEO to companies: Pay attention to "societal impact." *Wall Street Journal*, January 16. www.wsj.com/articles/blackrock-ceo-to-companies-pay-attention-to-societal-impact-1516120840.
35. Goranova, M., Abouk, R., Nystrom, P. C., & Soofi, E. S. (2017). Corporate governance antecedents to shareholder activism: A zero-inflated process. *Strategic Management Journal* 38(2): 415–435.
36. Lombardo, C. (2020). Carl Icahn boosts occidental stake to almost 10% as shares plummet. *Wall Street Journal*, March 11. www.wsj.com/articles/carl-icahn-boosts-occidental-stake-to-almost-10-as-shares-plummet-11583969050.
37. Terlep, S., & Benoit, B. (2017). P&G concedes proxy fight, adds Nelson Peltz to its board. *Wall Street Journal*, www.wsj.com, December 15.

38. Isidore, C., & Goldman, D. D. (2017). Procter & Gamble declares victory in expensive proxy fight. CNN Business, October 10.

39. Gantchev, N. (2013). The costs of shareholder activism: Evidence from a sequential decision model. *Journal of Financial Economics* 107(3): 610–631.

40. Shleifer, A., & Vishny, R. W. (1997). A survey of corporate governance. *Journal of Finance* 52(2): 737–783.

41. Nini, G., Smith, D. C., & Sufi, A. (2012). Creditor control rights, corporate governance, and firm value. *Review of Financial Studies* 25(6): 1713–1761.

42. Ibid.

43. Ibid.

44. Jandik, T., & McCumber, W. R. (2018). *Creditor governance.* Available at SSRN. https://dx. doi. org/10. 2139/ssrn. 3209460.

45. Aguilera, R. V., & Cuervo-Cazurra, A. (2004). Codes of good governance worldwide: what is the trigger? *Organization Studies* 25(3): 415–443.

46. La Porta, R., Lopez-de-Silanes, F., Shleifer, A., & Vishny, R. W. (1998). Law and finance. *Journal of Political Economy* 106(6): 1113–1155.

47. Liang, H., & Renneboog, L. (2017). On the foundations of corporate social responsibility. *Journal of Finance* 72(2): 853–910.

48. Cohen, L., Frazzini, A., & Malloy, C. J. (2012). Hiring cheerleaders: Board appointments of "independent" directors. *Management Science* 58(6): 1039–1058.

49. Shi, W., & Connelly, B. L. (2018). Is regulatory adoption ceremonial? Evidence from lead director appointments. *Strategic Management Journal* 39(8): 2386–2413.

50. Bromley, P., & Powell, W. W. (2012). From smoke and mirrors to walking the talk: Decoupling in the contemporary world. *Academy of Management Annals* 6: 483–530.

51. Shi, W., Aguilera, R., & Wang, K. (2020). State ownership and securities fraud: A political governance perspective. *Corporate Governance: An International Review* 28(2): 157–176.

52. Inoue, C. F., K. V., Lazzarini, S. G., & Musacchio, A. (2013). Leviathan as a minority shareholder: Firm–level implications of state equity purchases. *Academy of Management Journal* 56(6): 1775–1801.

53. Naughton, B. (2006). Claiming profit for the state: SASAC and the capital management budget. *China Leadership Monitor* 18: 1–9.

54. Heffernan, G. (2013). What happened after the Foxconn suicides. CBS News, August 7. www.cbsnews. com/news/what-happened-after-the-foxconn-suicides.

55. Johnsen, R. E., & Ford, D. (2008). Exploring the concept of asymmetry: A typology for analyzing customer–supplier relationships. *Industrial Marketing Management* 37(4): 471–483.

56. Fee, C. E., Hadlock, C. J., & Thomas, S. (2006). Corporate equity ownership and the governance of product market relationships. *Journal of Finance* 61(3): 1217–1251.

57. Allen, J. W., & Phillips, G. M. (2000). Corporate equity ownership, strategic alliances, and product market relationships. *Journal of Finance* 55(6): 2791–2815.

58. Bommaraju, R., Ahearne, M., Krause, R., & Tirunillai, S. (2019). Does a customer on the board of directors affect business-to-business firm performance? *Journal of Marketing* 83(1): 8–23.
59. Clarke, D. C. (2007). Three concepts of the independent director. *Delaware Journal of Corporate Law* 32(1): 73–112.
60. Dai, R., Liang, H., & Ng, L. (2020). Socially responsible corporate customers. *Journal of Financial Economics*.
61. Yu, T., Sengul, M., & Lester, R. H. (2008). Misery loves company: The spread of negative impacts resulting from an organizational crisis. *Academy of Management Review* 33(2): 452–472.
62. Albuquerque, R., Brandão-Marques, L., Ferreira, M. A., & Matos, P. (2019). International corporate governance spillovers: Evidence from cross-border mergers and acquisitions. *Review of Financial Studies* 32(2): 738–770.
63. Jia, Y., Wang, Z., Wu, J., & Zhang, Z. (2020). *The spillover effect of customer CEO myopia on supplier firms*. Available at SSRN.
64. Johnsen & Ford. Exploring the concept of asymmetry.
65. Drummond, B. (2006). One share, one vote: Short selling short-circuits the system. *International Herald Tribune*, March 1: 20.
66. Shi, W., King, D., & Connelly, B. (2021). Closing the deal: Managerial responses to short sellers following M&A announcement. *Journal of Business Research* 130: 188–199.
67. Pisani, B. (2021). What pro traders, the Reddit crowd and regulators may do next in the GameStop short squeeze saga. *CNBC*. January 29. www.cnbc.com/2021/01/29/gamestop-short-squeeze-what-pro-traders-the-reddit-crowd-and-regulators-may-do-next.html.
68. Diether, K. B., Lee, K. H., & Werner, I. M. (2009). It's SHO time! Short-sale price tests and market quality. *Journal of Finance* 64(1): 37–73; Massa, M., Qian, W., Xu, W., & Zhang, H. (2015). Competition of the informed: Does the presence of short sellers affect insider selling? *Journal of Financial Economics* 118(2): 268–288.
69. Frazzee, G. (2019). Why Elon Musk's tweets matter to the SEC. PBS.
70. Celarler, M. (2015). Valeant 'short' smells smoke — even when there's no fire. *New York Post*, October 27. https://nypost.com/2015/10/27/valeant-short-smells-smoke-even-when-theres-no-fire.
71. Shi, Ndofor, & Hoskisson. Disciplining role of short sellers.
72. Engelberg, J. E., Reed, A. V., & Ringgenberg, M. C. (2012). How are shorts informed? Short sellers, news, and information processing. *Journal of Financial Economics* 105(2): 260–278.
73. Christophe, S. E., Ferri, M. G., & Hsieh, J. (2010). Informed trading before analyst downgrades: Evidence from short sellers. *Journal of Financial Economics* 95(1): 85–106.
74. Karpoff, J. M., & Lou, X. (2010). Short sellers and financial misconduct. *Journal of Finance* 65(5): 1879–1913.

75. Shi, W., Ndofor, H. A., & Hoskisson, R. E. (2020). Disciplining role of short sellers: evidence from M&A activity. *Journal of Management*. 0149206320912307.

76. De Angelis, D., Grullon, G., & Michenaud, S. (2017). The effects of short-selling threats on incentive contracts: Evidence from an experiment. *Review of Financial Studies* 30(5): 1627–1659.

77. Shi, King, & Connelly. Closing the deal.

78. Activist Insight. (2020). *The activist investing annual review: The seventh annual review of trends in shareholder activism.*

79. Freeman, R. E. (1984). *Strategic management: A stakeholder approach.* Boston: Pitman.

80. Giroud, X., & Mueller, H. M. (2011). Corporate governance, product market competition, and equity prices. *Journal of Finance* 66(2): 563–600.

81. Hicks, J. R. (1935). Annual survey of economic theory: The theory of monopoly. *Econometrica: Journal of the Econometric Society*: 1–20.

82. Giroud, X., & Mueller, H. M. (2010). Does corporate governance matter in competitive industries? *Journal of Financial Economics* 95(3): 312–331.

83. Bennett, V., Pierce, L., Snyder, J. A., & Toffel, M. W. (2013). Customer-driven misconduct: How competition corrupts business practices. *Management Science* 59(8): 1725–1742.

84. Kim, K. H., & Tsai, W. (2012). Social comparison among competing firms. *Strategic Management Journal* 33(2): 115–136.

85. Connelly, B. L., Li, Q. J., Shi, W., & Lee, K. (2020). CEO dismissal: Consequences for the strategic risk taking of competitor CEOs. *Strategic Management Journal*.

86. Acharya, V. V., & Volpin, P. F. (2009). Corporate governance externalities. *Review of Finance* 14(1): 1–33.

87. Cheng, I.-H. (2011). Corporate governance spillovers. Available at SSRN 1299652.

88. Brauer, M., & Wiersema, M. (2018). Analyzing analyst research: A review of past coverage and recommendations for future research. *Journal of Management* 44(1): 218–248.

89. Ashbaugh-Skaife, H., Collins, D. W., & LaFond, R. (2006). The effects of corporate governance on firms' credit ratings. *Journal of Accounting and Economics* 42(1): 203–243; Brauer, M., & Wiersema, M. (2018). Analyzing analyst research: A review of past coverage and recommendations for future research. *Journal of Management* 44(1): 218–248; Morgan, A., Poulsen, A., & Wolf, J. (2006). The evolution of shareholder voting for executive compensation schemes. *Journal of Corporate Finance* 12(4): 715–737.

90. Womack, K. L. (1996). Do brokerage analysts' recommendations have investment value? *Journal of Finance* 51(1): 137–167.

91. Malenko, N., & Shen, Y. (2016). The role of proxy advisory firms: Evidence from a regression-discontinuity design. *Review of Financial Studies* 29(12): 3394–3427.

92. Puffer, S. M., & Weintrop, J. B. (1991). Corporate performance and CEO turnover: The role of performance expectations. *Administrative Science Quarterly* 36(1): 1–19.

93. Wiersema, M. F., & Zhang, Y. (2011). CEO dismissal: The role of investment analysts. *Strategic Management Journal* 32(11): 1161–1182.

94. Chen, T., Harford, J., & Lin, C. (2015). Do analysts matter for governance? Evidence from natural experiments. *Journal of Financial Economics* 115(2): 383–410.

95. Yu, F. (2008). Analyst coverage and earnings management. *Journal of Financial Economics* 88(2): 245–271.

96. Graham, J. R., Harvey, C. R., & Rajgopal, S. (2005). The economic implications of corporate financial reporting. *Journal of Accounting and Economics* 40(1–3): 3–73.

97. He, J., & Tian, X. (2013). The dark side of analyst coverage: The case of innovation. *Journal of Financial Economics* 109(3): 856–878.

98. Shi, W., Connelly, B. L., & Hoskisson, R. E. (2017). External corporate governance and financial fraud: Cognitive evaluation theory insights on agency theory prescriptions. *Strategic Management Journal* 38(6): 1268–1286.

99. Larcker, D. F., McCall, A. L., & Ormazabal, G. (2015). Outsourcing shareholder voting to proxy advisory firms. *Journal of Law and Economics* 58(1): 173–204.

100. Larcker, D. F., McCall, A. L., & Ormazabal, G. (2013). Proxy advisory firms and stock option repricing. *Journal of Accounting and Economics* 56(2–3): 149–169.

101. Cai, J., Garner, J., & Walkling, R. (2010). Shareholder access to the boardroom: A survey of recent evidence. *Journal of Applied Finance* 20(2): 15.

102. Li, T. (2018). Outsourcing corporate governance: Conflicts of interest within the proxy advisory industry. *Management Science* 64(6): 2951–2971.

103. Copland, J., Larcker, D. F., & Tayan, B. (2018). The big thumb on the scale: An overview of the proxy advisory industry. Rock Center for Corporate Governance at Stanford University Closer Look Series: Topics, Issues and Controversies in Corporate Governance No. CGRP-72: 18–27.

104. Kiernan, P. (2020). SEC votes to regulate proxy advisers more closely. *Wall Street Journal*, July 22. www.wsj.com/articles/sec-votes-to-regulate-proxy-advisers-more-closely-11595432292.

105. Healy, P. M., & Palepu, K. G. (2001). Information asymmetry, corporate disclosure, and the capital markets: A review of the empirical disclosure literature. *Journal of Accounting and Economics* 31(1): 405–440.

106. Bosch, O., & Steffen, S. (2011). On syndicate composition, corporate structure and the certification effect of credit ratings. *Journal of Banking & Finance* 35(2): 290–299.

107. Papadimitri, P., Pasiouras, F., Tasiou, M., & Ventouri, A. (2020). The effects of board of directors' education on firms' credit ratings. *Journal of Business Research* 116: 294–313.

108. Karampatsas, N., Petmezas, D., & Travlos, N. G. (2014). Credit ratings and the choice of payment method in mergers and acquisitions. *Journal of Corporate Finance* 25: 474–493.

109. Bednar, M. K. (2012). Watchdog or lapdog? A behavioral view of the media as a corporate governance mechanism. *Academy of Management Journal* 55(1): 131–150.

110. Core, J. E., Guay, W., & Larcker, D. F. (2008). The power of the pen and executive compensation. *Journal of Financial Economics* 88(1): 1–25.

111. Bushee, B. J., Core, J. E., Guay, W., & Hamm, S. J. W. (2010). The role of the business press as an information intermediary. *Journal of Accounting Research* 48(1): 1–19.

112. Wiesenfeld, B. M., Wurthmann, K. A., & Hambrick, D. C. (2008). The stigmatization and devaluation of elites associated with corporate failures: A process model. *Academy of Management Review* 33(1): 231–251.

113. Deephouse, D. L. (2000). Media reputation as a strategic resource: An integration of mass communication and resource–based theories. *Journal of Management* 26(6): 1091–1112.

114. Joe, J. R., Louis, H., & Robinson, D. (2009). Managers' and investors' responses to media exposure of board ineffectiveness. *Journal of Financial and Quantitative Analysis*: 579–605.

115. Core, Guay, & Larcker. The power of the pen and executive compensation.

116. Bednar. Watchdog or lapdog?

117. Nguyen, B. D. (2015). Is more news good news? Media coverage of CEOs, firm value, and rent extraction. Quarterly *Journal of Finance* 5(4): 1550020.

118. Chatterjee, A., & Hambrick, D. C. (2011). Executive personality, capability cues, and risk taking: How narcissistic CEOs react to their successes and stumbles. *Administrative Science Quarterly* 56(2): 202–237; Hayward, M. L., & Hambrick, D. C. (1997). Explaining the premiums paid for large acquisitions: Evidence of CEO hubris. *Administrative Science Quarterly*: 103–127.

119. Vergne, J. -P., Wernicke, G., & Brenner, S. (2018). Signal incongruence and its consequences: A study of media disapproval and CEO overcompensation. *Organization Science* 29(5): 796–817.

120. Ang, J. S., Hsu, C., Tang, D., & Wu, C. (2020). The role of social media in corporate governance. *Accounting Review*, forthcoming.

121. Heavey, C., Simsek, Z., Kyprianou, C., & Risius, M. (2020). How do strategic leaders engage with social media? A theoretical framework for research and practice. *Strategic Management Journal* 41(8); 1490–1527.

122. Briscoe & Gupta. Social activism in and around organizations.

123. Lee, D. (2014). Mozilla boss Brendan Eich resigns after gay marriage storm. BBC, April 4.

124. Wakabayashi, D., Griffith, E., Tsang, A., & Conger, K. (2018). Google walkout: Employees stage protest over handling of sexual harassment. *New York Times*, November 1. www.nytimes.com/2018/11/01/technology/google-walkout-sexual-harassment. html.

125. Gray, C. B. (2020). Banks' energy boycott is an antitrust problem. *Wall Street Journal*, July 14. https://www.bbc. com/news/technology-26868536.

126. Benoit, D., & Grind, K. (2015). Activist investors' secret ally: Big mutual funds. *Wall Street Journal*, August 9.

127. He, J., Xia, H., & Zhao, Y. (2020). *"Pump and dump" through media tone: The role of cross-blockholders in corporate litigation*. Available at SSRN. https://papers. ssrn. com/sol3/papers. cfm?abstract_id=3584740.

128. Jackson, D., & Marx, G. (2020). Will the *Chicago Tribune* be the next newspaper picked to the bone? *New York Times,* 19 January. www.nytimes.com.

129. Randles, J., & Alpert, L. I. (2020). Hedge fund Chatham wins bankruptcy auction for McClatchy's newspapers. *Wall Street Journal*, July 12. www.wsj.com/articles/hedge-fund-chatham-wins-bankruptcy-auction-for-mcclatchys-newspapers-11594569095.

130. Copland, Larcker, & Tayan. The big thumb on the scale.

131. Ibid., 18–27.

132. Baumeister, R. F., Bratslavsky, E., Finkenauer, C., & Vohs, K. D. (2001). Bad is stronger than good. *Review of General Psychology* 5(4): 323–370.

133. Wapner, S. (2018). *When the wolves bite: Two billionaires, one company, and an epic Wall Street battle*. New York: PublicAffairs.

134. Navera, T. (2020). In compromise with activist investors, Big Lots changes its board. *Columbus Business First*, April 23.

135. Shi, & Connelly. Is regulatory adoption ceremonial?

136. Hadani, M., & Schuler, D. A. (2013). In search of El Dorado: The elusive financial returns on corporate political investments. *Strategic Management Journal* 34(2): 165–181.

137. Westphal, J. D., & Bednar, M. K. (2008). The pacification of institutional investors. *Administrative Science Quarterly* 53(1): 29–72.

138. Westphal, J. D., & Deephouse, D. L. (2011). Avoiding bad press: Interpersonal influence in relations between CEOs and journalists and the consequences for press reporting about firms and their leadership. *Organization Science* 22(4): 1061–1086.

139. Mitchell, R. K., Agle, B. R., & Wood, D. J. (1997). Toward a theory of stakeholder identification and salience: Defining the principle of who and what really counts. *Academy of Management Review* 22(4): 853–886.

CHAPTER 3

Governance Actors and Corporate Strategy

BOX 3.1   Strategic Governance Challenge: Difference in Optimal Levels of Corporate Diversification for Shareholders and Executives

To illustrate the effect of corporate governance on corporate strategy, we examine the tension that exists between shareholders and top executives on the question of how diversified a firm's portfolios of businesses should be. In Figure 3.1, Curve *S* shows shareholders' optimal utility level and their preferred point of corporate diversification, occurring lower than that of top managers, as reflected on Curve *M*. This assumption rests on the logic that shareholders do not need firms to diversify their investments because they diversify their own portfolios by buying varied equities.

Of course, the optimum level of firm diversification that shareholders seek (Point *A* on Curve *S*) varies from firm to firm. Factors that affect shareholders' preferences include the company's primary industry, the intensity of rivalry among competitors in that industry, the top management team's

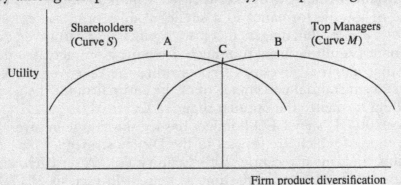

FIGURE 3.1   Shareholders' and top managers' utility and diversification.

experience with implementing diversification strategies, and the firm's perceived expertise in potential, new diversified businesses and their effects on other firm strategies, such as entry into international markets. Generally, however, shareholders seem to prefer focused diversification that may center on a dominant product or a set of related products or services.

The tension between shareholders and managers often becomes evident when activist investors seek to reduce the diversification level by divesting or selling off business units that seem superfluous to them. In 2015, for example, executives at major diversified corporations, including General Electric, AIG, Dow Chemical, DuPont, Qualcomm, Alcoa, Symantec, eBay, Yahoo!, and Amgen, either undertook or considered undertaking divestitures at the behest of activist investors, even while these divestitures would generally reduce overall firm product diversification.

As shown in Figure 3.1, top-level managers' optimal level of diversification (Point B on Curve M) is greater than that of shareholders. One reason rests on firm size, since diversification increases firm size and the size of a firm positively impacts executive compensation and external recognition, enhancing executives' social status in the business community. Diversification also increases the complexity of managing a firm and its network of businesses, usually requiring additional managerial pay. Also, product diversification and the resulting diversification of the firm's portfolio of businesses can reduce top-level *managerial employment risk*, or the risk of job loss, loss of compensation, and loss of managerial reputation. The risk decreases because a firm and its upper-level managers become less vulnerable to the reduction in demand associated with a single or limited number of product lines or businesses. Diversification also smoothens the cyclical nature of cash flows relative to a single product or narrow market-focused firm. If a company is acquired because of low performance in a single-product firm, the employment risk for its top-level managers increases significantly. However, declining performance resulting from too much diversification increases the probability that external investors (representing the takeover market) will purchase a substantial percentage of or the entire firm for the purpose of controlling it—hence the optimal shape of Curve M.

Since 2005, Disney CEO Bob Iger has led the charge in several acquisitions, four of which are central to the Disney strategy: Pixar, Marvel, Lucasfilm, and, most recently, 20th Century Fox. After each successful acquisition, his total compensation increased. In fact, in 2017, as part of the board's decision to extend his contract to 2021 to enable him to finish the integration of Fox—the largest of the acquisitions—his annual pay increased by about 60 percent to $48.5 million, in addition to stock awards worth about $100 million that will vest over the years after the acquisition, depending on the company's stock return. However, the board lowered his pay in 2019 prompted by a negative vote on his compensation by external shareholders after Glass Lewis, a proxy advisory intermediary, advised against Disney's say-on-pay proposal. Nevertheless, these acquisitions have attracted attention from the business media and boosted Iger's social recognition. He was named Businessperson of 2019 by *Time* magazine.

Through diversification, as in the case of Disney, top management teams receive higher compensation while also developing a strategy more immune to cycle volatility. However, managers seek to remain short of the point at which diversification increases their employment risk and reduces employment opportunities. Iger, for example, pursued acquisitions related to the movie industry, since movie themes are used to promote new attractions in Disney theme parks and also produce new retail opportunities by selling paraphernalia associated with the icons from the movies.

When no power differential exists between shareholders and owners, the compromise on firm diversification falls at point C, which is suboptimal for both shareholders and top managers.

Sources: Luscombe, B. (2019). Businessperson of the year. *Time.* https://time.com/businessperson-of-the-year-2019-bob-iger/; Whitten, S. (2019). 14 years, 4 acquisitions, 1 Bob Iger: How Disney's CEO revitalized an iconic American brand, *CNBC,* www.cnbc.com, August 6; Chen, S., & Feldman, E. R. (2018). Activist-impelled divestitures and shareholder value. *Strategic Management Journal* 39 (10), 2726–2744; Palmeri, C., & Kaskey, J. (2018). Disney investors offer say on executive pay, and dislike. *Bloomberg.com,* www.bloomberg.com, March 8; Stadler, M. Mayer, J., Hautz, J., & Matzler, K. (2018). International and product diversification: Which strategy suits family managers? *Global Strategy Journal* 8: 184–207; Hou, W. Priem, R. L. & Goranova, M. (2017). Does one size fit all? Investigating pay-future performance relationships over the "seasons" of CEO tenure, *Journal of Management* 43: 864–891; Hoskisson, R. E., Zyung, J. (Daniel), Gambeta, E., & Chirico, F. (2017). Managerial risk taking; A multitheoretical review and future research agenda. *Journal of Management* 43 (1): 137–169.; Shi, W., Zhang, A., & Hoskisson, R. (2017). Ripple effects of CEO awards: Investigating the acquisition activities of superstar CEOs' competitors. *Strategic Management Journal* 38 (10): 2080–2102; Wang, H., Zhao, S., & Chen, G. (2017). Firm-specific knowledge assets and employment arrangements: Evidence from CEO compensation design and CEO dismissal. *Strategic Management Journal* 38 (9): 1875–1894 C.; Mackey, T. B. Barney, J. B. & Dotson, J. P. (2017). Corporate diversification and the value of individual firms: A Bayesian approach. *Strategic Management Journal* 38: 322–341; De Cesari, A., Gonenc, H., & Ozkan, N. (2016). The effects of corporate acquisitions on CEO compensation and CEO turnover of family firms. *Journal of Corporate Finance* 38: 294–317; Amihud, Y. & Lev, B. (1981). Risk reduction as a managerial motive for conglomerate mergers. *Bell Journal of Economics* 12: 605–617.

As noted in the Strategic Governance Challenge (Box 3.1) and Figure 3.1, shareholders prefer firms to pursue riskier strategies with more focused diversification. Shareholders reduce their risk by holding a diversified portfolio of investments. While shareholders reduce their risk by holding a diversified portfolio of investments, executives cannot balance their managerial employment risk by working for a diverse portfolio of firms. Executives therefore prefer a level of corporate diversification that maximizes firm size, especially through acquisitions, as the Disney example in the challenge box shows. As in the case of Disney's Iger, top executives' compensations can dramatically increase through large diversifying acquisitions, while at the same time reducing their employment risk. But finding the appropriate level of diversification may be difficult for managers who might overdiversify, leading to lower performance and the potential for a hostile takeover. Too much diversification can also have negative effects on the firm's ability to create innovation (creating an incentive for managers to take on lower risks) and diverts managerial attention from other important activities such as corporate social responsibility.[1] Nevertheless, focused diversification that complements the firm's capabilities can enhance its innovation output.[2]

Product diversification forms a critical component of corporate strategy, which addresses the decision to determine in which businesses the firm should compete. Under the domain of corporate strategy, executives determine whether to enter new businesses through acquisitions and thus increase product diversification, or to exit existing business through divestitures and thus reduce business scope. The goal of corporate strategy is to create corporate advantage—the value created from owning multiple businesses together rather than separately. But although product diversification has the potential to generate corporate advantage, the action presents a potential agency problem that could result in shareholders incurring costs to control managerial behaviors. The potential tension between shareholders and top-level managers, as shown in Figure 3.1, coupled with the dilemma of determining which managers might act opportunistically, demonstrates why shareholders establish governance mechanisms, such as board monitoring or incentive compensation. However, the firm incurs costs when using one or more governance mechanisms. These agency costs refer to the sum of incentives, monitoring, and enforcement costs, as well as individual financial losses incurred by shareholders because governance mechanisms cannot guarantee total compliance by top executives. Monitoring may prove costly because board members, especially outside directors who are not associated with day-to-day firm operations, may find it difficult to monitor managers. These costs increase with larger and more complex firm operations, and go up quite dramatically upon diversification, given the additional complexity.[3]

Conventional thinking based on agency theory presumes that power lies within the CEO, and that agency costs are borne by the firm to rein in this power by boards or owners using authority bestowed on them by stakeholders.[4] However, another perspective, under resource dependence theory, points out that CEO power comes from multiple sources and resides in a variety of relationships with important stakeholders,[5] and this power cannot be exercised without the assent of these key stakeholders including employees. Though power allows CEOs to prioritize their own preferences, for the executives to maintain command, they must manage relationships with parties that underpin their sources of power,[6] suggesting that they must exercise their power and control judiciously. We will analyze their sources and limitations of power as we delve into the oftentimes tense and delicate relationship between top executives and governance actors, mainly shareholders and boards of directors, but also financial analysts and media players, especially where these influencers impact diversification strategies.

GOVERNANCE ACTORS AND DIVERSIFICATION STRATEGIES

As Figure 3.1 suggests, a persistent tension exists between shareholders and top managers about diversification strategy. Governance actors manage this tension through available governance devices.

Institutional Investors and Diversification Strategy

Over time, as noted in Chapter 2, institutional owners, or financial institutions such as stock mutual funds and pension funds, have become the dominant ownership group in the United States and the United Kingdom.[7] Because firms do not in general become overly diversified when they are owned by a high percentage of institutional investors, just having a large number of these investors can reduce managerial overdiversification and the need for divestiture.[8] Yet some institutional investors are more active in governance than others. Activist investors, who exercise their power through dialogues or direct threats, can reduce the level of diversification more effectively than other types of investors.[9] Activist Carl Icahn used this strategy effectively. During the 1960s and 1970s, executives of US public companies tended to run organizations in ways designed to increase their size while minimizing financial risk, with heavy emphasis on corporate diversification. Yet Icahn successfully challenged corporate managers throughout the 1970s and 1980s by buying blocks of shares in companies that he believed were undervalued and then demanding board seats and other changes in corporate governance

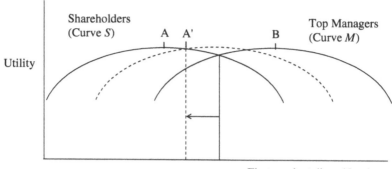

FIGURE 3.2   Shareholders' and top managers' utility and diversification as power shifts to shareholders.

and management.[10] This approach often meant a reduced level of diversification by selling off business units peripheral to the company's central strategy.

Activist investors continue the approach today. In 2018, Icahn held 6.7 percent in highly diversified Newell Brands, maker of variety products like Goody hair ties and Graco baby strollers. Another activist investor entered the fray. In a settlement with activist investor, Starboard, Newell allowed four activist-nominated board seats to be nominated in addition to appointing a new board chair to help the company focus its strategy by selling some of its business units and shedding factories that were not pertinent to Newell's revised strategy.[11] This activity also led to the former CEO leaving the company.

With increased activist owners and those institutional investors that support them, diversification is moving more in favor of owners' utility, as illustrated in Figure 3.2. Firms exhibit a shift toward lower levels of diversification as activist owners have gained power through more intense activism and appointment of board members that favor these actions. Meanwhile, as could be expected, activist-led divestitures can lead to increased shareholder wealth.[12]

BOARD MONITORING, EXECUTIVE COMPENSATION, AND DIVERSIFICATION STRATEGY

Boards have become more actively engaged in corporate strategic decisions as illustrated in Chapter 1. First, activist shareholders have gained power with the support of previously less engaged institutional investors. Second, boards are required to have more independent outside directors because of regulation imposed by the Sarbanes-Oxley Act of 2003. But dominant market exchanges in New York, London, and others are also contributing to the strength of outside directors through an increasing requirement to have these directors chair key board committees, such as the compensation, nomination, and audit committees. In the United States, this requirement has resulted in 40 percent of firms having only one inside director—the CEO,[13] which increases monitoring intensity by outside directors.

However, as we also noted in Chapter 1, when boards switch to a majority of outside directors, they focus their monitoring of top managers on more financial rather than strategic control, especially without sufficient insiders to help inform outside board members about firm-specific operations.[14] This form of monitoring often restricts managers from engaging in complex, long-term strategic decisions and reduces managerial risk taking, resulting in the potential for long-term underperformance. Boards should increase the effectiveness of their supervision to ensure that risk does not shift inappropriately to managers. This goal can be accomplished by monitoring practices that incorporate more emphasis on strategic control in the evaluation system rather than relying primarily on financial outcomes.[15] In other words, managers would be evaluated not only on financial outcomes but also on the quality of their strategic formulation with agreement of the board. Yet this more-balanced approach to monitoring becomes almost impossible without more inside directors[16] and is not the current reality due to the noted regulatory restrictions on having inside board members.

As the intensity of governance increases with more active investors and board members, managers become less able to reduce their employment risk by diversifying corporate assets. Since shareholders tend to be vigilant monitors, making sure that managers do not overdiversify the firm,[17] managers face higher employment risk—that is, risk shifts their way—as represented by the lower dashed line under the top managers curve in the lower right quadrant of Figure 3.3. If increased diversification is not a possibility (see Point B' of Figure 3.3), given the added risk they have incurred, managers are likely to require higher compensation.

A consequence of intensified governance that shifts risks to CEOs[18] is an increase in CEO turnover, especially as activist owners begin to engage with the company, as we saw with the departure of the CEO at Newell. As one governance consultant states: "The factors pushing CEOs out are only intensifying. CEOs are going to be held to greater account by the public, by investors, by employees, and the board."[19] Governance mechanisms, like board monitoring, incentives, or ownership concentrations, may work together as substitutes—that is, higher ownership concentration may be related to less need for board vigilance *concurrently*.[20] However, when one control mechanism becomes more intense than the other, the relationship may become negatively reinforcing as

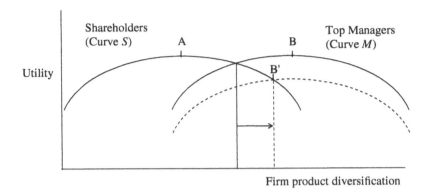

FIGURE 3.3   Shareholders' and top managers' utility and diversification as risk is shifted to managers.

undue risk is shifted to managers over time. If prominent risk shifting, strong ownership, and board monitoring prevent increased diversification, as might be the case in the US, then asking for increased compensation becomes an essential option for executives. For example, if a CEO is dismissed by a board due to an increased sensitivity to monitoring firm performance (such as due to a failed diversification strategy), a replacement CEO would enter either a failed situation or one requiring a revamped strategy—both of which are risky undertakings, whether the executive comes from the outside or inside. Accordingly, the new hire would seek protection by negotiating a higher salary, improved incentive compensation to encourage risk taking, and a *golden parachute* (compensation for early termination because of a change in ownership if the CEO's strategy does not work out) to take on the greater risk associated with the increasingly intensive monitoring environment.[21]

This depiction is supported by the evidence that CEO tenures are decreasing, as shown in Figure 3.4. Decreases in tenure indicate increased CEO risk. The increased emphasis on performance or financial outcome controls due to having predominantly outside board members[22] cause CEOs not only to lose their jobs, but also often their human and social capital, as they may become stigmatized or suffer other reputational losses that damage their market value and limit their chances of finding a new executive position.[23] As a new CEO takes over managing a firm, he or she will certainly recognize the more intense monitoring environment and the associated increase in employment risk, and, as such, may likely seek improved incentives that compensate for this risk, especially if diversification is not an option. Interestingly, Figure 3.4 suggests that CEO salary has been increasing. This observation implies that more compensation ensues from the need to encourage risk taking by executives. Still, in some cases, intensified monitoring has led some managers to

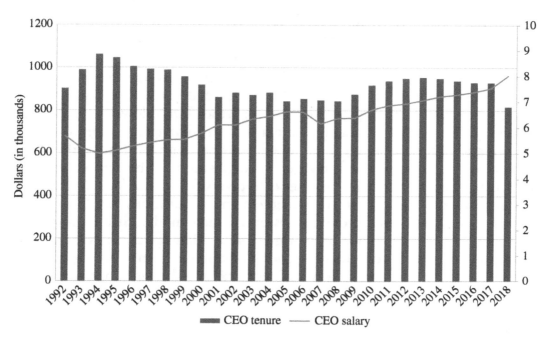

FIGURE 3.4 Average CEO salary and tenure of S&P 1500 firms.
Data source: ExecuComp

engage in financial misconduct to "boost" the appearance of improved firm performance.[24]

We have described the connection between increased monitoring in publicly traded firms and executive compensation through the principle of risk shifting. These two main governance devices founded in agency theory have created a cycle in which managers are paid excessively, requiring that corporate governance becomes more stringent and, as corporate governance becomes more stringent, managers require ever-higher pay. But the trend toward excessive compensation has resulted in more regulation, such as the "say-on-pay" proxy voting, where large outside owners can vote on the top executives' compensation packages during the annual proxy season. This approach has dampened pay somewhat, as we saw in the case of Disney, when Bob Iger's pay package received a negative vote.[25] Meanwhile, decrying an environment of excessive executive compensation may seem reasonable, but public outcry may lead to efforts to legislate pay limits, leaving CEOs forced to bear inappropriate amounts of risk, which they may choose to offset in indirect ways such as through implementing less risky strategies, in turn leading to lower innovation rates (to be discussed in Chapter 4). Alternative ways to approach corporate strategy exist, however, which may, in effect, increase diversification. Cooperative strategy by partnering with other firms is one such approach, which we will discuss next.

GOVERNANCE AND STRATEGIC ALLIANCES

Forester Consulting noted in a survey of 452 firms that over half of the companies surveyed (52 percent) received more than 20 percent of their revenue from the partnership channel.[26] The growing trend may be explained by the diversification that strategic alliances and partnerships allow. These avenues, especially diversifying alliances, create a way for managers to improve their performance by diversifying their operations through a means other than internal organic growth or a merger or acquisition.[27] The options become particularly beneficial when a firm seeks to diversify into markets in which the host nation's government prevents mergers and acquisitions (see Chapter 6). In these cases, alliances represent an essential entry mode. Airline companies, for instance, have joined one of the three major alliance networks (Star, Oneworld, and SkyTeam) due to restrictions on foreign firms owning national flag airlines. These alliances allow airlines to expand their international routes and sometime maintenance in other countries they are not currently serving without significant investment.

Corporate-level strategic alliances can also be attractive compared with acquisitions, particularly because they typically require fewer fixed asset investments and allow for greater flexibility but provide sought-after diversification through partner operations.[28] An alliance can also be used to determine whether the partners might benefit from a future merger or acquisition between them. Partners are also able to reduce information asymmetry between the potential acquirer and target.[29] Not surprisingly, prior alliance experiences enable acquirers to gain information helpful for post-acquisition integration.[30] Alliances also become attractive when dedicated institutional investors provide patient capital to make long-term exploratory joint ventures successful, such as when a new product is being created by two partnering independent firms.[31] Meanwhile, firms with a board with a good reputation are more likely to participate in strategic alliances because of their positive reputation.[32] Because trust is important, especially in long-term alliances, a history of good governance and relational governance capabilities (that is, a trustworthy reputation) enables firms to undertake such partnerships more readily.[33]

Although alliances can be a useful corporate strategy approach, they make governance more complex to evaluate, especially for outside governance actors. As the number and complexity of strategic alliances and partnerships grow, the governance costs also rise, causing diversifying strategic alliances to stir similar tensions between shareholders and managers as those due to the pursuit of mergers and acquisitions.[34] Like overdiversification, governance costs of excessive strategic alliances and partnership formations can outweigh the value to stakeholders, in particular shareholders. In fact, research shows that highly complex partnering strategies and alliances, especially when there are multiple forms of governance types (for instance, a mixture of nonequity and equity alliances) lead to lower firm performance and decreased shareholder value.[35]

GOVERNANCE AND ACQUISITIONS

As we noted in the introduction, one of the central means to diversify a firm occurs through mergers and acquisitions, but institutional investors tend to reduce the number of acquisitions, which leads to improved acquisition quality.[36] Over time, however, research has become more fine-grained, finding that institutional investors, especially those that are more active in regard to monitoring, create a two-edged sword for firms: they prevent bad acquisitions, but also reduce the number of risky acquisitions that might result in bigger gains for investors.[37] Cross-border acquisitions, for example, though often complex given possible differences in country cultures, may prove successful, especially when blockholding investors are involved. However, a curvilinear (inverted U-shaped) relationship occurs between country diversity of blockholders and cross-border acquisition performance. Some country cultural diversity can increase the quality of investor advice regarding the acquisition, but too much diversity and associated complexity can become detrimental because diverse country backgrounds and varying regulations regarding governance come into play.[38] Meanwhile, institutional investor involvement from the side of the target firm may also help increase the success of an acquisition transaction in favor of the purchased firm. Specifically, monitoring by institutional investors who are target firm owners leads to greater bid completion rates, higher (target) premiums, and lower acquirer returns, especially when the target has a significant weight in the institutional investor's portfolio.[39]

Monitoring by board members can add value to acquisition deals. Let us consider that board members have two main legal fiduciary duties: The *duty of care* focused on their oversight role requires that directors be informed and exercise appropriate diligence and good faith as they make business decisions; and the *duty of loyalty* requires that a director act in the best interests of the corporation, including in the acquisition context (not in their own interest or the interest of top management). Yet even when fulfilling these duties, many acquisitions do not realize improved returns for the acquiring firm;[40] in fact, shareholders typically earn returns that are close to zero, which reflects investors' skepticism about the likelihood that the firm will be able to achieve the synergies required to justify the target firm premium.[41] However, a transaction can work in the acquiring firm's favor if there is uncertainty about the target firm's value.[42] For example, in the Disney acquisition of Pixar in 2006, both firms had worked together previously, and both were publicly traded firms so there was not a lot of uncertainty about deal pricing. Accordingly, the boards of both the acquiring and target firms need to examine proposed deals closely to fulfill their fiduciary responsibilities.

We have mentioned how having many outside board members can create some setbacks for firms involved in merger and acquisition transactions. Because outside board members typically do not have contact with the company's day-to-day operations or ready access to detailed information about managers and their skills, they lack the insights required to evaluate their decisions and initiatives fully and effectively, especially when they are busy serving on multiple boards.[43] Outsiders can, however, obtain valuable information through frequent interactions with inside board members and during board meetings to better understand managers' decisions. In this way, they could allow a CEO greater strategic leeway (discretion regarding strategy), enabling them to impact firm performance.[44] But as activist shareholders dominate the reins of strategic control through their board member surrogates, performance has been detrimentally affected due to encumbrance on the strategic leeway needed by CEOs to enact appropriate strategies.[45] In this regard, there may be tradeoffs between the CEO and active outside board members who usurp strategic control. In fact, sometimes less-active board members who are friendly with the CEO allow the executive to be open to advice during the acquisition process.[46] In other instances, an acquiring CEO who has power (more discretion) to retain a target CEO, and thus garner the human capital, might derive that power from takeover defenses such as a staggered board, which might prevent a powerful activist investor from intervening in the acquisition process.[47] Therefore, a balance between overly active governance and strategic control of the CEO is critical to make appropriate acquisition decisions.

For example, a group of activist shareholders at embattled Swiss-Irish baked goods company Aryzta, with Cuisine de France as the flagship brand, have succeeded in their efforts to bring significant changes to the board. At an extraordinary general meeting (EGM) in Switzerland, shareholders removed CEO Kevin Toland from the company's board. The company has been losing significant value, but the board had opposed the motion put forward by the activist shareholder group, comprised of Veraison and the firm's largest shareholder, Spain-based Cobas Asset Management. In the EGM, the investors voted in Urs Jordi as chairman of the board to replace outgoing chairman Gary McCann. They also voted to put two new outside directors on the board. Previously, the board lacked baked goods industry experience and connections, and Urs Jordi, as well as the new board members brought the experience. It was also revealed that the board had been in discussions with hedge fund Elliott Management about a potential takeover. The question had become: can the firm stay independent while CEO Toland, who has been CEO for three years, executes a turnaround strategy under such a scenario? However, he is no longer on the board after the EGM and under the threat of a takeover by Elliot Management, although Jordi, the new board chair, suggests that the timing of a sale at the bottom is the worst time to sell.[48] In this example, shareholders would be better off allowing the turnaround strategy to mature rather than sell at the worst possible point in the process.

The Strategic Governance Highlight (Box 3.2) shows the importance of oversight by the board on the acquisition decision process and what a board can do to realize favorable acquisitions. To underscore the importance of this oversight, if an acquisition fails, it can have a devastating effect on the firm's stakeholders. For example, Daimler Benz acquired Chrysler in 1998 for $36 billion. In May 2007, DaimlerChrysler, the merged firm, sold the Chrysler business to a consortium of private equity investors led by Cerberus Capital Management LP for $7.4 billion.[49] Of the $7.4 billion provided by private equity firm, $5 billion was put into the operations of Chrysler and approximately $1 billion into Chrysler Financial Services, with the rest going to pay miscellaneous expenses. DaimlerChrysler only got approximately $1.35 billion. Although a recession at the time created extenuating circumstances, language and cultural differences as well as misjudged product launches quickly eroded Chrysler's market share. In the end, Daimler did not get much out of its original $36 billion investment, but it did unload $18 billion in Chrysler pension and health-care liabilities from its books.[50]

Board oversight can become of greater importance when an unexpected hostile takeover bid is presented, leaving little time to examine the deal thoroughly. In a *hostile takeover*, an acquiring firm accomplishes the acquisition of a target company not by coming to an agreement with the target company's management and board but by going directly to the company's shareholders for approval. As the takeover market has intensified, firms and their boards have developed a variety of defense tactics to deflect potential takeover bids. One such tactic, a *golden parachute*, usually forms part of an executive's employment agreement during hiring negotiations. The parachute is triggered in the event of a hostile takeover and increases the CEO's exit pay if the takeover succeeds. A new, incoming CEO will have had no control over the past failures that led to the takeover and therefore also requires the golden parachute clause as an incentive to enter a risk-filled environment. While a parachute may change the threshold level at which a CEO is willing to support a sale of his or her firm, it does not create a conflict with

BOX 3.2   Strategic Governance Highlight: Board Actions During the Acquisition Process

Boards play a key role in the merger and acquisition (M&A) process. Their fiduciary duties for oversight (duty of care) and acting in the best interest of the corporation (duty of loyalty) become accentuated in the sizable commitment a firm makes in staging an acquisition. Board members need to be involved in the following processes: a thorough strategic review of the potential target, a risk analysis of the deal, due diligence regarding the actual target portrayal of facts, analysis of the deal structure and target pricing, oversight on the integration process, and post-integration analysis regarding the deal outcomes for the firm. If a firm carries out a significant number of acquisitions, much of this oversight can be delegated to a board M&A committee.

In the strategic review of the acquisition, directors should ask many questions. What are the potential and unique benefits to the acquisition, and does it fit with the long-term strategy of the company? Will the intended synergies actually be realized, and what is the plan to facilitate synergy accomplishment upon target integration? In making judgments about a potential target, much can go wrong, especially if the CEO overestimates the firm's potential to realize the synergies involved. Directors should hence carry out a risk analysis, crucial in understanding possible problem factors that may take the venture astray.

If the deal moves further toward execution, the next step requires taking time to validate the target firm's accounting information and the rationale for the acquisition relative to accomplishing the intended strategy. As such, oversight and involvement in the due diligence process is essential. In fact, due diligence involves not only an analysis of the accounting and financial risks, but also nonfinancial matters such as technology (e.g., reported technology capabilities, information system integration), reputation among suppliers and customers, operational and engineering aspects, potential environmental liabilities, and perhaps violations associated with the Foreign Corrupt Practices Act—that is, involvement in possible corruption with foreign partners. Board members must be able to assure that a large acquisition will pass government regulators' assessment and often, if the target firm is a large, multinational corporation, attain regulatory approval in North America, Europe, and Asia for the same deal. Research suggests that understanding the political affinity between different countries can affect acquisition approval and integration success.

Once the deal gets past the due diligence hurdle, structuring and pricing the deal appropriately should follow. Paying too much for a target can lead to the need to lay off critical human capital to pay for the premium and may signal trouble, as can significant goodwill write-offs and other signs of acquisition failure. Sometimes a firm can legitimately price a deal more than competitors because the potential synergies are worth more to the focal firm than to potential rivals. Structuring the capital of the deal is equally important; how much should the focal firm use its stock versus cash to pay for the deal?

Once the pricing concludes and the deal is executed, the board should evaluate the oversight of the integration process and the team involved. What technical problems may arise between the two firms? Will the company cultures actually align, and how will they deal with cultural roadblocks? How can they retain critical human capital in the acquired firm?

Meanwhile, once the two firms integrate, a new board needs to be formed with board members from both companies. Usually, the acquiring firm receives the most board members (83 percent) on the combined board, while the target retains about one third of its members (34 percent of the inside directors and 29 percent of the outside directors). This process often implies that the combined board increases in size.

Once fully integrated, board directors should conduct a post-integration evaluation. Because many shareholders will be pleased and many disappointed with the merged firm, shareholder lawsuits and other litigation by customers and suppliers and also government regulators often occur, which underscores the importance of board members overseeing the process and carrying out their fiduciary duties. Consulting with legal professionals is highly recommended. The evaluation process can improve the capability of the firm when it pursues additional acquisitions.

Sources: Hasija, D., Liou, R., & Ellstrand, A. (2020). Navigating the new normal: Political affinity and multinationals' post-acquisition performance. *Journal of Management Studies* 57(3): 569–596; Cossin, D. & Lu, A. H. (2016). An M&A oversight framework for boards. IMD Global Board Center, https://www.imd.org/research-knowledge/articles/MAOversightFramework/; PwC (2016). Considering an acquisition? What boards need to do before, during, and after the deal. PwC's Governance Insights Center, http://broadrooms.com/wp-content/uploads/2017/05/pwc-what-boards-need-to-know-about-acquisitions.pdf; Lajoux, L.A. (2015). Role of the board in M&A. Harvard Law School Center on Corporate Governance, https://corpgov.law.harvard.edu/2015/09/07/role-of-the-board-in-ma/, September 7; Krishnan, H. A., Hitt, M. A., & Park, D. (2007). Acquisition premiums, subsequent workforce reductions and post-acquisition performance. *Journal of Management Studies* 44(5): 709–732.

respect to the CEO's negotiation of merger premium. However, side payments may be added to increase the CEO's incentive to get the deal done if both boards agree.[51]

Interestingly, these defense tactics may also raise the premium that a target firm receives from the acquiring firm when the target has many independent directors who seem to be able to use takeover defenses as resistance tactics.[52] Additionally, independent directors tend to hold the target CEO responsible when he or she refuses a good deal.[53] In these cases, within three years, the CEO is often terminated, possibly because the executive sought entrenchment (to maintain the CEO position, which is lost when a firm is taken over). Friendly deals realize lower premiums for the target firm, but this may be traded off for more control for the target CEO in the merged firm after assimilation into the acquiring firm.[54] Therefore, the board needs to weigh the need to retain human capital versus paying a higher premium.

GOVERNANCE AND DIVESTITURES

Divestiture or restructuring strategies are commonly used to correct or manage the results of ineffective mergers and acquisitions. As noted, firms can become overdiversified, prompting owners, especially activist owners, to urge firm executives to divest nonessential businesses, usually those unrelated to the firm's core businesses. Excessive diversification driven by acquisitions can be motivated by a CEO's appetite for compensation, as previously mentioned, but also for social status and prestige. For example, competitor CEOs are found to conduct 22 percent more acquisitions in the post-award period after a focal industry firm CEO wins a chief executive award and thus earns superstar status.[55] The competitor's acquisitions also grow larger, since larger acquisitions realize high status and recognition, and earn the top managers more compensation as well, which adds to their gained status. Owners and boards of directors should be aware of these alternative motivations behind acquisition activity.

Activist owners lead the way on many divestitures, especially when they perceive the firm to have diversified beyond its core businesses. However, even when an activist investor has not started an activist campaign, if the fund has a small ownership position, company leaders may still pursue defensive restructuring divestitures to avoid an activist campaign.[56] As the following Strategic Governance Highlight (Box 3.3) about Trian Partner's proxy battle with DuPont indicates, even when a proxy battle is defended by a firm successfully, as CEO Ellen Kullman discovered, you can win the battle but lose the war.

However, if a firm has a vigilant board made up of independent directors, and if a takeover attempt fails, the firm is less likely to restructure (sell off businesses) because board members may believe the diversification strategy to be appropriate given high pre-takeover vigilance.[57] Nevertheless, a firm may sell off businesses not only due to governance activism but also for competitive reasons such as market share loss or a change in the marketplace due to technological disruption.[58] Still some divestitures occur because a holding company or private equity fund uses a restructuring strategy in which they buy a firm at a lower price, restructure the assets, and sell the business, hopefully at a higher price.[59] The diversification level at which this happens varies across companies because each firm has different capabilities to manage diversification.[60]

Some firms have founding or legacy businesses. Once top executives have acquired a target and made it part of the strategic legacy, the CEO can be reluctant to divest the acquired business even when the need for the detachment seems clear.[61] Giving up parts of the firm proves difficult for executives involved in such decisions, especially when the unit is the original legacy business.[62] When Jeffrey Immelt announced in 2015 that General Electric would divest its banking business, GE Capital, one analyst noted wryly that Immelt "[comes across] as a painfully reluctant capital allocator—at least when allocating capital means selling businesses that he cares about."[63] Immelt had spent much of his career building that part of the business. Aware of status quo bias, or the strong commitment that CEOs employ toward current strategies and practices,[64] governance actors are likely to be involved to help these top executives articulate the appropriate action when shareholders feel uneasy with the firm's strategy and require divestiture.[65]

OTHER GOVERNANCE ACTORS: PROXY INTERMEDIARIES, FINANCIAL ANALYSTS, AND THE MEDIA

Although activist investors are spearheading the change, other governance actors also play a significant role in corporate restructuring, although more indirectly. As noted in the Strategic Governance Highlight (Box 3.3) regarding the activist campaign by Trian Partners against DuPont, ISS, a proxy intermediary, supported the proxy vote to elect Trian nominated board members to DuPont's board. In this manner, ISS and others such as Glass Lewis provide support for activists, which leads potentially more passive institutional investors to become engaged in the proxy voting process, which is the main tool for activists today. Since an activist campaign

BOX 3.3   Strategic Governance Highlight: Activist Investors Often Lead to Proxy Battles and Restructuring

Trian Partners, a hedge fund headed by Nelson Peltz, has a history of targeting large firms to get managers to change their strategies. In the past, Trian has approached large firms such as DuPont, General Electric, and Procter & Gamble. In the activist campaign against DuPont, CEO Ellen Kullman successfully defended the firm during a proxy vote. However, in the end, she lost her job, DuPont's board saw reforms, and the strategy changed to be more in line with the activist's recommendations. The "poison pill" defense mechanism that was effective in fending off hostile takeovers becomes less effective in the case of activist investors. A *poison pill* is called a shareholder's right plan where a firm's current shareholder can purchase two shares for the price of one, when an acquiring firm purchases, for example, 10 percent of the target firm. This in effect raises the premium price that an acquiring firm must pay.

Often, the fund activist managers will write a white paper outlining the strategic approach that they think the target company board should pursue. For example, in 2014, Trian wrote a letter to DuPont's board of directors suggesting that "DuPont's conglomerate structure is destroying value," and proposed that shareholder value could be maximized by splitting DuPont's seven major business lines into three separate companies. If the firm did not agree, the activist investor was prepared to undertake a proxy campaign to replace board members with its own representatives. As the case progressed, with the public wavering in support between the board and the activist, the underlying rationale for the firm's corporate strategy became exposed publicly to owners and financial analysts. Oftentimes, as in DuPont's case, proxy intermediaries such as ISS may support the activist investor proxy proposal for new board members. Over time and with the weakness of DuPont's strategy, the CEO lost her position even though the activist proxy vote narrowly failed. Ultimately, Trian instigated the transformation of DuPont into three independent companies after it first merged with Dow Chemical.

In September 2020, the hedge fund bought a position in Comcast, one of the largest firms approached by activist investors. While the outcome of the position remains inconclusive, Trian has announced on its website that the fund has begun "constructive discussions with Comcast's management team."

Source: Driebusch, C. (2020). Activist Trian Fund management takes stake in Comcast. *Wall Street Journal*, www.wsj.com, September 21; Jing, C. (2018). DowDuPont names three planned spin offs. *Chemical Week*, February 26; Tita, B., & Lublin, J. S. (2016). Breen's Tyco experience will guide him in dismantling DowDuPont, *Wall Street Journal*, www.wsj.com, January 6; Harper, B. R. (2016). The Dupont proxy battle: Successful defense measures against shareholder activism. *Delaware Journal of Corporate Law* 41 (1): 117–138; Benoit, D. (2015). ISS backs DuPont board seat for Peltz. *Wall Street Journal*, April 28, B1–B2.

mostly aims to create value through downscoping or reducing diversification through divestitures and spinoffs, activist shareholders do not need as significant an ownership position to trigger change if they achieve placement of a member or two on the board of the target firm to argue for favored positions.

For financial analysts, diversification can be difficult to assess due to the asymmetry between the information that analysts have access to and inside information that may not be discernable publicly through quarterly earnings reports.[66] In fact, managers may actively strive to keep some information, especially pertaining to the firm's core strategy, out of the public eye to avoid exposure to competitors and maintain the firm's competitive advantage. But by keeping information private, executives cause the knowledge asymmetry that leads financial analysts to discount the stock and reduce their coverage.[67] However, in instances of divestitures or spinoffs, firm transparency increases, augmenting analysts' coverage and "buy" recommendations, and thus positively affecting the stock price.[68]

In these indirect ways, proxy intermediaries and financial analysts support the activities of activist investors, especially in actions that narrow the scope of the firm through divestitures and spinoffs. Media contributes by providing news of events and actions undertaken by activist investors and proxy intermediaries, as well as by announcing buy or sell recommendations from analysts. For example, firms tend to divest assets that have been stigmatized by the media.[69] For example, BorgWarner divested its remaining asbestos business, a product that has been proven to be related to cancer, to Enstar, a firm that specializes in managing assets with liabilities.[70] Also, research suggests that the negative tone of media coverage about an acquisition can influence managers' decisions to abandon the purchase[71] and reduce company leaders' willingness to engage in acquisitions in the future.[72] These studies indicate that the media can provide important external performance feedback regarding firm strategic decisions, which in turn shapes future managerial decisions.

INSTITUTIONAL CHANGE, GOVERNANCE, AND RESTRUCTURING OF DIVERSIFIED BUSINESS GROUPS

Emerging economies tend to exemplify less-than-perfect market institutions and business environments with scarce factor resources relative to developed economies.[73] Nonetheless, because of their recent rapid development, relatively large population bases, and increased share in world trade, emerging economies have become increasingly important in the global market. Understanding governance and corporate refocusing in the emerging economy context is particularly relevant.

Emerging economies traditionally suffer from deficiencies in areas such as transportation and telecommunications,[74] making it more costly for firms to transact with other firms. As a result of inefficient distribution systems, import restrictions, and a lack of necessary capital, key raw materials are often unavailable to firms. Besides this lack of basic factor and infrastructure resources, the underdevelopment of necessary market institutions greatly affects local firms.[75] Missing market institutions can include economic reporting transparency; a stable currency; a stable government; liquid, well-functioning equity and lending markets to fuel expansion and growth; and a strong legal system to provide aggressive enforcement of property rights and a brake on opportunism, graft, and corruption. If legal infrastructure is not in place to protect contractual relationships, transaction costs may be high, and firms will be less likely to engage in economic deals. The lacking environment makes corporate governance increasingly important in these countries. Under these conditions, business groups—a collection of parent and subsidiary companies that function as a single economic entity through a common source of control—can act as substitutes for missing market institutions. The network of firms enables trust, suggesting that transactions take place more safely when they are accomplished in a network of relationships and ownership among group firms.[76]

Often, then, business groups make use of unrelated diversification, or the addition of new or unrelated product lines to enter new markets, among affiliate firms. The Achilles' heel for firms using the unrelated diversification strategy in a developed economy lies in competitors' ability to imitate financial economies and resource allocation more easily than they can replicate the value gained from the economies of scope developed through operational and corporate relatedness among the firms' business units. In other words, in economies with mature market institutions,[77] related diversification produces better performance than an unrelated diversification strategy.[78] However, this issue signifies less of a problem in emerging economies, in which the absence of strong market institutions encourages the use of the unrelated

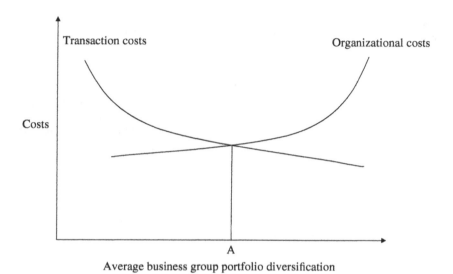

FIGURE 3.5   Costs and diversification.

diversification strategy within business groups. In fact, in emerging economies such as Taiwan, India, Chile, and others, diversification increases the performance of firms affiliated within large, diversified business groups, like the Tata group in India.[79] Yet, as market institutions improve in emerging economies, business groups still enjoy a dominant position,[80] but diversification becomes a less potent factor in facilitating group and affiliate firm performance.[81]

Figure 3.5 shows the proposed relationships between business group diversification and transaction and organizational costs. The downward-sloping transaction cost curve (TCC) represents the overall transaction costs in an economy produced by the legal infrastructure and the available market institutions. The upward-sloping curve represents the average organizational cost curve (OCC) that a diversified business group experiences to conduct internal transactions in an emerging country. The overall cost from the given set of market institutions would be realized at the intersection of the transaction and organizational cost curves, where the combined costs are the lowest. Thus, the overall optimal combined transaction and organizational costs would be realized at point A, representing the set point for the average level of group portfolio diversification based on these costs in an emerging economy.

Meanwhile, Figure 3.6 illustrates that when market institutions evolve to allow better legal protection for transactions, more capital available in the market, better financial intermediaries, and a more developed product market, overall transaction costs decrease, as seen by curve TCC1. The new, lower overall transaction cost level reduces the need for internal group markets and broad levels of diversification in diversified business groups, causing their

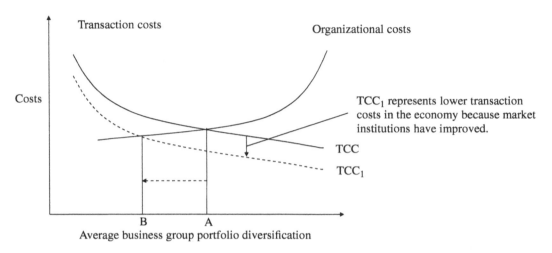

FIGURE 3.6 Lower transaction costs and diversification.

optimal level of diversification in the overall economy to also lower (point B). Accordingly, in emerging economies such as those in Latin America, business groups have an incentive to refocus so as to lower the level of diversification.[82] In effect, the large, unrelated diversified business groups become less necessary as substitutes for market institutions, and experience pressure to reduce their levels of diversification under the continued development of institutions. Let us note, though, that institution change takes time and other reasons for business groups to maintain their product diversification exist, such as to maintain family ownership and control. Likewise, government ownership of business groups can disrupt the potential pressure to restructure.[83]

The type of restructuring that might occur is shaped by governance and, in particular, the ownership configuration of business groups.[84] Family ownership is likely to increase related diversification. Similarly, foreign pension funds might encourage more related diversification similar to the power of more activist investors (see the shift toward shareholders in Figure 3.2). Alternatively, banks and government ownership might lead to maintaining unrelated diversification. In India, for instance, large, diversified groups who had significant bank ownership maintained an unrelated portfolio of group affiliated firms.[85] Connection to these large business groups allows a bank to increase the number of firms with which it can receive interest and fees and reduce the number of transactions because bank transactions are facilitated with its relationship to business group headquarters. Government ownership might realize less related business refocusing because priority issues include employment and social welfare more than performance. This focus explains why Chinese government-dominated business groups are more likely to do unrelated acquisitions in their own provinces.[86] Specifically, local officials are likely to support weak firms being purchased by strong firms even though the businesses are unrelated in order to maintain social welfare goals such as stable provincial employment levels.

As shareholder activism spreads across borders as opportunities (supply of good deals) are reduced in the United States and other countries with strong institutions. Activist investors probe the question of where they may most likely find success. Meanwhile top managers contend with the question of how to best respond to their attacks and engagements. As the examples in the Strategic Governance Highlight in Box 3.4 suggest, activists need to find places with strong market institutions and sufficient rule of law to allow for their ownership positions and proxy voting governance strategies to find support in the courts. Sufficient change in the institutional environment in South Korea had occurred to sustain Elliott's efforts in the controversy over several businesses in the Samsung Group, enough to cause a political scandal that put the country's president in jail for bribery and abuse of power. In Japan, although there are active shareholder engagements, the overall culture and legal infrastructure have not allowed these engagements to realize much improvement in performance through corporate restructuring. In the next section, we summarize the opportunities presented in different institutional environments and the suggested strategy opportunities for successful change.

SUMMARY OF FIT OR MISFIT BETWEEN MARKET INSTITUTIONS AND CURRENT DIVERSIFICATION STRATEGY

Figure 3.7 presents a framework that showcases, in Quadrant I (focused product diversification) and III (broad or unrelated product diversification), a strong fit between the current diversification strategy and the institutional environment. In Quadrants II and IV, we find a misfit between the two categories. In Quadrant I, representing scenarios with strong country market institutions and in which shareholders have significant information transparency, most firms remain relatively focused. When firms overdiversify, activist investors and their supporters (active institutional investors and analysts) try to influence these firms to reduce diversification. Of course, as we have noted, diversification levels might vary significantly because firms may have different capabilities to manage the ventures.[87] There also may be significant acquisitions and divestitures, as well as alliances, as business evolves over time.[88] Yet, the overall set point for diversification is low because of the strong institutional environment.

BOX 3.4   Strategic Governance Highlight: Foreign Shareholder Activism and Corporate Restructuring

In Box 2.3, we introduced the trend of shareholder activism going across borders. For example, Oasis Management, an activist investor located in Hong Kong, Texas and the Cayman Islands, has approached large Japanese corporations such as Nintendo, Panasonic, and Toshiba. As we will see, these foreign activist investors are shaping corporate strategy of target companies.

In Japan, 19 formally launched activist campaigns occurred in 2019, an almost five times increase from 2015, when Japan adopted a new governance code that strongly emphasized the importance of firms electing many more independent outside directors. Although until recently activist shareholders had traditionally been absent in the country, more active shareholders were labeled "engagement" funds soon after these changes. For example, the Japanese Government Pension Investment Fund has chosen a US engagement investor, the Taiyo Pacific Partners LP, to manage its $1 trillion assets. Also, the Japanese Financial Services Agency has introduced a "stewardship code" that calls on investors to "press for greater returns." Since 2019, the approach of activist funds is similar to that in the United States in seeking to foster significant corporate restructuring. As such, the engagement approach is now more aggressive.

In South Korea, shareholder returns improve when foreign institutional investors take a position in a Korean firm. The improvement augments if the investor has previously signaled that they are an "activist." Returns improve even more if the investors come from a country with strong market institutions. However, South Korea has a relatively strong legal infrastructure to support activists. Its institutional background is enhanced if the activist firm comes from a country with likewise strong market institutions.

An interesting example involved Elliott Management, a US activist fund that, in 2015, opposed the combination of two Samsung units, which would solidify Samsung's founding family's grip over corporate strategy and the business group. Business groups, especially family owners, can extract private benefits (called *tunneling*) relative to minority investors such as Elliott through voting right controls. Through tunneling, Elliott narrowly lost the proxy fight due to the support of the government-run National Pension Service. However, Elliott filed suit claiming a loss of

$770 million due to the government's unfair interference in the deal. The subsequent investigation led to a massive corruption scandal in which the presidential office allegedly pressured the minister in charge of the pension fund to side with Samsung. In the end, Park Geun-hye, South Korea's first female president, was found guilty of bribery and abuse of power and sentenced to 24 years in prison.

If a country provides fewer control rights to foreign institutional investors, as in China, activist investors will have fewer opportunities to have successful activist campaigns to foster corporate restructuring. Research suggests that foreign institutional investors may even create more tunneling if they partner with business groups because of the thin trading and lack of legal constraints to protect minority shareholders against tunneling such as that experienced by Elliott. As such, the legal infrastructure as well as the freedom to trade may affect the ability of foreign activist investors to succeed in cross-border corporate restructuring campaigns.

Source: Lewis, L., & Inagaki, K. 2020. How Japan Inc became a target for activist investors. *Financial Times*. February 3. https://www.ft.com/content/4a36f3b0-4419-11ea-a43a-c4b328d9061c; Becht, M., Franks, J., Grant, J., & Wagner, H. (2019). The early returns to international hedge fund activism: 2000–2010. *Journal of Applied Corporate Finance* 31(1): 62–80; Deveau, S. (2018). Elliott seeks $770 million from South Korea in Samsung fight. *Bloomberg*, www.bloomberg.com, July 13; Kim, W., Sung, T., & Wei, S.-J. (2017). The diffusion of corporate governance to emerging markets: Evaluating two dimensions of investor heterogeneity. *Journal of International Money & Finance* 70: 406–432; Zhang, X., Yang, X., Strange, R., & Zhang, Q. (2017). Informed trading by foreign institutional investors as a constraint on tunneling: Evidence from China. *Corporate Governance: An International Review* 25(4): 222–235.

Quadrant III, associated with countries with weak institutions and a matching strategy of relatively broad levels of diversification, stands as the opposite to Quadrant I. In this third quadrant, many emerging economies have broadly diversified business groups, which may dominate the economies. The influential groups are called, *qiye jituan* in China, *business houses* in India, *grupos economicos* in Latin American countries, *chaebol* in South Korea, *guanxi qiye* in Taiwan, and *family holdings* in Turkey.[89] Because of the lack of strong market institutions, these large, diversified business groups internalize transactions, which are more safely carried out within a network of relationships among family owners, director networks, or interpersonal ties.

Moving to Quadrant II, as institutions change over time, a mismatch may occur between the strategy that has evolved and the nature of a country's

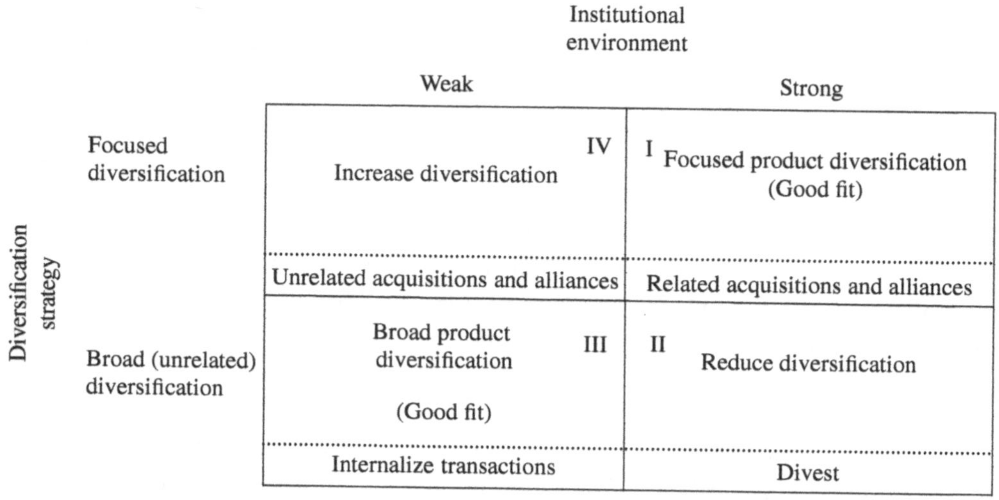

Institutional
environment

FIGURE 3.7 Institutional environments and dominant corporate diversification strategies.

institutions. In South Korea, for example, institutions evolved and many of the large, diversified chaebol needed to change after the currency crisis. During this time, better market institutions emerged, leading chaebols to carry out massive restructuring and many refocusing divestitures. However, there can be different approaches to refocusing strategies. For example, South Korean firm LG reduced its business scope, measured by the number of two-digit SIC codes (a measure of unrelatedness), from 21 in late 1997 to 16 by the end of 2000. Because a controlling family managed the subsidiaries, the business group was heavily centralized. Through restructuring, the business group became decentralized, and hence more fitting to manage an unrelated set of businesses. Hyundai, on the other hand, divested many of its unrelated businesses and maintained a centralized control structure by implementing a related diversification strategy that focused on its automotive business, which included financing for its automotive sales.[90]

In Quadrant IV, firms from countries with weak institutional environments need to match their diversification strategy with such environments. Specifically, the weaker the institutional system, the more firms turn to unrelated diversification because a focused one may not realize the best performance. In India, unrelated diversification improved performance until market reforms took root. At this point, the approach lowered performance whereas related diversification improved it.[91] A similar observation took place in Western Europe.[92] Firms in countries with relatively less developed market institutions experienced a positive relationship between diversification and performance, whereas more focused ones had a positive relation to performance in countries with more developed market institutions. State ownership plays a role, too. Because institutionally weaker countries tend to lack funds for entrepreneurial activities, the support from state ownership can spur diversification.[93] Hence, business groups that have substantial state ownership diversify to overcome the lack of market institutions.

LEVERAGING GOVERNANCE ACTORS TO PURSUE AN EFFECTIVE CORPORATE STRATEGY

Under an environment of weak institutions, governance will often be weaker as well, since inadequate regulations do not demand that outside directors be independent. Meanwhile, as family ownership dominates in many emerging economies, significantly more inside managers sit on boards. Also, financial analysts face the daunting task of analyzing the complex ownership and diversification strategies of business groups. Therefore, governance actors in Quadrants III and IV in countries with weaker institutions encounter a salient governance challenge. For these countries, as we will see, foreign institutional investors can make a difference. In Quadrants I and II with strong market institutions, activist investors are able to team up with other, more passive institutional investors and have a more defining impact.

Leverage, Engage, and Defend

Managers of firms that fall within Quadrant I have no choice but to engage and communicate with their boards, as suggested in Figure 3.8. Having a broadly diverse and experienced board allows firm executives to meet head on the challenge posed by activist investors in countries with strong market institutions. In these countries, activist investors often pursue their campaigns in *wolf packs* and seek to engage other institutional investors in their activism. Yet, as the activist shareholders often write *white papers* with a focus on the strategy of target firms, their insights into which business units the firm should focus on may prove valuable. Leveraging their ideas can be useful. For the same reason, and as a consequence of activist campaigns, activist representatives are often nominated and voted onto boards.[94] Leveraging the ideas of activists can sometimes realize positive results. In 2006, Trian Partners pushed for fast-food chain Wendy's to spin off its Tim Hortons coffee and donut business to increase value. The spinoff was supported by other shareholders and the board agreed.[95] Wendy's subsequently was better able to focus on competing with its key rivals, Burger King and McDonald's.

Country institutions	Resource provision	Governance actor	Strategy
Strong	Yes	Activist investors Boards	Leverage, engage and defend
Strong	No	Regulators Rating agencies Financial analysts	Acquiesce and defend
Weak	Yes	Boards Foreign institutional investors Government owners	Compromise and change
Weak	No	Politicians Regulators	Connect and avoid

FIGURE 3.8   Response strategies to different governance actors.

However, managers should consider engaging institutional investors more broadly, not just activists, since these less-active investors also have an interest in improving governance and strategy. Additionally, because institutional investors have a strong say on executive compensation and other governance issues, such as the separation of CEO and board chair positions, having a good investor relations group who can readily communicate with large and small owners about the company's proxy statement or strategy helps to improve evaluations by investor.[96]

At times, companies need to defend against activist proposals that may be short-term oriented and not in the interest of long-term company performance. At other times, firms may preemptively divest businesses that are unrelated to the firms' legacy businesses, as often happens when an activist shareholder has an ownership position in the firm but has not yet launched an activist campaign.[97] Defending against an activist may be difficult but not impossible. Leadership should have a well-designed action plan in place as well as a strong team of external financial and legal advisors and a united board who believes in the firm's strategy and CEO. Nelson Peltz at Trian Fund Management pushed PepsiCo to separate its snack food and soft drinks businesses. Yet, with support from the board and other shareholders who united behind the firm's strategy, CEO Indra Nooyi of PepsiCo was able to overcome this push and keep the company intact.[98] Although the company received complaints that main competitor Coca-Cola outperformed PepsiCo in the long term,[99] the disruption of PepsiCo's complementary businesses may have caused further underperformance, like the significant underperformance that occurred at Sears and JCPenney after activist campaigns.

Acquiesce and Defend

If broadly diversified and headquartered in a country with strong market institutions (see Quadrant II of Figure 3.7), a company is likely to be targeted by activist investors. Honeywell, United Technology, and other multi-industry diversified firms currently find themselves acquiescing to "rightsizing" pressures. General Electric (GE), a historic conglomerate, has been attacked incessantly by activists, probably for good reason. GE was so complex that board members did not seem to understand the strategy that top managers pursued. Because of GE's aggressive accounting,[100] the board had a hard time uncovering GE's underperformance and failed to prevent the firm from bad strategic acquisitions.[101]

Managers and inside governance actors face increased pressure to justify both their related and, mostly, unrelated acquisitions decisions. The onslaught is coming not only from activist investors, but also from sell-side analysts who find the complexity so hard to fathom that they discount the firm's stock price.[102] As such, the CEO, CFO, and investor relations officers need to provide clear explanations to defend their decisions. Yet, analysts generally provide a sell recommendation for broadly diversified firms as a way of discounting the stock. This discount can also apply to related diversified firms when "synergy" or interrelatedness between businesses is opaque and difficult to explain.[103] Related diversification through acquisitions carries its own challenges because these ventures can be perceived to dampen competition and harm consumers' welfare (see Chapter 5); thus, companies need to be well prepared to defend such acquisitions to antitrust and justice department regulators.

Compromise and Change

Enterprises located in countries with weak market institutions and which are broadly diversified (see Quadrant III of Figure 3.7) are a good match for this quadrant setting. Internal governance actors prove relatively weak while strong family and government owners wield control. In many Asian countries, for instance, boards consist of inside managers, often with family owners dictating the firm's direction. With changes in corporate governance taking place, more outside directors are required, but managers might focus on outside directors who have political connections to help smooth firm relations during regulatory struggles.[104] However, family-dominated firms have been forced to compromise by focusing on businesses in areas that fulfill national policy objectives while directed to be "national champions" and attract foreign investment. Under such a policy in South Korea, chaebols were established to become national leaders across many industries,[105] such as Hyundai in the auto manufacturing business and Samsung in the electronic and semi-conductor industry.

As many emerging market firms grow in size and seek to enter foreign markets both within their local regions and beyond, growth strategies require more investment. Meanwhile, foreign institutional investors from more developed countries seek to diversify across borders as well. Foreign institutional investors who identify themselves as "activists" and come from countries with strong market systems have been shown to improve South Korean firms' financial returns after their block purchases.[106] However, when market institutions were not as advanced in the country, local institutional investors provided more impact than foreign ones because these local investors had less information asymmetry than foreign counterparts.[107] Managers might consider whether they are in an industry that is transparent or opaque and pursue local or foreign institutional investors who can invest appropriately. Also, if firm leaders seek to invest abroad into countries with strong institutional environments, having foreign institutional investors and foreign directors from these target countries might lead to more successful strategy formulation and implementation.

Connect and Avoid

In Quadrant IV of Figure 3.7, firms that have pursued a focused diversification strategy and are from countries with weak market institutions may evolve toward more unrelated diversification. In cases of government ownership, unrelated diversification may proceed to maintain local employment levels as shown in China.[108] The importance of political connections proves critical in countries with weak market institutions but can transform over time. For example, when Taiwan was closed to foreign investment, formal government ties such as government ownership led to diversification through governmental support for resources.[109] Yet, as Taiwan opened to foreign investment, informal ties to government leaders also increased diversification. As we can see, firms in countries with weak market institutions should maintain both formal and informal government and political ties to boost growth primarily through increased diversification.

Once market institutions become more established and political connections less important, firm leaders may nevertheless maintain political ties to keep pressure off from regulators. In periods of institutional friction during which old institutions are displaced by new market-oriented ones, business groups might see value in continuing to leverage their political connections to secure favorable contracts from government agencies and avoid reducing diversification.[110] However, as markets change and foreign entry becomes inevitable, government support wanes, and more capital is available through better capital markets. As a result, unrelated diversification becomes less desirable, especially when shareholders become more prominent investors versus the government. For example, firm performance improves as affiliate group firms individually become publicly traded and as business groups carry more transparency into their inner workings because of increased public reporting (each affiliate has its own board and own annual reporting requirement through public stock exchanges).[111] Managers face the need to adapt over time to their firm country's level of institutional change and the correspondingly appropriate level of diversification. To adjust their strategy as needed, managers can leverage their board member expertise as well as that of foreign and local institutional investors. Also, if part of a business group, the firm's headquarters as well as other network affiliate firms might prove helpful in adjusting appropriately to these changes.[112]

Given both weak and strong institutional environments as indicated in Figure 3.8, engaging, leveraging, and defending against governance actors at times while connecting and acquiescing to others represents a challenging dilemma that boards and managers need to balance. As the power of governance actors grows over time, the failure to manage governance actors can be detrimental to designing and implementing an effective corporate strategy.

NOTES

1. Kang, J. (2013). The relationship between corporate diversification and corporate social performance. *Strategic Management Journal* 34: 94–109.
2. Arthurs, J. D., Sahaym, A., & Cullen, J. B. (2013). Search behavior of the diversified firm: The impact of fit on innovation, *Strategic Management Journal* 34: 999–1009.
3. Baysinger, B., & Hoskisson, R. E. (1990). The composition of boards of directors and strategic control: Effects on corporate strategy. *Academy of Management Review* 15: 72–87.
4. Golden, B. R., & Zajac, E. J. (2001). When will boards influence strategy? Inclination × power = strategic change. *Strategic Management Journal* 22: 1087–1111.
5. Emerson, R. M. (1962). Power-dependence relations. *American Sociological Review* 27: 31–41. Pfeffer, J., & Salancik, G. R. (1978). *The external control of organizations: A resource-dependence perspective*. New York: Harper & Row.
6. Pfeffer & Salancik, The external control of organizations.
7. Useem, M. (1996). *Investor capitalism: How money managers are changing the face of corporate America*. New York: Basic Books/HarperCollins; Gillan, S. L., & Starks, L. T. (2007). The evolution of shareholder activism in the United States. *Journal of Applied Corporate Finance* 19(1): 55–73.

8. Hoskisson, R. E., Johnson, R. A., & Moesel, D. D. (1994). Corporate divestiture intensity in restructuring firms: Effects of governance, strategy and performance. *Academy of Management Journal* 37, 1207–1251.
9. Chen, S., & Feldman, E. R. (2018). Activist-impelled divestitures and shareholder value. *Strategic Management Journal* 39(10): 2726–2744.
10. Carlisle, T. (2014). The Icahn manifesto. *Journal of Applied Corporate Finance* 26(4): 89–97.
11. Lombardo, C. (2018). Starboard pursuing proxy fight at Newell Brands despite deal with Icahn. *Wall Street Journal*, www.wsj.com, April 4.
12. Chen & Feldman. Activist-impelled divestitures and shareholder value.
13. Zorn, M. L., Shropshire, C., Martin, J. A., Combs, J. G., & Ketchen, D. J. (2017). Home alone: the effects of lone-insider boards on CEO pay, financial misconduct, and firm performance. *Strategic Management Journal* 38(13): 2623–2646.
14. Baysinger & Hoskisson. The composition of boards of directors and strategic control.
15. Thomas, R. J., Schrage, M., Bellin, J. B., & Marcote, G. (2009). How boards can be better—a manifesto. *MIT Sloan Management Review* 50(2): 69–74.
16. Baysinger & Hoskisson. The composition of boards of directors and strategic control.
17. Hoskisson, Johnson, & Moesel. Corporate divestiture intensity in restructuring firms.
18. Hoskisson, R. E., Castleton, M. W., & Withers, M. C. (2009). Complementarity in monitoring and bonding: More intense monitoring leads to higher executive compensation. *Academy of Management Perspectives*, 23(2): 57–74.
19. Krantz, M. (2019). CEOs are bailing out in droves; do they know something? *Investor's Business Daily*, www.ibd.com, December 19.
20. Rediker, K. J., & Seth, A. (1995). Boards of directors and substitution effects of alternative governance mechanisms. *Strategic Management Journal* 16(2): 85–99.
21. Hoskisson, Castleton, & Withers. Complementarity in monitoring and bonding.
22. Eisenhardt, K. M. (1989). Agency theory: An assessment and review. *Academy of Management Review* 14(1): 57–74.
23. Wiesenfeld, B. M., Wurthmann, K. A., & Hambrick, D. C. (2008). The stigmatization and devaluation of elites associated with corporate failure: A process model. *Academy of Management Review* 33(1): 231–251.
24. Shi, W., Connelly, B. L., & Hoskisson, R. E. (2017). External corporate governance and financial fraud: Cognitive evaluation theory insights on agency theory prescriptions. *Strategic Management Journal* 38(6): 1268–1286.
25. Palmeri, C., & Kaskey, J. (2018). Disney investors offer say on executive pay, and dislike. *Bloomberg*, www.bloomberg.com, March 8.
26. Forester Consulting(2019). Invest in partnerships to drive growth and competitive advantage. https://go.impact.com/rs/280-XQP-994/images/PDFdownload-PC-AW-InvestinPartnerships.pdf, June.
27. Capron, L., & Mitchell, W. (2012). *Build, borrow or buy: Solving the growth dilemma*. Cambridge: Harvard Business Review Press.

28. McCann, B. T., Reuer, J. J., & Lahiri, N. (2016). Agglomeration and the choice between acquisitions and alliances: An information economics perspective. *Strategic Management Journal* 37: 1085–1106.
29. Chang, S. & Tsai, M. (2013). The effect of prior alliance experience on acquisition performance. *Applied Economics* 45: 765–773; Zollo, M., & Reuer, J. J. (2010). Experience spillovers across corporate development activities. *Organization Science* 21(6): 1195–1212.
30. Cho, S. Y., & Arthurs, J. D. (2018). The influence of alliance experience on acquisition premiums and post-acquisition performance. *Journal of Business Research* 88: 1–10.
31. Connelly, B., Shi, W., Hoskisson, R., & Koka, B. (2019). Shareholder influence on joint venture exploration. *Journal of Management* 45(8): 3178–3203.
32. Bodnaruk, A., Massa, M., & Simonov, A. (2013). Alliances and corporate governance. *Journal of Financial Economics* 107(3): 671–693.
33. Hansen, M. H., Hoskisson, R. E., & Barney, J. B. (2008). Competitive advantage in alliance governance: Resolving the opportunism minimization–gain maximization paradox. *Managerial and Decision Economics* 29: 191–208.
34. Reuer, J. J., & Ragozzino, R. (2006). Agency hazards and alliance portfolios. *Strategic Management Journal* 27(1): 27–43.
35. Jiang, R. J., Tao, Q. T., & Santoro, M. D. (2010). Alliance portfolio diversity and firm performance. *Strategic Management Journal* 31(10): 1136–1144.
36. Gillan, S. L., & Starks, L. T. (2000). Corporate governance proposals and shareholder activism: the role of institutional investors. *Journal of Financial Economics* 57(2): 275–305.
37. Goranova, M. L., Priem, R. L., Ndofor, H. A., & Trahms, C. A. (2017). Is there a "dark side" to monitoring? Board and shareholder monitoring effects on M&A performance extremeness. *Strategic Management Journal* 38(11): 2285–2297.
38. Chen, V. Z. (2019). Shareholder wealth effects of cultural diversity among blockholders: Evidence from cross-border acquisitions by U.S.-listed companies. *Corporate Governance: An International Review* 27(3): 186–209.
39. Fich, E. M., Harford, J., & Tran, A. L. (2015). Motivated monitors: The importance of institutional investors' portfolio weights. *Journal of Financial Economics* 118(1): 21–48.
40. Bruner, R. F. (2002). Does M&A pay? A survey of evidence for the decision-maker. *Journal of Applied Finance* 12(1): 48–68.
41. Cho, S. Y., Arthurs, J. D., Townsend, D. M., Miller, D. R., & Barden, J. Q. (2016). Performance deviations and acquisition premiums: The impact of CEO celebrity on managerial risk-taking. *Strategic Management Journal* 37(13): 2677–2694.
42. Li, L., & Tong, W. H. S. (2018). Information uncertainty and target valuation in mergers and acquisitions. *Journal of Empirical Finance* 45: 84–107.
43. Hauser, R. (2018). Busy directors and firm performance: Evidence from mergers. *Journal of Financial Economics* 128: 16–37.
44. Quigley, T. J., & Hambrick, D. C. (2014). Has the "CEO effect" increased in recent decades? A new explanation for the great rise in America's attention to corporate leaders. *Strategic Management Journal* 36, 821–830.

45. Ponomareva, Y., Shen, W., & Umans, T. (2019). Organizational discretion, board control, and shareholder wealth: A contingency perspective. *Corporate Governance: An International Review* 27(4): 248–260.

46. Schmidt, B. (2015). Costs and benefits of friendly boards during mergers and acquisitions. *Journal of Financial Economics* 117(2): 424–447.

47. Wulf, J., & Singh, H. (2011). How do acquirers retain successful target CEOs? The role of governance. *Management Science* 57(12): 2101–2114.

48. Brennen, J. (2020). Aryzta sale in doubt as dissidents score boardroom coup. *The Irish Times*, September 16. www.irishtimes.com/business/agribusiness-and-food/aryzta-sale-in-doubt-as-dissidents-score-boardroom-coup-1. 4356167.

49. Fox, J. (2007): Buying a used Chrysler. *Time,* May 28: 46.

50. Welch, DS., Byrnes, N., & Bianco, A. (2007). A deal that could save Detroit: A Chrysler sale to Cerberus may spark a plan to eliminate most of the health-care liabilities crushing carmakers, *Businessweek,* May 28: 30.

51. Broughman, B. (2017). CEO side payments in mergers and acquisitions. *Brigham Young University Law Review* 2017(1): 67–115.

52. Cotter, J. F., Shivdasani, A., & Zenner, M. (1997). Do independent directors enhance target shareholder wealth during tender offers? *Journal of Financial Economics* 43(2): 195–218.

53. Bates, T. W., & Becher, D. A. (2017). Bid resistance by takeover targets: Managerial bargaining or bad faith? *Journal of Financial & Quantitative Analysis* 52: 837–866.

54. Wulf, J. (2004). Do CEOs in mergers trade power for premium? Evidence from "mergers of equals." *Journal of Law, Economics & Organization* 20(1): 60–101.

55. Shi, W., Zhang, Y., & Hoskisson, R. E. (2017): Ripple effects of CEO awards: Investigating the acquisition activities of superstar CEOs' competitors. *Strategic Management Journal* 38: 2080–2102.

56. Shi, W., Connelly, B. L., Hoskisson, R. E, & Ketchen, D. J. (2020). Portfolio spillover of institutional investor activism: An awareness-motivation-capability perspective. *Academy of Management Journal* 63(6): 1865–1892.

57. Chatterjee, S., Harrison, J. S., & Bergh, D. D. (2003). Failed takeover attempts, corporate governance and refocusing. *Strategic Management Journal* 24(1): 87–96.

58. Vidal, E., & Mitchell, W. (2018). Virtuous or vicious cycles? The role of divestitures as a complementary Penrose effect within resource-based theory. *Strategic Management Journal* 39(1): 131–154.

59. Hoskisson, R. E., & Hitt, M. A. (1994). *Downscoping: How to tame the diversified firm.* New York: Oxford University Press.

60. Mackey, T. B., Barney, J. B., & Dotson, J. P. (2017). Corporate diversification and the value of individual firms: A Bayesian approach. *Strategic Management Journal* 38: 322–341.

61. Chiu, S.-C., Johnson, R. A., Hoskisson, R. E., & Pathak, S. (2016). The impact of CEO successor origin on corporate divestiture scale and scope change, *Leadership Quarterly* 27: 617–633.

62. Feldman, E. (2014). Legacy divestitures: Motives and implications. *Organization Science* 25: 815–832.

63. Fox, J. (2015). Jeff Immelt, reluctant capital allocator. *Bloomberg Opinion*, www.bloomberg.com, March 17.

64. Hambrick, D. C., Geletkanycz, M. A., & Fredrickson, J. W. (1993). Top executive commitment to the status quo: Some tests of its determinants. *Strategic Management Journal* 14: 401–418.

65. Chiu, S. C., Pathak, S., Hoskisson, R. E. & Johnson, R. A. (in press). Managerial commitment to the status quo an corporate divestitures: Can power motivate openness to change: *Leadership Quarterly*.

66. Benner, M. J., & Zenger, T. (2016). The lemons problem in markets for strategy. *Strategy Science* 1(2): 71–89.

67. Litov, L. P., Moreton, P., Zenger, T. R. (2012). Corporate strategy, analyst coverage, and the uniqueness paradox. *Management Science* 58(10): 1797–1815.

68. Feldman, E. R. (2016). Corporate spinoffs and analysts' coverage decisions: The implications for diversified firms. *Strategic Management Journal* 37: 1196–1219.

69. Durand, R., & Vergne, J.-P. (2015). Asset divestment as a response to media attacks in stigmatized industries. *Strategic Management Journal* 36(8): 1205–1223.

70. BorgWarner. (2019). BorgWarner announces divestiture of BorgWarner Morse TEC LLC to Enstar. October 10. https://www.borgwarner.com/newsroom/press-releases/2019/10/30/borgwarner-announces-divestiture-of-borgwarner-morse-tec-llc-to-enstar.

71. Liu, B., & McConnell J. J. (2013). The role of the media in corporate governance: Do the media influence managers' capital allocation decisions? *Journal of Financial Economics* 110(1): 1–17.

72. Gamache, D. L., & McNamara, G. (2019). Responding to bad press: How CEO temporal focus influences the sensitivity to negative media coverage of acquisitions. *Academy of Management Journal* 62(3): 918–943.

73. Wan, W. P., & Hoskisson, R. (2003). Home country environments, corporate diversification strategies, and firm performance. *Academy of Management Journal* 46, 27–45; Wan, W. P. (2005). Country resource environments, firm capabilities, and corporate diversification strategies. *Journal of Management Studies* 42: 161–182.

74. Wan & Hoskisson. Home country environments, corporate diversification strategies, and firm performance.

75. Wan. Country resource environments, firm capabilities, and corporate diversification strategies.

76. Yiu, D. W., Lu, Y., Bruton, G. D., & Hoskisson, R. E. (2007). Business groups: An integrated model to focus future research. *Journal of Management Studies* 44(8): 1551–1579.

77. Wan & Hoskisson. Home country environments, corporate diversification strategies, and firm performance.

78. Hoskisson, R. E. (1987). Multidivisional structure and performance: The diversification strategy contingency. *Academy of Management Journal* 30: 625–644.

79. Ramaswamy, K., Li, M., & Petitt, B. (2012). Why do business groups continue to matter? A study of market failure and performance among Indian manufacturers. *Asia Pacific Journal of Management* 29(3): 643–658.

80. Larrain, B., & Urzúa, I. F. (2016). Do business groups change with market development? *Journal of Economics & Management Strategy* 25: 750–784.

81. Holmes, M., Holcomb, T., Hoskisson, R. E., Kim, H., & Wan, W. (2018). International strategy and business groups: A review and future research agenda. *Journal of World Business* 53: 134–150.

82. Hoskisson, R. E., Cannella, A. A., Tihanyi, L., & Faraci, R. (2004). Asset restructuring and business group affiliation in French civil law countries. *Strategic Management Journal* 25: 525–539.

83. Hoskisson, R. E., Johnson, R. A., Tihanyi, L. & White, R. E. (2005). Diversified business groups and corporate refocusing in emerging economies. *Journal of Management*, 31: 941–965.

84. Ibid., 941–965.

85. Ramaswamy, K., Li, M., & Veliyath, R. (2002). Variations in ownership behavior and propensity to diversify: A study of the Indian corporate context. *Strategic Management Journal* 23: 345–358.

86. Arnoldi, J., & Muratova, Y. (2019). Unrelated acquisitions in China: The role of political ownership and political connections. *Asia Pacific Journal of Management* 36(1): 113–134.

87. Mackey, Barney, & Dotson. Corporate diversification and the value of individual firms.

88. Helfat, C. E., & Eisenhardt, K. M. (2004). Inter-temporal economies of scope, organizational modularity, and the dynamics of diversification. *Strategic Management Journal* 5(13): 1217–1232; Capron & Mitchell. Build, borrow or buy.

89. Granovetter, M. (1994). Business groups. In N. J. Smelser & R. Swedberg (Eds): *Handbook of economic sociology*. Princeton, NJ: Princeton University Press.

90. Kim, H., Hoskisson, R. E., Tihanyi, L., and Hong, J. (2004). Evolution and restructuring of diversified business groups in emerging markets: The lessons from chaebols in Korea. *Asia Pacific Journal of Management* 21: 25–48.

91. Ramaswamy, K., Purkayastha, S., & Petitt, B. S. (2017). How do institutional transitions impact the efficacy of related and unrelated diversification strategies used by business groups? *Journal of Business Research* 72: 1–13.

92. Wan & Hoskisson. Home country environments, corporate diversification strategies, and firm performance.

93. Musacchio, A., Lazzarini, S. G., & Aguilera, R. V. (2015). New varieties of state capitalism: Strategic and governance implications. *Academy of Management Perspectives* 29(1): 115–131.

94. Bebchuk, L. A., Brav, A., Jiang, W., & Keusch, T. (2020). Dancing with activists. *Journal of Financial Economics* 137(1): 1–41

95. Austen, I. (2005). Wendy's moving to spin off its Canadian doughnut chain. *New York Times*, July 30. https://www.nytimes.com/2005/07/30business/wendy-moving-to-spin-off-its-canadian-doughnut-chain.html.

96. Karolyi, G. A., Kim, D., & Liao, R. (2020). The theory and practice of investor relations: A global perspective. *Management Science* 66(10): 4746–4771.

97. Shi, Connelly, Hoskisson, and Ketchen. Portfolio spillover of institutional investor activism.

98. George, B., & Lorsch, J. W. (2014). How to outsmart activist investors. *Harvard Business Review* 92(5): 88–95.

99. Duprey, R. (2018). PepsiCo investors should be happy CEO Indra Nooyi is out. *Motley Fool*, www.fool.com, August 18.

100. Engen, J. (2018). Rightsizing a mammoth. *Global Finance*, October, 18–19.

101. Messenbock, R., Morieux, Y., Backx, J., & Wunderlich, D. (2018). How complicated is your company? www.bcg.com, January 16.

102. Benner & Zenger. The lemons problem in markets for strategy.

103. Litov, Moreton, & Zenger. Corporate strategy, analyst coverage, and the uniqueness paradox.

104. Shin, J. Y., Hyun, J., Oh, S., & Yang, H. (2018). The effects of politically connected outside directors on firm performance: Evidence from Korean chaebol firms. *Corporate Governance: An International Review* 26(1): 23–44.

105. Song, O.-R. (2002). The legacy of controlling minority structure: A kaleidoscope of corporate governance reform in Korean chaebol. *Law and Policy in International Business* 34(1): 183–245.

106. Kim, W., Sung, T., & Wei, S.-J. (2017). The diffusion of corporate governance to emerging markets: Evaluating two dimensions of investor heterogeneity. *Journal of International Money & Finance* 70: 406–432.

107. Baik, B., Kang, J.-K., & Kim, J.-M. (2010). Local institutional investors, information asymmetries, and equity returns. *Journal of Financial Economics* 97(1): 81–106.

108. Arnoldi & Muratova. Unrelated acquisitions in China: The role of political ownership and political connections.

109. Mahmood, I., Chung, C., & Mitchell, W. (2017). Political connections and business strategy in dynamic environments: How types and destinations of political ties affect business diversification in closed and open political economic contexts. *Global Strategy Journal* 7(4): 375–399.

110. Kim, H., Kim, H., & Hoskisson, R. E. (2010). Does market–oriented institutional change in an emerging economy make business–group–affiliated multinationals perform better? An institution–based view. *Journal of International Business Studies* 41: 1141–1160.

111. Chittoor, R., Kale, P., & Puranam, P. (2015). Business groups in developing capital markets: Towards a complementarity perspective. *Strategic Management Journal* 36(9): 1277–1296.

112. Kim, Kim, & Hoskisson. Does market–oriented institutional change in an emerging economy make business–group–affiliated multinationals perform better?

CHAPTER 4

Governance Actors and Innovation Strategy

BOX 4.1   Strategic Governance Challenge: How Should Boards Be Structured to Foster Innovation?

From the 1970s to the 1990s, boards were populated with many inside directors—those with direct ties to the company, such as employees or officers—but in the early 2000s, with the implementation of the Sarbanes-Oxley Act, most boards of publicly traded firms became comprised with a majority of outside independent directors. With the implementation of this regulation, the intensity with which board members monitor executive decisions increased. Although mandated regulations are often associated with ceremonial and symbolic implementation with little effective change, one needs to explore the impact on decision-making by boards in sensitive areas such as forward-looking expenditures focused on innovation, both in countries with strong market institutions as well as in those with weak institutional foundations.

In Chapter 3, we suggest that boards that have a preponderance of outside directors might implement financial control with little understanding of the inside strategic operations, unless there are enough inside directors to help inform them of the strategic nature of innovation investment. Indeed, research shows that intense board monitoring may reduce excess CEO compensation and lower earnings management, but at the expense of decreased innovation expenditure. Specifically, in the presence of more inside directors, research and development expenditures become more effective, leading to better value creation, especially in R&D intensive firms such as those in the pharmaceutical industry. Human capital on the board, such as board members with science backgrounds, industry experience, and more diversity (e.g., more women), can also help foster better R&D investment, especially in countries with strong market institutions.

Yet, in countries with weak institutional bases, outside directors become more important because leadership might tend to reduce R&D expenditure and become involved in corrupt practices that occur in such countries (see Chapter 8). Under this scenario, outside directors help ensure that innovation expenditures are appropriate. Meanwhile, in countries with stronger market institutions, when firms are mature, have a high level of free cash flow, and function in less innovative intensive industries in which R&D expenditures are less important, agency problems might be more problematic and thus outside board members might ameliorate shareholders' concerns of managerial missteps like R&D overinvestment.

Company leaders need to make sure that boards are structured appropriately for the industry and the country environment in which they are headquartered, as well as in subsidiary locations internationally. Outside directors can help in many ways to alleviate excessive managerial self-interest, but their excessive monitoring, especially of complex decisions that are future oriented in research intensive industries and in countries with strong market institutions, can get in the way of effective decision-making relative to R&D activities.

Sources: Valenti, A., & Horner, S. (2020). The human capital of boards of directors and innovation: An empirical examination of the pharmaceutical industry. *International Journal of Innovation Management* 24(6), 205056; Sena, V., Duygun, M., Lubrano, G., Marra, M., & Shaban, M. (2018). Board independence, corruption and innovation. Some evidence on UK subsidiaries. *Journal of Corporate Finance* 50, 22–43; Shaikh, I. A., & Peters, L. (2018). The value of board monitoring in promoting R&D: a test of agency-theory in the US context. *Journal of Management & Governance* 22(2): 339–363; Shi, W., & Connelly, B. L. (2018). Is regulatory adoption ceremonial? Evidence from lead director appointments. *Strategic Management Journal* 39(8): 2386–2413; Guldiken, O., & Darendeli, I. S. (2016). Too much of a good thing: Board monitoring and R&D investments. *Journal of Business Research*, 69(8): 2931–2938; Faleye, O., Hoitash, R., & Hoitash, U. (2011). The costs of intense board monitoring. *Journal of Financial Economics* 101(1), 160–181; Coles, J. L., Daniel, N. D., & Naveen, L. (2008). Boards: Does one size fit all? *Journal of Financial Economics* 87(2): 329–356.

*I*nnovation signifies an important element for success for firms and countries, as advancements and associated research and development activities enable the introduction of new products and processes that fuel a firm's, as well as a country's, economic growth. Not surprisingly, researchers and practitioners alike strive to understand how governance actors influence innovation investment, since this influence may play a critical role in the firm's ultimate competitiveness. At the board level, as we suggest in the Strategic Governance Challenge (Box 4.1), structuring the board in a way that allows members to help top managers shape a firm's innovation strategy is essential. But, as we will see, ownership by short-term oriented institutional owners and activist investors, might lead to lower research and development (R&D) expenditures and create incentives for managers to improve short-term performance at the expense of long-run R&D activities. More dedicated institutional investors, however, might help foster lengthier time horizons for top managers, allowing for longer term R&D investment.[1] Meanwhile, as Box 4.1 also indicates, different country institutional environments produce different governance orientations at a national level, which in turn create varying effects on investment in innovation.[2] To make innovation decisions that can lead to a sustainable competitive advantage, managers and board members should take into consideration the varying industry and country characteristics.

Corporate innovation strategy extends beyond internal firm R&D expenditures, as there are other ways for firms to create innovation or gain knowledge (such as through corporate venture capital investment). The direction pursued may largely depend on governance actors' orientations toward innovation, which we will discuss in detail. Top managers and boards can leverage the various orientations, such as toward monitoring and resource provisions, to accentuate a long-term innovation focus and provide engagement, as well as to establish defensive activities to counteract those that would reduce focus on innovation in a way that may not be in the firm's best interest.

INNOVATION STRATEGY

Although innovation is important for countries to foster growth and progress, not all companies function in industries in which high innovation investment represents an essential element to maintain a competitive edge. For firms in mature industries, novel products may not be as important as in industries in which disruptive product innovation occurs more frequently. A company's goals also play a role. When companies emphasize a low-cost strategy, for example, to lower manufacturing costs may be more important than product innovation. Also, because digitalization and in particular platform strategies used by Amazon, Facebook, Uber, Airbnb, and Apple increasingly cause disruption in many industries, such as retail, advertising, taxi, lodging, and software applications, respectively, paying attention to possible disruptive innovation today becomes more important than ever.[3] In this business environment, governance actors need to be aware of a firm's innovation strategy and industry trends and ensure that top managers of the companies that they are responsible for, investing in, or monitoring are also paying attention to nuances in choosing an innovation strategy.

A firm can engage in innovation strategy in various ways. The most typical approach consists of investing capital in research and development to generate product and process innovation internally.[4] However, some company leadership teams engage in corporate entrepreneurship by investing in startup firms through corporate venture capital funds that may be used to gain knowledge and, if successful, then acquire the firm.[5] For example, Salesforce leadership, which is currently seeking to acquire Slack, a company messaging system producer, has had private investments in companies like Dropbox, Zoom, and Snowflake. Microsoft, a Salesforce competitor, is investing in C3.ai, a firm that facilitates the artificial intelligence service application for companies and is on the verge of going public.[6] Still other company leaders might form a joint venture with another firm to create innovation in which the two firms have complementary capabilities that neither one would have alone.[7] Alternatively, a firm might buy another firm on the open market to enter a new market, although this strategy is expensive because of the acquisition premiums that need to be paid, which may result in lower future innovation investment.[8]

GOVERNANCE ACTORS' INFLUENCE ON INNOVATION

Figure 4.1 introduces the various types of governance actors and their time frame orientations (on the *horizontal* axis) as well as their governance orientations (on the *vertical* axis). As the figure illustrates, governance actors foster perspectives focused on either short-term or long-term outlooks, either discouraging or facilitating investment in R&D activities and associated innovation strategies. The influencers' approaches also depend on their governance objectives, whether to monitor and provide resources or to seek information disclosure for their decision-making processes.

Monitoring and Resource Provision Governance Actors with a Short-Term Orientation

Outcome-monitoring-oriented board members, activist investors, and creditors, such as large banks that lend money to firms, fall under Quadrant I of Figure 4.1. All of these governance actors monitor firms, especially with regard to financial outcomes. Lenders, for example, monitor because their

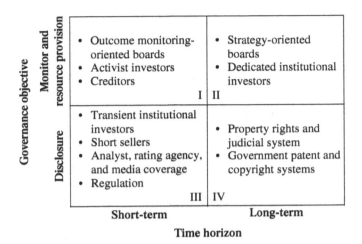

FIGURE 4.1 Governance actors and orientation toward innovation.

loaned capital depends on a firm's cash flow prospects. Some governance actors such as activist investors can provide top managers with strategic advice, or resource provision, but the advice is usually directed at improving short-term financial returns.

Outcome-Oriented Boards   As discussed in detail in Chapter 3, when boards have a preponderance of independent outside directors, who have little inside company information, these directors often emphasize outcome controls focused on financial returns rather than on future-oriented strategy formulation and advice.[9] This inclination becomes especially true for broadly diversified firms with complex innovation strategies, which are difficult for outside directors to evaluate. In these cases, headquarters often delegate strategic control to divisional managers, evaluate financial outcomes at the business level, and then allocate resources based on the divisional financial performance.[10] When strategy formulation takes place at this divisional level, the decision-making process is even more distant from the board since corporate officers, also removed from the process, cannot fully inform other board members about the strategy's details. Meanwhile, when the corporate office emphasizes divisional financial outcomes, the board will similarly place emphasis on the financial outcomes that come from the divisions. Since R&D investment typically harms a division's short-term performance because these long-term investments are expensed in the current period at the divisional level, firms with broad diversification tend to have a low level of R&D expenditure.[11]

As such, intensive monitoring by the board of directors, especially when focused on financial outcomes, can lead to a tradeoff in innovation as described in the opening Strategic Governance Challenge (Box 4.1). In contrast, when there are informed insiders on the board who do not focus entirely on financial outcomes, especially for R&D intensive firms, R&D expenditures are more effective in improving longer term firm value.[12]

Activist Investor Monitoring and Resource Provision   Research shows that hedge fund activist campaigns against target firms have significant tradeoffs regarding long-term strategy sustainability. In particular, research and development investment decreases not only in the short-term but also three to five years later.[13] Furthermore, long-term capital investments suffer, as does corporate social responsibility investment (see Chapter 7). In 2017, in response to an activist campaign by Nelson Peltz's Trian Fund, for example, the CEO of Procter & Gamble (P&G), David Taylor, said: "He's proposed some things that could be very dangerous to the short term, which is reorganize the company right now, and he's proposed something very dangerous for the long-term future of this company, and that is eliminating our corporate R&D."[14] Also, Peltz wanted to be on the board and facilitate splitting the company into three separate firms. Interestingly, although Taylor initially won the proxy battle to keep Peltz off the board, ultimately Peltz was appointed and the parties achieved a strategic compromise, which was successful.[15]

Although substantial research suggests that activist shareholders create short-termism among top managers, some researchers hold an opposite opinion. Once activists get on the board, they become longer-term investors because of their board participation and a closer inside view of the strategy being pursued by the firm.[16] This is apparently what happened in the P&G example above.

Creditors   When banks lend money to firms, they often require debt covenants attached to assets and monitor such investments intensely to ensure that companies have substantial cash flow with which to make periodic debt payments.[17] As innovation investment can generally harm short-term cash flow; top management teams typically reduce innovation expenditure in the presence of a high level of bank debt.[18] But the role of creditors in shaping innovation expenditures becomes particularly salient in the context of leveraged buyouts where public firms are taken private, usually replacing equity capital with debt capital. Research suggests that, after leveraged buyouts, firms have fewer patents, fewer patent citations, and fewer radical patents.[19] When firms have heavy debt loads, they have less cash flow available for longer-term expenditures. Yet, we should differentiate between institutional and management buyouts. Institutional buyouts are usually made by leveraged buyout firms that are seeking to turn around the assets in a short time period after restructuring the firm and then reselling the assets. In management buyouts, executives (who often have an ownership stake) seek to manage the business over a longer time horizon. Institutional buyouts have less innovation output compared to management buyouts, since executive owners have long-term goals, even though both scenarios may present similar amounts of debt. However, the negative relationship between debt and innovation is reduced when the debt is public rather than bank financed; bank-financed debt is more attached to assets and make managers more risk averse, whereas public bonds are often unsecured by assets. Also, long-term expenditures are facilitated by reducing the risk of debt through credit default swaps, which hedges the risk of debt, increasing managers' willingness to invest in the long term.[20]

Resource Provision and Monitoring Governance Actors with a Long-Term Orientation

Boards with a focus on strategic control as well as dedicated institutional investors influence firms' investment in innovation for the long term, as seen in Quadrant II of Figure 4.1.

Strategy-Oriented Boards As noted earlier, when boards have some balance between inside managers and independent outsiders, members can participate in strategy formulation and provide worthy advice to CEOs.[21] This kind of board likewise allows CEOs more strategic leeway because directors have a better understanding of the strategy that the top managers are pursuing and can wait to see fruition rather than pursuing more rapid discipline than boards do when they are more focused on performance outcomes. Balanced boards improve the "strategic action capability" of the top management team[22] and allow for better risk taking, especially among high-technology firms that are R&D intensive. Monitoring by boards with a strategic focus can improve underinvestment for R&D intensive firms and likewise reduce overinvestment when firms spend too much money on research and development.[23]

As the business environment has grown more complex and chaotic, more strategic input from board members benefits top managers. As one experienced board commentator noted: "Boards need to have strategy discussions with management and the CEO all year long. It can't be a 'once and done' event—strategy needs to be discussed at literally every meeting."[24]

Dedicated Institutional Investors Dedicated institutional investors typically pursue a *buy-and-hold strategy* for the firms they own.[25] Generally, they hold their stock positions for the long-term relative to transient institutional owners and, as such, they are known as "relational investors."[26] These investors place emphasis on strategic control more than on financial outcome, which allows them deeper insight into the value creation process.[27] In this manner, they can shield the firm from short-term market pressures. The patient capital provided by dedicated institutional investors can encourage firms to invest in long-term oriented R&D and other innovation activities.[28] In Chapter 5, we discuss how Berkshire Hathaway uses its dedicated ownership positions to foster a longer-term orientation in the firms that it retains in its investment portfolio.

Short-Term Oriented Governance Actors with a Focus on Information Disclosure

For Quadrant III of Figure 4.1, we discuss governance actors that pursue information disclosure and transparency and are associated with a short-term time horizon, including transient institutional investors, short sellers, rating agencies, media, and regulators pertaining to certain types of regulation.

Transient Institutional Investors   Transient institutional investors focus on short-term earnings reports and buy and sell quickly depending on earning prospects, leading to rapid turnover in their portfolios,[29] often of 80 percent or more per year. Accordingly, these investors are less concerned about long-term investments such as R&D.[30] They often turn a blind eye to governance issues and depend on outside independent directors who monitor mostly for financial outcomes. Transient investors are interested in information disclosure about *external innovation,* such as announcements of acquisitions or joint ventures, rather than scrutiny of the strategic process associated with complex value creation through innovation of new products because announcements of external innovation can trigger market reactions, creating short-term trading opportunities.[31] In other words, these investors are event-transaction-oriented rather than strategy-oriented.

Short Sellers   Short sellers borrow shares from owners, usually on a short-term basis, and make money if the share price goes down. With this purpose, they look for information disclosed on the firm, especially that which puts the company in a negative light, to then disseminate the negative data to the market and depress the stock price. Understandably, this downward pressure can lead companies to cut long-term expenditures such as R&D and investment in mergers and acquisitions[32] and lower firm growth activities.[33] CEOs routinely lobby for tighter short-selling restrictions because the negative information disseminated by short sellers lacks balance, highlighting negative news, and overlooking or suppressing the positive.[34]

Analysts, Rating Agencies, and Media Coverage Financial analysts concern themselves with company disclosure as they seek inside information about the strategies that managers are pursuing. R&D intensive firms often employ complex strategies because they are developing new products and processes that leadership wants to keep secret to not expose their new ideas to competitors and thus stay ahead of the competition. Yet, as analyst coverage increases, firms face growing pressure to increase transparency. As a result, firms reduce their internal R&D activities[35] and rely on more transparent external innovation strategies such as acquisitions and corporate venture capital investments in startups.[36] Such transactions often require public information disclosure that analysts can read and analyze to reach more informed judgments.

Similarly, corporate credit rating agencies examining R&D-intensive firms must weigh concerns about firms' future potential given high research and development investments. Hence, in the near term, the evaluators impose higher borrowing costs than the firm's past performance and risk characteristics would seem to reasonably justify.[37] However, this practice makes a firm's R&D investment more efficient because the company pays relatively higher credit costs, but the overall capital that research intensive firms would invest is lower. In the long term, if the firm's R&D spending continues to be efficient, its credit rating improves along with its reputation for realizing positive results from innovation investment, and ultimately its borrowing costs go down.

Firms are experiencing short-term market pressure to meet earnings expectations, accentuated by short sellers magnifying negative performance information. This pressure becomes even more pronounced by media exposure, especially if earnings fall below expectations. In contrast to the typically vague description of firms' long-run performance prospects, a news release announcing a firm's short-term performance is likely to be breaking news and thereby attracts greater investor attention. Meanwhile, innovation is an output of long-term investment; thus, the threat of media coverage can impede firm innovation. In addition, media coverage of innovation activities can reduce firms' innovation incentives and outputs because top managers are weary of critical news being disclosed to rivals. Overall, research shows that increased media exposure leads to decreased investments in innovation.[38]

Regulation Regulation has been a significant constraint on innovation activities. Notably, the Sarbanes-Oxley (SOX) Act, which increased the number of outside independent directors required, also emphasized the importance for firms to meet internal control requirements (SOX Section 404), which leads to tighter financial controls. This part of the SOX Act has been shown to dampen risk taking and innovation expenditures.[39] In addition, the Act enables actions to improve audit quality, which can lead top managers to reduce risk taking and innovation expenditures.[40]

Another type of regulation has to do with the government's new product approval process, such as for new pharmaceuticals and medical equipment. A rigorous approval process seeks to screen out unhealthy byproducts of new drugs and medical devices to protect the consumer. In the United States, the Food and Drug Administration supervises this approval process. A firm must submit extensive evidence about the drug's efficacy and safety, which corporate leaders collect through a series of clinical trials with increasingly larger numbers of recipients.[41] Even with a usually extensive review time and a stringent process, many side effects may not appear until the drug is approved and widespread use begins across the population. This scenario often leads to expensive litigation and risk associated with product liability if the firm's research team does not carefully conduct its clinical trials. For this reason, many firms choose to focus on generic drugs once a patented remedy expires.

Teva Pharmaceutical Industries is the largest generic drug producer. Instead of focusing on new products, the company pursues the less risky approach of buying innovation through acquisitions, especially if a firm's patented drugs will soon go off patent protection.[42] However, because acquisitions often require paying a premium price and patented drugs are hard to evaluate, Teva has had poor performance. Over time, as the drug approval process has become more stringent, fewer firms are spending the necessary dollars needed to pursue basic R&D innovation processes for breakthrough drugs, even though this approach has been shown to be the most profitable approach.[43]

Regulations can also indirectly influence firm innovation strategy by shaping the competitive environments. When regulators enact anticompetitive laws to prevent the unlawful reduction of competition, firms may become more motivated to make innovation investments because failure to innovate can weaken their positions in product market competition. Consistent with this, research shows that more stringent competition laws are associated with increases in firms' self-generated patents, the patent citation-impact, and the explorative nature of those patents.[44] By the same token, when regulators enact laws to constrain competition, firm motivation to invest in innovation decreases. For example, in 2007, the US government introduced the Foreign Investment and National Security Act (FINSA), which makes it difficult for foreign companies to acquire US companies based on the US company having assets that are in the nation's security interest. For instance, Broadcom's hostile takeover of Qualcomm was disapproved because it was feared that its foreign operation might expose trade secrets to foreign players.[45] The problem is that, after the passage of the law, companies in the industries protected by FINSA reduced R&D investment, likely due to weaker foreign rival competition.[46]

Long-Term Oriented Governance Actors with a Focus on Information Disclosure

The governance actors in Quadrant IV of Figure 4.1 help to ensure property rights and facilitate information disclosure to assist long-term innovation, while likewise encouraging growth-oriented intellectual property.[47] Regulators oversee a system of governance for establishing research patents and copyrights, which firms pursue to establish intellectual property rights. Patents help establish an appropriability regime by establishing property rights and allowing for an exclusive market position, which encourages inventors to innovate. The patenting system requires information disclosure and thereby creates a market for purchasing licensing or full property rights to a patent and at the same time allows broad information diffusion about the innovation. As the innovation is disclosed, other scientists might explore associated ideas and seek to advance their own patent or use the licensing rights to incorporate a patent idea into their own innovation or production process.[48] However, the patenting system that establishes appropriability rights and information disclosure only works to incentivize innovation if there is a strong judicial system that supports these structures. Having a judiciary and court system that will uphold intellectual property rights in contracts during conflicts creates an incentive for firms to engage in basic science and engineering to develop new products and processes. If the institutional environment is weak, with long-term patent property rights not contractually protected and courts lax in enforcing such contracts, firms will experience less enticement to pursue risky, long-term, and expensive research, which otherwise fuels economic growth and firm value creation. In fact, research shows that strong market institutions with accompanying legal protections is more important than tax credits or financial incentive in promoting innovation.[49]

Many emerging economy firms patent in the United States to not only establish property rights, but also maintain legal protection of exclusivity[50] because of the strong legal system. Yet, an ongoing patenting surge is occurring in many developing economies, such as China.[51] Often, foreign firms patent in the Chinese system to preemptively establish their property rights there. But, although the Chinese system has improved formal institutional protections in accordance with international agreements, actual enforcement of patent property rights is lacking.[52] In the end, the patenting system encourages technology transfer into China because of the establishment of better regulation, which otherwise would not take place. Although the judicial system protections and enforcement are lacking, especially for foreign firms, the system creates growth opportunities and advancement for Chinese companies. Nevertheless, when there are both formal patenting laws and strong legal enforcement to ensure exclusivity for intellectual property rights, firms will have stronger incentives to innovate. Of course, each country needs to be evaluated for its strengths and weaknesses when entry is considered.

Full information disclosure forms another important aspect of the patent process. If complete information is not fully disclosed in the patent application, the protective document can be invalidated and the property rights and associated appropriability lost. For example, as illustrated in the Strategic Governance Highlight (Box 4.2), Pfizer lost patent rights to Viagra, an erectile dysfunction remedy, early because of a lack of full disclosure in its patent application, resulting in a huge loss for the company, given Viagra's wide use.

LEVERAGING GOVERNANCE ACTORS TO FOSTER APPROPRIATE INNOVATION STRATEGY

In Figure 4.2, we provide a framework that addresses the situations as outlined in Figure 4.1 and offer four strategies as guidance toward leveraging governance actors associated with each quadrant:
  I. Engage and defend
 II. Connect and engage
III. Disclose, manage, and engage
IV. Disclose and comply, lobby, and adjudicate

Engage and Defend

With activist investors increasing the number of campaigns that they launch against target firms, board members must engage them or face stiffer challenges and demands for change. One commentator notes that if consensus is not reached between company leadership and the activist investor, the latter may make their demands public through open letters, white paper reports, shareholder proposals, and proxy contests. The expert further notes that activists' agenda typically involves issues related to corporate governance, such as replacing management, dividend payouts, new director appointments, and executive compensation, but an increasing number of activists seek influence within the strategy domain, which was traditionally the prerogative of executives.[53] If engagement can bring a consensus, from a cost–benefit perspective, less money will be spent in defending against an escalating activist campaign. Activist campaigns have been more effective when large institutional investors

BOX 4.2   Strategic Governance Highlight: The Patenting Bargain: Time-Limited Monopoly for Scientific Disclosure

The patenting bargain refers quite simply to scientific advancement, which can be the fundamental ingredient for the development of a particular product, that is given a time of limited monopoly (usually 20 years) in return for "a full and complete disclosure of the invention." The essence of this disclosure entails that someone wanting to duplicate the ingredient and develop associated products once the patent expires will have enough information to do so. The patenting system functions on the logic that the disclosure will allow scientific advancement for society in general while granting time-limited monopoly and exclusive appropriability for the company inventing the ingredient and associated products.

Pfizer, which patented the drug Viagra, an erectile dysfunction pharmaceutical, was challenged in court by Teva Pharmaceutical Industries Ltd., a generic drug producer. Interestingly, courts upheld Pfizer's patent in the United States, Spain, Norway, and New Zealand. However, the Supreme Court in Canada invalidated the patent, arguing that Pfizer had failed to state the exact specific active ingredient that created the foundation for the drug. In announcing the decision, one justice said: "Pfizer gained a benefit from the [Patent] Act—exclusive monopoly rights— while withholding disclosure in spite of its disclosure obligations under the Act. As a matter of policy and sound interpretation, patentees cannot be allowed to 'game' the system in this way. [The patent] is invalid."

Almost immediately, Pfizer lowered its prices on Viagra, since generics were bound to enter the market. The invalidation happened in 2014 and Pfizer lost significant profits that would have lasted until 2020, thanks to the action of not entirely complying with full disclosure. To avoid such costly mistakes, board members should seek to establish rules specifying that full disclosure be readily apparent in patent applications. In this manner, company leadership can ensure that shareholders and stakeholders, and society at large, receive the full benefit created by a strong patenting system.

Sources: Nocera, J. (2017). Viagra history from sex icon to generic drug. *Bloomberg*, www. bloomberg.com, December 6; Lorenzetti, L. (2014). Pfizer beats estimates as Viagra loses patent protections. *Fortune*, www.fortune.com, July 30; Fenwick, M. (2013). Pfizer case proves disclosure is the best policy. *Canadian Chemical News*, July/August 15; Canada cancels Pfizer's Viagra patent. (2012). *Biotechnology Law Report* 31(6): 593; Viagra patent invalidated in Canada. (2012). *Chain Drug Review*, November 19, 62; Loftus, P., & Rockoff, J. D. (2011). Pfizer Viagra patent upheld [in the US]. *Wall Street Journal*, August 16, B2.

Time Horizon	Resource Provision or Monitoring	Governance Actor	Strategy
Short-term	Monitoring and resource provisions	Activist investors outcome-oriented boards Creditors	Engage and defend
Long-term	Resource provisions and monitoring	Strategy-oriented boards Dedicated institutional investors	Connect and engage
Short-term	Monitor	Transient Institutional Investors Short sellers Analysts, rating agencies and media coverage Regulation	Disclose, manage, and engage
Long-term	No	Property rights and judicial system Regulators	Disclose and comply lobby, and adjudicate

FIGURE 4.2　Governance actors' response strategies to foster innovation.

(even passive ones) are involved with the activist because such campaigns are perceived to have more ownership support, which foreshadows success for any proxy vote by owners. Also there is an incentive for institutional owners to become involved because activist campaigns generally yield improved short-term financial performance for the investors involved.[54] In addition, activist campaigns have become more effective against target firms over time as their strategies have become more fine-tuned.[55] However, as the supply of easy targets has diminished, there have been a higher percentage of failed campaigns as target firms have become better at defending against such activist attacks.[56] As noted in Chapter 3, for example, PepsiCo was able to successfully defend against a significant activist campaign.

Though top management teams may find a strong cost–benefit rationale to engage with activist investors, which can improve short-term efficiency, if major strategic problems are created by an activist's proposal, potentially resulting in less capital available for innovation and development necessary for strategy implementation, then defending against an activist campaign becomes a more salient alternative. As with the P&G case noted earlier, CEO David Taylor indicated that the Nelson Peltz's Trian Management proposal was problematic in the short run for the company's strategy implementation, and problematic in the long run for development purposes. The P&G team fought and won the campaign, although Peltz was brought onto the board later anyway. Also, as noted in Chapter 3, Trian lost an initial board seat in a proxy vote campaign against PepsiCo, but later gained a board seat through a compromise. However, a year after gaining the board seat, the fund divested its stake in the company without waiting for the implementation of the key goal of their campaign, making a 50 percent return on its investment,[57] which is indicative of the time horizon that activist investors such as Trian often pursue. Such strategies can frequently weaken commitment by long-term stakeholders and harm value creation for minority shareholders. Interestingly, research shows that more value is dissipated in the long term and that other stakeholders (employees) are impaired by activist owners campaigns suggesting that value created by activist investors may be short-term oriented.[58] However, there is also research, which suggests that if a firm is over diversified (and diversification is negatively related to R&D intensity—see Chapter 3), then divestitures can reduce the excessive diversification allowing a firm to increase its R&D investment.[59]

As seen with P&G and PepsiCo, a defensive approach, though expensive, is at times warranted to protect the long-term viability of the innovation strategy. However, the defense approach may be compromised when a board is composed of short-term, outcome-oriented independent directors who lack the necessary strategic knowledge to put up a strong fight and form a cohesive coalition. To avoid costly losses in defense, board members must increasingly recognize the importance of thoroughly understanding firm long-term strategy, though the task becomes difficult for outsiders who do not have a day-to-day relationship with the company. Board rules can require that directors be long-term investors in the firm without an overly busy schedule (not on too many boards)[60] to instill a longer-term orientation and motivation to engage strategically and defend against the active nature of hedge funds and supporting longer-term institutional investors when appropriate.

Directors should also look to build strong board cohesion and chemistry to ensure board member commitment to the strategic orientation of the firm. Despite the various benefits of board diversity, this characteristic can create difficulty to form an effective board coalition and thus creates vulnerability to activist investors.[61] Sometimes companies may implement the proposal of outside investors to improve short-term performance, but boards need to actively get involved to ensure that the firms are adhering to the strategy agreed to by directors. Often, what happens is the activist investors put forward a whitepaper about what they think the strategic direction of the firm should be. When this happens the firm's strategy gets extra scrutiny by investors and the top management team needs to be able to strongly counter the activist investor arguments with their own position to defend the long-term strategy. This is what PepsiCo was able to do in countering the proposal by Nelson Peltz's Trian Partners. Furthermore, companies may consider having outside legal and investment bank help lined up in advance to provide advice when necessary to help defend their strategic arguments.[62]

Boards also need to make sure that the capital structure is appropriate for the strategy being pursued. As noted, the financing system, especially through bank debt, can be negatively related to firm R&D expenditures. If fostering innovation and R&D investment is competitively important, then a preponderance of bank debt would probably not signify the right decision.[63] Boards need to understand the dynamic with creditor governance actors and thus defend the appropriate capital structure to protect investments in innovation.

Connect and Engage

Unlike activist hedge fund investors who are event-oriented (such as seeking a divestiture or an acquisition), dedicated institutional investors are long-term investors who seek relationships with firms and monitor them to understand their long-term strategic direction. Dedicated institutional investors have a collaborative rather than adversarial approach. In fact, as we previously discussed, these governance actors can encourage firms to make investments in R&D.[64] Strategy-oriented boards may engage with dedicated institutional investors to keep the latter informed and providing support when faced with pressures from other investors with short-term performance goals. Dedicated institutional investors can provide key support to boards, for example, when favoring strong, long-term compensation incentives, such as restricted stock ownership, for top managers to keep them incentivized toward long-term strategic visions.[65]

Firm leaders may engage with investors who seek strategic disclosure, especially dedicated institutional investors, by creating investor relations departments that help disseminate the information to investors. Research indicates that investor relations departments become increasingly important when firms have a complex strategy and when engagement can help disclose appropriate information to relationship-oriented investors.[66] Such departments are especially significant in countries with weak market institutions, where disclosure requirements can be lax. Investor relations in these countries can foster better disclosure and reduce the cost of capital, which in turn can improve overall firm performance. Also, during occasions when board members speak directly to institutional investors, a beneficial practice might be for investor relations personnel to be present and thus establish a standing protocol to meet fair disclosure rules that require disclosure to all investors rather than giving certain ones an information advantage.[67]

As strategy-oriented boards can help managers take a long-term focus, company leaders should strive to put together a board that fits the firm's strategic situation.[68] Although most boards of publicly traded firms are required to have a preponderance of outside directors, a few insiders on the board can help inform outsiders who do not have a day-to-day relationship with the firm by providing critical insights on major strategic issues.[69] Bringing in outsiders with related industry experience can also help inform boards on strategy, especially related to innovation issues.[70] Leaders can likewise look to individuals who have special functional expertise or are experienced CEOs at other firms to provide strategic insights. Board diversity, such as including female members, further facilitates better strategic decisions that reduce risk.[71] Additionally, other boards that board members serve on or that they have relationships with can create network connections that may help improve strategic understanding among directors and executives,[72] but when board members serve on too many boards, they may not have the time to provide substantive input.

Disclose, Manage, and Engage

Compared to dedicated institutional investors, transient institutional investors have a short-term focus and can create short-term earnings pressure for top managers. Such pressure leads to short-term earnings improvement but decreases long-term oriented expenditures, such as R&D and longer-term capital investments. Over time, especially after an influx of investors with short-time horizons,[73] companies experience lower performance and less strategic sustainability. Often associated with mutual funds, transient institutional investors' portfolios turn over rapidly, often 60 and even 100 percent annually, making these investors apathetic toward corporate governance.[74]

However, transient investors are very interested in disclosure, especially regarding earnings and large strategic events, such as acquisitions, divestitures, and joint ventures[75] and accordingly watch news announcements carefully, especially when they expect movements in the stock price. Short sellers are likewise interested in disclosure, especially in negative events that will drive down the stock price and increase the value of their investment.[76] When negative events take place, short sellers seek to magnify them. To counter, firms should not only disclose such events, but if possible, also manage disclosure so that news of negative events are bundled together rather than separately announced to avoid a perceived pattern of negativity, giving short sellers more incentive to pursue the firm. Such a strategy, known as the *big bath*, can be used to manage earnings when there is some managerial discretion in regard to timing, such as when a firm is divesting some of its assets.[77] Another example is the recent write off of nonperforming assets among large energy giants such as Shell, Exxon Mobil, and Chevron during the Covid-19 pandemic.[78] When there are large asset write-offs firm earnings look better in future quarters and there are tax advantages to such write-downs.

Because of fair disclosure regulations, quarterly earnings announcements serve to not only disclose earnings and other news but also to engage
financial analysts and business media journalists, especially during question-
and-answer periods when these governance actors probe for additional information. Because analysts seek clarity, they may discount complex strategies
when clarity is not forthcoming. Their recommendations, along with media
coverage, can lead to a short-term orientation and reduced potential for innovation.[79] Top managers must therefore manage public announcements, such
as quarterly earnings reports, in such a way that not only provides strategic
clarity but also fosters the firm's image and reputation with a long-term view-
point and standing.[80] As we suggest in the Strategic Governance Highlight
(Box 4.3), managers can seek to engage analysts and journalists and manage
their reactions as a useful information disclosure strategy by using impression
management techniques to improve the impact of events. Investor conference forums are also a way to leverage the impressions that these governance
actors receive and still meet fair disclosure regulations.

Disclose and Comply, Lobby, and Adjudicate

As previously noted, Pfizer, which lost patent protection early for Viagra,
learned of the need to fully disclose innovation procedures on patent applications to maintain attractive patent property rights. Teva Pharmaceutical
Industries was able to get access to the scientific advancement of Viagra much
earlier than necessary because of Pfizer's lax disclosure regarding the remedy.
The case was adjudicated many times in courts around the world and it took
only one loss (in Canada) for the patent to be invalidated worldwide. Boards
should heed the harsh lesson and ensure that their firms fully comply with
patent application regulations and meet legal requirements so that corporate
intellectual property can be protected. By not only disclosing data but also
complying with full disclosure guidelines, firms gain an advantage to sustain
the rights to a strong patent. The same applies to copyrights and other intellectual property.

However, in regard to CEOs who aim for breakthrough innovations,
board members should be cautious when CEOs target technological success
over execution. In this scenario, boards might pair a technology-oriented
CEO with an executive, such as a chief operational officer (COO), who has
strong implementation skills. For example, SpaceX has found success with
Elon Musk as a technology visionary linked with Gwynne Shotwell, the
company's COO, who provides the necessary execution to make SpaceX a
success.[81] Of course, without strong property rights, the Space X advancement may never have been attempted in the first place. But the protection of

BOX 4.3   Strategic Governance Highlight: Impression Management Strategy

Organizational impression management (IM) involves the process by which company executives aim to control or influence external stakeholders' reactions to events or decisions by intentionally presenting or limiting available information. Executives face the problem of potentially disclosing too much information about a new product, making the news known to competitors, which may reduce the firm's competitive advantage. Thus, top managers at firms like Apple discuss and foreshadow future products without giving too much detail about their new inventions and associated products. There is even a "rumor" website (https:// www.macrumors.com) to which Apple watchers and possibly insiders leak information to the public that "foreshadows" future potential products and possible announcements.

Much of the strategy associated with this approach is called anticipatory IM. Executives engage in anticipatory IM when they are unclear about the market reaction that an event will generate. The approach can also be effective by using analysts to help announce a negative event before a general announcement to the public. Analysts favor information that is easy to attain, especially when managers provide strong rationales for events yet to be announced, and hence help with the preannouncements. But preannouncements also serve to influence analysts using future information as leverage, since by providing the information publicly in a more favorable light, the analysts will continue to get access. These analyst announcements usually fit into fair disclosure regulations because the news comes in the form of a public announcement as long as no one has profited from the previously undisclosed information.

Further, as noted, executives can decide on the "right" time to release negative, as well as positive, news. For instance, research shows that firm leaders tend to release more negative news immediately before stock options grants because their top executives might benefit from lower stock prices on the day of receiving the grants, allowing them to enjoy higher profits when exercising options. Although such a specific approach is not recommended because it can, as it did in this case, lead to CEOs and boards being stigmatized: among the 171 firms investigated for backdating issues, more than half saw turnover at the "C-suite" level. The example however suggests that timing can be an important tool for managing both positive and negative anticipatory and reactive IM.

Sources: Jin, J., Li, H., & Hoskisson, R. E. (2020). The use of strategic noise in reactive impression management: How do market reactions matter? *Academy of Management Journal*, in press; Janney, J. J., Gove, S., Chun, R., Argandoña, A., Choirat, C., & Siegel, D. S. (2019). Do executive departures to signal the end of a scandal create or reduce uncertainty? An examination of market reaction in stock option backdating scandal events. *Business & Society* 58(6): 1209–1233; Busenbark, J. R., Lange, D., & Certo, S. T. (2017). Foreshadowing as impression management: Illuminating the path for security analysts. *Strategic Management Journal* 38(12): 2486–2507; Graffin, S. D., Haleblian, J. J., & Kiley, J. T. (2016). Ready, AIM, acquire: Impression offsetting and acquisitions. *Academy of Management Journal* 59(1): 232–252; Whittington, R., Yakis-Douglas, B., & Ahn, K. (2016). Cheap talk? Strategy presentations as a form of chief executive officer impression management. *Strategic Management Journal* 37(1): 2413–2424; Washburn, M., & Bromiley, P. (2014). Managers and analysts: An examination of mutual influence. *Academy of Management Journal* 57(3): 849–868; Arndt, M., & Bigelow, B. (2000). Presenting structural innovation in an institutional environment: Hospitals' use of impression management. *Administrative Science Quarterly* 45(3): 494–522; Yermack, D. (1997). Good timing: CEO stock option awards and company news announcements. *Journal of Finance* 52(2): 449–476.

intellectual property rights is not the only governance issue that needed to be considered; strong execution is also needed to realize value creation from intellectual property discovery.

In countries with weak intellectual property laws, governments often compensate for weak regulations by granting licenses and sometimes subsidies to firms. In these situations, firm managers should learn to lobby governments for licensing rights as well as research and development subsidies. For example, when government leaders develop a policy to strategically pursue an industry in order to establish global competitiveness, they often license such rights and provide associated subsidies to jumpstart the industry, such as in Korea for the development of strong auto and semi-conductor industries. The Korean government granted rights to large, diversified, family-controlled companies (chaebols), such as Hyundai and Kia in the auto industry and Samsung in semi-conductors, to create stronger bases for the targeted industries.[82]

Of note, once a country is allowed entrance into global trading systems, its government can no longer protect home industries from foreign competition. Boards need to have expertise in global trade to understand how entry across borders is facilitated both formally and informally. Some countries have formal laws on the books, but the judicial system may lack the will or ability to enforce contracts and protect intellectual property.[83] Boards and top managers need to analyze whether a market presents a culture of bribery, bureaucratic complexity, or lax enforcement of contracts, among many other details, in target countries when considering foreign direct investment.

In developed countries, lobbying can be an important tool in industries that depend on government contracts, such as in the defense industry (see

Chapter 8). Many countries have large research agencies that provide funding, like the National Science Foundation and the National Institute of Health in the United States. Top managers should recognize the need for strong writing talent, as grant writing skills can be critical for firms to attain funding support from these agencies.[84] Companies may also consider working with government agencies to propel innovation activities. For instance, the US Department of Agriculture has funded the development of a strong science-based agriculture industry through university land grant institutions. Through this program, each state has a lead university to foster agriculture advancement and technological diffusion through a county extension agent in each state county. Many agricultural businesses build research and science-based processing systems located close to these centers of learning to take advantage of these systems of innovation and diffusion, as well as of the opportunity to source science-based human capital.

Many firms use legal strategies to prosecute other firms who copy their patent protected technology. Qualcomm and Apple have had a long-running battle in which Apple has accused Qualcomm of charging too much in royalties for their patents, raising the price of mobile phones to such a degree that it becomes anticompetitive, suggesting that Qualcomm is breaking antitrust laws. However, Qualcomm has won recent lawsuits in China, Germany, and finally the United States, which upheld three of its patents and awarded a $31 million claim against Apple in the United States.[85]

Patenting does not represent the only strategy to protect intellectual property. Nondisclosure agreements (NDAs), too, form an essential tool in managing critical trade secrets, especially in service industries or in manufacturing process innovations.[86] NDAs are also especially important for smaller firms who cannot afford the cost of patenting and fighting legal patent battles like the ones between Apple and Qualcomm. Patent protection has been found to be better for new product introductions compared to NDAs, but many firms use both strategies to protect their intellectual property. Yet, both the patenting system and trade secret protections under NDAs are only as good as the ability of firms to adjudicate these protections in the legal system.[87] If contract laws are not supported by a strong legal system, ensuring viable intellectual property protection becomes difficult. As noted above, many companies from less developed countries will come to countries with better legal protection to patent their intellectual property and often do so in multiple countries.

Our suggestions for response strategies to foster advancement in industries and markets must follow managers' and board members' careful assessment of a firm's position to determine an appropriate innovation strategy. As creative destruction occurs and disruptive technology appears on the horizon, both executives and governance actors need to adapt their innovation strategy to meet the future challenges faced by a firm. The strategy need not only aim for investment in innovations developed inside the firm but may also consist of joint creations through joint ventures that combine complementary capabilities, investment in potential startups through a corporate venture capital fund, or even the buying of innovation through an acquisition. Leveraging governance actors to further innovation efforts becomes an important activity of top managers and boards, whose members need to understand and commit to a firm's overall strategy, and especially innovation strategy, as continual pressure occurs from outside governance actors to short-change a firm's strategy and innovation potential.

NOTES

1. Hoskisson, R. E., Hitt, M. A., Johnson, R. A., & Grossman, W. (2002). Conflicting voices: The effects of ownership heterogeneity and internal governance on corporate strategy. *Academy of Management Journal* 45: 697–716.
2. James, B. E., & McGuire, J. B. (2016). Transactional-institutional fit: Corporate governance of R&D investment in different institutional contexts. *Journal of Business Research* 69(9): 3478–3486.
3. Fenwick, M., McCahery, J. A., & Vermeulen, E. P. M. (2020). The end of 'corporate' governance: Hello 'platform' governance. *European Business Organization Law Review* 20: 171–199.
4. Capron, L., & Mitchell, W. (2012). *Build, borrow, or buy: solving the growth dilemma*. Boston: Harvard Business Review Press.
5. Ceccagnoli, M., Higgins, M. J., & Kang, H. D. (2018). Corporate venture capital as a real option in the markets for technology. *Strategic Management Journal* 39(13): 3355–3381.
6. Novet, J. (2020). Microsoft doubles its money after backing C3.ai as it goes public. www.cnbc.com, December 9.
7. Inkpen, A. C. (2000). Learning through joint ventures: A framework of knowledge acquisition. *Journal of Management Studies* 37(7): 1019–1043. Lane, P., Salk, I. E., and Lyles, M. A. (2001) Absorptive capacity, learning and performance in international joint ventures. *Strategic Management Journal* 22(12): 1139–1161.
8. Lee, J., & Kim, M. (2016). Market-driven technological innovation through acquisitions. *Journal of Management* 42(7): 1934–1963; Makri, M., Hitt, M. A., & Lane, P. J. (2010). Complementary technologies, knowledge relatedness, and invention outcomes in high technology mergers and acquisitions. *Strategic Management Journal* 31: 602–628.
9. Baysinger, B., & Hoskisson, R.E. 1990. The composition of boards of directors and strategic control: Effects on corporate strategy. *Academy of Management Review* 15: 72–87.

10. Hoskisson, R. E., Hill, C. W. L., & Kim, H. 1993. The multidivisional structure: Organizational fossil or source of value? *Journal of Management* 19: 269–298.

11. Baysinger, B., & Hoskisson, R. E. 1989. Diversification strategy and R&D intensity in large multiproduct firms. *Academy of Management Journal* 32: 310–332; Hoskisson, R. E., & Hitt, M. A. 1988. Strategic control systems and relative R&D investment in large multiproduct firms. *Strategic Management Journal* 9: 605–621.

12. Coles, J. L., Daniel, N. D., & Naveen, L. (2008). Boards: Does one size fit all? *Journal of Financial Economics* 87(2): 329–356.

13. DesJardine, M. R., & Durand, R. (2020). Disentangling the effects of hedge fund activism on firm financial and social performance. *Strategic Management Journal* 41(6): 1054–1082.

14. Gurdus, L. (2017). P&G CEO calls Nelson Peltz's proposals 'very dangerous' in short and long term. www.cnbc.com, September 17.

15. Brunsman, B. J. (2019). P&G CEO Taylor, activist investor Peltz laugh off proxy battle as stock soars. *Cincinnati Business Courier*. September 20. www.bizjournals.com/cincinnati/news/2019/09/20/p-g-ceo-taylor-activist-investor-peltz-laugh-off.html.

16. Christie, A. L. (2019). The new hedge fund activism: Activist directors and the market for corporate quasi-control. *Journal of Corporate Law Studies* 19(1): 1–41.

17. Atanassov, J. (2015). Arm's length financing and innovation: Evidence from publicly traded firms. *Management Science* 62: 128–155.

18. Kerr, W. R., & Nanda, R. (2015). Financing innovation. *Annual Review of Financial Economics* 7: 445–462.

19. Cumming, D., Peter, R., & Tarsalewska, M. (2020). Public-to-private buyouts and innovation. *British Journal of Management* 31(4): 811–829.

20. Mann, W. (2018). Creditor rights and innovation: Evidence from patent collateral. *Journal of Financial Economics* 130(1): 25–47.

21. Baysinger & Hoskisson. The composition of boards of directors and strategic control.

22. Kim, B., Burns, M. L., & Prescott, J. E. (2009). The strategic role of the board: The impact of board structure on top management team strategic action capability. *Corporate Governance: An International Review* 17(6): 728–743.

23. Shaikh, I. A., & Peters, L. (2018). The value of board monitoring in promoting R&D: A test of agency-theory in the US context. *Journal of Management & Governance* 22(2): 339–363.

24. Cliffe, S. (2017). The board view: Directors must balance all interests. *Harvard Business Review* 95(3): 64–66.

25. David, P., O'Brien, J., Yoshikawa, T., & Delios, A. (2010). Do shareholders or stakeholders appropriate the rents from corporate diversification? The influence of ownership structure. *Academy of Management Journal* 53: 636–654.

26. Bhagat, S., Black, B. S., & Blair, M. M. (2004). Relational investing and firm performance. *Journal of Financial Research* 27: 1–30.

27. Connelly, B. L., Hoskisson, R. E., Tihanyi, L., & Certo, S. T. (2010). Owner-ship as a form of corporate governance. *Journal of Management Studies* 47: 1561–1589.

28. Hoskisson, Hitt, Johnson, & Grossman. Conflicting voices, 697–716; Bushee, B. J. (2001). Do institutional investors prefer near-term earnings over long-run value? *Contemporary Accounting Research* 18: 207–246.

29. Ibid., 207–246.

30. Ibid., 697–716.

31. Ibid., 697–716.

32. Shi, W., Ndofor, H. A., & Hoskisson, R, E. (2021). Disciplining role of short sell-ers: Evidence from M&A activity, *Journal of Management* 47(5): 1103–1133.

33. Shi, W., Connelly, B. L., & Cirik, K. (2018). Short seller influence on firm growth: A threat rigidity perspective. *Academy of Management Journal* 61(5): 1892–1919.

34. Massa, A. (2017). NYSE president calls short sellers 'Icky.' Bloomberg, www.bloomberg.com, June 27.

35. He, J., & Tian, X. (2013). The dark side of analyst coverage: The case of innova-tion. *Journal of Financial Economics* 109, 856–878.

36. Guo, B., Pérez-Castrillo, D., & Toldrà-Simats, A. (2019). Firms' innovation strategy under the shadow of analyst coverage. *Journal of Financial Economics* 131(2): 456–483.

37. Griffin, P. A., Hong, H. A., & Ryou, J. W. (2018). Corporate innovative efficiency: Evidence of effects on credit ratings. *Journal of Corporate Finance* 51: 352–373.

38. Dai, L., Shen, R., & Zhang, B. (2020). Does the media spotlight burn or spur innovation? *Review of Accounting Studies,* forthcoming.

39. Gao, H., & Zhang, J. (2019). SOX Section 404 and corporate innovation. *Jour-nal of Financial & Quantitative Analysis* 54(2): 759–787.

40. Nguyen, L., Vu, L., & Yin, X. (2020). The undesirable effect of audit quality: Evidence from firm innovation. *British Accounting Review*, 52(6).

41. Polidoro, F. (2020). Knowledge, routines, and cognitive effects in nonmarket selection environments: An examination of the regulatory review of innova-tions. *Strategic Management Journal* forthcoming.

42. Danzon, P., Epstein, A., & Nicholson, S. (2007). Mergers and acquisitions in the pharmaceutical and biotech industries. *Managerial and Decision Economics* 28: 307–328.

43. Mahlich, J., & Yurtoglu, B. B. (2019). Returns on different types of investment in the global pharmaceutical industry. *Managerial and Decision Economics* 40(1): 16–36.

44. Levine, R., Lin, C., Wei, L., & Xie, W. (2020). Competition laws and corporate innovation. National Bureau of Economic Research.

45. Greenwald, T. (2018). Qualcomm evaded Broadcom's bid; now, CEO has a lot to prove, *Wall Street Journal,* www.wsj.com, March 20.

46. Shi, W. (2019). In the name of national security: Foreign takeover protection and firm innovation. Available at SSRN 3431964.

47. Holmes, R. M., Zahra, S. A., Hoskisson, R. E., Deghetto, K., & Sutton, T. (2016). Two way streets: The role of institutions and technology policy for firms' corporate entrepreneurship and political strategies. *Academy of Management Perspectives* 30(3): 247–272.

48. de Rassenfosse, G., Palangkaraya, A., & Webster, E. (2016). Why do patents facilitate trade in technology? Testing the disclosure and appropriation effects. *Research Policy* 45(7): 1326–1336.

49. Brown, J. R., Martinsson, G., & Petersen, B. C. (2017). What promotes R&D? Comparative evidence from around the world. *Research Policy* 46(2): 447–462.

50. Yang, C.-H., & Kuo, N.-F. (2008). Trade-related influences, foreign intellectual property rights and outbound international patenting. *Research Policy* 37(3): 446–459.

51. Hu, A. G. (2010). Propensity to patent, competition and China's foreign patenting surge. *Research Policy* 39(7): 985–993.

52. Papageorgiadis, N., Cross, A. R., & Alexiou, C. (2013). The impact of the institution of patent protection and enforcement on entry mode strategy: A panel data investigation of US firms. *International Business Review* 22(1): 278–292.

53. Ponomareva, Y. (2018). Shareholder activism is on the rise: Caution required. *Forbes*. www.forbes.com, December 18.

54. Appel, I. R., Gormley, T. A., & Keim, D. B. (2019). Standing on the shoulders of giants: The effect of passive investors on activism. *Review of Financial Studies* 32(7): 2720–2774.

55. Denes, M. R., Karpoff, J. M., & McWilliams, V. B. (2017). Thirty years of shareholder activism: A survey of empirical research. *Journal of Corporate Finance* 44, 405–424.

56. Croce, B. (2020). Activist investors making more attempts, having less success in 2020—report. *Pension & Investments*, July 13. https://www.pionline.com/esg/activist-investors-making-more-attempts-having-less-success-2020-report.

57. Ponomareva. Shareholder activism is on the rise.

58. DesJardine & Durand. Disentangling the effects of hedge fund activism on firm financial and social performance.

59. Hoskisson, R. E., & Johnson, R. A. (1992). Corporate restructuring and strategic change: The effect on diversification strategy and R&D intensity. *Strategic Management Journal* 13: 625–634.

60. Redor, E. (2016). Board attributes and shareholder wealth in mergers and acquisitions: A survey of the literature. *Journal of Management & Governance* 20(4): 789–821.

61. DesJardine, M. R., Shi, W., & Marti, E. 2020. Board demographic diversity as an opportunity for shareholder activism. Working paper. University of Miami.

62. George, B., & Lorsch, J. W. (2014). How to outsmart activist investors. *Harvard Business Review* 92(5): 88–95.

63. Renneboog, L., Szilagyi, P., & Vansteenkiste, C. (2017). Creditor rights, claims enforcement, and bond performance in mergers and acquisitions. *Journal of International Business Studies* 48(2): 174–194.

64. Hoskisson, Hitt, Johnson, & Grossman. Conflicting voices, 697–716; Bushee. Do institutional investors prefer near-term earnings over long-run value?

65. Makri, M., Lane, P. J., & Gómez-Mejia, L. R. (2006). CEO incentives, innovation, and performance in technology-intensive firms: A reconciliation of outcome and behavior-based incentive schemes. *Strategic Management Journal* 27(11): 1057–1080.

66. Karolyi, G. A., Kim, D., & Liao, R. (2020). The theory and practice of investor relations: A global perspective. *Management Science* 66(10): 4746–4771.

67. Deiso, P. (2019). When should boards consider communicating directly with shareholders? NACD Directorship, 45(6): 66.

68. Hill, L. A., & Davis, G. (2017). The board's new innovation imperative: Directors need to rethink their roles and their attitude to risk. *Harvard Business Review* 95(6): 102–109.

69. Baysinger & Hoskisson. The composition of boards of directors and strategic control, 72–87.

70. Klarner, P., Probst, G., & Useem, M. (2020). Opening the black box: Unpacking board involvement in innovation. *Strategic Organization* 18(4): 487–519.

71. Bear, S., Rahman, N., & Post, C. (2010). The impact of board diversity and gender composition on corporate social responsibility and firm reputation. *Journal of Business Ethics* 97(2): 207–221.

72. Carpenter, M. A., & Westphal, J. D. (2001). The strategic context of external network ties: Examining the impact of director appointments on board involvement in strategic decision making. *Academy of Management Journal* 44(4): 639–660.

73. Cremers, M., Pareek, A., & Sautner, Z. (2020). Short-term investors, long-term investments, and firm value: Evidence from Russell 2000 index inclusions. *Management Science* 66(10): 4535–4551.

74. Hoskisson, Hitt, Johnson, & Grossman. Conflicting voices, 697–716.

75. Ibid., 697–716; Connelly, B., Shi, W., Hoskisson, R., & Koka, B. (2019). Shareholder influence on joint venture exploration. *Journal of Management* 45(8): 3178–3203.

76. Shi, Connelly, & Cirik. Short seller influence on firm growth, 1892–1919.

77. Campa, D., Cao, T., & Donnelly, R. (2019). Asset disposal as a method of real earnings management: Evidence from the UK. *Abacus* 55(2): 306–332.

78. McFarlane, S. (2020). Shell signals another poor quarter for oil majors: Energy giant warns of third-consecutive quarterly loss for its oil-and-gas production business, and a further write-down. *Wall Street Journal,* www.wsj.com, December 22.

79. Guo & Toldrà-Simats. Firms' innovation strategy under the shadow of analyst coverage, 456–483; Dai, L., Shen, R., & Zhang, B. (2020). Does the media spotlight burn or spur innovation? *Review of Accounting Studies,* forthcoming.

80. Busenbark, J. R., Lange, D., & Certo, S. T. (2017). Foreshadowing as impression management: Illuminating the path for security analysts. *Strategic Management Journal* 38(12): 2486–2507.

81. Wal, N., Boone, C., Gilsing, V., & Walrave, B. (2020). CEO research orientation, organizational context, and innovation in the pharmaceutical industry. *R&D Management* 50(2): 239–254.
82. Chang, J., Cho, Y. J., & Shin, H. H. (2007). The change in corporate transparency of Korean firms after the Asian financial crisis: An analysis using analysts' forecast data. *Corporate Governance: An International Review* 15, 1144–1167. Shin, J. Y., Hyun, J., Oh, S., & Yang, H. (2018). The effects of politically connected outside directors on firm performance: Evidence from Korean chaebol firms. *Corporate Governance: An International Review* 26(1): 23–44.
83. Liu, Y., Liang, C. C., & Phillips, F. (2020). Precursors of intellectual property rights enforcement in East and Southeast Asia. *Industrial Marketing Management* 90: 133–142.
84. Holmes, Zahra, Hoskisson, Deghetto, & Sutton. Two way streets, 247–272.
85. Nieva, R. (2019). Apple dealt legal blow as jury awards Qualcomm $32 million. *CNET*, www.cnet.com, March 15.
86. Crass, D., Valero, F. G., Pitton, F., & Rammer, C. (2019). Protecting innovation through patents and trade secrets: Evidence for firms with a single innovation. *International Journal of the Economics of Business* 26(1): 117–156.
87. Ibid., 117–156.

CHAPTER 5

Governance Actors and Competitive Strategy

BOX 5.1 Strategic Governance Challenge: Strategic or Tactical Competitive Actions?

Technological change, globalization, and privatization and deregulation have given rise to a new age of competition. Firms face an increasingly competitive business environment. Let us consider the global mobile phone industry. In early 2000s, Nokia and Motorola together owned 55 percent of the world mobile phone market. In 2007, the landscape changed completely with the first iPhone introduced by Apple. In the last decade, Apple sold at least 1.4 billion iPhones according to its official sales figures. Although Apple reshaped the industry, Samsung from South Korea was the No. 1 smartphone player in the world in terms of the number of units shipped. Yet, Huawei from China overtook Samsung and Apple to become the world's biggest smartphone player in the second quarter of 2020. Meanwhile, Google bought Motorola for $12.5 billion in 2012 and Microsoft bought Nokia for $7.6 billion in 2013.

Within such a fast-paced, ever-changing environment, business leaders may often be driven toward intense forms of corporate rivalry, such as corporate spying. In 2000, growing competition led Oracle Corporation to hire a detective firm to investigate groups sympathetic to Microsoft, to yield documents harmful to Microsoft in the midst of its antitrust battle with the government. Larry Ellison, CEO of Oracle, defended his company's decision to spy on Microsoft as "a public service" and "civic duty," arguing that its efforts were justified because of Microsoft's business practices.

Spying is an extreme case of competitive actions among industry rivals. More often, firms use two types of competitive actions to cope with increased competition from domestic and foreign rivals: *strategic actions*, such as acquisitions of industry peers and business expansions, require substantial commitment of resources to specific projects that are challenging to implement and reverse, whereas *tactical actions*, such as price cuts and marketing campaigns, involve fewer resources than strategic actions and are easier to implement and reverse. Although strategic actions may help sustain a firm's long-run competitiveness, they may not boost a firm's short-term financial performance, since payoffs from such actions take a long period of time to realize. In contrast, tactical actions can help firms earn market shares rapidly but may not ensure long-run competitiveness.

Boards and executives must allocate resources wisely to balance firms' short-term survival through tactical actions, as well as long-term competitiveness through strategic actions. Meanwhile, as discussed in Chapters 1 and 2, governance actors have heterogeneous demands and influences on firms, creating complexity for boards' and executives' decision-making. For example, business expansion may be important for a firm to consolidate its competitive position; however, short-term shareholders may prefer that the firm use its free cash flow to buy back shares. Similarly, although offshoring production to low labor-cost countries can improve a firm's cost position against rivals, employees may oppose the strategic decision because such actions may create employee layoffs. Navigating varied demands from governance actors has become a top priority for executives to formulate effective competitive strategy.

Sources: Kharpal, A. (2020). Huawei overtakes Samsung to be No. 1 smartphone player in the world thanks to China as overseas sales drop. *CNBC*. July 30. https://www.cnbc.com/2020/07/30/huawei-overtakes-samsung-to-be-no-1-smartphone-maker-thanks-to-china.html; Keswing, K. (2019). The iPhone decade: How Apple's phone created and destroyed industries and changed the world. *CNBC*. December 16. https://www.cnbc.com/2019/12/16/apples-iphone-created-industries-and-changed-the-world-this-decade.html; Microsoft (2013). Microsoft to acquire Nokia's devices & services business, license Nokia's patents and mapping services. September 3. https://news.microsoft.com/2013/09/03/microsoft-to-acquire-nokias-devices-services-business-license-nokias-patents-and-mapping-services; Goldman, D. (2012). Google seals $13 billion Motorola buy. *CNN Money*. May 22. https://money.cnn.com/2012/05/22/technology/google-motorola/index.htm; Markoff, J., & Richtel, M. (2000). Oracle hired a detective agency to investigate Microsoft's allies. *New York Times*. June 28. https://www.nytimes.com/2000/06/28/business/oracle-hired-a-detective-agency-to-investigate-microsoft-s-allies.html; Grimm, C. M., & Smith, K. G. (1997). *Strategy as action: Industry rivalry and coordination*. Cincinnati: South-Western; Hambrick, D. C., Cho, T. S., & Chen, M.-J. (1996). The influence of top management team heterogeneity on firms' competitive moves. *Administrative Science Quarterly*: 659–684; Smith, K. G., Grimm, C. M., Gannon, M. J., & Chen, M.-J. (1991). Organizational information processing, competitive responses, and performance in the US domestic airline industry. *Academy of Management Journal* 34(1): 60–85.

In Chapter 4, we detailed the influence of governance actors on corporate innovation strategy and how a firm's leadership can leverage this influence to make a winning innovation strategy. In Chapter 5, we focus on how governance actors can impact strategic choices pertaining to *competitive strategy*, an action plan to gain competitive advantage, and how firm leaders can capitalize on these actors to achieve long-run competitiveness. While the focus of corporate strategy (see Chapter 3) rests on creating value through holding a portfolio of businesses, competitive strategy pertains to how a firm can do better than its rivals in product market competition,[1] such as introducing new iPhone models by Apple to compete with Samsung in the smartphone business.

Governance actors exercise their influence on executives of firms, wielding their power in high-stakes scenarios that intend to push decisions toward their visions. Executives, in turn, must find ways to both leverage the benefits and manage the threats posed by these governance influencers in their decision considerations. Steering the company towards effective competitive strategies may hinge on this delicate balancing act. Our discussion below will lead us to suggested paths for executives to leverage different governance actors to construct a successful competitive strategy.

To help us understand the kinds of influences that they exert and their individual goals in acting a certain way towards the firms in their purview, we classify governance actors along two dimensions, as shown in Figure 5.1: those who provide resources to the firms (the *vertical* axis) and those who engage in relationships with the firms (the *horizontal* axis). Some governance actors, including board members and dedicated institutional investors, feel motivated to provide resources such as information that can be critical to a successful competitive strategy. Yet others, including financial analysts and the media, may instead focus on collecting information about a firm's competitive actions with the goal of reducing information asymmetry with external constituents. Similarly, board members may have an engaged relationship with firms while others, such as short sellers, may have only a transactional relationship. As they differ along the two dimensions, the governance actors exert varying forms of influence on strategic choices pertaining to competitive strategy.

RESOURCE PROVISION AND ENGAGED GOVERNANCE ACTORS

Governance actors that provide resources and carry an engaged relationship with the firm, as seen in Quadrant I of Figure 5.1, include board members, dedicated institutional investors, family shareholders, and employees. Each

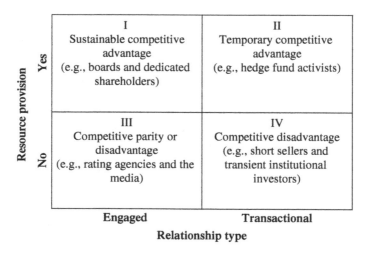

FIGURE 5.1   Governance actors and competitive strategy.

one represents an important source of knowledge for the executive, who should look to them for wisdom but with caution, understanding the particular motives behind each.

Board of Directors

Corporate directors from S&P 1500 firms hold an average tenure of over 8 years,[2] suggesting that directors have a long-term relationship with the firms through their board service. In addition, board members' reputation is closely tied to these firms. When a company has engaged in negative events, such as financial fraud, or has poor performance, board members' reputation can be at peril.[3] Therefore having an engaged relationship with the firms that they serve, directors have the responsibility not only to monitor executives for potential self-serving behaviors at the expense of other stakeholders, but also to play a critical role in advising executives.[4] As a matter of fact, a survey of board members suggests that directors place more emphasis on their advisory role in making firm strategy than on monitoring executives,[5] highlighting the resource-provision role of directors.

With such close relationships, directors inevitably influence a firm's competitive strategy. First, directors inform top managers during the process of strategy decision making based on their expertise, experience, and connections. Most board members are executives with extensive industry experience, which guides strategic competitive decisions.[6] Likewise, we note research in Chapter 4 that shows that directors with industry experience facilitate better strategic control, realizing more effective innovation strategy. For example, in regard to competitive strategy, directors who are either executives or directors of firms in one of the related upstream or downstream industries can bring potentially valuable knowledge about their own industries and facilitate the firm's access to contacts in those industries, reducing information asymmetry with suppliers and customers.[7] This related industry knowledge can potentially increase firms' bargaining power over suppliers and customers, granting a competitive advantage over rivals. Likewise, directors who have prior experience in the focal industry can help executives make more effective competitive strategies and achieve better performance.[8]

In the United States, the Clayton Act prohibits interlocking directorates among firms that compete in the same industry, if combining these firms could violate antitrust laws. As Google and Apple started to compete in the same product market, Eric E. Schmidt, Google's former chief executive, stepped down from Apple's board to alleviate the antitrust concern.[9] In 2019, Walt Disney's CEO Robert Iger resigned from Apple's board as both firms prepared to launch competing video-streaming services.[10] Though rivals may not be able to access each other's information directly through board members, firms can manage competitive uncertainty through appointing the friends of competitors' CEOs to their boards.[11] On the surface, this may seem to be a way to thwart antitrust regulation, but it is more likely to facilitate increased rivalry by providing information about a competitor's strategy, especially if there are multiple competitors in the same space.

Second, the characteristics of boards can shape how the board processes information,[12] thereby influencing a firm's competitive actions. Since competitive strategy is in essence a repertoire of strategic and tactical actions,[13] companies are associated with a high level of *competitive aggressiveness* when leadership engages intensively with rivals by launching many significant competitive actions.[14] For example, as female board members are more cognizant of the firm's surrounding industry and the changes in the external environment, firms with a large number of female directors tend to engage in more complex and aggressive competitive actions.[15] In addition, firms tend to undertake more aggressive competitive actions when directors have more human capital (e.g., knowledge, skills, and abilities) and social capital (e.g., social connections) in that these directors can help firms identify opportunities and threats in external environment to launch competitive actions.[16]

Third, the board of directors can shape executives' extrinsic motivation, or the desire to obtain tangible and intangible external rewards.[17] Through the introduction of pay-for-performance remuneration arrangements or equity plans, corporate boards may motivate top executives to undertake intensive competitive actions to defend firms' market positions.[18] Alternatively, the board can increase the pay gap between the CEO and the rest of the members of the top management team to stimulate competition among top executives with the goal of motivating them to undertake more aggressive[19] and complex competitive actions.[20] Yet, corporate boards need to be cautious with providing top executives with high-powered incentives because such incentives can motivate executives to undertake aggressive competitive actions with the goal of expanding short-term market shares at the expense of long-term competitiveness.[21]

Relatedly, granting executives high-powered incentives may demotivate them from making long-term investment critical to their strategic position, which refers to how a firm distinguishes itself in a valuable way from its rivals in a product market, whether through cost leadership or differentiation.[22] Firms pursuing a cost-leadership position attempt to create the same or similar value for customers by delivering products or services at a lower cost than rivals. Walmart leads in this strategic position, achieving competitive advantage based primarily on low costs and the corresponding low selling prices of goods. In contrast, firms pursuing a differentiation strategic position seek to create higher value for customers than that created by competitors through delivering products and services with unique features or better customer service, while keeping costs at the same or similar levels. Zappos, an online shoe and clothing retailer owned by Amazon, differentiates itself from other online retailers by offering superior customer service and free returns. A company pursuing a cost-leadership strategic position needs to continuously invest in process innovation, redesign standardized procedures, and train employees to improve their efficiency. Yet, if Walmart would tie executives' compensation to its short-term financial performance, executives may feel demotivated to make such investments, which may take a long time to yield benefits (see Chapter 4 for additional arguments about the effect on incentives and innovation). By the same token, firms pursuing a differentiation strategic position may need to make substantial investment in product innovation that can lead to next breakthrough products. As a result, if Zappos connected its executive pay to short-term financial returns, this could discourage its executives from making the needed investment to differentiate itself from its competitors.

Dedicated Shareholders

In Chapter 2, we saw that shareholders exhibit significant heterogeneity among themselves. Some shareholders such as dedicated institutional investors have a long-term investment horizon and engage in direct dialog with executives, whereas *transient* institutional investors, also called *transactional*, have short-term investment goals and do not attempt to understand the businesses of portfolio firms.[23] Dedicated investors, also known as relational shareholders, have a long-term focus that motivates them to not only monitor managers but also provide resources critical to effective strategic decisions.[24] These institutional investors can develop insights about an industry through their dedicated research functions. In fact, many institutional investment brokerages have entire divisions focused solely on conducting industry research, either for internal use to help investment managers make informed trades or for sale to outside investors.[25] But investors can go further by engaging executives through meetings and one-on-one phone calls,[26] giving the investors specialized insights into industries and firms that they may then transmit to executives of other firms. Take Berkshire Hathaway, a holding company for a multitude of businesses run by Warren Buffett and his executive team. As a dedicated institutional investor, Berkshire Hathaway invests in only a handful of industries and sectors, and its top 10 holdings by market value have been held for an average of 7.5 years.[27] Berkshire Hathaway not only provides capital but also advises its holding company executives, bringing insight from the various industries the corporate office is exposed to and analyzes rival firms to potentially shape the competitive strategy of a particular portfolio firm.

As discussed in Box 5.1, there are two types of competitive actions: *strategic* and *tactical*. Strategic actions, such as major business expansions and acquisitions, are critical to building and sustaining a firm's long-run position in a product market, whereas tactical actions, such as price cuts and marketing campaigns, can help a firm rapidly increase market shares. Tactical competitive actions may also involve engaging in legal actions. In 2016, for example, Salesforce was reported to press regulators in the United States and Europe to block Microsoft's acquisition of LinkedIn, claiming that the deal would be detrimental to competition by granting its business-software rival too much control over the social networking company's data.[28] Relatedly, in 2019, a number of Facebook's current and former rivals conveyed to FTC investigators that the social-media giant's business practices include many hardball tactics to thwart competition.[29] These two examples illustrate that rivals may resort to legal actions tactically to enhance their own competitive positions.

Thanks to the long-term investment horizon and support of dedicated institutional investors, firms with a high level of ownership by these investors tend to experiment with a diverse set of competitive actions.[30] Given the relational investment approach adopted by Berkshire Hathaway, this enables it to give its portfolio firms a high level of decision autonomy and allows the firms to focus on long-term strategic actions (see Chapter 4 for additional arguments with regard to these relational investors and innovation strategy).

In addition to dedicated institutional investors, company executives may also find help from nonfinancial corporate investors. These investors gain minority stakes in firms for strategic reasons, such as to secure tangible and intangible resources or to seek new or expanded markets;[31] thus, corporate investors, such as through corporate venture capital funds, can also be considered as dedicated shareholders. Given their focus on strategic issues, corporate investors are willing to help firms strengthen their competitive positions. These investors have often accumulated much experience and knowledge about the industries and the firms in which they invest in,[32] signifying a resource for top management teams to better scan external environments and identify potential opportunities and threats in the marketplace.[33] Through engagement with executives, corporate investors help devise effective competitive strategies and contribute to a firm's competitive advantage.

Ownership by corporate investors can also be in the form of cross holdings. In Japan, companies with interlocking business relationships engage in cross shareholdings. Such cross shareholding helps insulate companies from stock market fluctuations and takeover attempts, enabling executives to focus on a long-term investment horizon. For example, Toyota has cross-ownership with many of its suppliers, and such an ownership structure deepens trust, collaboration, and mutual investment, facilitating long-term relationships.[34]

Family shareholders represent another type of dedicated investor willing to provide resources to firm executives. Since these family owners exhibit a strong commitment to intergenerational wealth—as the older generation uses their financial capability to assist the younger generation to build affluence—family ownership in a company can not only reduce agency costs through owner control but also lengthen investment time horizons.[35] In addition, family ownership can facilitate intraorganizational trust and the development of an organizational structure that facilitates fast communication and swift decision-making.[36] Given these benefits, this type of investor can help firms identify and exploit profitable opportunities in the competitive landscape, increasing organizational flexibility.[37] Such flexibility allows firms to respond to competitive actions by rivals in an organized manner and avoid dysfunctional competitive actions, contributing to a firm's competitive advantage.[38] For example, half of the equity in Walmart's outstanding shares are held by heirs of founder Sam Walton. Interestingly, Walmart has been quickly and successfully catching up with Amazon by building a successful pickup grocery business and launching a membership program called Walmart Plus that gives members unlimited same-day delivery from more than half of its 4,700 stores.[39]

Employees

Like board members and dedicated shareholders, employees act as a type of engaged governance actor that provides important resources to firm leadership. Employees' job security and personal wealth are closely tied to a company's competitiveness and performance. Meanwhile, human capital embedded in employees is a critical source of sustainable competitive advantage for the company.[40] In this sense, employees provide critical resources to their firms. If leadership can design the right reward systems to align the interests of employees and the company, employees will have a strong motivation to provide first-hand information that they have collected from their interactions with suppliers, customers, and competitors, enabling executives to better understand competitors' moves.[41] On the contrary, if employees do not support firms' competitive actions, such actions are less likely to be implemented effectively and may not improve firm performance.[42]

Given the importance of employee human capital, the mobility of key employees to rival companies can be detrimental to a firm's competitiveness and harm performance.[43] To prevent excessive employee turnover, leadership may grant equity ownership to key employees and share firm profits with them.[44] For example, among the 800 companies that applied for *Fortune* magazine's 100 Best Companies to Work For 2005 to 2007, about one-fifth of them had employee stock ownership plans or another form of profit sharing although companies with employee ownership accounted for only about 10 percent of all sales and employment in the United States at the time.[45]

In sum, because governance actors in Quadrant I of Figure 5.1 are willing to not only engage with top managers but also provide resources for managerial decision making, these governance actors can support firms' competitive advantages that tend to be sustainable and long-lasting.

TRANSACTIONAL GOVERNANCE ACTORS THAT PROVIDE RESOURCES

Turning our attention to Quadrant II of Figure 5.1, we focus on hedge fund activists in our discussion of resource provision and transactional governance actors. Akin to directors and dedicated shareholders, hedge fund activists are motivated to provide resources and support to top management teams so that they can formulate effective competitive strategies. Yet, unlike directors and dedicated shareholders, these activist shareholders have a transactional relationship with the firms, as they have a median holding period of 423 days,[46] much shorter than dedicated shareholders.

In Chapter 3, we extensively discussed the influence of hedge fund activists on targeted firms' corporate strategy, but hedge fund activists can also affect targeted firms' competitive strategy. First, prior to targeting a firm for operational or strategic change, activist shareholders often conduct extensive research on the firm and its industry and can provide new insights that can help competitive strategy formulation. However, when it comes time to targeting for activism to shape desired change, hedge fund activists often develop detailed operational and strategic analyses, or "white papers," and generally discuss their views privately with the management team. If this engagement approach does not work, activist shareholders sometimes issue a white paper to the public. In September 2019, Elliott Management, a hedge fund activist, released a 25-page white paper addressed to the board of directors of AT&T after taking a $3.2 billion stake in the company. In the letter, Elliott outlined a four-part plan to increase AT&T's strategic focus and improve operational efficiency and made specific recommendations for competitive and strategic moves that AT&T should pursue. AT&T CEO and Chairman Randall Stephenson made a resolution with Elliott and commented, "I think our interests are 100 percent aligned. Seriously . . . And these guys [Elliott] are pretty good . . . had some really good insights and thoughts."[47]

Second, hedge fund activists can shape what type of competitive strategy a targeted firm may pursue. As noted in Chapter 1, a firm's competitive strategy can be classified into prospectors, defenders, analyzers, and reactors based on its co-alignment with the environment.[48] *Prospectors* maintain high organizational flexibility to combat environmental change and attempt to explore new product and market opportunities. For example, the Miller Brewing Company, which successfully promoted "light" beer and undertook aggressive, innovative advertising campaigns, had to close a brand-new brewery when management overestimated market demand. *Defenders* perceive the environment to be stable and certain and concentrate on one segment of a product market. The Adolph Coors Company, which for many years emphasized production efficiency in its one Colorado brewery and virtually ignored marketing, is a good example of a defender. *Analyzers* emphasize both flexibility and stability and respond to prospectors through imitation while simultaneously maintaining high operational efficiency, like Anheuser-Busch, which can follow a defender orientation to protect its massive market share in US beer and a prospector orientation to generate sales in its amusement parks. *Reactors* lack a consistent strategic choice and passively respond to the external environment. For instance, because of numerous takeover attempts, the Pabst Brewing Company has failed to follow a consistent strategy to keep its sales from dropping.

As hedge fund activists focus on cost-cutting and efficiency-enhancement measures and push companies to narrow corporate scope,[49] their influence may lead firm management teams to pursue a defender business strategy. See the example of Harley Davidson in Box 1.1 in Chapter 1 where the firm retreated to a defender position. Using a sample of 944 firms targeted by hedge fund activists (based on 13D filings) between 2000 and 2018, we found that the likelihood of a firm pursuing a defender strategy increases by 12 percent from the preattack to the postattack period, ehilr the likelihood of pursuing a prospector strategy decreases around 30 percent, attesting to the profound influence of hedge fund activists on competitive strategy. The switch to a defender strategy is partially driven by firms' declining commitment to R&D investment which was discussed in Chapter 4 as hedge fund activists may find it difficult to evaluate the direct consequence of such investment on firm short-term performance.[50] For example, after Starboard Value, a hedge fund activist, owned 10.7 percent of the Israeli chipmaker Mellanox Technologies, the activist voiced its concerns about the firm's R&D investment: "Mellanox is spending too much on research and development and other corporate expenses to try to boost revenue, sacrificing margins compared with peers."[51] Although a cut in R&D may help Mellanox improve its short-term financial returns, this could harm its ability to come up with breakthrough products (see Chapter 4 for a discussion of activist investor effects on innovation strategy).

As hedge fund activists pose a salient and severe threat to targeted managers, firms tend to reduce the number of competitive actions as a way to conserve resources and avoid making strategic pitfalls after being targeted by hedge fund activists.[52] But hedge fund activists do not only shape the competitive strategies of target firms. Nontarget firms may adjust their strategies as well to avoid becoming high potential targets of the activism. Direct rivals of targeted firms respond to hedge fund activism not only by reducing prices but also by improving their own productivity, cost and capital allocation efficiency, and product differentiation.[53] Hedge fund activists may hence boost the competitiveness of targeted firms as well as nontargeted rivals through enhancing operational efficiency and implementing cost-cutting measures, but such a boost tends to be short-lived.[54] In other words, hedge fund activists can lead firms to enjoy a temporary competitive advantage, which occurs when firms outperform industry rivals for a short period of time. To achieve sustainable competitive strategy, executives need to manage and isolate the influence of hedge fund activists, which will be discussed in detail later.

ENGAGED GOVERNANCE ACTORS WITHOUT RESOURCE PROVISION

Unlike the governance actors in Quadrant I, financial analysts and the media, which fall under Quadrant III of Figure 5.1, do not provide resources directly to firms. Instead of supporting firms with needed resources and information, these entities extract information from executives and then disclose it to external stakeholders. Financial analysts ask executives tough questions during earnings conference calls to gain additional insights, allowing them to make accurate forecasts, and the media collects information about firms from various sources to write stories appealing to readers. For instance, in an earning conference call held in November 2020 by Walmart, financial analysts asked Walmart executives about how the company's new membership program could improve its long-term competitiveness, reducing information asymmetry between Walmart and its stakeholders. Recent media coverage of antitrust lawsuits against Google enables stakeholders to develop a better insight into the company's business practices. Although financial analysts and journalists do not bestow firms with resources and information, they are motivated to cultivate favorable relationships with executives to gain access to "proprietary" information.[55] In this manner, financial analysts and the media have an engaged relationship with firms.

Financial analysts can affect a firm's competitive strategy by creating short-term earnings pressure as explained in Chapter 4, leading executives to adjust their competitive strategy.[56] Ted Turner, founder of CNN, once commented: "When all companies are quarterly earnings-obsessed, the market starts punishing companies that aren't yielding an instant return. This not only creates a big incentive for bogus accounting, but also it inhibits the kind of investment that builds economic value."[57] Given the importance of meeting earnings expectations to firms' stock prices, executives under strong earnings pressure may exploit market power opportunities and reduce output to improve current profits, even though such actions can encourage rivals to expand their output and harm the firms' long-term competitiveness.[58] Also, high levels of ownership by dedicated institutional investors can help alleviate the impact of earnings pressure on initiating tactical competitive actions, as these investors focus on long-term performance and do not trade based on short-term earnings.[59] As a matter of fact, dedicated institutional investors can help firms foster reliable relations with primary stakeholders such as employees, suppliers, and customers by enabling a long-term focus.[60]

Financial analysts may also affect competitive strategy in a more subtle way. Due to their limited expertise on specific industries, these governance actors are unable to understand novel, unique strategic moves with which they are unfamiliar.[61] As a result, executives divest businesses to facilitate analysts' valuation of their shares.[62] For the same reason, company leaders may pursue simpler competitive moves with the goal of attaining favorable recommendations by analysts who may better understand the rationale behind such moves and thus issue more favorable recommendations. Although reducing competitive complexity can help firms receive positive recommendations from financial analysts, this action may harm a firm's competitiveness in the long run.[63]

We have so far focused on the influence of analysts on focal firms' competitive strategy. If a firm and its rivals are all covered by financial analysts, they will all be exposed to earnings pressure from the analysts, resulting in competitive parity—achieving a performance level similar to rivals. However, negative earnings by analysts can create attack opportunities for rivals. Specifically, a firm's negative earnings surprise can be perceived by its rivals as an opportunity to exploit its vulnerability, thereby triggering aggressive competitive actions.[64] In August 2003, Dell announced an across-the-board price cut the day after Hewlett-Packard, its biggest personal computer rival, revealed disappointing earnings.[65]

The media's influence on a firm's competitive strategy is akin to the influence from financial analysts (see Chapter 4). Although positive media coverage of a firm can help it cultivate a good reputation,[66] extensive media coverage can reduce a firm's information asymmetry with its rivals, which may actually harm its competitiveness by exposing the details of its strategy. Meanwhile, rivals closely analyzing a firm's social media to better understand the latter's customers can put the firm at a disadvantageous position.[67] In addition, when a company's negative events are extensively covered by the media, the company may lose the support from stakeholders, rendering them vulnerable to competitive actions from rivals. In December 2020, Walmart was sued by the Department of Justice for helping to fuel the US opioid crisis by inadequately screening for questionable prescriptions despite repeated warnings from its own pharmacists.[68] The suit was extensively covered by business press and inevitably harms the reputation of Walmart.

In addition to financial analysts and journalists, competition regulators—government agencies that regulate and enforce competition laws—also belong to Quadrant III. Countries around the world establish antitrust policy and laws to ensure evenhanded competition and protect the interests of consumers. In the United States, the Federal Trade Commission (FTC) and the US Department of Justice Antitrust Division are responsible for enforcing civil US antitrust law and the promotion of consumer protection. The European Competition Commission, together with the national competition authorities, enforce European Union (EU) competition rules. The Ministry of Commerce of China is responsible for regulating market competition and consumer protection in the country.

In February 2020, the FTC investigated Amazon for anticompetitive business practices, such as favoring products on its site that pay for Amazon services.[69] In the same month, the FTC issued Special Orders to five large technology firms (Alphabet, Amazon, Apple, Facebook, and Microsoft), requiring them to provide information and documents on the terms, scope, structure, and purpose of transactions (e.g., prior acquisitions) that each company consummated between January 1, 2010, and December 31, 2019.

A primary goal of the FTC is to understand whether large tech companies are collectively making potentially anticompetitive acquisitions of nascent or potential competitors that fall below the thresholds to be reported to the antitrust agencies. In June 2020, the European Competition Commission was reported to open a formal antitrust investigation to assess whether Amazon's use of sensitive data from independent retailers who sell on its marketplace is in breach of EU competition rules.[70] As governmental bodies, competition regulators do not provide direct resources to firms; on the contrary, these regulators constantly monitor firm behaviors and enforce violations of competition laws. However, company leaders need to develop an engaged relationship with regulators who are in charge of monitoring their competitive strategies.

Antitrust laws and regulations that are effectively enforced by competition regulators create a fair competitive environment, but do not help a firm with a dominant market position achieve competitive advantage since the threat of potential investigation can complicate the process of designing an effective competitive strategy. As large firms with high profit margins face a high level of scrutiny from regulatory authorities that suspect them of anticompetitive practices,[71] these firms may refrain from certain competitive actions to avoid becoming an investigation target. Yet, for medium- or small-sized firms, antitrust laws can promote a fair competitive environment and create a more level playing field, critical for these firms to foster competitive advantages.

TRANSACTIONAL GOVERNANCE ACTORS WITHOUT RESOURCE PROVISION

As noted in Chapter 2, short selling can be an expensive strategy, so investors tend not to hold a short position for a long period of time. Short sellers hence have a transactional relationship with shorted firms. Also, because short sellers are motivated to drive down share prices through revealing negative information or spreading rumors, these investors are unlikely to offer firms resources that facilitate the development of a successful competitive strategy. These governance actors fall under Quadrant IV of Figure 5.1 because they have only a transactional relationship and provide no resources for strategic decisions.

Short sellers can affect strategic choices pertaining to competitive strategy, mainly because of their ability to depress stock prices. When a firm's competitive actions fail to generate anticipated benefits, the scenario can dampen its short-term financial performance and create short-selling opportunities. The threat from short sellers can in fact lead companies to refrain from under-taking a large volume of competitive actions.[72] In addition, being attacked by activist short sellers can make a company vulnerable to attacks from its rivals. When activist short seller Chris Brown labeled Energous, a wireless charging company, "a worthless equity" and claimed that Apple would not adopt the company's wireless charging technology,[73] his comment created opportunities for Energous's rivals to take over its market share. For exam-ple, according to data from Capital IQ, Pioneer Power Solutions, Energous's rival, announced that it had received several large contracts two months after Brown attacked Energous.

Transient institutional investors trade in and out of portfolio firms and lack the motivation to understand the businesses of their portfolio firms. These investors are not motivated to hold direct conversations with execu-tives; moreover, they lack the expertise to provide information that can be used in competitive strategy. Instead, transient institutional investors try to capitalize on private information that they can collect to inform their trading strategies. Given their focus on short-term financial returns, transient insti-tutional investors can lead firms to undertake tactical competitive actions, such as price cuts and new product launches, that are effective in improving competitive position and profitability in the short run. But when firms have high levels of transient institutional investor ownership, executives will hesi-tate to implement complex competitive repertoires and will instead focus on a set of familiar competitive actions.[74] Short sellers and transient institutional investors alike do not provide resources directly to firms in making effective competitive strategies and can instead create opportunities for rivals to attack or lead firms to focus on tactical actions that yield only short-term gains. Thus, short sellers and transient institutional investors can result in competi-tive disadvantage for firms. Our recommendations on addressing the adverse influence of short sellers and transient institutional investors will be discussed in the next section.

As discussed in the Strategic Governance Highlight (Box 5.2), institutional investors can influence portfolio firms' competitive strategy through common ownership, where an institutional investor hold shares of multiple rival firms. The rise of common ownership suggests that firms cannot be considered independent decision makers in the product market. In particular, when an institutional investor has a blockholding stake in two rivals, the investor can facilitate coordination and collaboration between the rivals. Consequently, rivals held by the same institutional blockholder are more likely to engage in within-industry strategic alliances and acquisitions than rivals without this link.[75] In this sense, institutional investors can help portfolio firms achieve temporary competitive advantages through cross holding in rivals.

BOX 5.2   Strategic Governance Highlight: Common Ownership and Competitive Strategy

For half a century, the United States experienced a steady increase in institutional ownership and a decline in the share of the average public company owned by retail investors. This trend resulted in institutional investors holding ownership in many competitors within the same industry, a situation referred to as *common ownership*. For example, as of 2017, Vanguard, a large mutual fund, held at least a 6 percent share in the six largest domestic airlines, and Berkshire Hathaway held at least 7 percent in four of these same firms. Institutional investors have both the incentive and ability to dampen competition among rivals in their portfolios as lessened competition can generate higher profits. Common ownership can also reduce competition and improve portfolio firm performance through adopting dissimilar competitive actions, which has become a salient concern to regulators.

Although dampened competition can be in the interest of competing firms, it can be detrimental to the interest of consumers. Dampened competition triggered by common ownership leaves consumers vulnerable to higher prices and lesser quality or innovation of products. For example, when the same institutional investors are the largest shareholders in branded drug companies and generic drug companies, the latter are less likely to offer cheaper versions of the brand-name makers' drugs. This concerns antitrust regulators that put together proposals requiring index funds, large shareholders of many companies, to notify regulators in advance of acquiring a significant number of shares in a company.

One way to cope with the deleterious effect of common ownership on competition is to restructure executive compensation in a way that puts less weight on competitive benchmarks. Regulators may also consider encouraging competition from foreign competitors, as it is relatively rare for US institutional investors to hold large stakes in firms from other countries. Unfortunately, in 2007, the US government introduced the Foreign Investment and National Security Act (FINSA) and gave the Committee on Foreign Investment broad authority to investigate foreign takeovers, making it difficult for foreign firms to acquire US companies and enter US markets, ultimately creating barriers that dampen foreign competition. As a result, as noted in Chapter 4, US firms may lack the motivation to innovate and introduce new products.

Although common ownership and increasing barriers for foreign competition may result in a favorable external environment for top executives in the short term, new technological development makes industry boundaries less visible, and executives need to constantly monitor rivalry from substituting products and services. In other words, designing a winning competitive strategy requires firms to be aware not only of actions by direct rivals but also be attentive to potential rivals from other industries and how governance might shape competitive rivalry.

Sources: McLaughlin, D., & Massa, A. (2020). The funds that owned too much? *Bloomberg Businessweek.* 21 December: 20–21; Boller, L., Morton, F. S. (2019). Testing the theory of common stock ownership. Working paper; Connelly, B. L., Lee, K. B., Tihanyi, L., Certo, S. T., & Johnson, J. L. (2019). Something in common: Competitive dissimilarity and performance of rivals with common shareholders. *Academy of Management Journal* 62: 1–21; Schmalz, M. C. (2018). Common-ownership concentration and corporate conduct. *Annual Review of Financial Economics* 10: 413–448; Shi, W., (2019). In the name of national security: Foreign takeover protection and firm innovation. Working paper, University of Miami; Antón, M., Ederer, F., Giné, M., & Schmalz, M. C. (2018). Common ownership, competition, and top management incentives. Working paper, University of Michigan.

MANAGING GOVERNANCE ACTORS FOR A WINNING COMPETITIVE STRATEGY

We have explained how different governance actors influence competitive strategy. Although governance actors in Quadrant I of Figure 5.1 can be conducive for firms to achieve competitive advantages, there are some pitfalls that executives need to avoid when relying on expertise and information from these governing influencers. As governance actors in the other three quadrants may not contribute to a firm's sustainable competitive advantage and some can even result in competitive disadvantage, it is important for executives to manage these governance actors to design a successful competitive strategy. Figure 5.2 describes four types of strategies that executives may consider in making competitive strategy.

Engage and Evaluate

Through engagement and evaluation, executives can manage governance actors that provide resources for competitive strategic decisions and have an engaged relationship. Engagement takes place when executives actively seek suggestions and help from these influencing actors. Building a board made up of directors with diverse expertise and experiences is the first step for effective

Relationship Type	Resource Provision	Example	Strategy
Engaged	Yes	Boards	Engage and evaluate
Transactional	Yes	Hedge fund activists	Leverage and defend
Engaged	No	Financial analysts	Manage and co-opt
Transactional	No	Short sellers	Isolate

FIGURE 5.2 Managing governance actors for a winning competitive strategy.

engagement. When directors do not believe in the mission and goal of the company, executives may have a hard time engaging them through active communication—the most important aspect of engagement. Communication can take place collectively when executives address all directors simultaneously during board meetings. But a more effective communication strategy lies in conducting one-to-one meetings. One-to-one communication helps executives cultivate personal bonds with individual directors, and more importantly provides directors with opportunities to discuss issues and share information that they may not be willing to raise in the presence of other directors.

Frequent engagement allows directors to share with executives their industry insights and management experiences, and such insights and experiences can be crucial inputs to designing a successful competitive strategy. However, executives need to *critically* evaluate suggestions from board members. Because board members are responsible for disciplining executives and setting their compensation levels, the managers may blindly follow their suggestions, which may potentially cause bias in strategic decision-making. Research[76] has shown that, under conditions of high uncertainty, a higher proportion of board members whose primary professional experience is within the focal firm's industry can actually detract from effective decision-making and increase the probability of organizational failure because such experience can result in group overconfidence and myopia and thus constrain constructive discussions. Indiscriminately following board members' suggestions can limit exploration of a multitude of competitive options, resulting in less optimal competitive strategies.

Unlike board members, dedicated shareholders may lack formal channels to engage with executives. Dedicated institutional investors and corporate shareholders often have done extensive due diligence about invested firms and their industries. Meanwhile, family shareholders are not only socioemotionally attached to firms in which they have ownership but also are familiar with business operations.[77] Top managers should therefore create platforms that enable communication with these shareholders. Communicating with dedicated shareholders is not simply the task of the investor relations department but requires active participation from executives and board members. For example, executives can hold day events to update investors on the health and direction of the company. Direct communication between executives and these shareholders allow the latter to better understand firm strategy and ease potential performance concerns. More important, such communication provides a platform for dedicated shareholders to directly share their insights with executives.

Again, we highlight the importance of critically evaluating dedicated shareholders' preferences and insights. In other words, executives should avoid blindly following the suggestions from these shareholders in efforts to appease them, given the power that they can wield. Executives need to evaluate, for example, whether dedicated shareholders have ownership in their rivals. Common ownership can distort the shareholders' incentives because high common ownership in rival firms can steer their focus toward the overall performance of their portfolio of firms rather than on the interests of the individual firm.

Leverage and Defend

To manage governance actors that can provide resources to the firm but have a transactional relationship (Quadrant II), executives may consider leveraging the expertise of and information provided by these influencers and defend their competitive strategy through communicating with and seeking support from other governance actors. Our discussion will focus on capitalizing on hedge fund activists' expertise, knowledge, and information to make successful competitive strategy.

Most hedge fund activists, such as Carl Icahn, Pershing Square, Trian, and Starboard Value, conduct thorough analyses of potential target firms' business models and strategic decisions prior to launching activist campaigns.[78] Hedge fund activists can hence provide an external diagnosis of the firm's competitive strategy. Under such a scenario, even if executives disagree with all the requests by the investor, it may not be wise for them always to take a defensive position and dismiss all the activists' suggestions. In 2017, Trian Fund Management invested $3.5 billion in Procter & Gamble (P&G) and requested board seats as the company's efforts to slim down did not boost its stock price significantly. P&G took a defensive position by communicating to shareholders via letters, presentations, and press releases to refute Trian's claims. Eventually, P&G and Trian engaged in a proxy contest, which P&G won, but Nelson Peltz, CEO of Trian was ultimately put on the board anyway. Peltz remarked about the contest: "Think about that, $100 million, all this sales and effort, to keep me off the board."[79] It can be deleterious for executives to take a defensive position. Instead, executives may need to better understand the rationale behind hedge fund activists' views and incorporate the suggestions that can potentially strengthen the firm's competitive position.

However, succumbing entirely to the pressure from hedge fund activists can be detrimental to a firm's long-term competitiveness because most of these investors focus on short-term financial returns and can constrain firms from making long-term strategic commitments.[80] To defend against hedge fund activists, executives can seek support from other governance actors. Hedge fund activists can wield disproportionate power because index managers such as BlackRock and Vanguard, as well as mutual funds and pension funds such as Capital Group and Fidelity, support them.[81] If executives hold frequent communication with other institutional investors and garner support for a strategic commitment, executives can be more effective in defending against activist campaigns and implementing a long-term competitive strategy.[82]

Manage and Co-Opt

As we previously discussed, governance actors in Quadrant III of Figure 5.1 do not provide resources to firms and instead demand information in their attempt to reduce information asymmetry with external constituents. Although these governance actors, such as financial analysts, the media, and regulators, have an engaged relationship with firms, their interests are not necessarily aligned. And yet they can profoundly shape a firm's direction by influencing stakeholder views or the company's operational environment.

Executives can alleviate the adverse implications of these governing influencers on competitive advantage through symbolic management and co-optation.[83] Impression management can be in the form of rendering personal and professional favors to financial analysts who are following the firm,[84] including personally disclosing industry knowledge or keeping them in touch with knowledgeable industry parties, such as customer and supplier firms.[85] Providing more general industry knowledge, would not likely violate fair disclosure rules. Executives can also build personal connections and provide a range of personal favors, such as recommending them for job positions and offering career advice.[86] Favor rendering directed at financial analysts can help firms avoid negative outcomes.[87] For example, analysts who received favors from executives are less likely to downgrade a firm following the disclosure of negative earnings or the announcement of a diversifying acquisition.[88] Of course, such personal favors need to be managed carefully; otherwise, they could be perceived as a form of kickback and thus backfire. By engaging in impression management (see Box 4.3 in Chapter 4), executives can achieve the support of external stakeholders and enhance organizational legitimacy while maintaining their decision discretion.

Impression management tactics can also help executives cultivate their relationships with journalists. For instance, executives can collect beneficial information or engage in ingratiatory behavior such as complimenting journalists' work or expressing when in agreement with their point of view on business issues. This form of impression management can help executives avoid negative coverage at times of low earnings.[89] Yet, impression management could distract executives' strategic focus and be carried out to advance their own interests.[90] Fostering good relationships with financial analysts and journalist also include invitations to events or participation in more personal gatherings to make a good impression that do not include rendering favors or breaking fair disclosure rules. Managing relationship with financial analysts and journalists can help shield executives from external pressure and enable them to develop a long-term competitive strategy.

Beyond impression management, an executive's ability to manage governance actors should include reducing their dependence on regulators. Firm leaders can manage the external uncertainty posed by regulators through co-option via corporate political activities, which we will discuss in detail in Chapter 8. For now, lobbying serves as an example. According to data from OpenSecrets, a nonprofit organization tracking political spending, Microsoft and Facebook spent over $10 million and $16 million, respectively, in lobbying in 2019. Company leadership may also appoint board members with political connections and other nonmarket activities to co-opt the influence of regulators.[91] Interestingly, acquirers and targets located in the political districts of powerful US congressional members serving on committees with antitrust regulatory oversight receive relatively favorable antitrust review outcomes.[92] Smaller companies may not have the financial muscle to appoint high-profile political directors or engage in lobbying individually, but they could lobby through industry associations to ensure that they can compete in a fair marketplace. In essence, corporate political activities can help firms manage political uncertainty and reduce investigation by competition regulators.

Isolate

To address governance actors that have a transactional relationship with firms and do not provide resources, such as short sellers and transient institutional investors (Quadrant IV), managers can isolate these influencers and minimize their adverse impact by building coalitions with other governance actors, such as dedicated shareholders. Although short-selling activities have been on the rise in the United States, the average of shares shorted only accounts for around 5 percent of total shares outstanding among S&P 1500 firms,[93] suggesting that short sellers may not be able to dampen firm stock prices on their own and may need to rely on other long-term shareholders to impose a downward pressure on stock prices. Under such a scenario, executives can shield themselves from short seller threat by engaging and communicating with dedicated shareholders. With support from dedicated shareholders, executives will be less concerned about consequences of failed strategic competitive actions. For example, Edward Lampert, a billionaire investor and businessman, is known for building positions in undervalued companies and collaborating with them to improve their performance. Such investors can help executives of portfolio firms undertake competitive actions that produce long-term value.[94] Likewise, company managers can isolate the negative influence of short sellers on stock prices by engaging with primary stakeholders such as employees, suppliers, and customers.[95]

By the same token, with the support from dedicated shareholders and primary stakeholders, executives may not need to pursue tactical competitive actions to satisfy the short-term performance focus of transient institutional investors. Company leaders can also consider engaging in impression management to attain the support from quasi-indexer institutional investors. Specifically, executives can use ingratiatory tactics to create rapport with and persuade representatives of institutional investors like fund managers that the company has the right strategy.[96] Through creating a coalition with dedicated shareholders, executives can isolate short sellers and transient institutional investors and enable a long-term competitive strategy.

As summarized in Figure 5.2, by unengaging owners and analyzing competitive situations with boards of directors, top managers can use the resources provided by relational owners to advance the firms' competitive advantage. Likewise, they need to leverage the input of activist owner, but defend their strategic position when their input might tend to erode the firms' competitive advantage in the long term. In regard to analysts and the media, boards and top managers need to manage and coopt them to support their firms' competitive positioning. Finally, if there are transaction-oriented investors, managers need to isolate these investors from other investors to avoid weakening the firms' competitive positioning with an overemphasis on short-term competitive actions.

NOTES

1. Porter, M. E. (1980). *Competitive strategy: Techniques for analyzing industries and competitors.* New York: Free Press.
2. Huang, S., & Hilary, G. (2018). Zombie board: Board tenure and firm performance. *Journal of Accounting Research* 56(4): 1285–1329.
3. Fich, E. M., & Shivdasani, A. (2007). Financial fraud, director reputation, and shareholder wealth. *Journal of Financial Economics* 86(2): 306–336.
4. Hillman, A. J., & Dalziel, T. (2003). Boards of directors and firm performance: Integrating agency and resource dependence perspectives. *Academy of Management Review* 28(3): 383–396.
5. Adams, R. (2009). Asking directors about their dual roles. *Finance and Corporate Governance Conference 2010 Paper.*
6. Oehmichen, J., Schrapp, S., & Wolff, M. (2017). Who needs experts most? Board industry expertise and strategic change—a contingency perspective. *Strategic Management Journal* 38(3): 645–656.
7. Dass, N., Kini, O., Nanda, V., Onal, B., & Wang, J. (2013). Board expertise: Do directors from related industries help bridge the information gap? *Review of Financial Studies* 27(5): 1533–1592.
8. Faleye, O., Hoitash, R., & Hoitash, U. (2018). Industry expertise on corporate boards. *Review of Quantitative Finance and Accounting* 50(2): 441–479.
9. Stone, B. (2009). Google Chief Gives Up Board Seat at Apple. *New York Times,* August 4. www.nytimes.com/2009/08/04/technology/companies/04apple.html.
10. Mickle, T., & Smith, E. (2019). Disney Chief Executive Robert Iger Resigns from Apple's Board. *Wall Street Journal,* September 13. www.wsj.com/articles/disney-chief-executive-robert-iger-resigns-from-apples-board-11568411573.
11. Westphal, J. D., & Zhu, D. H. (2019). Under the radar: How firms manage competitive uncertainty by appointing friends of other chief executive officers to their boards. *Strategic Management Journal* 40(1): 79–107.
12. Khanna, P., Jones, C. D., & Boivie, S. (2014). Director human capital, information processing demands, and board effectiveness. *Journal of Management* 40(2): 557–585.
13. Ferrier, W. J., & Lee, H. (2002). Strategic aggressiveness, variation, and surprise: How the sequential pattern of competitive rivalry influences stock market returns. *Journal of Managerial Issues*: 162–180. Ferrier, W. J. (2001). Navigating the competitive landscape: The drivers and consequences of competitive aggressiveness. *Academy of Management Journal* 44(4): 858–877.
14. Yu, T. Y., Subramaniam, M., & Cannella, A. A. (2009). Rivalry deterrence in international markets: contingencies governing the mutual forbearance hypothesis. *Academy of Management Journal* 52(1): 127–147.
15. Kolev, K., Hughes-Morgan, M., & Rehbein, K. (2019). The role of female directors in the boardroom: Examining their impact on competitive dynamics. *Business & Society.* doi.org/10.117/0007650319847477.
16. Offstein, E. H., Gnyawali, D. R., & Cobb, A. T. (2005). A strategic human resource perspective of firm competitive behavior. *Human Resource Management Review* 15(4): 305–318.

17. Brief, A. P., & Aldag, R. J. (1977). The intrinsic-extrinsic dichotomy: Toward conceptual clarity. *Academy of Management Review* 2(3): 496–500.

18. Offstein, Gnyawali, & Cobb. A strategic human resource perspective of firm competitive behavior, 305–318.

19. Gnyawali, D. R., Offstein, E. H., & Lau, R. S. (2008). The impact of the CEO pay gap on firm competitive behavior. *Group & Organization Management*, 33(4): 453–484.

20. Connelly, B. L., Tihanyi, L., Ketchen, D. J., Carnes, C., & Ferrier, W. (2017). Competitive repertoire complexity: Governance antecedents and performance outcomes. *Strategic Management Journal* 38(5): 1151–1173.

21. Shi, W., Connelly, B. L., & Sanders, W. G. (2016). Buying bad behavior: Tournament incentives and securities class action lawsuits. *Strategic Management Journal* 37(7): 1354–1378.

22. Porter. *Competitive strategy*; Porter, M. E. (1985). *Competitive advantage: Creating and sustaining superior performance*. New York: Free Press.

23. Bushee, B. J. (1998). The influence of institutional investors on myopic R&D investment behavior. *Accounting Review* 73(3): 305–333.

24. Foss, N. J., Klein, P. G., Lien, L. B., Zellweger, T., & Zenger, T. (2020). Ownership competence. *Strategic Management Journal*. Palter, R. N., Rehm, W., & Shih, J. (2008). Communicating with the right investors. McKinsey on Finance: McKinsey.

25. Madureira, L., & Underwood, S. (2008). Information, sell-side research, and market making. *Journal of Financial Economics* 90(2): 105–126.

26. Bushee, B. J., Gerakos, J., & Lee, L. F. (2018). Corporate jets and private meetings with investors. *Journal of Accounting and Economics* 65(2–3): 358–379.

27. Bushee, B. J. (2004). Identifying and attracting the "right" investors: Evidence on the behavior of institutional investors. *Journal of Applied Corporate Finance*, 16(4): 28–35.

28. King, R. (2016). Salesforce.com to press regulators to block Microsoft-LinkedIn Deal. *Wall Street Journal*. www.wsj.com, September 29.

29. Wells, G. L., & Seetharaman, D. (2019). Snap detailed Facebook's aggressive tactics in "Project Voldemort" dossier. *Wall Street Journal*, September 24. https://www.wsj.com/articles/snap-detailed-facebooks-aggressive-tactics-in-project-voldemort-dossier-11569236404.

30. Connelly, B. L., Tihanyi, L., Certo, S. T., & Hitt, M. A. (2010). Marching to the beat of different drummers: The influence of institutional owners on competitive actions. *Academy of Management Journal* 53(4): 723–742. Connelly, B. L., Tihanyi, L., Ketchen, D. J., Carnes, C., & Ferrier, W. (2017). Competitive repertoire complexity: Governance antecedents and performance outcomes. *Strategic Management Journal* 38(5): 1151–1173.

31. Boh, W. F., Huang, C. J., & Wu, A. (2020). Investor experience and innovation performance: The mediating role of external cooperation. *Strategic Management Journal* 41 (1): 124–151.

32. Douma, S., George, R., & Kabir, R. (2006). Foreign and domestic ownership, business groups, and firm performance: Evidence from a large emerging market. *Strategic Management Journal* 27(7): 637–657.

33. Boh, Huang, & Wu. Investor experience and innovation performance, 124–151.

34. Aoki, K., & Thomas Taro, L. (2013). The new, improved keiretsu. *Harvard Business Review*, 91(9): 109–113.

35. Habbershon, T. G., Williams, M., & MacMillan, I. I. C. 20. (2003). A unified systems perspective of family firm performance. *Journal of Business Venturing* 18(4): 451–465.

36. Zahra, S. A., Hayton, J. C., Neubaum, D. O., Dibrell, C., & Craig, J. (2008). Culture of family commitment and strategic flexibility: The moderating effect of stewardship. *Entrepreneurship Theory and Practice* 32(6): 1035–1054.

37. Miller, D., & Le Breton-Miller, I. (2006). Family governance and firm performance: Agency, stewardship, and capabilities. *Family Business Review* 19(1): 73–87.

38. Zahra, Hayton, Neubaum, Dibrell, & Craig. Culture of family commitment and strategic flexibility, 1035–1054.

39. CBS (2020). "Walmart launching Walmart Plus to compete with Amazon Prime." *CBS*, September 2. www.cbsnews.com/news/walmart-plus-launch-amazon-prime-competitor/.

40. Campbell, B. A., Coff, R., & Kryscynski, D. (2012). Rethinking sustained competitive advantage from human capital. *Academy of Management Review* 37(3): 376–395. Coff, R. W. (1997). Human assets and management dilemmas: Coping with hazards on the road to resource-based theory. *Academy of Management Review* 22(2): 374–402.

41. Gottschalg, O., & Zollo, M. (2007). Interest alignment and competitive advantage. *Academy of Management Review* 32 (2): 418–437. Hoskisson, R., Gambeta, E., Green, C., & Li, T. (2018). Is my firm-specific investment protected? Overcoming the stakeholder investment dilemma in the resource based view. *Academy of Management Review* 43(2): 284–306.

42. Kim, K.-H., Kim, M., & Qian, C. (2018). Effects of corporate social responsibility on corporate financial performance: A competitive-action perspective. *Journal of Management* 44(3): 1097–1118.

43. Aime, F., Johnson, S., Ridge, J. W., & Hill, A. D. (2010). The routine may be stable but the advantage is not: competitive implications of key employee mobility. *Strategic Management Journal* 31(1): 75–87; Somaya, D., Williamson, I. O., & Lorinkova, N. (2008). Gone but not lost: The different performance impacts of employee mobility between cooperators versus competitors. *Academy of Management Journal* 51(5): 936–953.

44. Wang, H. C., He, J., & Mahoney, J. T. (2009). Firm-specific knowledge resources and competitive advantage: the roles of economic- and relationship-based employee governance mechanisms. *Strategic Management Journal* 30(12): 1265–1285.

45. Blasi, J., Kruse, D., & Conway, M. (2019). We found one simple trick to boost employee happiness: Give them ownership. *FastCompany*, June 7. www.fastcompany.com/90360409/employee-ownership-of-companies-boosts-retention-and-profits.

46. Martin, R. L. (2018). Activist hedge funds aren't good for companies or investors, so why do they exist? *Harvard Business Review Digital Articles*, www.hbs.com, 2–4.

47. Goldman, D., & Stelter, B. (2019). Big changes are coming to AT&T after shareholder battle. *CNN*, www.cnn.com, October 28.

48. Miles, R., & Snow, C. (1978). *Organization strategy, structure and process.* New York: McGraw-Hill.

49. Brav, A., Jiang, W., & Kim, H. (2015). The real effects of hedge fund activism: Productivity, asset allocation, and labor outcomes. *Review of Financial Studies,* 28(10): 2723–2769.

50. Ibid., 2723–2769.

51. Scheer, S. (2017). Mellanox shares jump 11 percent after Starboard stake purchase.

52. DesJardine, M., Shi, W., & Sun, Z. (2021). Different horizons: The effects of hedge fund activism versus corporate shareholder activism on strategic actions. *Journal of Management.*

53. Aslan, H., & Kumar, P. (2016). The product market effects of hedge fund activism. *Journal of Financial Economics* 119(1): 226–248.

54. DesJardine, M. R., & Durand, R. (2020). Disentangling the effects of hedge fund activism on firm financial and social performance. *Strategic Management Journal* 41(6): 1054–1082.

55. Westphal, J. D., & Clement, M. B. (2008). Sociopolitical dynamics in relations between top managers and security analysts: Favor rendering, reciprocity, and analyst stock recommendations. *Academy of Management Journal* 51(5): 873–897; Westphal, J. D., & Deephouse, D. L. (2011). Avoiding bad press: Interpersonal influence in relations between CEOs and journalists and the consequences for press reporting about firms and their leadership. *Organization Science* 22(4): 1061–1086.

56. Zhang, Y., & Gimeno, J. (2010). Earnings pressure and competitive behavior: Evidence from the US electricity industry. *Academy of Management Journal* 53(4): 743–768; Zhang, Y., & Gimeno, J. (2016). Earnings pressure and long-term corporate governance: Can long-term-oriented investors and managers reduce the quarterly earnings obsession? *Organization Science* 27(2): 354–372.

57. Turner, T. (2004). My beef with big media: How government protects big media and shuts out upstarts like me. *Federal Communications Law Journal* 57: 229.

58. Zhang, Y., & Gimeno, J. (2010). Earnings pressure and competitive behavior: Evidence from the US electricity industry. *Academy of Management Journal* 53(4): 743–768.

59. Zhang, Y., & Gimeno, J. (2016). Earnings pressure and long-term corporate governance: Can long-term-oriented investors and managers reduce the quarterly earnings obsession? *Organization Science* 27(2): 354–372.

60. Hoskisson, Gambeta, Green, & Li. Is my firm-specific investment protected? 284–306.

61. Litov, L. P., Moreton, P., & Zenger, T. R. (2012). Corporate strategy, analyst coverage, and the uniqueness paradox. *Management Science,* 58(10): 1797–1815.

62. Zuckerman, E. W. (2000). Focusing the corporate product: Securities analysts and de-diversification. *Administrative Science Quarterly* 45(3): 591–619.

63. Benner, M. J., & Zenger, T. (2016). The lemons problem in markets for strategy. *Strategy Science* 1(2): 71–89.

64. Guo, W., Sengul, M., & Yu, T. (2020). Rivals' negative earnings surprises, language signals, and firms' competitive actions. *Academy of Management Journal* 63(3): 637–659.

65. Huddleston, T. (2014). War of words: After H-P announces split, Dell doesn't miss a chance for a swipe back. *Fortune,* www.fortune.com, October 7.

66. Deephouse, D. L. (2000). Media reputation as a strategic resource: An integration of mass communication and resource-based theories. *Journal of Management* 26(6): 1091–1112; Pollock, T. G., & Rindova, V. P. (2003). Media legitimation effects in the market for initial public offerings. *Academy of Management Journal* 46(5): 631–642.

67. Gémar, G., & Jiménez-Quintero, J. A. (2015). Text mining social media for competitive analysis. *Tourism & Management Studies* 11(1): 84–90.

68. Puko, T., & Gurman, S. (2020). US sues Walmart, Alleging role in fueling opioid crisis. *Wall Street Journal*, December 22. www.wsj.com/articles/u-s-sues-walmart-alleging-role-in-fueling-opioid-crisis-11608661856.

69. Palmer, A. (2020). Unions push the FTC to investigate Amazon for "anticompetitive practices. " *CNBC*, February 28. www.cnbc.com/2020/02/28/unions-push-ftc-to-investigate-amazon-for-anti-competitive-practices.html.

70. Satariano, A. (2020). Amazon set to face antitrust charges in European Union. *New York Times*, June 11. www.nytimes.com/2020/06/11/technology/amazon-antitrust-european-union.html.

71. Agnihotri, A. (2015). How to avoid regulatory antitrust scrutiny: The behavioral defense. *Business Horizons* 58(4): 441–447.

72. Shi, W., Connelly, B. L., & Cirik, K. (2018). Short seller influence on firm growth: A threat-rigidity perspective. *Academy of Management Journal* 61(5): 1892–1919.

73. Zdinjak, N. (2019). 25 biggest activist short sellers in the hedge fund world. *Insider Monkey.* June 19. www.insidermonkey.com/blog/25-biggest-activist-short-sellers-in-the-hedge-fund-world-758552

74. Connelly, Tihanyi, Certo, & Hitt. Marching to the beat of different drummers, 723–742.

75. He, J. J., & Huang, J. (2017). Product market competition in a world of cross-ownership: Evidence from institutional blockholdings. *Review of Financial Studies* 30(8): 2674–2718.

76. Almandoz, J., & Tilcsik, A. (2016). When experts become liabilities: Domain experts on boards and organizational failure. *Academy of Management Journal* 59(4): 1124–1149.

77. Gómez-Mejía, L. R., Haynes, K. T., Nunez-Nickel, M., Jacobson, K. J. L., & Moyano-Fuentes, J. (2007). Socioemotional wealth and business risks in family-controlled firms: evidence from Spanish olive oil mills. *Administrative Science Quarterly* 52(1): 106–137.

78. An investor calls. (2015). *The Economist,* February 5. www.economist.com/briefing/2015/02/05/an-investor-calls.

79. Lovelace, B. (2017). Billionaire Nelson Peltz: P&G is making my board battle the "dumbest thing I've ever been involved in." *CNBC*, October 6. www.cnbc.

com/2017/10/06/billionaire-activist-peltz-my-proxy-fight-with-procter-gamble-will-be-close.html.

80. DesJardine & Durand. Disentangling the effects of hedge fund activism on firm financial and social performance, 1054–1082.

81. An investor calls, *The Economist*.

82. Westphal, J. D., & Bednar, M. K. (2008). The pacification of institutional investors. *Administrative Science Quarterly* 53(1): 29–72.

83. Westphal, J. D., & Park, S. H. 2020. *Symbolic management: Governance, strategy, and institutions*. Oxford, UK: Oxford University Press.

84. Westphal & Clement. Sociopolitical dynamics in relations between top managers and security analysts, 873–897.

85. Brown, L. D., Call, A. C., Clement, M. B., & Sharp, N. Y. (2015). Inside the "black box" of sell-side financial analysts. *Journal of Accounting Research* 53 (1): 1–47. Soltes, E. (2014). Private interaction between firm management and sell-side analysts. *Journal of Accounting Research* 52(1): 245–272.

86. Westphal & Park. *Symbolic management*.

87. Cialdini, R. (2008). *Influence: Science and practice*. Boston: Pearson.

88. Westphal & Park. *Symbolic management*.

89. Westphal, J. D., & Deephouse, D. L. (2011). Avoiding bad press: Interpersonal influence in relations between CEOs and journalists and the consequences for press reporting about firms and their leadership. *Organization Science* 22(4): 1061–1086.

90. Westphal, J. D., & Zajac, E. J. (2013). A behavioral theory of corporate governance: Explicating the mechanisms of socially situated and socially constituted agency. *Academy of Management Annals* 7(1): 607–661.

91. Hillman, A. J. (2005). Politicians on the board of directors: Do connections affect the bottom line? *Journal of Management* 31(3): 464–481. Hillman, A. J., Keim, G. D., & Schuler, D. (2004). Corporate political activity: A review and research agenda. *Journal of Management* 30(6): 837–857.

92. Mehta, M. N., Srinivasan, S., & Zhao, W. (2020). The politics of M&A antitrust. *Journal of Accounting Research* 58(1): 5–53.

93. Shi, W., Ndofor, H. A., & Hoskisson, R. E. (2021). Disciplining role of short sellers: Evidence from M&A activity. *Journal of Management* 47(5) 1103–1133.

94. Connelly, Tihanyi, Certo, & Hitt. Marching to the beat of different drummers, 723–742.

95. Hoskisson, Gambeta, Green, & Li. Is my firm-specific investment protected? 284–306.

96. Westphal, J. D., & Bednar, M. K. (2008). The pacification of institutional investors. *Administrative Science Quarterly* 53(1): 29–72.

CHAPTER 6

Governance Actors and
Global Strategy

BOX 6.1   Strategic Governance Challenge: The Location Choice Conundrum in Global Expansion

---

In global expansion, top managers face the challenge of identifying locations that can generate a stream of sustainable returns amid a moderate level of political and economic risks. In some countries, such as Western Europe and the United States, well-developed institutions lead to low political and economic risks, allowing for low but stable economic growth. As a result, expansion into these countries may not generate enormous profits. Meanwhile, although emerging economies such as China and India have less-developed institutions and are associated with high investment risks, the large populations in these countries represent a tremendous market potential to foreign firms. Expansion into these countries may signify little competition, enabling an early-mover advantage and high financial returns in the long run if the countries are able to sustain their economic growth.

General Motors entered China in 1997 through a joint venture. Although China did not have a well-developed infrastructure back then, GM did not face much competition in the Chinese automobile market. Ford had a late start in the country and did not begin to make a mark until 2012. Although China had a well-developed highway system and many Chinese consumers had the means to purchase a car, Ford faced strong competition from both domestic and foreign automakers.

But firms from countries with less developed market institutions may likewise find difficulties upon entering more developed ones. Although there is a strong trend of emerging market multinationals entering more developed economies, domestic firms in the developed countries may have competitive resources that have been honed through strong domestic competition. Foreign firms with less developed competitive resources may therefore struggle to compete, especially when facing strong cultural differences between host and home countries. In addition, emerging multinationals are facing rising political uncertainty in developed countries. For example, Chinese telecommunications giant Huawei was banned in the United States due to national security concerns.

Top managers need to carefully balance risks and returns in location decisions, as governance actors have different risk tolerance—or degree of variability in investment returns that an investor is willing to withstand. Family shareholders, for example, have their personal and family wealth heavily embedded in firms, as well as a strong socioemotional attachment to them, leaving the shareholders with a low level of risk tolerance. In contrast, transient institutional investors have a diversified portfolio of ownership and a high risk tolerance.

Sources: O' Keeffe, K., McKinnon, J. D., & Strumpf, D. (2019). Trump steps up assault on China's Huawei. *Wall Street Journal.* May 15. https://www.wsj.com/articles/trump-telecom-ban-takes-aim-at-china-huawei-11557953363; Hancock, T. (2019). Why Ford is stalling in China while Toyota succeeds. *Financial Times.* March 4. https://www.ft.com/content/6fd5a4c4-36c1-11e9-bd3a-8b2a211d90d5; Kim, H., & Hoskisson, R. E. (2015). A resource environment view of competitive advantage. In Tihanyi, L., Banalieva, E. R., Devinney, T. M., & Pederson, T. (Eds.), *Emerging Economies and Multinational Enterprises, Advances in International Management,* Vol. 28. Bingley, UK: Emerald Group Publishing, 95–140; Wiseman, R. M., & Gomez-Mejia, L. R. (1998). A behavioral agency model of managerial risk taking. *Academy of Management Review* 23, 133–153; Lieberman, M. B., & Montgomery, D. B. (1988). First-mover advantages. *Strategic Management Journal* 9, 41–58. Luo, Y. (2004). Building a strong foothold in an emerging market: A link between resource commitment and environment conditions. *Journal of Management Studies* 41(5): 749–773.

Business leaders expand to foreign countries and compete in international markets to achieve sales growth, obtain low-cost resources that increase firm efficiency, and diversify risks arising from a focus on a single market.[1] Although various market and operational reasons can drive global expansion, executives ultimately attempt to explore country-specific locational advantages arising from the resources, markets, and institutional characteristics of different countries.[2] Company leadership formulates a *global strategy*, or an action plan to compete and expand into the global market. In essence, global strategy refers to a series of strategic actions taken by firm leaders to explore locational advantages.

We note that strategic choices related to global strategy can overlap with those pertaining to corporate and competitive strategies. For example, the decision to acquire a new line of business in a foreign country (rather than at home) relates to both a firm's corporate and global strategies. Similarly, the decision to locate manufacturing facilities in a foreign country with cheap labor costs relates to both global strategy and competitive strategy, which focuses on achieving cost leadership. Despite their overlaps, however, global strategy differs from corporate and competitive ones in an important way. Whereas corporate strategy focuses on creating value from owning a portfolio of businesses (see Chapter 3) and competitive strategy concerns creating competitive advantage through undertaking competitive actions in a product market (see Chapter 5), global strategy pertains to exploring the advantages achieved by being located at a particular site or within a different government jurisdiction from its home country.[3]

Governance actors influence a firm's strategic choices about global strategy in varying degrees according to their risk tolerance. Executives must take actions to leverage the influence and achieve long-run competitiveness in global markets. We will explore the key concepts of strategizing globally under the impact of various governance actors, and offer guidance on how company leadership can regulate the impact of these governance actors to develop a successful global action plan. Our discussion will also reveal how governance actors can shape a firm's legitimacy in global expansion and ways to manage the arising legitimacy challenges.

GLOBAL STRATEGY

Global strategy consists of a variety of strategic decisions, ranging from international diversification to choosing which foreign country to enter and how. *International diversification* refers to a strategy through which a firm expands the sales of its goods or services across the borders of global regions and countries into different geographic locations or markets.[4] Unlike product diversification (see Chapter 3), which has a focus on expanding to new product areas, international diversification enables firms to create value through access to resources and customers in foreign markets.[5] A firm that engages in international diversification is often called a *multinational enterprise* (MNE).

Although international diversification allows firms to access foreign growth opportunities, build new capabilities, accumulate new knowledge from foreign operations, and exploit existing competencies abroad, the practice involves substantial risks. MNEs are subject to political risks that arise from instability in national governments and national and international wars.[6] In 2007, for example, due to nationalization efforts by the Venezuelan government, Exxon Mobil, and ConocoPhillips were forced to leave the country.[7] International diversification can also increase economic risks that stem from fluctuations in currency values. For instance, when the value of the US dollar appreciates against the Euro, the value of a US MNE's assets and earnings in European Union countries decreases. In 2018, the value of the Turkish lira decreased by more than 20 percent against the US dollar in a week. The change in currency value not only affected companies that borrowed dollars, but also made US MNEs' profits in Turkey less valuable for American shareholders.[8]

The *liability of foreignness*, which refers to additional costs of conducting business in an unfamiliar cultural and institutional environment and coordinating across different countries,[9] signifies another important internationalization risk. Amazon's exit of its domestic ecommerce business in China in 2019 is a case in point. Amazon entered China in 2004 by acquiring Joyo.com, an online Chinese book seller, but struggled to survive in the market. In addition to facing intense local competition, top managers failed to adapt to the different marketplace. Whereas Chinese online shoppers are highly price-sensitive for many goods and prefer instant delivery, Amazon controlled most of its own inventory and developed its own delivery infrastructure, which slowed delivery speed and increased costs. In contrast, Alibaba, its Chinese rival, chose to be only an online platform for small vendors and depend on local delivery to shorten delivery time and cut costs.[10] Amazon's lack of understanding of the Chinese market directly reflects the heavy costs that may result from the liability of foreignness.

The question of location creates another important strategic choice pertaining to global strategy. The performance of global expansion[11] and the ability of firms to exploit locational advantages hinge on the proper choice of countries to enter.[12] Developing effective location strategies requires substantial information about potential countries; however, top managers often lack the needed information,[13] which may cause considerable uncertainty under the global strategy.[14] Amazon's unsuccessful business expansion in China could be partially attributed to the lack of understanding of Chinese consumers. To reduce information gaps, company leaders often choose to expand to geographically close countries because a short geographic distance can facilitate information flows and collection.[15] Culturally proximate countries can also signify reduced risk in liability of foreignness and are associated with lower information collection costs.[16]

Making an optimal locational decision requires firms to balance the tradeoff between risks and returns, as indicated in the Strategic Challenge in Box 6.1. Although institutionally developed countries are associated with a low level of uncertainty and risks, the move implies forgoing potential growth and capability-development opportunities attained in institutionally less-developed countries. The disadvantage becomes particularly salient when MNEs face a high level of competition in the developed countries or when these markets grow at a slow pace. When a firm has abundant resources[17] or has accumulated much information about potential target countries from stakeholders,[18] executives will be less concerned about choosing target countries with high risks, such as those with extensive political corruption.[19]

Once top managers have decided which country to enter, the next decision becomes how. Firms can enter a foreign country using different *entry modes*. Some entry modes, such as mergers and acquisitions (M&As) or greenfield investments—in which firms build their fully owned foreign subsidiaries from scratch—require substantial capital, but give firms a high level of control. Cross-border M&As, or mergers and acquisitions of foreign targets, enable firms to have a controlling ownership in foreign target firms. Amazon, for example, entered the Chinese market through a cross-border M&A when it acquired Joyo.com. Meanwhile, Coca-Cola, McDonald's, and Starbucks have entered foreign countries mainly through greenfield investments. In contrast, producing products in one country and selling in another (exporting) does not call for much investment, but neither does it grant executives a high level of control. Similarly, strategic alliances, which provide resource contributions from partner firms, do not require as much capital investment as cross-border M&As or greenfield investments, but managers hold a lower level of control than in acquired targets or wholly owned foreign subsidiaries. For example, General Motors (GM) entered China through a joint venture (a type of strategic alliance) with the state-owned Shanghai Automotive Industry Corporation (SAIC) in 1997. Although GM did not have full control over the joint venture, having a Chinese partner reduced the capital commitment from GM and helped GM better navigate the Chinese market.

Governance actors can influence a firm's international diversification, location choices, and entry mode decisions—ultimately its ability to exploit locational advantages. As we show in Figure 6.1, governance actors fall along two dimensions: resource provision (the *vertical* axis) and risk tolerance (the *horizontal* axis). We have discussed the actors' resource provision role in Chapter 5. Those, such as board members and dedicated shareholders, like family shareholders, are motivated to provide information and resources that can assist with a firm's global expansion, whereas others, such as transient institutional investors, may not be able to afford such resources. Along the other dimension, governance actors vary in their threshold of the risk that they are willing to withstand. Compared with transient institutional investors, dedicated institutional investors invest in a small number of companies and do not have a diversified portfolio, thereby holding a low level of risk

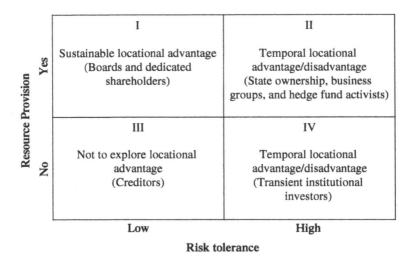

	Low	High
Yes	I Sustainable locational advantage (Boards and dedicated shareholders)	II Temporal locational advantage/disadvantage (State ownership, business groups, and hedge fund activists)
No	III Not to explore locational advantage (Creditors)	IV Temporal locational advantage/disadvantage (Transient institutional investors)

Resource Provision

Risk tolerance

FIGURE 6.1 Governance actors and global strategy.

tolerance. Because of differences in goals and approaches, governance actors exert varying influences on executives and their ability to pursue locational advantages.

RESOURCE-PROVISION GOVERNANCE ACTORS WITH LOW RISK TOLERANCE

Governance actors that provide resources to firms and have a low level of risk tolerance fall under Quadrant I of Figure 6.1. We will focus on how board members and dedicated shareholders like family owners can influence global strategy-related decisions.

Board of Directors

As we have discussed, a key function of the board of directors is to advise managers on strategic decisions. Through this advisory role, directors provide critical information that can be used in global strategy and to reduce information asymmetry that top managers face during global expansion. To align the interests of directors and firms, a significant portion of director compensation is paid in equity. According to data from the ISS Analytics, Russell 3000 companies pay approximately 60 percent of total director compensation in equity.[20] Because directors' personal wealth is tied to the performance of the companies in which they serve and is associated with a low level of portfolio diversification, they will be averse to strategic directions that harm their personal wealth, thereby exhibiting low risk tolerance.[21]

The board of directors can affect a firm's global strategy in three ways. First, directors with foreign experience and connections may provide critical information for an effective global strategy. By living or working in foreign countries, directors develop first-hand knowledge of foreign markets and establish a network of foreign contacts.[22] Such resources can alleviate uncertainty during global expansion and allow managers to make informed strategic decisions. As a result, top managers of firms with foreign independent directors make better cross-border M&A decisions when the targets are from the home regions of these board members.[23] Because directors' country-specific experiences help make effective foreign investment decisions, US firms appointed more outside directors with China-related experience after the US Congress granted permanent normal trade relations status to China in 2000, which made it easier for American firms to invest in China. Such directors have been shown to improve US firms' acquisition performance of Chinese firms.[24]

Second, directors with distinct characteristics can influence global strategy differently. Outside directors, for instance, devote more attention to international diversification than inside directors.[25] Their knowledge and international vision can help top managers cope with challenges in internationalization. For example, a higher ratio of outside directors can have a positive effect on export intensity, as they help expand a firm's knowledge base and horizon.[26] Similarly, a larger board size, associated with a high level of information processing capability, tends to lead to a higher level of international diversification.[27] Furthermore, directors with more ownership, thus more interests aligned with the firm,[28] are more likely to choose entry modes that provide the potential for greater long-term returns, such as cross-border M&As.

Third, directors monitor top managers and make decisions on their compensations, which in turn can shape a firm's global strategy. Because monitoring often-complex foreign operations may prove difficult for directors,[29] they grant CEOs a large percentage of long-term pay to align the chief executive's interests with the firm's. For the same reason, boards of companies with a high level of export intensity tend to give CEOs significant equity ownership.[30] As global expansion is associated with a large degree of complexity, board directors often grant CEOs substantial compensation to motivate more international diversification.[31] Granting CEOs a high level of long-term pay can also motivate them to prefer full control modes such as cross-border acquisitions and greenfield investments over shared-control entry modes like alliances.[32]

By providing information and resources to firms under a low level of risk tolerance, directors of boards can lead top managers to make well-reasoned

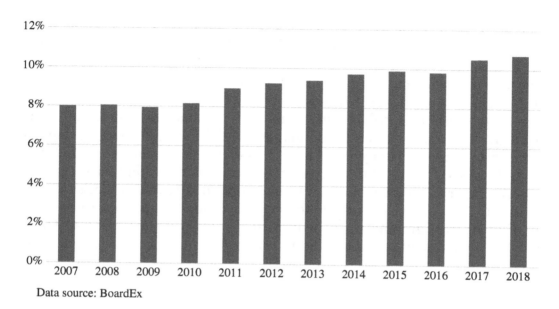

Data source: BoardEx

FIGURE 6.2   Foreign director ratio of S&P 1500 firms.

strategic choices in global expansion and achieve sustainable locational advantages. This leadership trend is particularly true for foreign directors given their unique experiences, which explains the growing number of foreign directors among US firms. As shown in Figure 6.2, the percentage of foreign directors among S&P 1500 firms increased from 8 percent in 2007 to 11 percent in 2018. Yet, the effectiveness of these directors to shape the quality of global strategy may hinge on a firm's home and host country institutions. Countries with high-quality institutions tend to have well-functioning capital markets and effective regulators, reducing the benefits of additional monitoring by foreign directors.[33] But for firms from emerging economies, directors with foreign experience can facilitate the adoption of strong corporate governance practices. Performance increases after firms hire directors with foreign experience in emerging economies such as China.[34]

Dedicated Shareholders

Dedicated shareholders, such as family owners or dedicated institutional investors, are committed to firms' long-term viability and competitiveness. Beyond providing patient capital, these shareholders are driven to build an enduring legacy for their foreign subsidiaries[35] and motivated to play an advisory role during global expansion. Since they have a desire to control risks because of the concentration of family wealth in a single organization,[36] these owners exhibit a low level of risk tolerance. As internationalization often requires expansion into countries with unfamiliar institutions and carries a long payoff period,[37] small- and medium-sized family firms find it difficult to amass resources needed to sustain a competitive advantage that can be exploited in the international context. Owners of these firms are less willing to engage in extensive internationalization.[38]

Family owners show great caution in deciding whether to pursue an increased involvement in international markets, but they may not necessarily avoid internationalization entirely. Internationalization provides new opportunities for value creation by gaining access to new resources, foreign stakeholders, and new knowledge and capability, which is critical to sustaining family owners' long-term wealth.[39] Once family owners decide to pursue internationalization, they will allocate resources to carefully assess international environments and formulate a detailed action plan for a fast but careful pace in internationalization, since resources are limited. In addition, family firms will avoid expanding to many countries at the same time to reduce risk arising from unfamiliarity with target countries.[40]

Family ownership can also influence entry mode choices in global expansion. These owners need to balance two key family-related goals: maintaining family control and keeping a long-term business orientation.[41] Carefully pursuing international opportunities allows family owners to ensure the company's long-term viability. To safeguard family control in international expansion, family founders tend to choose high equity and noncooperative entry modes, including cross-border M&As and greenfield investments, rather than entry modes like alliances and licensing.[42] For example, in 2017, Huntsman Corporation, a family-owned US chemical firm, announced it would acquire IFS Chemicals, a UK chemical firm, to expand its growing downstream chemical market in the United Kingdom.[43]

Beyond family owners, dedicated institutional investors who typically do not have a highly diversified portfolio of ownership are often willing to provide patient capital to their firms. Because dedicated institutional investors, such as pension funds, focus on long-term investment horizons, top managers are able to focus on risky forms of international diversification.[44] In addition to providing patient capital, dedicated institutional investors can supply managers with important information that can facilitate global expansion decisions. For example, with a strong motivation to provide knowledge about potential target countries, long-term foreign institutional investors can influence a firm's cross-border M&A location choice.[45]

In summary, governance actors in Quadrant I of Figure 6.1 show willingness to provide resources that can facilitate decisions for global expansion. However, these governance actors exhibit a low risk tolerance and are motivated to monitor managers' strategic decisions pertaining to global strategy.

Yet these characteristics can benefit top managers by leading them to pursue global strategies that give rise to sustainable locational advantages.

RESOURCE PROVISION GOVERNANCE ACTORS WITH HIGH RISK TOLERANCE

Quadrant II of Figure 6.1 outlines governance actors that provide resources to firms and have a higher level of risk tolerance, such as state owners and business group owners. State ownership refers to the ownership of an enterprise by the state or a public body. State-owned enterprises (SOEs), business entities over which the government or state holds significant control through full, majority, or significant minority ownership, loom large in both developed and emerging economies. In fact, SOEs have been among the largest and fastest expanding MNEs.[46] A recent International Monetary Fund report[47] suggests that 20 percent of the largest globally listed firms over the past decade are SOEs and that assets of SOEs around the world reach $45 trillion, equivalent to half of the global GDP. The report also suggests that SOEs operate in almost all the countries in the world but dominate in emerging countries such as China, India, Indonesia, Russia, and Saudi Arabia.

State owners provide capital to SOEs, but they may also use their political connections to support the enterprises' strategic growth. The tight connection between SOEs and the government, through ownership, boards of directors, and managers' political connections, enables these companies to obtain financial resources and policy support in ways that are unavailable to private firms.[48] In countries like China, state owners focus on social and political goals besides economic ones.[49] Also, as state owners of emerging economies like China and Brazil can have financial interests in companies of different industries, their risk tolerance increases. State owners of developed countries such as Norway and Singapore invest in diversified portfolios of firms through sovereign wealth funds (SWFs),[50] explained in Box 6.2, increasing their risk tolerance as well. Hence, as a governance actor, state owners provide important resources to firms and have a high level of risk tolerance.

State ownership can influence country choice for international expansion. Since the alignment between firm strategies and national interests creates a key factor in deciding location choices, SOE top managers tend to favor a host country that has sound diplomatic relations with the home government.[51] And because SOEs receive strong support from home governments, which helps meet the substantial resources required to expand to geographically distant countries, company executives are more likely to choose more distant countries than do leaders of privately-owned firms.[52] SOE executives

BOX 6.2   Strategic Governance Highlight: Sovereign Wealth Funds

Sovereign wealth funds (SWFs) refer to state-owned investment vehicles that invest globally in a variety of assets, from financial to real assets, and are often funded by commodity export revenues or the transfer of assets from foreign exchange reserves, government budget surpluses, or country pension funds. According to the Sovereign Wealth Fund Institute, the 89 largest SWFs managed assets estimated at US$7.83 trillion in 2020. SWFs act as a key player in today's financial market as they hold shares in one out of every five firms. The largest SWF is Norway Government Pension Fund Global with total assets of US$1.1 trillion, followed by China Investment Corporation with a total asset of US$940 billion.

The acquisition of significant, but noncontrolling stakes in domestic companies by SWFs has been controversial. Policymakers are concerned that SWF equity investments allow foreign governments to become major controllers of domestic firms and can pose a national security concern. In the United States, this concern is regulated through the Department of Treasury through the Committee on Foreign Investment in the United States (CFIUS). Although the United States has regulations focused on foreign investors that buy controlling stakes in American companies, and such regulations can lead to the termination of any deal based on the potential of a national security threat, SWF equity investments often do not fall under regulation by the government. One way to alleviate policymakers' national security concerns is to remove control rights associated with shares held by SWFs.

Although SWFs represent a type of indirect state ownership, they generally do not have controlling stakes in portfolio firms and do not directly provide resources for portfolio firms' international expansion, though this does not imply that SWF ownership cannot influence portfolio firms' cross-border investment. For example, as Norway Government Pension Fund Global seeks to establish legitimacy both at home and in the international community with the goal of alleviating concerns about the political and strategic intent of its investments, the intention may lead its portfolio firms to adopt responsible investment principles in cross-border investment. Capital provided by SWFs can also facilitate firms' global expansion. In 2019, Saudi Arabia's SWF invested $400 million in CloudKitchens, the operator of delivery-only restaurants in the commissaries, which funded the firm's rapid global expansion from multiple cities in the United States to China, India, and the UK.

Sources: SWFI. (2020). Top 89 largest sovereign wealth fund rankings by total assets. SWFI. www.swfinstitute.org/fund-rankings/sovereign-wealth-fund; Johes, R., & Winkler, R. (2019). Saudis back Travis Kalanick's new startup. *Wall Street Journal*. November 7. www.wsj.com/articles/saudis-back-travis-kalanicks-new-startup-11573122604; Fernandes, N. (2011). Sovereign wealth funds: Investment choices and implications around the world; Vasudeva, G. (2013). Weaving together the normative and regulative roles of government: How the Norwegian Sovereign Wealth Fund's responsible conduct is shaping firms' cross-border investments. *Organization Science* 24: 1662–1682; Butt, S., Shivdasani, A., Stendevad, C., & Wyman, A. (2008). Sovereign wealth funds: A growing global force in corporate finance. *Journal of Applied Corporate Finance* 20: 73–83; Gilson, R. J., & Milhaupt, C. J. (2007). Sovereign wealth funds and corporate governance: A minimalist response to the new mercantilism. *Stanford Law Review* 60: 1345–1370.

also need to consider cultural distance between their home and host countries, since a state-owned enterprise can represent a threat to host countries in terms of national security.[53] For instance, due to national security concerns, US politicians forced Dubai Ports World controlled by the United Arab Emirates government to give up its ownership stake in six US ports.[54]

The influence of state owners extends to entry mode choices. Research suggests that leaders of SOEs tend to choose high ownership entry modes through acquisitions.[55] The preferred choice of cross-border M&As by SOEs is partially attributable to the abundant resources with which SOEs are endowed. Meanwhile, state owners have an incentive to promote SOEs' global participation to gain control over key industry and value chains through dominant ownership control.[56] Yet, entering foreign countries through cross-border M&As can result in adverse outcomes. Because stakeholders generally have limited access to credible information about SOEs, research suggests that state ownership is negatively associated with market reactions to announcement of cross-border M&As[57] and low rates of acquisition completion.[58]

Debates about whether state ownership encourages or discourages international diversification are inconclusive. On the one hand, the government can provide SOEs with the financial and political help needed to fund foreign investments, especially when the government has explicit support policies to foster international growth.[59] On the other hand, some scholars suggest that state ownership can hinder the internationalization of SOEs because the enterprises have a strong dependence on the home country government[60] and bureaucratic control can lead to a lower likelihood of doing business in foreign markets.[61] Still other scholars[62] attempt to reconcile the two arguments by proposing a curvilinear relationship between state ownership and international diversification. Specifically, the influence of state ownership on foreign investments is an outcome of the interaction between the support and controls associated with different levels of the state ownership, leading to varying levels of international expansion. Local governments may hinder internationalization and seek more local investments instead, while central governments might push for far-reaching global expansion for political reasons—as is the case in China with the central "Go Global" policy.[63] Nevertheless, scholars generally agree that state ownership can play a critical role in firms' internationalization.[64]

Like state owners, business group owners belong to Quadrant II of Figure 6.1. A business group refers to an interorganizational network of semi-autonomous firms tied together through multiplex ownership, buyer-supplier, director interlock, and/or social ties. This type of network is comprised of a collection of parent and subsidiary companies that function as a single economic entity through a common source of control.[65] Business group member firms, or *affiliates*, retain legal independence, though they may share common objectives.[66] Business groups play a critical role in many emerging economies. In India, for example, 45 of the 50 largest enterprises are business groups.[67] Networks of affiliates help facilitate many countries' globalization. For instance, foreign exports by large South Korean *chaebol* (business groups) represented about 82 percent of the country's GDP in 2012.[68] But business groups also have a strong presence in some developed countries, with over 26,000 of them established throughout Western European nations.[69]

Business group affiliation can benefit firms by functioning as efficient internal capital and labor markets within the affiliate network and mobilizing valued resources for firms.[70] In this sense, business group owners can provide affiliates with financial and human resources needed for foreign strategic investment. These owners tend to have a diversified portfolio of businesses. For instance, the Samsung Group, a South Korean *chaebol*, directly or indirectly controls numerous affiliated businesses, most of which are united under the Samsung brand. As the largest business group in India, Reliance Industries Limited is engaged in a myriad of businesses including energy, petrochemicals, textiles, natural resources, retail, and telecommunications. Given their diversified portfolios, business group owners often have a high level of risk tolerance.

Similar to that of state ownership, the impact of business group affiliation on firms' internationalization is not uniform across firms. Some scholars argue that business group affiliation can facilitate international expansion because each affiliate can benefit from internal markets and intragroup learning.[71] Others argue that affiliates, due to their constraints within business groups and responsibility to other group members, exist within a structure of high complexity and inflexibility, which can restrain their international diversification.[72] This argument may explain why some Japanese *keiretsu* affiliates export less than standalone firms.[73] But the low level of internationalization by business group affiliates may also be due to a high level of liability of foreignness. Affiliates often find it difficult to transfer their business group resources, such as domestic political ties and reputations, to foreign markets.[74]

Business group affiliation can shape location choice decisions and entry mode choices. Japanese keiretsu affiliates, for example, tend to follow fellow group members into particular geographic regions when intragroup trade is greater.[75] In fact, as group members may have access to each other's information, expertise, human resources, and technology, small keiretsu affiliates are more likely to invest in politically unstable countries than do standalone firms.[76] Similarly, affiliates can benefit from fellow affiliates' entry mode experiences, making them inclined to choose the same entry mode as their fellows.[77] By enabling learning from fellow affiliates, keiretsu membership mitigates host country risk and weakens the risk's influence on firms' equity stakes in foreign subsidiaries.[78] In essence, business group resources and information from fellow affiliates may critically shape affiliates' location and entry mode decisions.

Although state ownership and business group affiliation can provide firms with substantial resources that enable international diversification, these owners often have nonprofit or political goals to achieve. SOEs may engage in international diversification only to satisfy the social and political objectives of state owners, while affiliates of business groups may need to reciprocate with each other and thus provide resources for international diversification. As a result, state ownership and business group affiliation may lead decision makers to engage in global expansion that does not lead to a sustainable locational advantage, and instead may lead to a temporary advantage, or even face a locational disadvantage.

Hedge fund activists, also belonging to Quadrant II, are motivated to advise top managers on strategic decisions and provide needed information, as we explored in Chapter 5. Although hedge funds may not have as highly diversified portfolios as do mutual funds, their investment strategies are characterized by high fees and high risks. In this sense, hedge fund activists can be associated with an elevated risk tolerance. But since activists often call for targeted firms to engage in restructuring to enhance operational efficiency and reduce organizational complexity, they will not support international diversification decisions by targeted companies. Hedge fund activists will constrain firms from pursuing locational advantages and lead top managers to focus on honing competitive advantages at home. In 2013, Tim Hortons, a Canadian coffee-and-doughnut chain, was confronted by two hedge fund activists—Scout Capital Management LLC and Highfields Capital Management LP. These activist investors called on Tim Hortons to curtail its foreign expansion in the United States and instead buy back more shares.[79] Ultimately, Tim Hortons was bought by Burger King, and in part the rationale was the tax saving purposes with Burger King being headquartered in Canada. Then Burger King was acquired by Restaurant Brands International Inc., which was facilitated by another activist investor, 3G, a Brazilian investor, along with support from Berkshire Hathaway. Restaurant Brands is a company pursuing an international set of restaurant chains with significant ownership by 3G.[80]

GOVERNANCE ACTORS WITH LOW RISK TOLERANCE BUT NO RESOURCE PROVISION

Quadrant III of Figure 6.1 shows governance actors that do not provide resources to firms and do not bear much risk. Creditors such as banks are representative of these actors. These governance actors grant loans to firms but do not provide information or other resources that can support strategic decisions. By the same token, and unlike shareholders, creditors may not directly benefit from firms' successful and profitable international diversification. Creditors focus on ensuring the safety of their principal and timely interest payments rather than on benefiting from borrowers' growth and profitability; thus, creditors may have a low level of risk tolerance. Nevertheless, these actors influence corporate decisions according to the level of debt that a company takes on. Although international diversification can reduce a firm's dependence on its domestic market and diversify revenue sources, it can also subject the company to all sorts of risks associated with operating businesses abroad, including political risk in host countries and foreign exchange risk. Consequently, firms with a high debt ratio may not choose to engage in intensive international diversification as readily as those with a low debt ratio.[81]

As creditors not only lack strong incentives to support firms' international diversification with valuable information but also possess a low tolerance for risk, they may hence create hurdles for firms to pursue locational advantages abroad by charging high interest for funding international expansion, particularly when the firms are from countries with large domestic markets, as in the United States and China. However, for firms located in home countries with relatively small domestic markets, like Switzerland and South Korea, these governance actors may not necessarily inhibit firms from pursuing locational advantages, as their firms have to expand internationally to grow. Also, international risk may be reduced when there are coalitions with lower trade barriers between countries, such as those in the European Union.

GOVERNANCE ACTORS WITH HIGH RISK TOLERANCE BUT NO RESOURCE PROVISION

Quadrant IV of Figure 6.1 captures governance actors such as transient institutional investors that have high risk tolerance but do not provide resources such as information to firms. Although internationalization is associated with high risks, announcements of international acquisitions by firms without previous international operations can trigger positive stock market returns, which may benefit transient institutional investors.[82] International diversification of portfolio firms can also help these transactional investors to indirectly diversify country-specific risks.[83] For these reasons, high levels of ownership by transient institutional investors can lead top managers to engage in international diversification and pursue locational advantages abroad.[84]

This type of investor can also impact location decisions. Transient institutional investors seek to garner short-term returns from portfolio firms' international expansion. They benefit from spreading their risks across their investment portfolios, hence firms' expansion into high-risk countries can lead to higher growth and profitability potential. Meanwhile, firms can achieve better diversification of risks when including expansion to countries unrelated to home. Therefore, ownership by transient institutional investors may motivate top managers of their portfolio firms to venture into higher risk and unexplored countries.[85]

The goal of transient institutional investors is to maximize the financial returns in their investment portfolio. Compared with partial control entry modes such as alliances or licensing, high decision control ownership options enable firms to achieve greater economies of scale, lower management costs, and better integration of assets and skills,[86] giving rise to higher financial return potential. Accounting rules on consolidation also play a role in the investors' preferred modes of entry. The International Financial Reporting Standards (IFRS) require parent firms to consolidate earnings proportionally to the level of ownership, and the Generally Accepted Accounting Principles (GAAP) of the United States only allow full consolidation of sales, expenses, taxes, and earnings of business holdings for subsidiaries with more than 50 percent ownership. Both accounting guidelines suggest that transient institutional investors can boost their potential earnings upon portfolio firms' announcements to enter foreign countries through full control. For these reasons, influence by these investors may lead executives of firms to choose controlling ownership entry modes, such as cross-border M&As or greenfield investments.[87]

BOX 6.3 Strategic Governance Highlight: Competitors and Global Strategy

In Chapter 2, we discuss the role of competitors as an external governance actor. Although competitors do not directly provide firms with resources used in international expansion, they can influence firm decisions indirectly for at least two reasons. First, firms engage in global expansion to maintain competitive balance with their rivals. When a firm expands to a foreign country, rival firms may also follow suit and choose the same country to establish multimarket contact. In 2018, for example, Walmart paid $16 billion to take control of India's largest ecommerce company Flipkart to expand its business in the country. In 2019, Amazon increased its investment in India by opening its biggest office building in the world in the Indian city of Hyderabad. Similarly, US telecom firms form global strategic alliances outside of the United States as managers observe competitive moves by rivals.

Second, international expansion is replete with uncertainties and risks. Firm executives can learn from competitors' international expansion experiences and imitate successful moves such as in location choices. In this way, rivals indirectly supply firms with information that can alleviate focal firm concerns about expansion uncertainties. Chinese SOEs have been a key player in China's international business expansion. Since the launch of the Belt and Road Initiative (BRI) by Chinese President Xi Jinping in 2013, more than 80 of the 97 SOEs owned by China's central government have undertaken over 3,100 projects worldwide. The experiences accumulated by these SOEs can significantly reduce information asymmetry faced by non-SOEs in their own international expansion.

Mimicry of competitors' international diversification is strongly linked to the structure of domestic competition. Specifically, more mimicry takes place among oligopolistic firms than among monopolistic ones. Nevertheless, managers need to be cautious about how competitors can influence their global strategy. Global expansion to maintain competitive balance or to imitate competitors may not help companies achieve sustainable locational advantages unless firms have the capabilities and resources to support the expansion.

Sources: Leutert, W. (2019). The overseas expansion and evolution of Chinese state-owned enterprises.https://medium.com/fairbank-center/the-overseas-expansion-and-evolution-of-chinese-state-owned-enterprises-3dc04134c5f2; Iyengar, R. (2019). Amazon just opened its biggest office building—and it's not in the United States, *CNN*. August 22. www.cnn.com/2019/08/22/tech/

amazon-hyderabad-new-office-building/index.html; Nassauer, S., & Abrams, C. (2018). Walmart agrees to buy 77% stake in Flipkart for $16 billion. *Wall Street Journal.* May 9. www.wsj.com/articles/walmart-agrees-to-buy-77-stake-in-flipkart-for-16-billion-1525864334; Gimeno, J., Hoskisson, R. E., Beal, B. D., & Wan, W. P. (2005). Explaining the clustering of international expansion moves: A critical test in the U.S. telecommunications industry. *Academy of Management Journal* 48: 297–319; Yu, C.-M. J., & Ito, K. (1988). Oligopolistic reaction and foreign direct investment: The case of the US tire and textiles industries. *Journal of International Business Studies* 19(3): 449–460.

As transient institutional investors may depress stock prices through threatening to sell their holdings, top managers may make global strategy decisions that can satisfy the demands of such investors but harm the firms' long-term competitiveness (see Chapter 4). Although transient institutional investors can lead firms to pursue locational advantages through international diversification, the advantages may not be sustainable because these investors focus on attaining stock value gains from announcements of such diversification.

Influence of Financial Analysts and Competitors on Global Strategy

As introduced in Chapter 3, financial analysts do not directly provide resources that can support firms' strategic decisions; instead, they collect information from top managers with the goal of making accurate forecasts about a firm's prospects. As the reputation of financial analysts hinges on their abilities to issue accurate recommendations, the analysts generally focus on firms in particular industries and develop in-depth industry expertise and knowledge.[88] By the same token, as it is difficult for analysts to develop expertise and knowledge on many countries, as such analysts make more precise earnings forecasts for firms in their country of residence than nonresident analysts.[89] In this sense, analysts may find it difficult to issue accurate forecasts for firms with high international diversification. Also, internationalization can increase a firm's organizational and business complexity and worsen internal control over overseas subsidiaries,[90] making it challenging for financial analysts to issue accurate forecasts.[91] As a result, financial analysts tend to exhibit a downward bias in their recommendations when firms are associated with high levels of international diversification.[92] Given the profound influence that analyst recommendations have on firm stock price, we may expect that top managers will refrain from international diversification when faced with pressure from financial analysts.[93] Although competitors, similar to financial analysts, cannot be mapped to Figure 6.1, they can also have a profound influence on firms' global strategy as discussed in Box 6.3.

MANAGING GOVERNANCE ACTORS FOR A WINNING GLOBAL STRATEGY

We have explained how governance actors exert varying influences on strategic decisions pertaining to global strategy. Although actors in the first quadrant of Figure 6.1 can lead firms to achieve sustainable locational advantages, their low risk tolerance may persuade managers to eschew some foreign investment opportunities. Meanwhile, although governance actors in Quadrants II and IV can facilitate decisions to explore locational advantages abroad, the long-term interests of these influencers may misalign with those of the firms. Managers may therefore need to resist the pressure from these governance actors to engage in global expansion. When under pressure by governance actors in Quadrant III, who can constrain firm leaders from exploring locational advantages, managers may need to alleviate the inhibition and nonetheless engage in international expansion critical to the company's competitiveness. Figure 6.3 describes four types of strategies that executives can use to help manage different governance actor tendencies.

Engage and Interact

Through engagement and interaction, managers can urge governance actors that offer resources to firms but have a low risk tolerance to enable the necessary global strategy actions for growth. Firms need to enable and equip

Resource Provision	Risk Tolerance	Example	Strategy
Yes	Low	Family shareholders	Engage and interact
Yes	High	State ownership	Leverage and balance
No	--	Financial analysts	Manage
No	High	Transient institutional investors	Resist and isolate

FIGURE 6.3 Managing governance actors for a successful global strategy.

top managers so that they can elicit and receive ideas and information from board members and dedicated institutional investors. Because directors with foreign work and living experiences can provide information valuable for executives to assess opportunities abroad, including which country to enter and how to enter, active engagement and interaction with such directors can help managers develop an effective global strategy. Top managers should also frequently engage with dedicated institutional investors who may have foreign investment experiences through designing a year-round engagement program around the proxy season, as they signify important sources of knowledge to help facilitate and evaluate opportunities, as well as challenges, in global expansion.

Although directors and dedicated shareholders are motivated to provide guidance during expansion, top managers need to *critically* evaluate information from these governance actors. As directors and dedicated shareholders (through imposing pressure on directors) can influence managers' compensation levels as well as job security, top managers may incorporate their advice indiscriminately as an ingratiation tactic. Uncritically following governance actors' guidance and suggestions can constrain firms from pursuing the most effective global strategy. For example, one director may have worked in a foreign country and recommends the country as a target for cross-border M&As. Managers may choose the country as the destination even if another country better fits the firm's strategic plans.

Given that dedicated shareholders do not readily tolerate risk, a key task for managers becomes to alleviate their concerns and seek their support for risky global investments. This task becomes particularly salient among family firms. Family shareholders show great caution about risky global investment because their portfolios are not as diversified as those of institutional investors, and they carry concerns of potential adverse influences on family control or a diluted family identity. To garner support from family owners and other dedicated shareholders, managers need to conduct detailed due diligence about foreign business opportunities and clearly identify potential challenges in global operations and devise a specific mitigation strategy.

Leverage and Balance

To manage governance actors that can provide resources and have high risk tolerance (Quadrant II of Table 6.1), executives may consider leveraging the expertise and information provided by these actors, but also balance the potential conflicts of interest between the influencers and the firm. State ownership can grant top managers political connections and access to resources controlled by the government such as subsidies and preferential policies, which managers should leverage and capitalize on for global expansion. However, the goal of state owners in some countries like China and Russia may differ from a firm's goals, requiring managers to balance such conflicting aims. For example, state owners may pressure firms with a minority state ownership to invest in a foreign country that does not have locational advantages because heads of government desire to establish better diplomatic relations with that country. Under such a scenario, company leaders may pacify the state owners by lobbying the government for resource support and minimizing the firm's own investment into the requested expansion. A similar case applies for business group affiliation. Other group members can supply affiliates with resources needed for international expansion, but they also expect the help in return when needed.[94] Affiliates need to balance their own firms' goals with those of the collective network.

Hedge fund activists tend to curtail firms' international expansion since the move may not generate short-term financial returns. In such a context, top managers need to leverage the expertise of these activists and balance their focus on short-term gains with the focus of the firm on long-term competitiveness. But hedge fund activists may push firms to divest international assets[95] in an effort to reduce firm redundancy and streamline business operations. Yet, not all activist-impelled divestitures may achieve these intended results.[96] For example, the activist investor Nelson Peltz pushed CEO Irene Rosenfeld of Kraft to acquire Cadbury Schweppes and then split the combined company into a global snacks business (Mondelēz) and a US grocery business (Kraft). Yet, Mondelēz struggled to compete with global giants such as Nestlé and Unilever.[97] As seen in this case, divestiture of international assets may lead to an improvement in firms' short-term performance, but it may also disrupt firms' global value chains and harm long-run competitiveness. In this situation, managers may need to align with other governance actors such as dedicated shareholders through hosting investor day events and communicating with them about firm strategic plans to resist hedge fund activists' divestiture proposals.

Top managers of new ventures that have not been listed need to cope with venture capitalists—private equity investors that provide capital to companies exhibiting high growth potential in exchange for equity stakes. Venture capitalists are a type of governance actor that provide substantial resources for firm growth and have a high level of risk tolerance. In some cases, venture capitalists give new ventures lavish funding, which can impel their rapid international expansion. Softbank, a Japanese multinational conglomerate holding company, invested over $10.3 billion through its Vision Fund, the world's largest technology-focused venture capital fund, in WeWork, a new office space leasing venture. The abundant funding drove WeWork executives to pursue fast global expansion with the goal of dominating the office share business but paid inadequate attention to risk control, which came with a cost. WeWork failed its initial public offering in September 2019 and Soft-Bank wrote down about 90 percent of its investment.[98] In 2021, WeWork was reported to agree with merging with a special-purpose acquisition company in a deal to take itself public nearly two years after its high-profile failure to launch a traditional initial public offering.[99] The debacle of WeWork attests to the importance of balancing venture capitalists' "aspirations" and the firm's own capabilities. Although SoftBank owners expected WeWork to dominate the leasing office business through fast-paced expansion, top managers of WeWork failed in their ability to manage such expansion successfully due to a lack of control over risks and cost.

Manage

Although financial analysts cannot directly influence firm global strategy, they exert an indirect influence on strategic decisions by shaping shareholder trading behaviors. As discussed, financial analysts tend to react negatively to excessive international diversification because it can increase a firm's organizational complexity and make it difficult for them to issue accurate forecasts. The key strategy for managers to cope with financial analysts lies in impression management. Top managers can resort to impression management tactics, including rendering personal favors such as facilitating connections with industry experts to cultivate a close bond with analysts. Such relationship building creates rapport between analysts and managers and thereby helps the executives avoid negative analyst recommendations even after announcing international expansion plans.

More important, executives can improve the markets' access to important strategic information by proactively communicating the rationale behind global expansion plans to financial analysts. Earnings conference calls provide an important platform for managers to convince financial analysts of the strategic importance of international expansion moves. In another approach, firms may pay for independent equity research and dissipate important strategic information to investors, a trend that has become increasingly common in recent years. If improving communication fails, managers may consider finding investors who believe in the firm's global strategy, which could mean taking the company private.[100]

Resist and Isolate

Transient institutional investors (Quadrant IV of Figure 6.1), who have a high-risk tolerance but do not provide resources to firms, may benefit from a company's pursuit of global opportunities in risky countries through a full control entry mode. Yet this form of global expansion may end up harming the firm's long-term competitiveness. Managers need to engage in a global strategy to satisfy the preferences of transient institutional investors but must focus on developing a plan that enables sustainable locational advantages. To manage the pressure from transient institutional investors, executives can isolate these governance actors and minimize their selling pressure by seeking support from other shareholders, such as board directors and quasi-indexer institutional investors. As shown in Chapter 2, transient institutional investors on average hold less than 5 percent of S&P 1500 firms; thus, these investors are unlikely to exert a profound influence on firm stock prices on their own. In contrast, quasi-indexer institutional investors hold more than 50 percent of firm ownership, making it difficult for managers to seek support from these investors. However, managers may consider engaging in impression management, specifically using ingratiatory tactics to create rapport with representatives of quasi-indexer institutional investors, like fund managers, and convince them of the soundness of their global strategy.[101] By creating a coalition with other shareholders, executives can then constrain the influence of transient institutional investors and focus on pursuing a longer-term global strategy.

GOVERNANCE ACTORS AND LEGITIMACY IN GLOBAL STRATEGY

Turning our attention to a salient issue in global strategy, we explore the challenges in establishing and maintaining organizational legitimacy,[102] which refers to the acceptance of the organization by environmental stakeholders such as customers.[103] Top managers of multinational enterprises need to cope with legitimacy issues in host countries as well as at home. Huawei, a Chinese telecommunications conglomerate, for example, is forbidden from doing business with federal agencies in the United States because US politicians believe that the Chinese government may have the potential to gather information from Huawei network products, which can put the US national security in peril.[104] But MNEs are also subject to legitimacy issues at home. In 2017, President Donald Trump criticized Ford for relocating a car plant to Mexico. Ford canceled the plan and instead invested $700 million in a Michigan facility to build electric vehicles.[105] Yet, under the new Biden administration, in March 2021, the firm announced plans to move new projects from a Ohio plant to a Mexican plant.[106] Top managers must understand legitimacy issues when formulating global strategy, including the variety of factors that may influence outcomes such as countries of origin[107] and poor corporate social performance,[108] but also governance actors.

Among the different types of ownership—from state owners to institutional investors as discussed in Chapter 2—state owners can have a profound influence on firms' legitimacy in global expansion, and such an influence is tied to owners' countries of origin. Compared to private firms, SOEs from autocratic countries function as more effective and centralized vehicles for the agenda of the state.[109] As a result, SOEs may lack organizational legitimacy and face resistance in host countries, as we saw in the Huawei example. This conflict is particularly true when SOEs' home and host countries have different political systems or difficult historical hostilities,[110] since state ownership under such scenarios represents a more salient threat to national security. Ownership by sovereign wealth funds can also affect legitimacy as concerns arise in host countries that SWFs make politically driven investments instead of economically driven ones,[111] posing national security doubts.

Firms with state or SWF ownership are likely to face more legitimacy-related issues as many countries have strengthened investment-related national security screening laws and regulations that restrict foreign investment.[112] In 2007, the United States introduced the Foreign Investment and National Security Act (FINSA) which gave the Committee on Foreign Investment in the United States (CFIUS) broad authority to investigate foreign takeovers. Canada amended its Investment Canada Act and enacted the National Security Review of Investments Regulations in 2009. In the same year, Germany introduced a general control mechanism for takeovers by investors outside the European Union and European Free Trade Association. In 2011, China enacted new regulations for the national security review system overseeing mergers and acquisitions of domestic firms by foreign ones. In 2018, the United Nations Committee for Trade and Development (UNCTAD) estimated that 55 nations introduced over 112 measures affecting foreign investment. Over one third of these reflect increased national security concerns about foreign ownership for critical infrastructure, core technologies, and other sensitive assets.[113] As foreign investment receives more scrutiny, executives of SOEs or SWF-owned firms face an increasing need to manage organizational legitimacy.

In addition to ownership structures, firm governance practices also shape the level of legitimacy that companies receive in host countries. Distinct governance practices may be perceived differently by country due to dissimilar institutional environments.[114] A firm with significant CEO compensation incentives, for example, may be perceived to have an effective corporate governance in the United States[115] and is therefore associated with a high level of organizational legitimacy. Yet, in Japan with a "communitarian" culture characterized by embedded social and cultural ties and reciprocal exchanges, a firm with a CEO who receives enormous incentive pay may be perceived negatively by stakeholders.[116]

The influence of a firm's governance practices on organizational legitimacy hinges on its home country institutions. As research shows, in the context of foreign initial public offerings (IPOs) in the United States, how a new venture's board structure and incentive compensation shape US investors' valuation is contingent on the venture's home country institutions.[117] Specifically, board independence does not seem to play as important a role in affecting investor perceptions as does executive incentives for new ventures from countries with strong investor protection, because such countries have institutions available to safeguard shareholders' fundamental interests and investors are more concerned about whether executives are motivated to perform. In other words, firms' organizational legitimacy associated with governance practices in foreign host countries is subject to the influence of these firms' home-country institutions. If the home country has less-developed market institutions, then the legitimacy signal of independent directors is less salient, as investors may be more worried about whether their contracts with stakeholders are enforceable, for example.

Leverage Governance Actors to Manage Legitimacy

Although a firm's governance actors can represent sources of organizational legitimacy issues in host countries, managers may leverage them for an increased likelihood of validity during global expansion. We have the following specific recommendations on how to tackle legitimacy issues in implementing global strategy.

First, create a board of directors that may enhance organizational legitimacy in the eyes of stakeholders in host countries. For example, new ventures with a higher percentage of outside directors and the separation of CEO and board chairs are associated with better initial public offering performance because these board structures signal high firm quality and are associated with strong organizational legitimacy in the eyes of investors.[118] Likewise, MNEs may establish a board of directors that local stakeholders in foreign host countries can perceive positively, especially when these stakeholders lack sufficient information to determine if MNEs will function as responsible corporate entities. For instance, if the government of the host country is concerned about national security associated with an MNE's foreign subsidiary, top managers may consider appointing directors with local political connections to the foreign subsidiary's board. Alternatively, if local communities have concerns about a foreign subsidiary's treatment of employees, the MNE can appoint employee representatives on the board. In essence, conforming to the expectations of local stakeholders may inspire their allegiance,[119] thereby elevating the legitimacy of the organization in their eyes.

Second, firms can leverage home and host country governments. Home country consulates abroad have the responsibility of nation-branding,[120] which can in part be achieved through strong diplomatic protections to safeguard the interests of firms in global competition.[121] Diplomatic agencies can not only help firms identify potential legal and regulatory traps in the foreign countries but also facilitate integration with host-country business networks through the agencies' information platforms.[122] More important, MNEs can shape their operating environment in host countries through political activities. Foreign firms engage in lobbying activities in the United States to elevate their legitimacy. In the face of increasing political scrutiny, many Chinese companies turn to lobbyists for help. After TikTok, a social media company owned by the China-based ByteDance became a target of the Trump administration over national security concerns, and firm executives hired more than 35 lobbyists to work on the company's behalf, including one with deep ties to President Trump.[123] Although the long-term outcomes of TikTok's lobbying efforts remain unclear as the case unfolds, research suggests that MNEs' political strategies can reduce exposure to host country risks, including legitimacy concerns, especially in emerging economies.[124]

Third, company executives can enhance legitimacy by cooperating with high-status local firms or joining local business communities. Although local stakeholders may lack information and judgment about a foreign company, they have developed their evaluations of local ones. MNEs may elevate their legitimacy through collaborations with high legitimacy local partners.[125] These local partners help certify the acceptability of MNE subsidiaries, creating interorganizational legitimacy spillover. In recent years, Hollywood studios have cooperated with Chinese studios to increase the legitimacy of Hollywood movies in the eyes of moviegoers in China. *The Great Wall*, a movie co-produced by both Hollywood and Chinese studios, achieved respectable commercial success in China, though it flopped in the United States.[126]

Relatedly, MNE entrants may improve social evaluations by becoming part of host country business communities.[127] These communities can serve as gatekeepers for MNEs to access local resources and consumers.[128] MNEs may, for instance, find it easier to integrate with host country value chains and understand local business practices. In the absence of endorsement by host country business communities, multinationals face increasing difficulty in understanding prevalent business norms,[129] which can slow its integration into value chains and harm the firm's ability to participate in local market competition.

In conclusion, governance actors can play a critical role in shaping strategic decisions pertaining to whether, where, and how to expand globally with the goal of pursuing locational advantages. Whereas some governance actors such as transient institutional investors may support firms' international diversification, others such as analysts may constrain firms from expanding internationally. A key task for top managers is to understand governance actors' preferences for global strategic choices and leverage such actors to better grasp opportunities abroad and tackle challenges to realize effective international expansion.

NOTES

1. Hitt M. A., Ireland R. D., & Hoskisson R. E. (2020). *Strategic management: competitiveness and globalization* (13th ed.). Mason, OH: South-Western.
2. Dunning, J. H. (1998). Location and the multinational enterprise: A neglected factor? *Journal of International Business Studies* 29(1): 45–66.
3. Ibid.
4. Hitt, Ireland, & Hoskisson. Strategic management.
5. Hitt, M. A., Tihanyi, L., Miller, T., & Connelly, B. (2006). International diversification: Antecedents, outcomes, and moderators. *Journal of Management* 32(6): 831–867.
6. Kobrin, S. J. (1979). Political risk: A review and reconsideration. *Journal of International Business Studies* 10(1): 67–80.
7. Pearson, N. O. (2007). Chávez finishes nationalizing Venezuela oil. *The Seattle Times*. May 2. www.seattletimes.com/nation-world/chvez-finishes-nationalizing-venezuela-oil.
8. Phillips, M. (2018). Why Turkey's lira crisis matters outside Turkey. *New York Times*. August 13. www.nytimes.com/2018/08/13/business/turkey-lira-emerging-markets.html.
9. Zaheer, S. (1995). Overcoming the liability of foreignness. *Academy of Management Journal* 38(2): 341–363.
10. Weise, K. (2019). Amazon gives up on Chinese domestic shopping business. *New York Times*. April 18. www.nytimes.com/2019/04/18/technology/amazon-china.html.
11. Dunning, J. H. (1977). Trade, location of economic activity and the MNE: A research for an eclectic approach. In *The International Allocation of Economic Activity*. Ohlin, B., Hesselborn, P. O., Wijkman, P. M. (Eds). New York: Holmes & Meier; Dunning, J. H. (1998). Location and the multinational enterprise: A neglected factor? *Journal of International Business Studies* 29(1): 45–66.
12. García–Canal, E., & Guillén, M. F. (2008). Risk and the strategy of foreign location choice in regulated industries. *Strategic Management Journal* 29(10): 1097–1115. Li, Y., Zhang, Y. A., & Shi, W. (2020). Navigating geographic and cultural distances in international expansion: The paradoxical roles of firm size, age, and ownership. *Strategic Management Journal* 41(5): 921–949.
13. Chakrabarti, A., & Mitchell, W. (2013). The persistent effect of geographic distance in acquisition target selection. *Organization Science* 24(6): 1805–1826.

14. Duncan, R. B. (1972). Characteristics of organizational environments and perceived environmental uncertainty. *Administrative Science Quarterly* 17(3): 313–327. Henisz, W. J., & Delios, A. (2001). Uncertainty, imitation, and plant location: Japanese multinational corporations, 1990–1996. *Administrative Science Quarterly* 46(3): 443–475; Miller, K. D. (1992). A framework for integrated risk management in international business. *Journal of International Business Studies* 23(2): 311–331.

15. Boeh, K. K., & Beamish, P. W. (2012). Travel time and the liability of distance in foreign direct investment: Location choice and entry mode. *Journal of International Business Studies* 43(5): 525–535; Ghemawat P. (2001). Distance still matters: The hard reality of global expansion. *Harvard Business Review* 79(8): 137–147; Ragozzino, R. (2009). The effects of geographic distance on the foreign acquisition activity of US firms. *Management International Review* 49(4): 509–535.

16. Shenkar, O. (2001). Cultural distance revisited: Towards a more rigorous conceptualization and measurement of cultural differences. *Journal of International Business Studies* 32(3): 519–535; Tihanyi, L., Griffith, D. A., & Russell, C. J. (2005). The effect of cultural distance on entry mode choice, international diversification, and MNE performance: a meta-analysis. *Journal of International Business Studies* 36(3): 270–283.

17. Henisz, W. J., & Delios, A. (2001). Uncertainty, imitation, and plant location: Japanese multinational corporations, 1990–1996. *Administrative Science Quarterly* 46(3): 443–475.

18. Laursen, K., & Salter, A. (2005). Open for innovation: The role of openness in explaining innovation performance among U. K. manufacturing firms. *Strategic Management Journal* 27: 131–150.

19. Cuervo-Cazurra, A. (2006). Who cares about corruption? *Journal of International Business Studies* 37(6): 807–822.

20. Papadopoulos, K. (2019). Update on U.S. director pay. Harvard Law School Forum on Corporate Governance. May 6. https://corpgov.law.harvard.edu/2019/05/06/update-on-u-s-director-pay.

21. Sanders, W. G. (2001). Behavioral responses of CEOs to stock ownership and stock option pay. *Academy of Management Journal* 44(3): 477–492.

22. Masulis, R. W., Wang, C., & Xie, F. (2012). Globalizing the boardroom—The effects of foreign directors on corporate governance and firm performance. *Journal of Accounting and Economics* 53(3): 527–554.

23. Ibid.

24. Chen, S. S., Chen, Y. S., Kang, J. K., & Peng, S. C. (2020). Board structure, director expertise, and advisory role of outside directors. *Journal of Financial Economics* 138(2), 483–503.

25. Tihanyi, L., Johnson, R. A., Hoskisson, R. E., & Hitt, M. A. (2003). Institutional ownership differences and international diversification: The effects of boards of directors and technological opportunity. *Academy of Management Journal* 46(2): 195–211.

26. Lu, J., Xu, B., & Liu, X. (2009). The effects of corporate governance and institutional environments on export behaviour in emerging economies. *Management International Review* 49(4): 455–478.
27. Sanders, W. G., & Carpenter, M. A. (1998). Internationalization and firm governance: The roles of CEO compensation, top team composition, and board structure. *Academy of Management Journal* 41(2): 158–178.
28. Musteen, M., Datta, D. K., & Herrmann, P. (2009). Ownership structure and CEO compensation: Implications for the choice of foreign market entry modes. *Journal of International Business Studies* 40(2): 321–338.
29. Sanders & Carpenter. Internationalization and firm governance.
30. Lu, J., Xu, B., & Liu, X. (2009). The effects of corporate governance and institutional environments on export behaviour in emerging economies. *Management International Review* 49(4): 455–478.
31. Sanders & Carpenter. Internationalization and firm governance.
32. Musteen, Datta, & Herrmann. Ownership structure and CEO compensation, 321–338.
33. Miletkov, M., Poulsen, A., & Wintoki, M. B. (2017). Foreign independent directors and the quality of legal institutions. *Journal of International Business Studies* 48(2): 267–292.
34. Giannetti, M., Liao, G., & Yu, X. (2015). The brain gain of corporate boards: Evidence from China. *Journal of Finance* 70(4): 1629–1682.
35. Gomez-Mejia, L. R., Cruz, C., Berrone, P., & De Castro, J. (2011). The bind that ties: Socioemotional wealth preservation in family firms. *Academy of Management Annals* 5(1): 653–707.
36. Gallo, M. Á., Tàpies, J., & Cappuyns, K. (2004).comparison of family and nonfamily business: Financial logic and personal preferences. *Family Business Review* 17(4): 303–318; Schulze, W. S., Lubatkin, M. H., & Dino, R. N. (2003). Exploring the agency consequences of ownership dispersion among the directors of private family firms. *Academy of Management Journal* 46(2): 179–194.
37. Hitt, Tihanyi, Miller, & Connelly. International diversification.
38. Fernández, Z., & Nieto, M. J. (2006). Impact of ownership on the international involvement of SMEs. *Journal of International Business Studies* 37(3): 340–351.
39. Zahra, S. A. (2003). International expansion of US manufacturing family businesses: The effect of ownership and involvement. *Journal of Business Venturing* 18(4): 495–512.
40. Lin, W-T. (2012). Family ownership and internationalization processes: Internationalization pace, internationalization scope, and internationalization rhythm. *European Management Journal* 30(1): 47–56.
41. Gómez-Mejía, L. R., Haynes, K. T., Núñez-Nickel, M., Jacobson, K. J., & Moyano-Fuentes, J. (2007). Socioemotional wealth and business risks in family-controlled firms: Evidence from Spanish olive oil mills. *Administrative Science Quarterly* 52(1): 106–137.
42. Pongelli, C., Caroli, M. G., & Cucculelli, M. (2016). Family business going abroad: The effect of family ownership on foreign market entry mode decisions. *Small Business Economics* 47(3): 787–801.

43. Huntsman (2017). Huntsman acquires UK polyurethane formulations company, IFS. *Borderless*, May 17. https://www.borderless.net/news/chemical-value-chain/huntsman-acquires-uk-polyurethane-formulations-company-ifs.

44. Tihanyi, Johnson, Hoskisson, & Hitt. Institutional ownership differences and international diversification.

45. Bu, J., & Shi, W. (2020). Foreign institutional investors and location choice of cross-border mergers and acquisitions. Working paper. University of Miami.

46. OECD (2020). The COVID-19 crisis and state ownership in the economy: Issues and policy considerations.

47. IMF (2020). *State-owned enterprises: The other government*. Washington, DC: International Monetary Fund.

48. Benito, G. R., & Rygh, A., & Lunnan, R. (2016). The benefits of internationalization for state-owned enterprises. *Global Strategy Journal* 6(4): 269–288.

49. Shi, W., Aguilera, R., & Wang, K. (2020). State ownership and securities fraud: A political governance perspective. *Corporate Governance: An International Review* 28(2): 157–176.

50. Alhashel, B. (2015). Sovereign wealth funds: A literature review. *Journal of Economics and Business* 78: 1–13;

51. Zhang, J., He, X. (2014). Economic nationalism and foreign acquisition completion: The case of China. *International Business Review* 23(1): 212–227.

52. Li, Y., Zhang, Y. A., & Shi, W. (2020b). Navigating geographic and cultural distances in international expansion: The paradoxical roles of firm size, age, and ownership. *Strategic Management Journal* 41(5): 921–949.

53. Shi, W., Hoskisson, R. E., & Zhang, Y. (2016). A geopolitical perspective into the opposition to globalizing state-owned enterprises in target states. *Global Strategy Journal* 6(1): 13–30.

54. Sanger, D. E. (2006). Under pressure, Dubai company drops port deal. *New York Times*. March 10. https://www.nytimes.com/2006/03/10/politics/under-pressure-dubai-company-drops-port-deal.html.

55. Cuervo-Cazurra, A., & Li, C. (2020). State ownership and internationalization: The advantage and disadvantage of stateness. *Journal of World Business*: https://doi.org/10.1016/j.jwb.2020.101112.

56. Kalotay, K., & Sulstarova, A. (2010). Modelling Russian outward FDI. *Journal of International Management* 16(2): 131–142.

57. Tao, F., Liu, X., Gao, L., & Xia, E. (2017). Do cross-border mergers and acquisitions increase short-term market performance? The case of Chinese firms. *International Business Review* 26(1): 189–202.

58. Li, J., Li, P., & Wang, B. (2019). The liability of opaqueness: State ownership and the likelihood of deal completion in international acquisitions by Chinese firms. *Strategic Management Journal* 40(2): 303–327.

59. Luo, Y., Xue, Q., & Han, B. (2010). How emerging market governments promote outward FDI: Experience from China. *Journal of World Business* 45(1): 68–79.

60. Deng, Z., Yan, J., & Van Essen, M. (2018). Heterogeneity of political connections and outward foreign direct investment. *International Business Review* 27(4): 893–903.

61. Mazzolini, R. 1979. European government-controlled enterprises: Explaining international strategic and policy decisions. *Journal of International Business Studies* 10(3): 16–26.

62. Kalasin, K., Cuervo-Cazurra, A., & Ramamurti, R. (2020). State ownership and international expansion: The S-curve relationship. *Global Strategy Journal* 10(2): 386–418. Wu, J. & Zhao, H. (2015). The dual effects of state ownership on export activities of emerging market firms: An inducement–constraint perspective. *Management International Review* 55(3): 421–451.

63. Kim, H., Wu, J., Schuler, D. A., & Hoskisson, R. E. (2019). Chinese multinationals' fast internationalization: Financial performance advantage in one region, disadvantage in another. *Journal of International Business Studies*: 1–31.

64. Cuervo-Cazurra & Li. State ownership and internationalization.

65. Holmes, R. M., Hoskisson, R. E., Kim, H., Wan, W. P., & Holcomb, T. R. (2018). International strategy and business groups: A review and future research agenda. *Journal of World Business* 53(2): 134–150.

66. Yiu, D., Bruton, G. D., & Lu, Y. (2005). Understanding business group performance in an emerging economy: Acquiring resources and capabilities in order to prosper. *Journal of Management Studies* 42(1): 183–206.

67. Ramachandran, J., Manikandan, K., & Pant, A. (2013). Why conglomerates thrive (outside the US). *Harvard Business Review* 91(12): 110–119.

68. Pesek, W. (2013). Koreans find breaking up with Chaebol hard to do. *Bloomberg*. www.bloomberg.com, July 8.

69. Belenzon, S., Berkovitz, T., & Rios, L. A. (2013). Capital markets and firm organization: How financial development shapes European corporate groups. *Management Science* 59(6): 1326–1343.

70. Khanna, T., & Palepu, K. 1997. Why focused strategies may be wrong for emerging markets. *Harvard Business Review* 75(6): 41–54.

71. Kim, H., Hoskisson, R. E., & Lee, S-H. (2014). Why strategic factor markets matter: "New" multinationals' geographic diversification and firm profitability. *Strategic Management Journal*. Singh, D. A., & Gaur, A. S. (2013). Governance structure, innovation and internationalization: Evidence from India. *Journal of International Management* 19(3): 300–309.

72. Kumar, V., Gaur, A. S., & Pattnaik, C. (2012). Product diversification and international expansion of business groups. *Management International Review* 52(2): 175–192.

73. Geringer, J. M., Tallman, S., & Olsen, D. M. 2000. Product and international diversification among Japanese multinational firms. *Strategic Management Journal* 21(1): 51–80.

74. Tan, D., & Meyer, K. E. (2010). Business groups' outward FDI: A managerial resources perspective. *Journal of International Management* 16(2): 154–164.

75. Belderbos, R., Olffen, W. V., & Zou, J. (2011). Generic and specific social learning mechanisms in foreign entry location choice. *Strategic Management Journal* 32(12): 1309–1330.

76. Alcantara, L. L., & Mitsuhashi, H. (2012). Make-or-break decisions in choosing foreign direct investment locations. *Journal of International Management* 18(4): 335–351.

77. Guillen, M. F. (2003). Experience, imitation, and the sequence of foreign entry: Wholly owned and joint-venture manufacturing by South Korean firms and business groups in China, 1987–1995. *Journal of International Business Studies* 34(2): 185–198.

78. Delios, A., & Henisz, W. I. (2000). Japanese firms' investment strategies in emerging economies. *Academy of Management Journal* 43(3): 305–323.

79. Johnson, K. (2013). Interview: Tim Hortons CEO talks expansion, activist Investors and . . . coffee. *Wall Street Journal*. September 17. www.wsj.com/articles/BL-CDRTB-2685.

80. Strauss, M. (2017). Tim Hortons' franchisee spat hurting sales, activist investor Ackman says. *The Globe and Mail*. November 16. https://www.theglobeand-mail.com/report-on-business/tim-hortons-franchisee-spat-hurting-sales-activist-investor-ackman-says/article37000363/.

81. Chen, C. J. P., Cheng, C. S. A., He, J. & Kim, I. 1997. An investigation of the relationship between international activities and capital structure. *Journal of International Business Studies* 28(3): 563–577; Lee, K. C., & Kwok, C. C. (1988). Multinational corporations vs. domestic corporations: International environmental factors and determinants of capital structure. *Journal of International Business Studies* 19(2): 195–217.

82. Doukas, J., & Travlos, N. G. (1988). The effect of corporate multinationalism on shareholders' wealth: Evidence from international acquisitions. *Journal of Finance* 43(5): 1161–1175.

83. Del Guercio, D., & Tkac, P. A. (2002). The determinants of the flow of funds of managed portfolios: Mutual funds vs. pension funds. *Journal of Financial and Quantitative Analysis*, 523–557.

84. Tihanyi, L., Johnson, R. A., Hoskisson, R. E., & Hitt, M. A. (2003). Institutional ownership differences and international diversification: The effects of boards of directors and technological opportunity. *Academy of Management Journal* 46(2): 195–211.

85. Lien, Y.-C., & Filatotchev, I. (2015). Ownership characteristics as determinants of FDI location decisions in emerging economies. *Journal of World Business* 50(4): 637–650.

86. Agarwal, S., & Ramaswami, S. N. (1992). Choice of foreign market entry mode: Impact of ownership, location and internalization factors. *Journal of International Business Studies* 23(1): 1–27.

87. Xu, K., Hitt, M. A., & Miller, S. R. (2020). The ownership structure contingency in the sequential international entry mode decision process: Family owners and institutional investors in family-dominant versus family-influenced firms. *Journal of International Business Studies* 51(2): 151–171.

88. Kadan, O., Madureira, L., Wang, R., & Zach, T. (2012). Analysts' industry expertise. *Journal of Accounting and Economics* 54(2–3): 95–120.

89. Bae, K.-H., Stulz, R. M., & Tan, H. (2008). Do local analysts know more? A cross-country study of the performance of local analysts and foreign analysts. *Journal of Financial Economics* 88(3): 581–606.

90. Lee, K. C., & Kwok, C. C. (1988). Multinational corporations vs. domestic corporations: International environmental factors and determinants of capital structure. *Journal of International Business Studies* 19(2): 195–217.
91. Duru, A., & Reeb, D. M. (2002). International diversification and analysts' forecast accuracy and bias. *Accounting Review* 77(2): 415–433.
92. Ibid.
93. Benner, M. J., & Zenger, T. (2016). The lemons problem in markets for strategy. *Strategy Science* 1(2): 71–89.
94. Wan, W. P., Yiu, D. W., Hoskisson, R. E., & Kim, H. (2008). The performance implications of relationship banking during macroeconomic expansion and contraction: A study of Japanese banks' social relationships and overseas expansion. *Journal of International Business Studies* 39(3): 406–427.
95. Brav, A., Jiang, W., & Kim, H. (2015). The real effects of hedge fund activism: Productivity, asset allocation, and labor outcomes. *Review of Financial Studies* 28(10): 2723–2769.
96. Shi, W., Connelly, B. L., Hoskisson, R., & Ketchen, D. (2020). Portfolio spillover of institutional investor activism: An awareness-motivation-capability perspective. *Academy of Management Journal* 63(6): 1865–1892.
97 George, B., & Lorsch, J. W. (2014). How to outsmart activist investors. *Harvard Business Review* 92(5): 88–95.
98. Sherman, E. (2019). SoftBank group writes down $9.2 billion on WeWork—and that's only the beginning of the bad news. *Fortune.* November 6. www.fortune.com.
99. Farrell, M., & Brown, E. (2021). WeWork agrees to SPAC deal that would take startup public. *Wall Street Journal.* March 26. www.wsj.com/articles/wework-agrees-to-spac-deal-that-would-take-startup-public-11616752804.
100. Zenger, T. (2013). Strategy: The uniqueness challenge. *Harvard Business Review* 91(11): 52–58.
101. Westphal, J. D., & Bednar, M. K. (2008). The pacification of institutional investors. *Administrative Science Quarterly* 53(1): 29–72.
102. Kostova, T., & Zaheer, S. 1999. Organizational legitimacy under conditions of complexity: The case of the multinational enterprise. *Academy of Management Review* 24(1): 64–81.
103. Suchman, M. C. (1995). Managing legitimacy: Strategic and institutional approaches. *Academy of Management Review* 20(3): 571–610.
104. Zhong, R. (2019). 'Prospective threat' of Chinese spying justifies Huawei ban, U.S. says. *New York Times.* July 5. www.nytimes.com/2019/07/05/technology/huawei-lawsuit-us-government.html.
105. Rogers, C. & Stoll, J. D. (2017). Ford cancels plan for new small car plant in Mexico. *Wall Street Journal.* January 3. www.wsj.com/articles/ford-cancelling-plan-for-new-small-car-plant-in-mexico-1483461051.
106. Naghton, N. (2021). UAW accuses Ford of shifting new vehicle production from Ohio to Mexico. *Wall Street Journal.* March 17. https://www.wsj.com/articles/uaw-accuses-ford-of-shifting-new-vehicle-production-from-ohio-to-mexico-11615990216.

107. Fiaschi, D., Giuliani, E., & Nieri, F. (2017). Overcoming the liability of origin by doing no-harm: Emerging country firms' social irresponsibility as they go global. *Journal of World Business* 52(4): 546–563.

108. Rathert, N. (2016). Strategies of legitimation: MNEs and the adoption of CSR in response to host-country institutions. *Journal of International Business Studies* 47(7): 858–879.

109. Clegg, L. J., Voss, H., & Tardios, J. A. (2018). The autocratic advantage: Internationalization of state-owned multinationals. *Journal of World Business* 53(5): 668–681.

110. Li, C., Arikan, I., Shenkar, O., & Arikan, A. (2020). The impact of country-dyadic military conflicts on market reaction to cross-border acquisitions. *Journal of International Business Studies* 51(3): 299–325. Shi, W., Hoskisson, R., & Zhang, Y. (2016). A geopolitical perspective into the opposition to globalizing state-owned enterprises in target states. *Global Strategy Journal* 6(1): 13–30.

111. Rose, P. (2008). Sovereigns as shareholders. *North Carolina Law Review* 87: 83.

112. Heinemann, A. (2012). Government control of cross-border M&A: Legitimate regulation or protectionism? *Journal of International Economic Law* 15(3): 843–870.

113. UNCTAD (2019). World Investment Report 2019, UNCTAD: United Nations.

114. Moore, C. B., Bell, R. G., Filatotchev, I., & Rasheed, A. A. (2012). Foreign IPO capital market choice: Understanding the institutional fit of corporate governance. *Strategic Management Journal* 33(8): 914–937.

115. Paruchuri, S., & Misangyi, V. F. (2015). Investor perceptions of financial misconduct: The heterogeneous contamination of bystander firms. *Academy of Management Journal* 58(1): 169–194.

116. Bradley, M., Schipani, C. A., Sundaram, A. K., & Walsh, J.P. (1999). The purposes and accountability of the corporation in contemporary society: Corporate governance at a crossroads. *Law and Contemporary Problems* 62(3): 9–86.

117. Bell, R. G., Filatotchev, I., & Aguilera, R. V. (2014). Corporate governance and investors' perceptions of foreign IPO value: An institutional perspective. *Academy of Management Journal* 57(1): 301–320.

118. Certo, S. T., Daily, C. M., & Dalton, D. R. (2001). Signaling firm value through board structure: An investigation of initial public offerings. *Entrepreneurship Theory and Practice* 26(2): 33–50. Deutsch, Y., & Ross, T. W. (2003). You are known by the directors you keep: Reputable directors as a signaling mechanism for young firms. *Management Science* 49(8): 1003–1017.

119. Suchman, M. C. (1995). Managing legitimacy: Strategic and institutional approaches. *Academy of Management Review* 20(3): 571–610.

120. Potter, E. H. (2004). Branding Canada: The renaissance of Canada's commercial diplomacy. *International Studies Perspectives* 5(1): 55–60.

121. Gertz, G. (2018). Commercial diplomacy and political risk. *International Studies Quarterly* 62(1): 94–107.

122. Han, X. (2020). Risk management, legitimacy, and the overseas subsidiary performance of emerging market MNEs. *International Business Review*: 101732.

123. Kang, C., Jakes, L., Swanson, A., & McCabe, D. (2020). TikTok enlists army of lobbyists as suspicions over China ties grow. *New York Times*. July 15. www.nytimes.com/2020/07/15/technology/tiktok-washington-lobbyist.html.

124. Puck, J. F., Rogers, H., & Mohr, A. T. (2013). Flying under the radar: Foreign firm visibility and the efficacy of political strategies in emerging economies. *International Business Review* 22(6): 1021–1033.

125. Nartey, L. J., Henisz, W.J., & Dorobantu, S. (2018). Status climbing vs. bridging: Multinational stakeholder engagement strategies. *Strategy Science* 3(2): 367–392.

126. Hornaday, A. (2017). "The Great Wall," Matt Damon and Hollywood's delicate dance with China. *Washington Post*. February 16. www.washingtonpost.com/lifestyle/style/the-great-wall-matt-damon-and-hollywoods-delicate-dance-with-china/2017/02/16/ddac0b7e-f464-11e6-8d72-263470bf0401_story.html.

127. Darendeli, I. S., & Hill, T. (2016). Uncovering the complex relationships between political risk and MNE firm legitimacy: Insights from Libya. *Journal of International Business Studies* 47(1): 68–92.

128. Han, X. (2020). Risk management, legitimacy, and the overseas subsidiary performance of emerging market MNEs. *International Business Review*: https://doi.org/10.1016/j.ibusrev.2020.101732.

129. Stevens, C. E., Xie. E., & Peng, M. W. (2016). Toward a legitimacy-based view of political risk: The case of Google and Yahoo in China. *Strategic Management Journal* 37(5): 945–963.

Governance Actors and Stakeholder Strategy

Employees represent a firm's most important asset and a key source of competitive advantage. Treating employees well leads to higher worker commitment and generally promotes organizational innovation. Yet, employee-related investments, such as workplace training and well-being programs, may not generate immediate financial returns. For this reason, employees' interests can be compromised when firms become the target of financially driven activist investors, who often push for organizational restructuring and a reduction of "unnecessary" spending with the goal of boosting short-term financial returns. Beyond activists, a headquarters system of "management by the numbers," or an internal control mechanism that emphasizes financial control over divisions even while headquarters managers have limited knowledge about the divisions' internal workings, also increases corporate wrongdoing and workplace safety violations.

Facing performance pressure from activist shareholders and management by the numbers systems, executives may put more workload on employees and cut "unnecessary" workplace safety programs. After their firms were targeted by activist investors, former employees of Fortune 500 companies commented: "Very stressful . . . management wants to add work and try to cut costs, but injury costs add up," and "So overworked we all got sick or injured." Even if top managers do not reduce workplace safety investment, they may still spend considerable attention dealing with activist investors and dedicate less time and attention to addressing employee concerns such as workplace safety. For example, in 2015 former Mondolez International CEO Irene Rosenfeld estimated that dealing with just two activist investors required 25 percent of her time.

As the comments above reflect, ownership by activist shareholders and management by the numbers systems can increase a firm's workplace injury rate. Neglecting workplace safety may boost firm productivity and reduce costs in the short run, but may also harm a firm's reputation and give rise to unnecessary turnover of productive employees, which in turn adversely affects the firm's competitiveness. As shareholder activism is on the rise, managers face the increasingly difficult task of balancing the conflicting interests of activist shareholders and employees.

Sources: Shi, W., Xia, C., & Meyer-Doyle, P. (2020). Who bleeds when activists attack? Activist institutional ownership and employee safety. Working paper, University of Miami; Chen, G., Meyer-Doyle, P. & Shi. W. (in press). Hedge fund investor activism and human capital loss. *Strategic Management Journal*; Langley, M. (2015). Activists put Mondelez CEO Irene Rosenfeld on the spot. *Wall Street Journal*. October 15. www.wsj.com/articles/two-activists-put-one-ceo-on-the-spot-1450230598; Campbell, B. A., Coff, R., & Kryscynski, D. (2012). Rethinking sustained competitive advantage from human capital. *Academy of Management Review* 37 (3): 376–395; Hill, C. W. L., Kelley, P. C., Agle, B. R., Hitt, M. A., & Hoskisson, R. E. (1992). An empirical examination of the cause of corporate wrongdoing in the United States. *Human Relations* 45: 1055–1076.

Top managers today must manage relationships with stakeholders because a firm's ability to sustain its competitive advantages hinges on support from the business participants.[1] Because governance actors affect managerial decisions, managers must take actions to leverage both governance actors and stakeholders by designing a successful *stakeholder strategy*. This strategy refers to an action plan to invest in and engage nonshareholder stakeholders, including employees, suppliers, customers, partners, and communities, to achieve strategic goals.

Since the *New York Times* published an essay by economist Milton Friedman titled "The Social Responsibility of Business Is to Increase Its Profits" in 1970, the United States business community has espoused the shareholder primacy model with focus on maximizing financial returns for shareholders. In 2019, however, nearly 200 CEOs from major US companies signed a "Business Roundtable" statement that asserts that the purpose of a corporation is to fulfill a "fundamental commitment to *all* of our stakeholders," a sign that the stakeholder primacy model may be gaining ground.[2] The shareholder versus stakeholder primacy debate centers around the normative question whether firms have an obligation to promote nonshareholder stakeholders' interests over and above firms' economic and legal obligations.[3] Our discussion differs from the debates about the primacy models by focusing on stakeholder strategy as an investment that firm leaders can make in stakeholders to achieve competitive advantages. If a firm's competitive advantage can be attributable to its investment in stakeholders, we can say that the firm enjoys a *stakeholder advantage*. We will explain why stakeholder investment can give rise to stakeholder advantage and look at the different types of stakeholder strategies. We will also consider the influence of various governance actors and the ways managers may leverage the influencers in pursuit of an effective stakeholder strategy.

STAKEHOLDER STRATEGY

Similar to other types of strategies, a successful stakeholder strategy requires continuous resource commitment, which may advance stakeholder interests through various ways. A focus on employees, for instance, can lead to programs that promote worker health and welfare, as well as to employee ownership plans that help retain talent. To further the interests of customers, managers may devote resources to enhance product safety and design comprehensive privacy policies and data security management systems that ensure customer data security. Firm leaders can also enhance supplier relationships by treating the providers fairly and improving related practices. For communities, executives can allocate resources to protect natural environments and make philanthropic donations to local communities.

Although stakeholder strategy can be broadly defined as actions undertaken by firm managers to engage nonshareholder stakeholders with the goal of creating competitive advantages,[4] it can be classified into different types based on various criteria. In Figure 7.1, we categorize stakeholder strategy into four types according to the scope of stakeholder focus and degree of decoupling. As reflected on the horizontal axis, some firms focus on a select group of stakeholders while others devote attention to a broader range. A focused stakeholder strategy is due to the practical reality of limited resources and managerial attention. Firm managers pursuing a focused stakeholder strategy need to identify participant groups most critical to their competitiveness.[5] Three attributes can help identify the right stakeholder to focus on: (i) whether a stakeholder possesses power over the firm; (ii) whether a stakeholder has a legitimate claim perceived to be valid and well accepted; and (iii) whether a stakeholder has an urgent claim calling for an immediate response.[6] In contrast, managers pursuing a broad stakeholder strategy do not attempt to differentiate their investment since all the stakeholders can vitally affect the

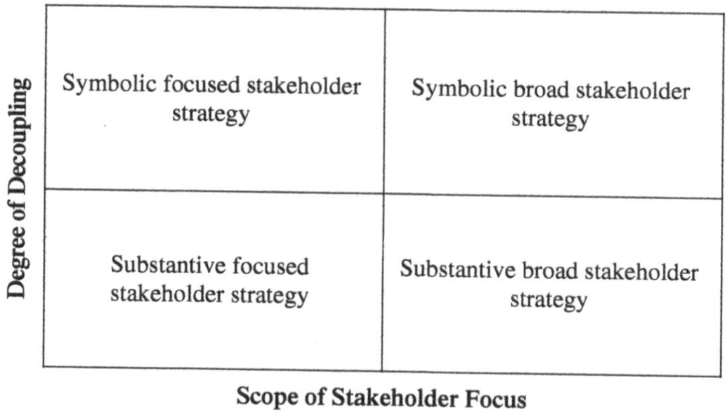

Symbolic focused stakeholder strategy	Symbolic broad stakeholder strategy
Substantive focused stakeholder strategy	Substantive broad stakeholder strategy

Degree of Decoupling

Scope of Stakeholder Focus

FIGURE 7.1   Different types of stakeholder strategy.

firm's competitiveness in the long run. A broad stakeholder strategy gives managers the discretion to respond to a comprehensive set of participants who can affect or be influenced by the firm.

The vertical dimension in Figure 7.1 refers to the degree of decoupling—the symbolic compliance with stakeholder demands but without making substantive changes.[7] Firm leaders pursue a symbolic stakeholder strategy by publicizing plans to invest in stakeholders but without undertaking specific actions, in essence decoupling actions from words. *Greenwashing,* or the act of overemphasizing positive aspects of a firm's environmental record with the goal of masking actual performance, represents a common symbolic stakeholder strategy. In contrast, executives pursuing a substantive stakeholder strategy do not decouple public statements from actual investment in stakeholders and are associated with a high level of authentic word–deed consistency. Based on these two dimensions, we have four types of stakeholder strategy: symbolic focused stakeholder strategy, symbolic broad stakeholder strategy, substantive focused stakeholder strategy, and substantive broad stakeholder strategy.

An effective stakeholder strategy potentially strengthens competitive advantages and creates a stakeholder advantage for four reasons. First, stakeholder investment can improve a firm's reputation. Companies with better treatment of stakeholders are perceived not only as more attractive business partners[8] but also more attractive employers to prospective workers.[9] In addition, customers are more likely to purchase and pay premium prices for products or services from firms that treat stakeholders fairly.[10] But whether stakeholder investment can enhance a company's reputation hinges on the visibility of such investment to existing and prospective participants.[11] Companies can raise external party awareness of their attention and investment through advertising or media coverage.[12] One type of investment that attracts significant attention from the media and elicits positive stakeholder reaction is philanthropic donations.[13] For example, the JDB Group, an unlisted manufacturer of a popular soft drink in China, announced that it would donate 100 million RMB after the 2008 Wenchuan earthquake in China, and this resulted in a sharp increase in sales.[14]

If leadership seeks to boost the firm's reputation in the short term, managers may pursue a symbolic stakeholder theory—making statements without necessarily following up with deeds. Yet, the approach carries significant risk in the long run as vested parties monitor a firm's information disclosure over time and may censor firms that have engaged in symbolic compliance.[15] For example, in 2013, British Petroleum, which touted itself as "Beyond Petroleum," received strong criticism from stakeholders for its poor, actual environmental record.[16] Thus, firm leaders aiming to build a sustainable reputation may need to consider a substantive stakeholder strategy, in which words and actions are more aligned.

Second, investment in stakeholders can trigger reciprocation.[17] When business participants experience benefits from corporate investments, they reciprocate by endorsing the firm, giving rise to more productive and enduring relationships.[18] For example, as employees benefit from practices that enable desired goals such as a safe work environment, fair pay, and professional development opportunities, they exhibit stronger commitment to firms[19] and prove more productive, even in the presence of monitoring mechanisms.[20] Local communities can also reciprocate to firms by granting a societal license to operate[21] and securing government procurement contracts.[22]

If company leaders aim for stakeholder reciprocation, they may consider a substantive focused stakeholder strategy. For example, Nike took a series of actions, such as appointing a director with rich labor practice expertise, creating a board-level corporate responsibility committee, and publishing standalone corporate responsibility reports to address labor issues in Nike's contract manufacturing factories.[23] Merely symbolically endorsing stakeholder practices without specific actions is unlikely to motivate participants to engage in social exchanges with firms. In addition, a focused stakeholder strategy can be more effective in encouraging stakeholder reciprocation than a broad one. Developing trust with the various business contributors takes time and continual, substantial investment. Yet managers, often constrained by limited resources and attention, are unlikely to build deep trust with all stakeholders. They may focus on building trust with key stakeholders, which helps build the perception that other primary stakeholders will be treated equally well.[24]

Third, in addition to the reputation-enhancement and stakeholder recip-rocation mechanisms, investment in stakeholders can help firm leaders reduce risks. Attention to the needs of vested parties may directly alleviate risks from violating stakeholders' rights and interests. Pollution prevention practices and employee health and safety programs, for example, can decrease the likelihood of litigation by communities and employees.[25] Also, stakeholder investment can indirectly reduce risk exposure through the closer relationships devel-oped with stakeholders, making them more willing to share information and enabling firm management to identify threats early.[26] In 2015, Volkswagen was found to have illegally installed software in its cars to evade standards for reducing air pollution. The scandal can be partly attributed to its authorita-tive corporate culture, which made employees hesitant to question and share bad news with their superiors.[27] If the firm had fostered a culture that encour-aged employees to speak out, its managers would have noticed the problem earlier and corrected it before facing a costly public scandal.[28]

Investment in a substantive focused stakeholder strategy can be most effective to achieve risk mitigation. To either reduce the risk of litigation or facilitate the early identification of threats, managers should install stake-holder management programs, since symbolic actions cannot deter accidents from taking place. Work safety protocols, for instance, could avoid worker-related accidents. Under a focused stakeholder strategy, managers scrutinize the sources of risk and make targeted investments into the stakeholders that expose firms to high risks. For instance, the reputation of Nike was severely damaged after revelation of unsafe workplace practices at its contract manu-facturing factories in the 1990s, and the company took a series of targeted actions discussed above. This kind of strategy does not require as much resource commitment as a broad one, and is perceived less often as a waste of firm resources by shareholders.[29]

Lastly, improving stakeholder treatment can help firm leaders identify new opportunities and spark innovation.[30] As noted, better stakeholder treat-ment can make the participants more willing to share information with firms, which can sow the seeds of innovative ideas. In addition, stakeholders are less likely to commit to innovation unless they are committed to firms in the long run, and this commitment can be enhanced by stakeholder investment.[31] Furthermore, the act itself of addressing stakeholders' interests requires the greater development of existing innovation capabilities, or triggers the cre-ation of new capabilities,[32] and allows for better product differentiation.[33] Danone, a multinational food products company, is a good case in point. Since the early 2000s, the firm has launched a series of societal projects in rural areas of developing countries, and such projects not only help local communities by improving local employee income but also allow the firm to develop capabilities in creating low-cost solutions that allow the company to reach a wider range of consumers.[34]

A substantive stakeholder strategy can be effective in enhancing a firm's innovation capabilities, whereas a symbolic one is unlikely to encourage stakeholders to disclose and share truthful information. Also, a broad strategy may be more effective than a focused one in facilitating stakeholders' information disclosure, since identifying which stakeholders can facilitate strong innovation capabilities before disclosure is challenging if not impossible. In other words, firm managers may consider a substantive broad stakeholder strategy if they attempt to cultivate strong innovation capabilities. Yet, treating stakeholders too well may create an inward focus on current product innovations and lead companies not to embrace new technological terrains. For example, research suggests that a strong emphasis on employee relations leads employees to become complacent, making it difficult to produce breakthrough innovation, although incremental innovation on the current portfolio of products does increase.[35]

We have introduced different types of stakeholder strategy and mechanisms that may help enhance a firm's competitive advantage. Now we turn our attention to the various governance actors and their influence on managers' pursuit of stakeholder strategy. To facilitate our discussion, we classify governance actors along two dimensions: relationship type (the *horizontal* axis) and strong emphasis on financial objectives (the *vertical* axis) in Figure 7.2. Governance actors differ in terms of relationship type with firms. Influencers such as board members and long-term shareholders (such as family shareholders) have an engaged relationship with firms, while others like transient institutional investors and hedge fund activists have a transactional relationship. Meanwhile, governance actors' emphasis on financial objectives also determines their influence on stakeholder-related decisions. Compared with transient institutional investors with a strong emphasis on financial returns, socially responsible ones seek to consider both financial returns and social and environmental causes when making investment decisions. Along these two dimensions, as depicted in Figure 7.2, governance actors exert different influences on firms' stakeholder strategy choices.

ENGAGED GOVERNANCE ACTORS WITH A STRONG EMPHASIS ON FINANCIAL OBJECTIVES

Quadrant I of Figure 7.2 describes governance actors that are strongly focused on financial goals and at the same time pursue an engaged relationship with firms. We will look specifically at long-term financial investors and suppliers.

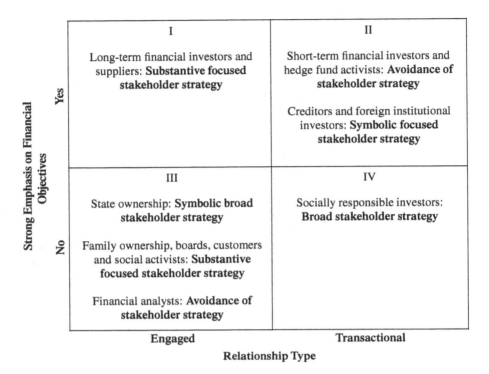

FIGURE 7.2 Governance actors and stakeholder strategy.

Long-Term Financial Investors

As discussed in Chapter 2, given their lasting investment horizon, long-term financial investors are motivated to develop an engaged relationship with firms and influence managerial decisions through direct dialogues. Long-term financial investors can lead managers to pursue a stakeholder strategy because the patient capital provided by such investors enables the company leaders to focus on long-term competitiveness, which can be created through treating stakeholders well. Research suggests that ownership by pension funds, a type of long-term financial investor, is positively associated with a firm's corporate social performance.[36]

Long-term financial investors may not only motivate executives to pay attention to corporate social performance but also affect the type of stakeholder strategy adopted. Although a symbolic stakeholder strategy may enhance a firm's reputation in the short run, it cannot mitigate risks and sharpen innovation capability nor create stakeholder reciprocation—all elements of long-term value. Since these investors focus on reaping financial returns over time, they will not support resource allocation to a symbolic stakeholder strategy. The ultimate focus of long-term investors is to generate financial returns from their investment, hence also steering them away from broad stakeholder investments that would allocate resources to a wide range of stakeholders and crowd out resources available for distribution to shareholders. These investors consequently pressure managers to focus only on the stakeholders most critical to firm competitiveness and to pursue a substantive focused stakeholder strategy.

Suppliers

A firm's suppliers also belong to Quadrant I of Figure 7.2. Suppliers often develop an engaged relationship with customer firms through supplier contracts or customer-specific investments. When suppliers have strong bargaining power (e.g., in the presence of few suppliers), they can directly push customer firms to pursue a stakeholder strategy.[37] But even if individual supplier firms do not exert high bargaining power, they can engage in collective actions with other suppliers to influence customer firms' attention to stakeholders. For example, although car manufacturers rolled back standards dating from the Obama administration that mandate a deep cut in auto emissions after the election of Donald Trump, auto suppliers urged automakers to maintain their commitment to green vehicles. In a joint statement issued by five auto part groups in 2018, the suppliers stated that it was "in the nation's best interest" that US automakers continue to develop and manufacture "the cleanest and most efficient vehicles in the world."[38] Auto part companies push for cleaner vehicle standards because tougher emissions rules spur automakers to equip their vehicles with new, more efficient technologies, which can benefit the parts manufacturers with new business opportunities and likely better profit margins.

Suppliers can lead firms to pursue a substantive focused stakeholder strategy. As the providers tend to develop a long-term relationship with customer firms, they will prefer the more beneficial approach for long-term horizons, which occurs under a substantive strategy. In addition, given that most suppliers make profits by supplying raw materials or parts, these suppliers lack the motivation to push customer firms to invest in stakeholders that cannot directly benefit themselves. In the example we discussed above, auto suppliers are mainly interested in promoting a focus on the environment because automakers' investment in environment-friendly vehicles can create new business opportunities and profit for these suppliers.

TRANSACTIONAL GOVERNANCE ACTORS WITH A STRONG EMPHASIS ON FINANCIAL OBJECTIVES

Quadrant II of Figure 7.2 refers to governance actors that have a transactional relationship with firms and have a strong emphasis on financial objectives, including short-term financial investors, hedge fund activists, creditors, and foreign institutional investors.

Short-Term Financial Investors

Short-term institutional financial investors such as banks and mutual funds that pursue a short-term investment horizon and focus solely on financial returns may not benefit from portfolio firms' stakeholder investments, since payoffs take a long period to materialize. This scenario is similar to the findings in diversification strategy research in which diversified firms that emphasize financial control weaken the relationship between diversification and stakeholder investment (see Chapter 3).[39] In addition, resources allocated to improving stakeholder relationships may reduce firms' dividend payments to shareholders. A high level of ownership by short-term financial investors may therefore constrain managers from pursuing a stakeholder strategy.[40]

Yet, short-term financial investors will not entirely oppose investment in stakeholders. If announcements of stakeholder investment can enhance a firm's short-term reputation and trigger positive stock market reactions, these investors may support a symbolic stakeholder strategy. Given that investment in some stakeholders, such as communities and environmentalists, may attract attention from the media and boost firm reputation, top managers, to satisfy short-term financial investors, may prioritize representational investment in these stakeholders. In other words, ownership by short-term institutional investors can lead managers to pursue a symbolic focused stakeholder strategy.

Hedge Fund Activists

Unlike short-term financial investors, hedge fund activists do not attempt to reap financial profits through opportunistic trading given their substantial holdings in targeted firms. Therefore, these activist investors will not push firm managers to pursue a symbolic stakeholder strategy with the goal of enhancing the company's short-term reputation. However, hedge fund activists nevertheless motivate managers to promote the short-term interests of shareholders and avoid stakeholder investment, even while they promote themselves as strong proponents of "shareholder democracy" and "don the mantle of the shareholders' champion and accuse the target company's board and management of subpar corporate governance."[41] One hedge fund manager commented in an interview, "Of course I would be glad to be ESG [environmental-social-governance] conscious and responsible, but if that means I'm going to underperform, I'm not going to do it."[42] As the comment implies, hedge fund activists focus mainly on financial returns rather than on the interests of other stakeholders.

Although investment in stakeholders may enhance a firm's long-run competitiveness, managers under the pressure of hedge fund activists may eschew a strategy attending to other business participants. Research suggests that firm executives reduce investment in stakeholder initiatives after being targeted by hedge fund activists.[43] The activists can also indirectly harm the interests of stakeholders by pushing firms to focus on cost cutting and efficiency improvement. Restructuring activities initiated by hedge fund activists can lead to layoffs and stagnation in work hours and wages, despite an increase in labor productivity.[44] Given the disruption and uncertainty that activist influence can trigger, capable employees may choose to leave their employers after being targeted by hedge fund activists, resulting in human capital loss.[45]

Creditors

As creditors, banks lend to firms with the goal of supporting their business growth. Because irresponsible treatment of stakeholders can represent a type of business risk, creditors call for firms to invest in stakeholders. The Commonwealth Bank of Australia stated in its annual report that "[t]he Bank and its controlled entities are not subject to any particular or significant environmental regulation under a law of the Commonwealth or of a State or Territory, but can incur environmental liabilities as a lender. The Bank has developed credit policies to ensure this is managed appropriately."[46] Bank JPMorgan Chase & Co integrates clients' environmental and social performance in its due diligence to reduce its risks.[47] Due to creditors' concerns, top managers may make investments in stakeholders to reduce the cost of debt.[48]

But because of information asymmetry between firms and creditors, the creditors may not be aware of firm investment into stakeholder interests unless management discloses the information.[49] This condition can motivate managers to pursue a symbolic stakeholder strategy. Also, as investment in some stakeholders may be more visible to creditors than others, executives will pursue a focused stakeholder strategy to target the right groups. Furthermore, research finds that firms that pursue public debt (bonds) versus private debt (banks) are more likely to pursue stakeholder investment disclosure.[50] Research also suggests that only corporate investment in green environmental causes may help reduce the cost of debt because these efforts are more observable to creditors.[51] Overall, creditors can lead firm leaders to pursue a symbolic focused stakeholder strategy.

Foreign Institutional Investors

Most foreign institutional investors are financial investors with the goal of reaping financial returns by investing in foreign firms (see Box 7.2). Since these investors may find it difficult to build relationships with foreign portfolio

BOX 7.2　Strategic Governance Highlight: Stakeholder Strategy across Countries

The role of stakeholder strategy in creating competitive advantages varies across countries with distinct institutions. Firms are embedded in different country institutions and the variances in the institutional systems can shape leadership's attention to stakeholders. For example, Japanese automakers Daihatsu and Kawasaki have considerably lower stakeholder performance than German automakers Daimler and BMW, although these firms all operate in the same industry. Research suggests that company leaders allocate less attention to stakeholders when they are in countries with higher levels of competition, higher levels of shareholder protection, lower levels of corruption, more prevalent labor unions, and lower availability of trained and skilled human capital. Perhaps one of the reasons for the difference between the auto companies in Japan and Germany is that there is stronger auto industry competition in Japan because there are so many producers.

The importance of stakeholder strategy varies across countries according to two types of capitalism: liberal market economies (LMEs) and coordinated market economies (CMEs). LMEs such as the United States, Canada, and the United Kingdom feature market-oriented financial systems, dynamic labor markets, and a focus on impersonal market transactions. CMEs are characterized by bank or state financing, rigid labor regulations that safeguard employees, and personal transactions taking place in existing firm networks. Japan, Norway, Germany, and even China would be examples of CME countries because of the importance of bank ownership (and state ownership, in the case of China). Since owners are the key stakeholders in LMEs, most of them will support stakeholder investment that can directly enhance firm value in the short run. In contrast, in CMEs, owners need to consider the interests of a broader set of stakeholders.

If the goal in a stakeholder strategy is to encourage stakeholder reciprocation, managers in LMEs will find more effective results in placing focus on business participants than will counterparts in CMEs, who struggle to differentiate their stakeholder practices from competitors. However, if the goal in stakeholder strategy is to enhance reputation, managers in CMEs will reach more effective results from favorable stakeholder treatment because, in these economies, such actions form a critical element to a firm's legitimacy; those that violate stakeholder interests may face social censorship. In sum, managers who develop stakeholder strategy need to take a country's institutional environment into consideration.

Sources: Desender, K., & Epure, M. (2020). The pressure behind corporate social performance: Ownership and institutional configurations. *Global Strategy Journal*; Ioannou, I., & Serafeim, G. (2012). What drives corporate social performance? The role of nation-level institutions. *Journal of International Business Studies* 43: 834–864; Hall, P. A., & Soskice, D. (2003). Varieties of capitalism and institutional change: A response to three critics. *Comparative European Politics* 1: 241–250; Porter, M. E. (1990). *The Competitive Advantage of Nations*. London: The Macmillan Press.

firms due to geographic distance, they tend to have a transactional relationship with invested firms. Concerned with risks facing portfolio companies that they have limited ways of impacting, foreign institutional investors prefer portfolio firms to invest in stakeholders since this form of investment can mitigate business risks in the long run. In fact, a study based on a sample of firms from 41 countries[52] suggests that foreign institutional ownership is positively associated with firms' environmental and social performance. However, as financial investors, foreign institutional owners will be wary of managers potentially misusing firm resources by allocating substantial means to all stakeholders without differentiation, therefore it is likely that they will promote a focused stakeholder strategy.

ENGAGED GOVERNANCE ACTORS WITHOUT A STRONG EMPHASIS ON FINANCIAL OBJECTIVES

Not all governance actors are ultimately driven by a strong focus on financial returns. Quadrant III of Figure 7.2 captures governance actors that have an engaged relationship with firms but whose behaviors are not entirely driven by financial pursuits. Although state owners, family owners, corporate boards, and customers all belong to this quadrant, their influences on stakeholder strategy vary.

State Ownership

Governments of various levels pursue both financial and political goals through their ownership. In this sense, state owners are not entirely driven by the pursuit of financial goals. Motivated also by governments' strategic goals, state owners tend to have a long-term holding period. They can also directly appoint top managers and board members. For these reasons, state owners can be perceived as engaged owners. A high level of state ownership can motivate firm leaders to invest in stakeholders, since treating stakeholders well can enhance a firm's reputation and legitimacy, which represents a key concern for state owners.[53] In addition, governments often pressure executives to invest in stakeholders as part of an overall welfare agenda[54] and are less constrained by the necessary resources to invest in stakeholders. Hence, state-owned enterprises (SOEs) tend to have better environmental performance than private firms.[55]

In essence, high levels of government influence can lead managers of SOEs to allocate more effort and attention to meeting expectations of government by investing in stakeholders.[56] Yet, ownership by sovereign wealth funds (SWFs) may not necessarily motivate investment in stakeholders because SWFs, as passive investors, focus on preventing losses from their investment rather than pushing portfolio firms to seek ways to force value-creating changes.[57] Yet, this dynamic could be changing. Recently, a hedge fund activist was appointed as the CEO of Norges Bank Investment Management, an SWF that manages Norwegian oil funds, as more active management boosts investment returns and lays the foundation for interacting with companies.[58]

Top managers may pursue a symbolic broad stakeholder strategy in the presence of high state ownership. Although the state as an owner can promote investment into the various business participants, officials may not effectively monitor managers to ensure successful implementation of stakeholder practices. As a result, managers of SOEs may engage in symbolic management and decouple stakeholder program implementation from announcement. Meanwhile, the broad focus of the strategy occurs because SOEs may receive subsidies that allow for resources for a more generalized approach to stakeholder practices. Also, harming any stakeholders' interests can be detrimental to the legitimacy of the state; hence managers maintain a broad perspective toward stakeholder strategy.

Family Ownership

The strategic objectives of family owners are complex, incorporating both financial wealth and noneconomic objectives arising from socioemotioal attachment to their firms.[59] Therefore, family owners hold both financial and nonfinancial goals and tend to have an engaged relationship with family firms. High stakeholder performance can allow the family firm to receive the support from key participant groups and increase the firm's reputation and recognition.[60] Stakeholder support can be perceived as a potentially valuable pool of goodwill to be tapped if needed at a future time.[61] Given that family owners give priority to building and maintaining family control, these owners can lead firms to pursue a stakeholder strategy to cultivate strong ties with both internal stakeholders, like employees, and external ones, like suppliers and customers.[62] Interviews of family owners suggest that they focus on the next generation and are inclined to embrace strategies that put customers and employees first, as well as emphasize social responsibility.[63] Leaders of family firms not only allocate substantial resources to protect the environment,[64] but also focus on developing eco-innovation to safeguard their reputation.[65]

Family owners often have a significantly long investment horizon. They are hence less likely to pressure firm managers to develop stakeholder investment for the purpose of boosting short-term reputation. Nevertheless, to encourage stakeholder reciprocation and mitigate risk, managers of family firms may be compelled to choose a substantive stakeholder strategy. Yet, they may not focus on a broad range of stakeholders. Family owners often exhibit *family altruism*—the priority of family interests over those of other stakeholders.[66] This sense of altruism can constrain leaders of family firms from attending to broader stakeholder interests because doing so requires substantial resource commitment. In this manner, family ownership can lead to a substantive focused stakeholder strategy.

The Board of Directors

Board members have the responsibility of monitoring and advising top managers; hence they hold engaged relationships with the company decision makers. But top managers may also serve as directors to receive financial compensation, as well as to enhance their reputation and social recognition.[67] In this sense, boards do not have a strong emphasis on financial objectives. Managers are nevertheless influenced by their boards in distinct preferences for stakeholder investment based on the boards' differential characteristics. Large boards represent diverse interests, leading their firms toward usually better corporate social performance.[68] Meanwhile, because independent directors are highly concerned about their reputation and violation of stakeholder rights can be detrimental to their reputation, these directors may help ensure managerial compliance with a wider range of stakeholder responsibility, thereby increasing stakeholder investment.[69] However, if boards are dominated by managers who focus on short-term profits, the dynamic can lead to a decreased investment in stakeholders.[70] In contrast, boards with high demographic diversity and external connections can steer managers to invest more in stakeholders.[71] In some countries (e.g., Germany), stakeholders have their own representatives on boards (such as local government and labor representatives), which inevitably lead boards to invest in the various participant groups. Directors can also influence stakeholder investment through shaping executive compensation. For example, fixed pay structures based on retrospective short-term financial goals may discourage investment in stakeholders,[72] and a higher percentage of bonus payments may motivate top managers to focus on short-term performance and neglect stakeholder investment.[73]

Board members generally prefer that managers adopt a substantive focused stakeholder strategy. According to Equilar, the average tenure of directors in 2016 was 7.5 years for companies belonging to the S&P 500 index and 6.1 years for small-cap companies (the bottom two-thirds of the Russell 3000 index, as measured by revenues). Since directors have a long-term relationship with firms, they are less likely to pressure managers to pursue stakeholder investment solely for symbolic management. But although it is critical for directors to take stakeholder interests into consideration in decision-making, in many countries they have a fiduciary responsibility with shareholders rather than stakeholders. They then push managers to identify a firm's most important stakeholders and adopt a substantive focused stakeholder strategy.

Customers

Customer firms do not usually have direct financial interests in a supplier company but are motivated to foster an engaged relationship with the providers due to potential search costs of identifying new suppliers. In this manner, customers represent a governance actor that belongs in Quadrant III of Figure 7.2. As noted in Chapter 2, in customer–supplier dyads, the buyers often have more power over the providers than the other way around. This power arrangement enables customers to directly require their suppliers to invest in stakeholders. In fact, research suggests that socially responsible corporate customers can infuse similar socially responsible business behavior in suppliers.[74] For example, in 2018, Microsoft started to require its suppliers and contractors to provide at least 12 weeks of paid time off to new parents.[75]

Customers are deeply concerned about suppliers' treatment of stakeholders because the actions can affect their reputation. In 2019, Apple's supplier Foxconn violated a Chinese labor rule by using too many temporary staff in the world's largest iPhone factory, tarnishing Apple's reputation.[76] The relational nature between customers and suppliers leads the buyers to push their providers to pursue a substantive stakeholder strategy, which may benefit the providers in the long run. Yet customers are most likely to focus on stakeholders that are of significant concern to themselves. Thus, Apple pressured Foxconn to adopt a series of measures to improve its treatment of employees.

Financial Analysts

To make accurate evaluations and recommendations, financial analysts tend to develop an engaged relationship with leaders of the firms that they cover.[77] However, they do not have direct financial interests in their covered firms; therefore, their decisions are not driven directly by financial objectives. Yet anecdotal evidence suggests that financial analysts do not regard stakeholder investment as a value-enhancing activity. A study by the United Nations Environment Program,[78] which conducts in-depth interviews with analysts from many countries, concludes, "Young analysts appear unconvinced over the materiality of most environmental, social, and governance issues to business." In other words, analysts may perceive investment in stakeholders as a misuse of firm resources and can lead firm managers to refrain from investing in the various vested parties. Faced with the pressure to meet analyst expectations, managers often sacrifice long-term economic value and refrain from investment in stakeholders that cannot generate immediate payoffs. This effect may explain why a reduction in analyst coverage can lead to an increase in firms' investment in stakeholders.[79]

Although analysts generally do not perceive stakeholder investment positively, their attitude has been changing over time. In the early 1990s, analysts issued more pessimistic recommendations for firms with high corporate performance ratings. However, analysts progressively assess these firms more optimistically by issuing more positive recommendations.[80] Under the changing social trends, firm managers may consider adopting a symbolic focused stakeholder strategy to encourage favorable recommendations from financial analysts. Symbolic stakeholder investment does not require substantial firm commitment and can free up resources for other investment projects, which can bear a more direct relationship with a firm's competitive advantages. In addition, executives may focus on investing in stakeholders that are most visible to financial analysts.

Social Activists

Social activists refer to individuals or organizations that engage in actions to bring about social change and attempt to find ways to end social injustice and create strong communities promoting economic, social, and psychological health. Social activists are not only taking on government policies but also putting companies in the spotlight. Starbucks, for example, experienced an unwanted, nationwide "Starbucks Appreciation Day" in August 2013, featuring visits from visibly armed gun owners supporting Starbucks' stance on "open carry"—a position the company subsequently reversed because of the public's and employees' response to the event. In 2013, Applebee faced an online social movement in support of a restaurant hostess who was fired after posting a nontipping customer's bill, which ultimately accumulated thousands of negative posts toward the company on social media. In 2014, the CEO of Mozilla was forced to step down after his prior financial support for California's Proposition 8, banning same-sex marriage, instigated protests inside and outside of the company. Given the rising power of social activists, company leaders need to constantly monitor potential risks from activist actions.

The activists often focus on a specific issue. In 2018, thousands walked out at Google over executives' handling of sexual harassment claims. In 2019, it was reported that over 4,200 Amazon employees had called on leadership to rethink how to address and contribute to fighting global warming and taking specific steps to "reduce [the company's] carbon footprint across its vast operations, not make piecemeal or vague announcements."[81] These employees also used the stock they receive as compensation to file a resolution to be voted on by investors during their annual meeting. As social activists closely monitor specific actions undertaken by executives to address stakeholder concerns, a symbolic stakeholder strategy may backfire. Instead, social activists may lead firm executives to pursue a substantive focused stakeholder strategy that produces more tangible results.

TRANSACTIONAL GOVERNANCE ACTORS WITHOUT A STRONG EMPHASIS ON FINANCIAL OBJECTIVES

Quadrant IV of Figure 7.2 captures governance actors that do not have a strong focus on financial returns and have a transactional relationship with firms. Our discussion focuses on socially responsible investing (SRI), which refers to an investment strategy that seeks to consider both financial returns and social and environmental good to bring about social change regarded as positive by proponents. Socially responsible investors promote corporate practices that enhance environmental and consumer rights protection, racial and gender diversity, and human rights. Some SRI investors avoid companies in businesses perceived to have negative social effects (such as alcohol, tobacco, gambling, fossil fuel production, or the military). This kind of investor pays particular attention to environmental, social, and governance (ESG) issues, usually devoting much attention to these issues at the stage of portfolio screening. They do not, however, appear to develop a relational relationship with firms and at times may be considered as transactional governance actors.

According to a 2017 McKinsey report, more than a quarter of assets under management are now invested with the thesis that ESG can influence a company's financial performance.[82] An increasing number of institutional investors subscribe to the United Nations' Principles for Responsible Investment, and 84 percent of millennial investors, who are set to inherit $30 trillion, report that ESG performance is important, according to the Institute of Sustainable Investing at Morgan Stanley.[83] Under such a context, firm leaders cannot afford to disappoint investor expectations with respect to industry standards for ESG performance if they want to access these rapidly growing pools of capital.

Since SRI investors focus on corporate social performance, a high level of ownership by SRI investors can encourage firm managers to attend to stakeholder relationships. As SRI carries a broad focus on stakeholder issues, the presence of SRI governance actors will encourage company executives to focus on a wide spectrum of stakeholders. In addition, given that SRI investors are highly attentive to stakeholder programs and practices, firms may engage in symbolic stakeholder investment to attract such investors.

LEVERAGE GOVERNANCE ACTORS TO PURSUE AN EFFECTIVE STAKEHOLDER STRATEGY

In an environment impacted by different governance actors requiring close evaluation for the best choice of stakeholder strategy, managers must be capable of leveraging the strengths of these influencers to enable the successful implementation of the chosen strategy. We have discussed the different types of stakeholder strategy and how governance actors affect the pursuit of the various choices. We now present two approaches that executives can use to manage governance pressures: evaluate and engage, and proactive disclosure and engagement (see Figure 7.3). As directors of corporate boards play a key role in establishing stakeholder strategy, we will also discuss key issues that board members must consider to help design and support the right strategy.

Strong Financial Emphasis	Relational Type	Example	Strategy
Yes	Transactional	Hedge fund activists	Evaluation and engagement
Yes	Engaged	Long-term shareholders	Evaluation and engagement
No	Transactional	Socially responsible investors	Proactive disclosure and engagement
No	Engaged	Financial analysts and social activists	Proactive disclosure and engagement

FIGURE 7.3 Leveraging governance actors in designing stakeholder strategy.

Evaluation and Engagement

Governance actors focused on the short term, such as hedge fund activists, seek to reap financial returns in a brief period of time. Due to performance pressure from these activists, executives may neglect the interests of stakeholders, which may prove detrimental to a firm's long-term competitiveness. Not attending to the interests of employees, for instance, can cause the loss of key talent to competitors. Similarly, neglecting suppliers' stakeholder practices can end up harming a firm's reputation.

Although performance pressure from hedge fund activists may lead managers to neglect stakeholders, we do not imply that the activists oppose corporate investment in key stakeholders. For example, in January 2017, JANA Partners, a hedge fund activist, and the California State Teachers' Retirement System, a public pension fund, send a letter to Apple's board of directors, stating, "We believe there is a clear need for Apple to offer parents more choices and tools to help them ensure that young consumers are using your products in an optimal manner."[84] The concern of hedge fund activists lies in whether executives misuse firm resources for their own affinities, like making philanthropic donations to foundations that meet their own preferences.[85] In the face of intensive scrutiny from hedge fund activists, executives need to evaluate which stakeholders are crucial to the firms' competitiveness and reduce investment in stakeholders that the hedge fund activists might perceive as a waste of firm resources. In other words, eliminating nonessential stakeholder programs can help avoid intervention by these activists.

Besides evaluating existing stakeholder programs, executives may engage with hedge fund activists when developing stakeholder strategy. Some hedge fund activists are beginning to pay attention to environmental and social issues. For example, Clifton S. Robbins, an activist investor, told his investors that he would urge company leaders to devote more attention to environmental and social issues such as climate change, diversity, and employee well-being programs because better stakeholder treatment can reduce the risks that portfolio firms face.[86] Elliott Management, known for waging campaigns for share buybacks and executive change, is now joining in the wave of socially responsible investing. In a public letter to Evergy, Elliott asked the utility company to consider reducing its carbon footprint. Jeff Ubben, an activist known for nudging companies to focus on their core businesses, has bought into BP as a vote of confidence in the British oil giant's recent plan to reduce its carbon emissions.[87] As hedge fund activists start to realize the worth of improving stakeholder treatment for value creation, executives may engage such investors to evaluate which stakeholders should be prioritized when mapping out a focused stakeholder strategy. Engagement should focus on how stakeholder investment can complement creating value for shareholders.

Evaluation and engagement during the design of a stakeholder strategy can also be used to leverage engaged and financially driven governance actors (see the example of Unilever in Chapter 9). Although long-term shareholders support firms' investments in stakeholders, they are also concerned about potential misuse of firm resources to advance managers' personal interests. As with short-term investors, managers of firms with a high level of ownership by long-term shareholders should evaluate all stakeholder programs and terminate the ones that cannot contribute to a firm's competitiveness. If managers allocate resources to a variety of stakeholders without creating differentiation, the action can send a signal to long-term shareholders of poor resource allocation. Executives can alleviate this concern by developing clear evaluation criteria and communicating such criteria to shareholders.

Importantly, executives should also engage with long-term shareholders in formulating stakeholder strategy. Through their portfolio holdings in other companies, these shareholders may have developed unique insights into what stakeholder programs and investment can be most effective in enhancing a firm's reputation, reducing risks, and motivating business participants. Frequent communication with long-term shareholders regarding the firms' investment in stakeholders, as well as to receive shareholder ideas for implementation, helps establish fruitful executive–shareholder engagements that allow for a successful stakeholder strategy.

PROACTIVE DISCLOSURE AND ENGAGEMENT

An effective strategy for managing socially responsible investors entails proactive disclosures. Most socially responsible investors are passive investors that evaluate firms' ESG performance prior to making investment, an assessment process known as negative screening. These investors use negative screening as a critical tool to constrain risks and exclude companies from a portfolio based on their performance with respect to ESG factors.[88] To alleviate investors' concerns regarding ESG risks, firm executives need to develop ESG standards through establishing a board-level corporate responsibility committee such as Nike and communicate how they are meeting such standards by proactively issuing ESG reports.

Some socially responsible investors believe that good ESG performance can generate long-term financial returns and consider ESG factors in their fundamental analyses. These investors pursue a positive screening strategy with the goal of identifying firms with the best social performance. For instance, the investments by Third Swedish National Pension Fund in green bonds doubled in 2016 to reduce the fund's carbon footprint with the belief that a portfolio

BOX 7.3 Strategic Governance Highlight: CEO Activism

CEOs are generally reluctant to publicly take a position on controversial social and environmental issues because doing so could turn away consumers who have a different position. Yet, faced with growing pressure from employees, CEOs are increasingly engaged in activism. CEO activism takes place when corporate leaders speak out on environmental and social issues not directly pertaining to their company's core business. In the last decade, the business community has experienced a significant increase in the cases of CEO activism. For example, Marc Benioff, CEO of Salesforce, and Tim Cook, CEO of Apple, expressed their support of LBTGT rights. Microsoft CEO Satya Nadella and Facebook CEO Mark Zuckerberg publicly communicated their stand on immigration. Kevin Plank, CEO of Under Armour, expressed his view on climate change and called for more actions to combat detrimental environmental changes; and Bob Iger, CEO of Walt Disney, called for swift actions to stop gun violence.

Although motivated by diverse interests, activist CEOs generally resort to two tactics: raising awareness and leveraging economic power. CEOs of large companies receive extensive media coverage and are highly visible public figures. Therefore, they can communicate and engage with stakeholders on issues that are of great concern to the business participants. In some cases, chief executive officers undertake collective actions to raise awareness. For instance, the CEOs of 14 large food companies, including General Mills, Coca-Cola, and Kellogg, called on governments to create a strong accord that would "meaningfully address the reality of climate change" in a letter cosigned by the company leaders. In addition to raising awareness, CEOs can impose pressure on political leaders by wielding their strong economic power to influence stakeholder interests more directly. In response to Indiana's Religious Freedom Restoration Act perceived to be anti-LGBTQ, the CEO of Angie's List dropped the plan to expand in Indiana and the CEO of Salesforce threatened to cancel all Salesforce employee travel to the state. Under pressure, state officials revised and approved a new version of the law, which forbids businesses from denying service to customers due to their sexual orientation.

Although public statements by CEOs can be perceived as toothless "cheap talk" by stakeholders and harm relationships with those who disagree, they can also trigger positive reactions from employees and customers who support the statements. When CEOs' public statements echo employees' values, the announcements can evoke strong employee identification with companies and motivate them to work harder. Some customers may likewise react positively to CEO activism and become more loyal buyers. Research suggests that CEOs of firms with important human capital are more likely to engage in activism. Also, the market responds positively to CEO activism news, implying that shareholders view activism by the chief executives constructively.

Sources: Gelle, D. (2021). Delta and Coca-Cola reverse course on Georgia voting law, stating "crystal clear" opposition. *New York Times.* www.nytimes.com, April 5; Mkrtchyan, A., Sandvik, J., & Zhu, V. (2020). CEO activism and firm value. Working paper; Chatterji, A. K., & Toffel, M. W. (2019). Assessing the impact of CEO activism. *Organization & Environment* 32(2): 159–185; Chatterji, A. K., & Toffel, M. W. (2018). The new CEO activists. *Harvard Business Review* 96(1): 78–89.

with high sustainability criteria can improve both the return and the risk profile of the fund.[89] Proactive disclosure of ESG activities can help executives gain the attention of socially responsible investors, who will consistently support the firm's goal of achieving competitive advantages through stakeholder investment. As noted in Box 7.3, CEO activism can be an effective way to gain the attention and support from ESG investors.

In addition to passive socially responsible investors, some active socially responsible investors attempt to enhance the ESG performance of portfolio firms by taking board seats or having direct dialogues with management. These investors may target firms with suboptimal ESG performance and acquire a stake attempting to improve their environmental and social governance. Sometimes, the active investors may collaborate with external parties to influence managers' ESG practices. Eumedion, a Dutch nonprofit foundation with a focus on enhancing corporate governance and environmental and social performance of listed companies, is an important collaborator for institutional investors to advance portfolio firms' ESG performance. Executives need to proactively engage with active socially responsible investors when designing a stakeholder strategy because these investors may be aware of the best ESG practices and help advance both financial and ESG performance.

As we have discussed, financial analysts may lead managers to avoid investment in social performance to protect resources from being diverted from shareholders and hence better meet their forecast expectations. Yet, though reducing investment in business participants may help executives improve short-term performance, the actions could turn away socially responsible investors and even increase firms' likelihood of being a target of active socially responsible investors. Also, financial analysts' attitudes have been changing over time and they are gradually acknowledging the importance of ESG investment to a firm's bottom line and to reduce risks that firms are exposed to.[90] Executives' proactive disclosure of stakeholder investments may help analysts develop more favorable recommendations as they gradually perceive these investments to reduce risks.[91]

Proactive engagement, including CEO activism, may likewise prove valuable to manage relationships with social activists. Whether internal (such as employees) or external (such as climate activists) to a firm, these activists have become a powerful force behind environmental and social company investments. Ignoring social activists during decision-making may be costly, as the governance actors can disrupt firms' normal operations and harm their reputation. Thus, CEOs can undertake activism activities (see Box 7.3) to proactively engage social activists through establishing a covert or overt coalition. For example, in 2007, Dow Chemical joined the US Climate Action Partnership—an alliance of major businesses and leading climate and environmental groups—to show the company's commitment to reducing greenhouse gas emissions.

Engagement includes the consideration of the nature of country institutions, as illuminated in Box 7.4, when designing a stakeholder strategy. Some strategies may not create differentiation for the firm, so that the strategy does not create competitive advantage. Thus, it is important to consider how the strategy not only conforms to the existing country institutions but also maximizes the ability of the strategy to signal the firm's distinctive approach to stakeholders—critical to creating competitive advantages.

RECOMMENDATIONS FOR BOARD MEMBERS

As executives must manage stakeholder relationships, boards should provide support and keen attention to the pressures from and impact of participants beyond shareholders. We highlight the importance of the role of boards in designing an effective stakeholder strategy as they carryout the task of securing their companies' long-term future. Many directors, however, often focus on short-term value maximization and disagree about the importance of paying attention to ESG issues. In fact, a survey of directors of more than 700 listed companies by PricewaterhouseCoopers in 2018 indicated that 56 percent of the directors believed that boards were overspending time on ESG issues.[92] We have the following three recommendations for board members to help enable a successful stakeholder strategy.

First, corporate board members need to be aware that stakeholders play an increasingly important role in shaping firm competitiveness and long-term

BOX 7.4   Strategic Governance Highlight: National Institutions and Stakeholder Engagement Strategy

As discussed in Box 7.2, national institutions can influence firms' investments in stakeholders, as well as the effectiveness of different stakeholder engagement strategies in creating competitive advantages and improving firm performance. Based on the degree of conformity and differentiation from firms' institutional environments, four types of stakeholder engagement strategy occur: (i) *complementary stakeholder strategy*, in which managers focus on exploiting complementarities between firm activities and dominant institutional forces with the goal of creating legitimacy; (ii) *substitutional stakeholder strategy*, in which managers are concerned with direct engagement with stakeholders that have not received significant attention from local institutions. For example, in countries with weak protection of labor rights, executives can differentiate their firms by using employee welfare programs; (iii) *minimalist stakeholder strategy*, in which managers do not engage in stakeholder activities beyond legal requirements; and (iv) *encompassing stakeholder strategy*, in which managers focus on activities complementing and substituting institutional contexts.

The effectiveness of these stakeholder strategies in influencing firm performance hinges on institutions. In countries with strong capital and weak labor institutions, such as in the United States, a substitutional stakeholder strategy has a stronger relation to firm performance, as such a strategy can help differentiate firms from competitors. The US has relatively weak institutions to protect labor rights and strong institutions to safeguard shareholder interests. Yet, some firms oppose pressure from activist investors to ensure that employee interests are not harmed. For example, 3M and Caterpillar have encouraged their shareholders to vote against governance proposals by activist investors that would reduce managers' ability to allocate resources to employees.

However, in countries holding both strong labor and capital institutions, including Germany and Finland, minimalist and encompassing engagement strategies can be most effective in promoting firm performance. Leaders of companies such as Volkswagen functioning in strong labor and capital institutions manage labor and capital pressures by offshoring their activities (minimalist stakeholder strategy). Konecranes, a Finnish company specialized in the manufacture and service of cranes and lifting equipment, adopted a series of measures to align the interests of employees and shareholders (encompassing stakeholder strategy). Yet, the pursuit of a complementary stakeholder strategy by attending to the particular stakeholder group represented by strong local institutions may not give rise to higher financial performance, since the strategy may not help managers differentiate their firms from competitors.

Effective stakeholder management requires executives to balance conformity and differentiation to achieve optimal distinctiveness. Conformity refers to the degree of adherence to country norm practices and differentiation pertains to the deviation from these practices. Firms are unlikely to be perceived differently by stakeholders if they only abide by country regulatory requirements. Differentiation from country stakeholder practices may help managers set their firm apart from other companies; however, they run the risk of backlash from shareholders who may perceive that managers have wasted firm resources in peripheral stakeholders.

Source: Gupta, K., Crilly, D., & Greckhamer, T. (2020). Stakeholder engagement strategies, national institutions, and firm performance: A configurational perspective. *Strategic Management Journal* 41(10): 1869–1900; Shi, W., & Veenstra, K. (2020). The moderating effect of cultural values on the relationship between corporate social performance and firm performance. *Journal of Business Ethics*: 1–19; Zhao, E. F., Fisher, G., Lounsbury, M., & Miller, D. (2017). Optimal distinctiveness: Broadening the interface between institutional theory and strategic management. *Strategic Management Journal* 38(1): 93–113.

financial performance. Entirely neglecting stakeholders' interests can cause a firm to not only become a target of social activists but also lose support from some socially responsible investors and possibly become the target of shareholder activism. Board diversity may help enhance board preparedness for a successful stakeholder strategy, as directors with different backgrounds can bring distinct insights and experiences to board discussions and identify firms' stakeholder threats and opportunities. In other words, a firm's business environment analysis needs to take into consideration both internal and external stakeholders. Directors may create specialized committees to scan the environment for social issues and exploit activism as a strategic opportunity. In 2008, Nike's two subcontractors in Honduras dismissed 1,800 employees without payment of about $2 million in severance. Although Nike was not legally responsible for the severance payments, the company was faced with pressure from universities and student groups across the United States to take care of their subcontractors' obligations. The company's corporate responsibility committee came up with an innovative arrangement whereby Nike created a workers' relief fund and provided support for vocational training and health coverage for the dismissed workers while the Honduran government would make the severance payments.[93] But being targeted by social activists requires firms to make substantial changes to their practices. It is best to avoid stakeholder violations in the first place by defensively scanning the environment.

Second, boards are responsible for approving capital allocation decisions. A successful stakeholder strategy requires directors to take stakeholders' responses into consideration. Directors need to carefully assess what reactions a firm's investment projects can trigger from the various stakeholders in addition to potential financial returns. This assessment will sometimes require board members to resist pressure from short-term shareholders, such as hedge fund activists who tend to focus on immediate financial returns. As noted in Box 7.4, in their analyses and resource allocation decisions, board members need to consider the firm's institutional environment to ensure that resource allocation to stakeholders not only conforms to the institutional environment but creates differentiation and increased competitive advantage.

Third, boards have the responsibility to establish the metrics used to compensate top managers. Motivating executives to take stakeholder strategy seriously requires board members to tie executive compensation to corporate social performance. The integration of corporate social performance criteria into executive compensation can lead to a greater long-term orientation, firm value, social and environmental initiatives, and green innovations.[94] Meanwhile, the metrics used to evaluate firms' social performance varies across firms and country institutional environments. For example, carbon missions may not be a target issue for a consulting company but will be critical for an oil company. In other words, firm leaders need to identify their primary stakeholders and how their institutional environments affect them. Airbnb, a vacation rental online marketplace, identifies guests, hosts, communities, shareholders, and employees as its stakeholders. It creates a "stakeholder committee" and ties executive bonuses to performance on the firm's social goals.[95] However, its stakeholder strategy may have to be adapted in different countries' institutional environments.

The successful management of stakeholder relationships is unlikely to take place in the absence of boards' commitment and participation. As policymakers and society start to pay growing attention to stakeholders' interests, directors need to work with top executives to ensure the formulation of an appropriate stakeholder strategy that can balance stakeholders' conflicting demands.

NOTES

1. Freeman, R. E., Harrison, J. S., & Wicks, A. C. (2007). *Managing for stakeholders: Survival, reputation, and success.* New Haven, Conn.: Yale University Press.

2. Harrison, J. S., Phillips, R. A., & Freeman, R. E. (2020). On the 2019 Business Roundtable "Statement on the Purpose of a Corporation." *Journal of Management* 46(7): 1223–1237.

3. Carroll, A. B. (1999). Corporate social responsibility: Evolution of a definitional construct. *Business & Society* 38(3): 268–295.

4. Hoskisson, R. E., Chirico, F., Zyung, J., & Gambeta, E. (2017). Managerial risk taking: A multitheoretical review and future research agenda. *Journal of Management* 43(1): 137–169.

5. Mitchell, R. K., Agle, B. R., & Wood, D. J. (1997). Toward a theory of stakeholder identification and salience: Defining the principle of who and what really counts. *Academy of Management Review* 22(4): 853–886.

6. Ibid., 853–886.

7. Meyer, J. W., & Rowan, B. (1977). Institutionalized organizations: Formal structure as myth and ceremony. *American Journal of Sociology* 83(2): 340–363.

8. Fombrun, C., & Shanley, M. (1990). What's in a name? Reputation building and corporate strategy. *Academy of Management Journal* 33(2): 233–258.

9. Turban, D. B., & Greening, D. W. (1997). Corporate social performance and organizational attractiveness to prospective employees. *Academy of Management Journal* 40(3): 658–672.

10. Homburg, C., Koschate, N., & Hoyer, W. D. (2005). Do satisfied customers really pay more? A study of the relationship between customer satisfaction and willingness to pay. *Journal of Marketing* 69(2): 84–96. Sen, S., & Bhattacharya, C. B. (2001). Does doing good always lead to doing better? Consumer reactions to corporate social responsibility. *Journal of Marketing Research* 38(2): 225–243.

11. Vishwanathan, P., van Oosterhout, H., Heugens, P. P., Duran, P., & Van Essen, M. (2020). Strategic CSR: A concept building meta–analysis. *Journal of Management Studies* 57(2): 314–350.

12. Deephouse, D. L., & Heugens, P. P. (2009). Linking social issues to organizational impact: The role of infomediaries and the infomediary process. *Journal of Business Ethics* 86(4): 541–553.

13. Wang, H. L., & Qian, C. L. (2011). Corporate philanthropy and corporate financial performance: The roles of stakeholder response and political access. *Academy of Management Journal* 54(6): 1159–1181.

14. Gao, F., Faff, R., & Navissi, F. (2012). Corporate philanthropy: Insights from the 2008 Wenchuan Earthquake in China. *Pacific-Basin Finance Journal* 20(3): 363–377.

15. Marquis, C., & Qian, C. (2013). Corporate social responsibility reporting in China: Symbol or substance? *Organization Science* 25(1): 127–148.

16. Lyon, T. P., & Maxwell, J. W. (2011). Greenwash: Corporate environmental disclosure under threat of audit. *Journal of Economics & Management Strategy* 20(1): 3–41.
17. Vishwanathan, van Oosterhout, Heugens, Duran, & Van Essen. Strategic CSR.
18. Bosse, D. A., & Coughlan, R. (2016). Stakeholder relationship bonds. *Journal of Management Studies* 53(7): 1197–1222.
19. El Akremi, A., Gond, J.-P., Swaen, V., De Roeck, K., & Igalens, J. (2018). How do employees perceive corporate responsibility? Development and validation of a multidimensional corporate stakeholder responsibility scale. *Journal of Management* 44(2): 619–657.
20. Jones, T. M. (1995). Instrumental stakeholder theory: A synthesis of ethics and economics. *Academy of Management Review* 20(2): 404–437.
21. Henisz, W. J., Dorobantu, S., & Nartey, L. J. (2014). Spinning gold: The financial returns to stakeholder engagement. *Strategic Management Journal* 35(12): 1727–1748.
22. Flammer, C. (2018). Competing for government procurement contracts: The role of corporate social responsibility. *Strategic Management Journal* 39(5): 1299–1324.
23. Paine, L. S. (2014). Sustainability in the boardroom. *Harvard Business Review* 92(7): 86–94.
24. Cording, M., Harrison, J. S., Hoskisson, R. E., & Jonsen, K. (2014). Walking the talk: A multistakeholder exploration of organizational authenticity, employee productivity, and post-merger performance. *Academy of Management Perspectives* 28(1): 38–56.
25. Vishwanathan, van Oosterhout, Heugens, Duran, & Van Essen. Strategic CSR.
26. Harrison, J. S., Bosse, D. A., & Phillips, R. A. (2010). Managing for stakeholders, stakeholder utility functions, and competitive advantage. *Strategic Management Journal* 31(1): 58–74.
27. Cremer, A., & Bergin, T. (2015). Fear and respect: VW's culture under Winterkorn. *Reuters, 10 October.*
28. Vishwanathan, van Oosterhout, Heugens, Duran, & Van Essen. Strategic CSR.
29. Harjoto, M. A., & Jo, H. (2011). Corporate governance and CSR nexus. *Journal of Business Ethics* 100(1): 45–67.
30. Harrison, Bosse, & Phillips. Managing for stakeholders, stakeholder utility functions, and competitive advantage.
31. Flammer, C., & Kacperczyk, A. (2015). The impact of stakeholder orientation on innovation: Evidence from a natural experiment. *Management Science* 62(7): 1982–2001.
32. Vishwanathan, van Oosterhout, Heugens, Duran, & Van Essen. Strategic CSR.
33. Hull, C. E., & Rothenberg, S. (2008). Firm performance: The interactions of corporate social performance with innovation and industry differentiation. *Strategic Management Journal* 29 (7): 781–789.

34. Humberg, K., & Braun, B. (2014). Social business and poverty alleviation: Lessons from Grameen Danone and Grameen Veolia. *Social Business*: 201–223: Springer.

35. Gambeta, E., Koka, B. R., & Hoskisson, R. E. (2019). Being too good for your own good: A stakeholder perspective on the differential effect of firm–employee relationships on innovation search. *Strategic Management Journal* 40(1): 108–126.

36. Johnson, R. A., & Greening, D. W. (1999). The effects of corporate governance and institutional ownership types on corporate social performance. *Academy of Management Journal* 42(5): 564–576. Neubaum, D. O., & Zahra, S. A. (2006). Institutional ownership and corporate social performance: The moderating effects of investment horizon, activism, and coordination. *Journal of Management* 32(1): 108–131.

37. Paranikas, P., Whiteford, G. P., Tevelson, B., & Belz, D. (2015). How to negotiate with powerful suppliers. *Harvard Business Review* 93(7): 90–96.

38. Tabuchi, H. (2018). Parts suppliers call for cleaner cars, splitting with their main customers: Automakers. *New York Times,* www.nytimes.com, March 1.

39. Kang, J. (2013). The relationship between corporate diversification and corporate social performance. *Strategic Management Journal* 34(1): 94–109.

40. Johnson, & Greening. The effects of corporate governance and institutional ownership types on corporate social performance; Neubaum, D. O., & Zahra, S. A. (2006). Institutional ownership and corporate social performance: The moderating effects of investment horizon, activism, and coordination. *Journal of Management* 32(1): 108–131.

41. Liekefett, K. H. (2018). *The hypocrisy of hedge fund activists*. Harvard Law School Forum on Corporate Governance and Financial Regulation, https://corpgov.law.harvard.edu. June 4.

42. DesJardine, M. R., & Durand, R. (2020). Disentangling the effects of hedge fund activism on firm financial and social performance. *Strategic Management Journal* 41(6): 1061.

43. Ibid., 1054–1082.

44. Brav, A., Jiang, W., & Kim, H. (2015). The real effects of hedge fund activism: Productivity, asset allocation, and labor outcomes. *Review of Financial Studies* 28(10): 2723–2769.

45. Chen, G., Meyer–Doyle, P., & Shi, W. (2020). Hedge fund investor activism and human capital loss. *Strategic Management Journal*, https://doi.org/10.1002/smj.3257.

46. Commonwealth Bank of Australia. (2004). Annual report. Sydney: Commonwealth Bank of Australia.

47. JPMorgan and Chase & Co. (2020). Environmental, Social & Governance Report. New York: JPMorgan Chase & Co.

48. Erragragui, E. (2018). Do creditors price firms' environmental, social and governance risks? *Research in International Business and Finance* 45: 197–207.

49. Chan, M. C., Watson, J., & Woodliff, D. (2014). Corporate governance quality and CSR disclosures. *Journal of Business Ethics* 125(1): 59–73.

50. Tan, W., Tsang, A., Wang, W., & Zhang, W. (2020). Corporate social responsibility (CSR) disclosure and the choice between bank debt and public debt. *Accounting Horizons*, 34(1): 151–173.

51. Erragragui. Do creditors price firms' environmental, social and governance risks?

52. Dyck, I., Lins, K., Roth, L., & Wagner, H. (2019). Do institutional investors drive corporate social responsibility? International evidence. *Journal of Financial Economics* 131(3): 693–714.

53. Roper, J., & Schoenberger-Orgad, M. (2011). State-owned enterprises: Issues of accountability and legitimacy. *Management Communication Quarterly* 25(4): 693–709.

54. Surroca, J., & Tribó, J. A. (2008). Managerial entrenchment and corporate social performance. *Journal of Business Finance & Accounting* 35(5–6): 748–789.

55. Chang, L., Li, W., & Lu, X. (2015). Government engagement, environmental policy, and environmental performance: Evidence from the most polluting Chinese listed firms. *Business Strategy and the Environment* 24(1): 1–19.

56. Bai, C.-E., Lu, J., & Tao, Z. (2006). The multitask theory of state enterprise reform: Empirical evidence from China. *American Economic Review* 96(2): 353–357.

57. Liang, H., & Renneboog, L. (2020). The global sustainability footprint of sovereign wealth funds. *Oxford Review of Economic Policy* 36(2): 380–426.

58. Steinberg, J. (2020). The world's largest sovereign wealth fund weighs a more active approach. *Wall Street Journal,* www.wsj.com, December 19.

59. Gómez-Mejía, L. R., Haynes, K. T., Núñez-Nickel, M., Jacobson, K. J., & Moyano-Fuentes, J. (2007). Socioemotional wealth and business risks in family-controlled firms: Evidence from Spanish olive oil mills. *Administrative Science Quarterly* 52(1): 106–137; Jiang, F., Shi, W., & Zheng, X. (2020). Board chairs and R&D investment: Evidence from Chinese family-controlled firms. *Journal of Business Research,* 112: 109–118.

60. Sirmon, D. G., & Hitt, M. A. (2003). Managing resources: linking unique resources, management, and wealth creation in family firms. *Entrepreneurship Theory and Practice* 27(4): 339–358.

61. Anderson, R. C., Mansi, S. A., & Reeb, D. M. (2003). Founding family ownership and the agency cost of debt. *Journal of Financial Economics* 68(2): 263–285.

62. Miller, D., Le Breton–Miller, I., & Scholnick, B. (2008). Stewardship vs. stagnation: An empirical comparison of small family and nonfamily businesses. *Journal of Management Studies* 45(1): 51–78.

63. Fernández-Aráoz, C., Iqbal, S., & Ritter, J. (2015). Leadership lessons from great family businesses. *Harvard Business Review* 93(4): 82–88.

64. Berrone, P., Cruz, C., Gomez-Mejia, L. R., & Larraza-Kintana, M. (2010). Socioemotional wealth and corporate responses to institutional pressures: Do family-controlled firms pollute less? *Administrative Science Quarterly* 55(1): 82–113.

65. Bammens, Y., & Hünermund, P. (2020). Nonfinancial considerations in eco-innovation decisions: The role of family ownership and reputation concerns. *Journal of Product Innovation Management* 37(5): 431–453.

66. Schulze, W. S., Lubatkin, M. H., & Dino, R. N. (2003). Toward a theory of agency and altruism in family firms. *Journal of Business Venturing* 18(4): 473–490.

67. Yermack, D. (2004). Remuneration, retention, and reputation incentives for outside directors. *Journal of Finance* 59(5): 2281–2308.

68. Kock, C. J., Santalo, J., & Diestre, L. (2012). Corporate governance and the environment: What type of governance creates greener companies? *Journal of Management Studies* 49(3): 492–514.

69. Luoma, P., & Goodstein, J. (1999). Stakeholders and corporate boards: Institutional influences on board composition and structure. *Academy of Management Journal* 42(5): 553–563.

70. Walls, J. L., & Hoffman, A. J. (2013). Exceptional boards: Environmental experience and positive deviance from institutional norms. *Journal of Organizational Behavior* 34(2): 253–271.

71. Ibid.

72. Berman, S. L., Wicks, A. C., Kotha, S., & Jones, T. M. (1999). Does stakeholder orientation matter? The relationship between stakeholder management models and firm financial performance. *Academy of Management Journal* 42(5): 488–506.

73. Stata, R., & Maidique, M. A. (1980). Bonus system for balanced strategy. *Harvard Business Review* 58(6): 156–163.

74. Dai, R., Liang, H., & Ng, L. (2020). Socially responsible corporate customers. *Journal of Financial Economics.*

75. Weber, L. (2018). Microsoft to require its suppliers, contractors to give paid family leave. *Wall Street Journal,* www.wsj.com, August 30.

76. Gurman, M. (2019). Apple, Foxconn broke a Chinese labor law to build latest iPhones. *Bloomberg,* www.bloomberg.com, September 8.

77. Soltes, E. (2014). Private interaction between firm management and sell-side analysts. *Journal of Accounting Research* 52(1): 245–272.

78. UNEP. (2004). *Generation lost: Young financial analysts and environmental, social and governance issues.* Geneva: UNEP Finance Initiative.

79. Qian, C., Lu, L. Y., & Yu, Y. (2019). Financial analyst coverage and corporate social performance: Evidence from natural experiments. *Strategic Management Journal* 40(13): 2271–2286.

80. Ioannou, I., & Serafeim, G. (2015). The impact of corporate social responsibility on investment recommendations: Analysts' perceptions and shifting institutional logics. *Strategic Management Journal* 36(7): 1053–1081.

81. Weise, K. (2019). Over 4,200 Amazon workers push for climate change action, including cutting ties to big oil. *New York Times,* www.nytimes.com, April 10.

82. Bernow, S., Klempner, B., & Magnin, C. (2017). *From 'why' to 'why not"; Sustainable investing as the new normal. McKinsey & Company,* www.mckinsey.com, October 25.

83. Ranawake, J. & Russo, I. (2019). Making sense of ESG investment capital. *International Financial Law Review,* December 23.

84. Eccles, R. G. (2018). Why an activist hedge fund cares whether Apple's devices are bad for kids. *Harvard Business Review*, January 16. https://hbr.org/2018/01/why-an-activist-hedge-fund-cares-whether-apples-devices-are-bad-for-kids.

85. Masulis, R. W., & Reza, S. W. (2014). Agency problems of corporate philanthropy. *Review of Financial Studies* 28(2): 592–636.

86. Benoit, D. (2017). Activist investor takes a page from Greenpeace, pushing companies for change. *Wall Street Journal*, www.wsj.com, March 19.

87. Driebusch, C. (2020). The next wave in shareholder activism: Socially responsible investing. *Wall Street Journal,* www.wsj.com, March 8.

88. Bernow, Klempner, & Magnin. *From 'why' to 'why not'.*

89. Ibid.

90. Hanson, D., Lyons, T., Bender, J., Bertocci, B., & Lamy, B. (2017). Analysts' roundtable on integrating ESG into investment decision-making. *Journal of Applied Corporate Finance* 29(2): 44–55.

91. Godfrey, P. C. (2005). The relationship between corporate philanthropy and shareholder wealth: A risk management perspective. *Academy of Management Review* 30(4): 777–798.

92. Eccles, R. G., Johnstone-Louis, M., Mayer, C., & Stroehle, J. C. (2020). The board's role in sustainability. *Harvard Business Review* 98(5): 48–51.

93. Paine. Sustainability in the boardroom.

94. Flammer, C., Hong, B., & Minor, D. (2019). Corporate governance and the rise of integrating corporate social responsibility criteria in executive compensation: Effectiveness and implications for firm outcomes. *Strategic Management Journal* 40(7): 1097–1122.

95. Stoll, J. D. (2020). Airbnb's new compensation plan asks shareholders to share with other stakeholders. *Wall Street Journal,* www.wsj.com, January 18.

CHAPTER 8

Governance Actors and Corporate Political Strategy

BOX 8.1   Strategic Governance Challenge: Corporate Governance and Corporate Political Activities

---

Corporate political activity (CPA), such as lobbying activities and political donations, provides important channels for company leaders to shape policies and create a favorable policy environment. CPA may also help firms gain government contracts and assistance. Although the COVID-19 pandemic has slowed down many businesses, the lobbying industry has not come to a pause. Instead, lobbyists have taken swift action to capitalize on the stimulus bills moving quickly through Congress. Some congressional aides have compared the lobbying blitz around the stimulus legislation to a gold rush.

Yet, despite the potential benefits that CPA can generate in the short and long terms, the activities may carry high risk. Discrepancies in corporate messaging, for example, may cause stakeholder concern. Walmart praises its employees for working during the pandemic, putting their health at risk, whereas it financed state attorneys general seeking to remove the Affordable Care Act that provides health insurance for millions of Americans during the crisis. AT&T espouses LGBTQ rights while it offered funds that supported local legislators who attempted to roll back these rights. Although company leaders have no control over how their political donations are spent in most cases, their firms' reputation can be put in peril when stakeholders perceive inconsistencies in their words and actions. Sometimes, top managers may use corporate funds for CPA to advance their personal interests such as gaining political positions after retirement. In other cases, managers may engage in illegal political activities including bribing officials to seek political favors, resulting in regulatory and civil penalties and sometimes criminal prosecution.

Given the potential risks and agency problems associated with CPA, shareholders are generally concerned about firm political spending and have called for the transparent disclosure of such spending. In January 2021, in the wake of a deadly riot against the Capitol, Congressman Andy Levin introduced the Transparency in Corporate Political Spending Act, which would reverse a law that prevents the Securities and Exchange Commission (SEC) from requiring companies to disclose their political spending. While CPA can potentially support favorable legislation and regulation, managers need to consider how to best allocate resources to political spending especially amid the rising power of shareholders and the causes that they support.

Sources: Levin introduces legislation promoting transparency in political spending. (2021). https:// andylevin.house.gov/media/press-releases/levin-introduces-legislation-promoting-transparency- political-spending; Sorkin, A. R. (2020). A company backs a cause. It funds a politician who doesn't. What gives? *New York Times*, July 21. https://www.nytimes.com/2020/07/21/busi- ness/dealbook/corporate-political-donations.html.; Vogel, K. P., Edmondson, C., & Drucker, J. (2020). Coronavirus stimulus package spurs a lobbying gold rush. *New York Times*, March 20. https://www.nytimes.com/2020/03/20/us/politics/coronavirus-stimulus-lobbying.html; Dahan, N. M., Hadani, M., & Schuler, D. A. (2013). The governance challenges of corporate political activ- ity. *Business & Society* 52(3): 365–387.

As the opening Strategic Governance Challenge (Box 8.1) suggests, governance actors may affect company leaders' pursuit of *corporate political strategy*, a strategic action plan to shape government policy in ways favorable to the firm.[1] Top managers must take actions that leverage the influence of the governance players to design a successful political strategy. In today's economy, sustained competitive advantages rely not only on addressing environment, social, and governance (ESG) concerns but also on managing relationships with govern- ments.[2] Governments, as an integral component of formal institutions, create laws and regulations by which companies need to abide. In turn, executives may use corporate political activity (CPA) to shape the laws and regulations, especially when a strong business rationale supports such activity. During the COVID-19 pandemic, for example, meat industry lobbyists, concerned about the shutting down of meatpacking plants by local health departments, con- vinced former President Trump to declare that the slaughtering and processing of beef, chicken, and pork represents an "essential business" and that federal agencies set the criteria for ensuring workers' safety.[3]

Governments may affect companies' bottom line directly because governing bodies can be important customers. In 2019, US federal agencies spent $6.9 trillion, according to USAspending.gov—a website managed by the Bureau of the Fiscal Service of the US Department of Treasury that tracks spending by government agencies. In the same year, China's government spent about 23.5 trillion yuan ($3.4 trillion), representing about 23 percent of its GDP.[4] Furthermore, governments can provide direct financial support such as through loans, tax relief, and cash grants to companies. Firms in some industries like agriculture also receive direct government subsidies in the form of cash payments and loans.

We will look at how corporate political activity can give rise to a firm's competitive advantages. For executives, the process includes pursuing different corporate political strategies while contending with the influence of governance actors. We will therefore discuss ways in which they may leverage the influencers to create a successful corporate political strategy.

CORPORATE POLITICAL STRATEGY

Company executives may manage relationships with government officials and shape policy environments through various ways. In the United States, companies represent important players in the political process using two primary forms of CPA:[5] lobbying and campaign contributions. Lobbying refers to communicating information to policymakers with the goal of influencing actions,[6] and campaign contributions usually occur through support of political action committees (PACs), or organizations that seek to influence policymakers, regulators, legislators, and election outcomes. In some countries, executives may build ties with governments by appointing directors who are former government officials[7] or by hosting visits by high-level officials.[8]

Although CPA potentially helps company managers further their long-term goals through creating a favorable policy and resource allocation environment, these activities bring risks as suggested by the examples in Box 8.1. PAC contributions, for instance, may foster a *quid pro quo* relationship in which company executives help enhance the electoral prospects of a candidate in exchange for acts that benefit the company's interests.[9] In some cases, top managers may use corporate resources to pursue CPA with the goal of advancing their own political preferences or personal interests.[10] Firm top managers might also engage in questionable gift-giving or money-giving activities, hire relatives of government officials, or pay officials honoraria for speaking as ways to build political connections. Also, under certain scenarios, CPA can adversely influence firm performance.[11] For instance, when executives with strong political ties depart the firm and join its competitor, the performance of the firm losing the executives can be harmed.

Company executives may pursue distinct corporate political strategies[12] that may be classified in multiple ways. For example, based on the level of participation, a firm's leadership can pursue CPA individually or collaboratively with other companies through trade associations to engage in collective actions.[13] We broadly classify corporate political strategy into four types, based on either an "approach" or "orientation" criterion (see Figure 8.1). Under approaches, a "relational" approach focuses on long-term and issue-spanning relationships whereas a "transactional" approach is more *ad hoc* and issue-specific.[14] In the second criterion, top managers pursuing a proactive orientation will actively inform government decision makers about the impact of potential legislation in attempts to reduce overly restrictive regulation over the firm. They will also work alongside or in trade associations to lobby, make campaign contributions, or engage in other activities to influence legislative and regulatory processes.[15] In contrast, companies adopting a reactive orientation will focus on tracking the development of legislation or regulation to ensure compliance when enacted. A proactive approach occurs as *buffering* actions focused on shaping public policy, whereas a reactive approach is focused on *bridging* actions directed at reducing information asymmetry between companies and governments.[16]

The two dimensions in Figure 8.1 allow for our classification into four types of CPA. *Engagement strategy* pertains to the pursuit of competitive advantages through adopting an engaged approach and a proactive orientation to CPA. Its opposite, *conformity strategy*, occurs when adopting a transactional approach and a reactive orientation. In addition, *opportunistic strategy* refers to a transactional approach and a proactive orientation, whereas

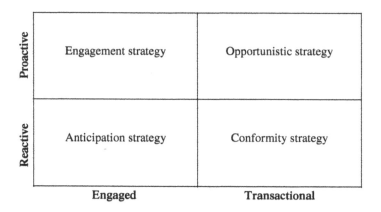

FIGURE 8.1 Types of corporate political strategy.

anticipation strategy takes place when a firm pursues an engaged approach and a reactive orientation. The corporate political strategy available may also hinge on the country in which the firm is headquartered. As shown in Box 8.2, as companies around the firm contend with different institutional environments, they may face unique risks and opportunities in managing political relationships.

Corporate political strategy potentially strengthens a company's competitive advantages and improves financial performance for several reasons. First, CPA can help secure government contracts or permits to operate, as well as provide a favorable competitive environment, which in turn enhances financial performance. The practice of lobbying executive branch agencies has been shown to effectively establish government contracts.[17] In 2001, the US Air Force began a procurement process to replace its aging refueling tankers. In 2011, it finally offered a contract with a value of $49 billion to Boeing. To gain the contract, Boeing increased its lobbying expenditures by over 82 percent in the three years leading up to the awarding of the contract, from $29 million between 2005 and 2007 to $53 million between 2008 and 2010.[18]

CPA can also complement a firm's competitive strategy. Walt Disney and other Hollywood studios have engaged in intensive CPA to prevent the spread of Section 230 abroad. Section 230 of the Communication Decency Act of 1996 holds the people who post content on social media platform providers such as Facebook and YouTube responsible for libel or other legal issues but does not hold platform providers responsible. In other words, Section 230 makes it nearly impossible to sue platform providers for posts by users, creating difficulty to enforce copyrights. For this reason, Disney executives strongly oppose the protection of platform providers and engaged in intensive lobbying activities to urge the Trump administration not to allow the Section 230 protection in a trade deal with Britain, which would make it difficult for film companies to enforce copyrights in Britain.[19] In June 2020, President Trump signed an executive order to strip legal protections for social media platforms from litigation over content posted by users on their sites.[20]

Second, CPA helps facilitate support from governments, especially in countries whose governments control substantial resources. In China, politically connected firms are significantly more likely to obtain subsidies than nonconnected firms.[21] Similarly, companies that have hosted visits by high-level officials tend to receive subsidiaries from these governments.[22] But such scenarios might also take place in companies from countries with more developed institutions. Moreover, firms that have spent more on lobbying have been found to gain larger proceeds from the disbursements of the antidumping duties to the injured firms.[23] In addition, CPA may assist firms to gain lucrative business opportunities. The Trump Administration accused the Chinese-owned

BOX 8.2   Strategic Governance Highlight: Corporate Political Activity around the World

Executives around the world may engage in varying forms of corporate political activity (CPA) due to differences in formal and informal institutions. In particular, the political system within which business and government agents interact can exert a strong influence on CPA. In fact, democratic and autocratic political systems may determine the value of CPA. In autocratic countries, as power is concentrated in the hands of an autocratic leader, firm managers need to engage in CPA that can connect them to the leader or people close to the leader. Yet, a change in autocratic regimes can turn CPAs into liabilities. In Indonesia, firms with strong connections with former President Suharto experienced a sharp drop in value after his resignation. In democratic countries like the United States and the United Kingdom, as change between political parties is common, top managers need to balance their CPA toward different possible election outcomes.

Even within democratic nations, CPA decisions should balance the differing electoral systems. In the United States and the United Kingdom, engagement with local constituencies of specific candidates or campaign donations to them can be critical in shaping law-making processes. In these systems of proportional representation, political parties tend to carry more importance than individual members of parliament, and therefore CPA should focus on building connections with key decision makers in political parties or affecting the public opinion with which parties attempt to align.

A country's enforcement mechanisms and informal norms may influence firms' CPA. Developed countries typically require a high level of transparency on business-to-government interactions, which may increase public scrutiny. Although corruption is an illegal form of CPA around the world, firm leaders in less developed countries may be tempted to engage in bribery because of low risk of detection and weak punishment.

Managers of foreign subsidiaries of multinational enterprises (MNEs) face unique challenges in pursuing corporate political strategy. On the one hand, the subsidiaries must engage in CPA to build their legitimacy in host countries. Thus, MNEs tend to choose outside professional lobbyists to signal legitimacy. On the other hand, subsidiaries need to abide by the laws and regulations of their home countries. US firms, for example, are subject to the Foreign Corrupt Practices Act of 1977, which prohibits US citizens and entities from bribing foreign government officials to benefit their business interests.

Sources: Kim, J. H. (2019). Is your playing field unleveled? US defense contracts and foreign firm lobbying. *Strategic Management Journal* 40(12): 1911–1937; Cui, L., Hu, H. W., Li, S., & Meyer, K. E. (2018). Corporate political connections in global strategy. *Global Strategy Journal* 8(3): 379–398; Zheng, W., Singh, K., & Chung, C. N. (2017). Ties to unbind: Political ties and firm sell-offs during institutional transition. *Journal of Management* 43(7): 2005–2036; Leuz, C., & Oberholzer-Gee, F. (2006). Political relationships, global financing, and corporate transparency: Evidence from Indonesia. *Journal of Financial Economics* 81(2): 411–439; Lambsdorff, J. G. (2002). Making corrupt deals: Contracting in the shadow of the law. *Journal of Economic Behavior and Organization* 48(3): 221–241; Hillman, A., & Keim, G. (1995). International variation in the business-government interface: Institutional and organizational considerations. *Academy of Management Review* 20(1): 193–214.

video-sharing social networking service TikTok of being a threat to national security and demanded a full sale of TikTok to an American owner. Although several large US companies like Microsoft and Walmart were interested in the purchase, TikTok executives chose Oracle as the company's business partner in the US ostensibly because of Oracle's close ties to the Trump administration.[24]

Third, corporate political activity may help create a policy environment favorable to firms. When proposed legislation threatens the interests of some companies, executives may respond with CPA directed toward blocking the legislation. As a matter of fact, only 6 percent of legislative proposals are passed by Congress into law; hence, defeating threatening legislation can have a high success rate.[25] In the early 1990s, Ocean Spray, an American agricultural cooperative of growers of cranberry and grapefruit, began lobbying Congress to block a proposed policy requiring fruit drink manufacturers to reveal the actual percentage of juice contained in a product. Yet, its offerings contained only about 25 percent of juice compared with 100 percent for orange juice products. Company leaders spent around $3 million on CPA to delay the change until 1994, by which Ocean Spray had modified some of its products to contain 100 percent juice. This example illustrates that CPA can serve to buffer the firm from governmental threats, contributing to desirable financial performance.[26] A favorable policy environment may also create competitive advantages through CPA that shapes the enactment of laws and regulations. Aware that copyright on the Mickey Mouse character was about to expire in the late 1990s, Disney's management team spent around $6.3 million in political contributions to pass the Sonny Bono Copyright Term Extension Act, enabling the company to maintain its copyright on Mickey for another two decades.

Fourth, political connections can enhance companies' legitimacy and give rise to favorable treatment by stakeholders. Banks, for instance, charge lower interest rates for S&P 500 companies with political connections because such connections help improve the borrower's credit worthiness.[27] In China, visits by high-level political leaders can enhance legitimacy of host firms and trigger positive stock market reactions.[28] The importance of political connections in boosting acceptability becomes particularly salient for foreign companies. Faced with the challenges of legitimizing their operations in host countries, foreign companies can establish connections with influential members of the host country's political elite.[29]

Although political connections can create positive perceptions in foreign countries, activities such as political contributions are often portrayed in domestic media as the functional equivalent of bribes. For example, the *Washington Post* wrote, "To judge from polls, Americans are deeply concerned about political corruption. They share a widespread belief that members of Congress are unethical, with lobbyists as the only group seen as more unethical."[30] In other cases, retaliation from key stakeholders for supporting the "wrong" cause or candidate can take the form of online campaigns, negative media coverage, and consumer boycotts.[31] In the early 2000s, Starbucks lobbied to have coffee bean roasting considered as a type of manufacturing to win a tax break worth millions of dollars. This resulted in a wave of negative editorials and news reports about the company for pursuing a "money-grubbing" special interest, harming the company's image in the eyes of consumers.[32] The increased risks and potential harm to competitive advantages due to CPA become particularly salient in a politically divided country such as the United States. In today's environment, taking sides on a controversial topic can alienate half of a company's primary stakeholders, including investors, customers, suppliers, and employees.

GOVERNANCE ACTORS AND CHOICE OF CORPORATE POLITICAL STRATEGY

Having introduced different types of corporate political strategy and mechanisms through which firms can enhance competitive advantage, we next explain how governance actors may influence executives' pursuit of political strategy. To facilitate our discussion, we classify governance actors into four categories based on two dimensions (see Figure 8.2). The horizontal axis pertains to the relationship type between governance actors and firms. As discussed in prior chapters, some governance actors such as short-term investors have a transactional relationship with firms whereas others such as long-term investors have an engaged relationship. The vertical axis is concerned with whether governance actors provide firms with resources and information.

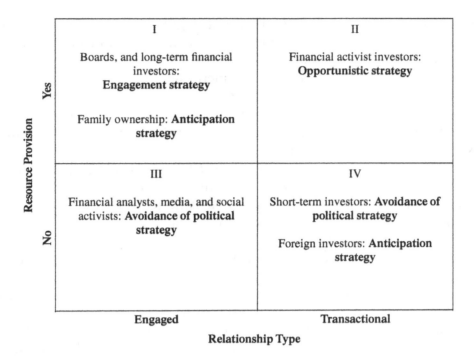

	Engaged	**Transactional**
Yes	**I** Boards, and long-term financial investors: **Engagement strategy** Family ownership: **Anticipation strategy**	**II** Financial activist investors: **Opportunistic strategy**
No	**III** Financial analysts, media, and social activists: **Avoidance of political strategy**	**IV** Short-term investors: **Avoidance of political strategy** Foreign investors: **Anticipation strategy**

Resource Provision (vertical axis) / Relationship Type (horizontal axis)

FIGURE 8.2 Governance actors and corporate political strategy.

Financial analysts, for instance, do not play a resource provision role, while board members, in one of their key functions, provide managers with human and social capital resources and information allowing the latter to make effective strategic decisions.

Engaged Governance Actors with a Resource Provision Role

Quadrant I of Figure 8.2 describes engaged governance actors that provide resources to firms. As we will see, boards, long-term shareholders, state ownership, and family ownership influence executives' corporate political strategy.

Boards The appointment of directors with political connections can form an essential component of a firm's political strategy. As directors, ex-politicians may bring important political links and inform company leaders about the public policy process, as well as establish communication channels and access to incumbent politicians.[33] In some countries, directors with political connections help increase the legitimacy of a firm in the eyes of external stakeholders because of the information and resources that they bring. These politically affiliated appointments occur as an engaged (rather than transactional) approach to CPA given that the average director tenure is over seven years for S&P 1500 firms. Because companies in regulated industries are exposed to a high level of policy uncertainty, board members tend to appoint political directors to help manage the uncertainty.[34] Also, political directors can directly improve a firm's bottom line by increasing the likelihood of its ability to win government procurement contracts.[35]

Directors influence CPA through their monitoring role. Although corporate political activity helps give rise to a favorable policy environment and helps firms attain government contracts, the activities can go awry in the absence of board monitoring. In October 2020, the leadership at Goldman Sachs admitted criminal wrongdoing by employees in its Malaysian subsidiary. The employees had taken part in a scheme to pay $1 billion in bribes to foreign officials to win a license to sell local bonds. The bank was also requested to pay more than $5 billion in penalties to regulating bodies around the world.[36] This example highlights the risk of illegal CPA such as bribery and suggests the importance of having an effective board monitoring function to reduce the threats. Board members also need to constrain value-destroying CPA driven by top managers' motives to advance their own private interests. Managers inclined to use corporate funds to make political donations, instead of using such funds to invest in value-creating areas, like R&D, may cause lower stock market returns. This danger may be thwarted by establishing a smaller board size and a board chair independent of the CEO, which facilitate better board monitoring and generally lead to a lower level of political donations.[37]

Board members will generally prefer an *engagement* strategy. As board members are engaged governance actors, they will favor a long-term oriented relational approach to CPA, which may entail appointing politically connected directors or lobbying Congress on important policy issues. In contrast, a transactional approach could consist of lobbying executive branch leaders with the goal of winning government contracts, or offering paid travel or honoraria for speaking. But managers can potentially appear to be bribing officials to attain political favors to boost short-term financial performance using a transactional approach. Because the transactional approach represents a high risk in the eyes of directors, this can keep managers more focused on an engaged approach. In addition, most directors of firms in heavily regulated industries prefer to manage political relationships *proactively* to weaken government regulation and influence the legislative and regulatory processes for a favorable external environment.[38]

Meanwhile, directors must actively manage potential risks associated with CPA to ensure that the political activity stays consistent with firm strategy and messaging to stakeholders. Failure to do so can backfire. For example, Aetna ran into shareholder resolutions and a lawsuit after news revealed an undisclosed $7.5 billion lobbying expenditure used to attack the federal Affordable Care Act, despite the company's public support for the healthcare legislation.[39]

Long-Term Shareholders With lasting investment horizons, long-term shareholders tend to have an engaged relationship with leadership teams of portfolio firms and are motivated to provide resources and information that can improve executive decision-making. These shareholders may be concerned about agency problems associated with corporate political spending and thus rely on internal governance mechanisms, including submission of shareholder proposals, to reduce this spending.[40] Yet, for the spending that does occur, failure by company leaders to manage political relationships can be detrimental to companies' value creation due to the critical role of governments in creating and sustaining competitive advantages. Currently, leaders of pharmaceutical companies, concerned about proposals that would peg drug prices in the United States to prices paid overseas and force firms to pay rebates for drugs whose price increase is higher than the rate of inflation, are engaging in active lobbying to defeat the proposals.[41] Shareholders of these pharmaceutical companies could benefit if the lobbying activities prove successful in helping to defeat these proposals.

A high level of ownership by long-term shareholders can lead managers of firms with strong political dependence—referring to their reliance on the government for resources or legitimacy[42]—to pursue an engagement strategy. Although a transactional approach to CPA can prove effective in the short run, it tends to be associated with high risks. For instance, bribing governmental officials can help firms attain lucrative contracts, but may significantly damage a firm's reputation and result in enormous penalties as shown by the Goldman Sachs example, in which the company must now pay a hefty penalty fee. In contrast, as an engaged approach carries emphasis on reducing firms' policy uncertainty in a systematic manner, the approach can take the form of subtle CPA, such as lobbying, involving a lower level of risk. In addition, since long-term shareholders are motivated to monitor managerial behaviors, they help ensure that firms' relational investment in CPA serve the interests of shareholders rather than managers.

Relational investment in CPA can lead to regulations favorable to only some firms. For example, in Norway, the world's largest producer and exporter of salmon, small fish farming firms have strongly opposed new standards of environmental regulation whereas large and multinational firms have supported or even demanded stricter environmental regulation, since the latter can use environmental regulation strategically to strengthen their competitive advantages at the expense of the smaller and weaker rivals.[43] Accordingly, owners, including shareholders and stakeholders, of large and small fish-farming firms may benefit differently from environmental regulations.

Similar to directors, long-term shareholders of firms with strong political dependence will prefer a proactive approach rather than a reactive one since performance is subject to a high level of policy uncertainty. In some cases, these shareholders engage in political spending to help buffer their portfolio firms from policy uncertainty. In 2018, New York Governor Andrew Cuomo called for legalizing marijuana "once and for all," leading the MedMen Opportunity Fund, with extensive investment in marijuana businesses, to contribute $65,000 to Cuomo's third-term campaign.[44] According to data from the Center for Responsive Politics, since 2012, institutional investors have been the single largest source of political contributions in the United States, donating a total of $154.56 million in the 2019–2020 political cycle. As a long-term shareholder, Berkshire Hathaway spent over $4 million on lobbying in 2019, with lobbying expenditure (2008–2019) as shown in Figure 8.3. This expenditure may help portfolio firms in the same industry benefit from favorable industry policies.

Family Ownership   The owners or managers of family firms tend to have a long-term presence in the firms and often have direct control over financial resources and strategic decisions; therefore, family owners are less concerned that managers might use corporate resources to engage in CPA that advances their personal

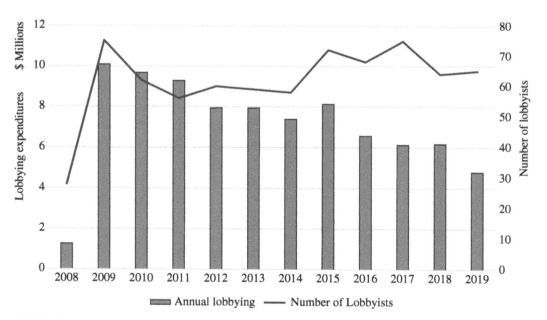

FIGURE 8.3   Berkshire Hathaway lobbying expenditure.
Data source: Center for Responsive Politics

motives. In Chapter 3, we discuss family dominant owners of large diversified business groups (Chaebols) and how they were designated by firm-connected government officials to create leading business in industries (e.g. automobile and semiconductors) considered strategic by the government. Meanwhile, CPA can reduce the firms' long-term risks from the possible consequences of legislative outcomes on market strategies and on firms' business environment. In particular, CPA allows managers of family-owned firms to gain political access and monitor political processes, which translates into insurance against negative future events.[45] In this manner, CPA can be perceived as a nonmarket, risk-reducing strategy. As family owners are less diversified than other types of shareholders and often keep most of their wealth in their owned companies, they are motivated to pursue strategies that reduce their risks and benefit firms in the long run. Family-owned firms therefore tend to pursue a higher level of CPA than comparable non-family-owned firms.[46]

Family ownership can lead to an engagement strategy, enabling a relational approach to CPA, as the political activity represents a holistic strategy focusing on the long term, aligned with the time horizon of the owners. Family firms therefore tend to have a more permanent lobbying staff (in-house lobbyists) on a continuous basis rather than hiring external lobbyists for specific purposes.[47] In addition, family ownership can motivate the company leaders to pursue a proactive approach, specifically in supporting political candidates and issues aligned with the family's values. Leaders of Chick-Fil-A, a fast-food chain owned by a Baptist family, has for years given millions of dollars to organizations fighting same-sex marriage and supporting heterosexual ones, and its CEO Dan Cathy said supporting same-sex marriage would invite God's judgment on the country. Despite strong backlash from consumers due to its political contributions in 2012, Chick-Fil-A has not stopped making donations to anti-LGBTQ groups.[48] Leaders of family firms are willing to take a stand on controversial issues to safeguard their family values.

Transactional Governance Actors with a Resource Provision Role

Quadrant II of Figure 8.2 describes governance actors that have a transactional relationship with firms and are motivated to provide resources. Our discussion will focus on financial activist investors. As noted in previous chapters, financial activists, often including hedge funds and other types of institutional investor activists, attempt to reap financial returns through launching shareholder activism. These activist investors typically exit their holdings after they make financial returns (i.e., a transactional relationship with invested firms), but are motivated to provide targeted companies with resources to enable short-term gains.

Financial activist investors focus on efficient and effective use of firm resources. They likely reduce the level of CPA among targeted firms with low political dependence since CPA in these cases may seem a waste of firm resources. Using a sample of 1,330 firms targeted by activist investors for shareholder activism but whose large customers do not include governments, our research finds that these firms reduce lobbying expenditures by over 35 percent from the pre-activism period to the post-activism period. The decline appears especially sharp for lobbying expenditures oriented toward Congress because influencing the law-making process requires a long payoff period and involves high uncertainty.[49]

For companies with high political dependence, financial activist investors will motivate company executives to pursue a transactional approach to CPA, including endeavors for government contracts and favorable executive orders. Based on a sample of 158 firms targeted by activist institutional investors and with governments as large clients, research finds that these companies almost double their lobbying expenditure from the pre-activism period to the post-activism period. The increase is mainly driven by a jump in lobbying expenditure toward the executive branch rather than the Congress because lobbying toward the executive branch proves more effective in helping firms attain government contracts and beneficial policy environment.[50]

In addition, financial activist investors will pressure executives to take a proactive approach to CPA since these investors themselves are active players in the political arena. In fact, hedge funds have emerged as a significant political player since 2007. Based on data from the Center for Responsive Politics, we graph hedge funds' political contributions in Figure 8.4. In the 2018 election cycle, hedge funds contributed $101 million to federal candidates, political action committees, and outside spending groups, 85 percent going to Democratic candidates and incumbents and 15 percent going to Republican ones. Given the rising role of hedge funds in politics, executives of firms targeted by hedge fund activists may engage in CPA proactively.

Engaged Governance Actors without a Resource Provision Role

Quadrant III of Figure 8.2 describes governance actors, including financial analysts, the media, and social activists, that do not provide resources to firms but have an engaged relationship with company leadership.

Financial Analysts Although corporate political activity can potentially improve a firm's financial performance, analysts generally dislike the practice because political favoritism triggered by CPA usually occurs covertly and complicates analysts' ability to perform their forecasting tasks successfully. As a

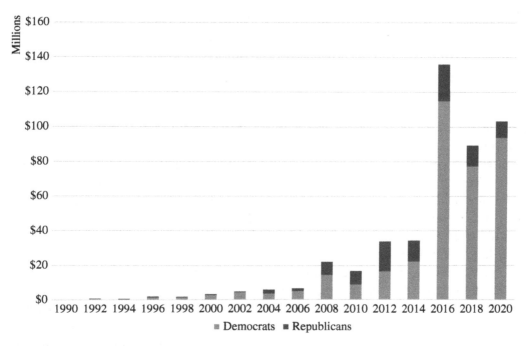

FIGURE 8.4   Hedge fund political contributions.
Data source: Center for Responsive Politics

result, analysts tend to issue less accurate earnings forecasts for firms with political connections than for firms without such connections.[51] The negative influence of political connections on earnings forecast accuracy becomes particularly strong in countries with high levels of corruption because politicians tend to transfer benefits to connected firms under corrupt systems.[52] When facing strong pressure from financial analysts, managers will most often hesitate to engage in CPA.

Media   Extensive media coverage can also lead executives to refrain from CPA. The media investigates companies suspected of inappropriate behavior and distributes the information to external stakeholders.[53] Not surprisingly, therefore, major business newspapers are replete with often negatively toned articles about the role of big businesses' influence on politics. For example, the *Wall Street Journal* and *New York Times* have written extensively about Facebook's engagement in political contributions to affect government legislation with respect to net neutrality, data privacy, and censorship. The coverage can give rise to less favorable perceptions by consumers and adversely affect corporate reputation.

Being targeted by social media can influence CPA disclosure. In fact, companies face the need for increased transparency in political spending disclosure when their CPA is targeted frequently in Twitter messages.[54] Although the disclosure of a company's CPA is generally favored by shareholders, the release of information potentially augments the challenge for firm leaders to benefit from their political connections. In this manner, scrutiny from the media may lead managers to refrain from CPA.

Social Activists   Social activists are dedicated to changing social institutions and can have profound influences on governments by shaping public opinion and culture.[55] Companies targeted by social activists may undergo detrimental effects to its reputation, complicating executives' chances of accessing political stakeholders. For example, boycotts by social activists may lead to significant increases in the proportion of refunded political contributions and retracted government contracts, highlighting the impact of these activists on firm leaders' relationships with political stakeholders.[56]

Nevertheless, corporate political activity may improve executives' ability to resist the pressure from social activists who seek to influence company policies and practices on a variety of issues.[57] Politically active S&P 500 firms, for instance, are more likely to challenge socially oriented shareholder proposals, and therefore are less likely to reach agreements with social activists than with their less politically active counterparts.[58] More specifically, for S&P 500 firms, the Securities and Exchange Commission (SEC) allows the omission of proxy ballot proposals more frequently for those firms more active in CPA, since the political activity may serve to influence or preempt decisions by regulators at the SEC and other supervisory agencies that can cause disruptions to firms.[59] For example, in 2015, Walmart successfully excluded from its proxy a proposal from Trinity Church banning the sale of firearms.[60] Nevertheless, "in 2015, it stopped selling assault-style rifles and it stopped selling handguns" so that this issue would not be revived again through a proxy battle.[61]

Transactional Governance Actors without a Resource Provision Role

Quadrant IV of Figure 8.1 describes transactional governance actors that do not provide resources to firms. Two types of shareholders, short-term and foreign shareholders, belong to this quadrant.

Short-Term Shareholders   Since payoffs from CPA generally take a long period of time to realize, short-term shareholders, who focus on garnering quick financial returns, may not espouse corporate political activities. These shareholders are not motivated to monitor managerial behaviors to ensure that resources for CPA are well spent. Thus, investing in CPA may lead to sell-offs by short-term shareholders, particularly among firms with low political dependence in which financial performance does not depend on improved political relationship management. Yet, although short-term shareholders oppose executive decisions to pursue an engaged approach to CPA, they may not prevent executives of firms with high political dependence from pursuing a transactional approach that may lead to immediate financial payoffs. Our analyses based on a sample of 6,545 US companies suggest that ownership by transient institutional investors is negatively associated with lobbying expenditures that focus solely on the Congress, but not with lobbying expenditures that focus on the executive branch, which likely offer quicker payoffs.

Foreign Shareholders Geographic distance creates difficulty for foreign shareholders to monitor portfolio firms, making these shareholders less likely to adopt a relational approach in investment. But due to the liability of foreignness, they may be greatly concerned about political uncertainty in host countries, and therefore favor their portfolio firms to engage in CPA. Foreign ownership can also increase a firm's political dependence. When a foreign interest has the direct or indirect power to direct or decide matters affecting the management or operations of a US company, the company could be deemed to be operating under Foreign Ownership, Control or Influence (FOCI) regulation and therefore subject to close government scrutiny and stringent regulatory compliance[62]. As foreign ownership can represent a direct type of control by a foreign interest, US firms with this kind of ownership carry a high level of political dependence on their home country's government. To manage the dependence, executives of firms with high foreign institutional ownership tend to engage in intensive CPA.[63]

One particular type of foreign shareholder that merits special attention is sovereign wealth fund (SWF) ownership. Host country governments have concern that foreign states deploy SWFs to defend or advance foreign sovereign interests. Host country government officials will often highlight national security concerns with regard to SWFs. But foreign sovereigns can circumvent the federal ban on foreign entities' making political contributions to gain access to the US political process through SWF ownership of firms engaged in US political contributions, as there are no restrictions on foreign ownership of US-listed firms. As a result, firm campaign contributions increase after SWF investment, especially in industries vulnerable to legislation capable of inhibiting or expunging foreign investment.[64]

Foreign shareholders prefer that firm leaders pursue an anticipation strategy—a strategy characterized by a relational and reactive approach to CPA. As foreign shareholders are concerned about portfolio firms' political dependence, managing such dependence requires executives to develop an engaged approach through building relationships with politicians (e.g. lobbying). Consistent with such an argument, our analyses of a large sample of US firms suggest that foreign institutional ownership can lead to an increase in lobbying expenditures focused on the Congress but does not affect lobbying expenditures focused on the executive branch. Also, firms with high foreign ownership will choose a reactive approach, since a proactive one could be perceived as foreign influence on domestic politics.

MANAGING GOVERNANCE ACTORS TO CREATE POLITICAL ADVANTAGES

We have discussed different types of corporate political strategy and how governance actors affect company leaders' choices of such strategy. We will now explain the process of how managers can draw on governance actors to gain political advantages, which arise from managing political relationships. The process starts with evaluating governance actors' preferences for CPA, as shown in Figure 8.5.

Step 1. Evaluate Governance Actors' Preferences

We have suggested that governance actors have distinct preferences for corporate political activity. Some, such as board directors and long-term shareholders, may prefer executives to engage in CPA, whereas analysts and the media tend to have a less favorable view of the activity and may make top managers reluctant to invest in CPA. Managers therefore need to carefully evaluate governance actors' preferences especially if the influencers' support is critical to the firm's legitimacy and survival.

Top managers need to assess the degree of political dependence to which their firm is subject and decide whether they should undertake CPA. They

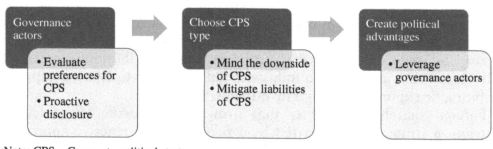

Note: CPS = Corporate political strategy

FIGURE 8.5   Manage governance actors for a successful corporate political strategy.

should not necessarily avoid political activity because of preferences expressed by certain governance actors. In the United States, political uncertainty has intensified as a consequence of partisan policy disputes.[65] Executives face increased political intervention in their business activities. The Committee on Foreign Investment in the United States (CFIUS), an inter-agency committee of the US government that reviews the national security implications of foreign investments in American companies or operations, revealed in its 2019 annual report to Congress that its review of the 231 notices of covered transactions filed in 2019 subsequently led to an investigation of 113 of the 231 notices—the most in the history of the CFIUS. Given the growing role of political uncertainty, executives that neglect corporate political strategy may cause the uncertainty to impact normal business operations and transactions. When the Trump administration moved to block US chipmakers from supplying to Huawei, a Chinese telecom giant, due to national security concerns, this inevitably harmed the performance of these US headquartered chipmakers.[66]

A firm's level of political dependence may also be impacted by other companies whose corporate political activities may potentially lead to competitive disadvantages for the focal firm. For example, nonlobbying firms can be negatively affected when a new piece of regulation influenced by lobbying firms is approved by Congress. In fact, in one study the aggregate firm loss in value per one legislative bill for nonlobbying firms was $1.9 billion.[67] Yet, lobbying firms' direct competitors experience a smaller loss because these competitors potentially benefit from the passed legislation. Lobbying by Google, Twitter, or Facebook, for instance, may harm the interests of traditional media companies but benefit companies distributing online content, since the lobbyists for the leading online platforms push regulators to enact laws and regulations favorable to digital media rather than traditional media.

If, upon assessment, managers determine that CPA represents a crucial element for the firm's long-term competitiveness, they should not avoid engaging and instead foster the company's political capabilities that contribute to value creation and maintenance. At the same time, executives need to intensify political disclosure to alleviate governance actors' concerns about managerial motives behind CPA. The disclosure of corporate spending has come to the forefront of the investor agenda, attracting much attention from regulators, media, and the corporate community at large.[68] Figure 8.6 presents the number of shareholder proposals calling for firms to increase political spending disclosure from 2006 to 2019. The number of such proposals was 42 in 2006 and reached its peak of 137 in 2013 and 2014.

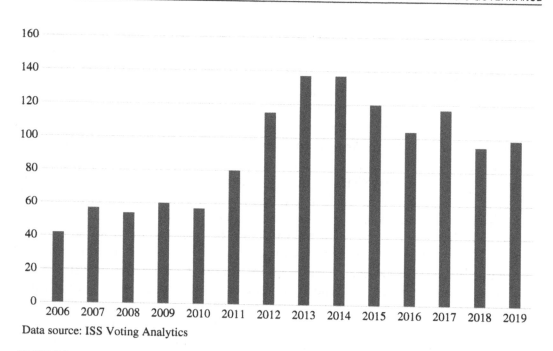

Data source: ISS Voting Analytics

FIGURE 8.6 Number of shareholder proposals on political spending.

Disclosure through mandatory filings with different government offices does not allow executives to explain the strategic rationale behind their political spending. Therefore, voluntary disclosures provide a means for them to communicate their commitment to value-enhancing political activities. In particular, because institutional investors (especially socially responsible investors) are highly aware of and concerned about CPA, executives of firms with a high level of ownership by such investors should manage their political disclosure more actively. Research has documented the potential benefits of voluntary political spending disclosure.[69] For instance, the disclosure can give rise to higher analyst following and lower forecast error.

The following caveats can be helpful for managers when engaging in voluntary political disclosure:

1. Corporate political spending reflects the company's interests and not the preferences of directors or top managers.
2. The firm has a committee (which be a committee of the board) to monitor, supervise, and evaluate corporate political spending.
3. The disclosure of corporate political spending is complete and transparent; incomplete disclosure can backfire if stakeholders later reveal undisclosed spending.
4. The disclosure is updated regularly.

These suggested stipulations are developed more fully in Box 8.3, outlining ethical considerations.

Step 2. Mind the Downside of Corporate Political Strategy

If governance actors prefer CPA engagement, managers may need to pursue a corporate political strategy favored by the actors, as shown in Figure 8.2. Yet, each corporate political strategy has its inherent downside, which needs to be actively managed. Although an engagement strategy may allow firms to reap long-term benefits from political ties, the strategy may lead to resources being wasted on political activity that may not lead to benefits. In some cases, the activity can cause managerial entrenchment, since strong political connections potentially shield managers from being disciplined by external governance actors. Also, because strong political connections can delay the acquisition process and make it difficult for a firm to be acquired,[70] the connections can protect managers from hostile takeovers, but, on the other hand, can potentially lead to managerial entrenchment. Furthermore, executives with deep political ties are less likely to receive penalties after the revelation of corporate fraud by regulatory bodies.[71] Relatedly, CEOs use their political ties to shield themselves from forced departure, even when the firm performs poorly.[72] In sum, although political ties can be critical to business viability and competitiveness,[73] such connections built through CPA can also give rise to managerial entrenchment and ineffective corporate governance. Directors and long-term shareholders must therefore play an active monitoring role to minimize and mitigate the downside of a political engagement strategy.

An opportunistic strategy also carries high risk. This strategy may not call for substantial resource commitment nor give rise to managerial entrenchment, but can heighten risks when managers pursue extreme actions. Bribing government officials might provide an immediate way to attain lucrative contracts and business opportunities. However, the revelation of bribery can adversely influence a firm's reputation and in some cases result in enormous penalties. Based on the data from Stanford Law School, the average penalty for 658 enforcement actions in violation of the Foreign Corrupt Practices Act amounts to $38 million per enforcement action. In addition, a transactional relationship with political officials built through an opportunistic strategy can expose firms to a high level of risk. In some cases, firms may build political ties with officials who are political rivals and these ties can harm firms' legitimacy and performance.[74] To minimize the risks associated with an opportunistic strategy, company leaders need to design an effective internal control system and develop a culture that can discourage managers from illegal political activities at home and abroad.

BOX 8.3   Strategic Governance Highlight: Ethics Issues in Implementing Corporate Political Strategy

Ethical CPA consists of activities that pursue appropriate goals (intentions) using suitable means and processes, hence resulting in proper consequences. Yet, when pursued by unethical means, CPA can create an unfair business environment that adversely influences overall socioeconomic development, particularly in countries with less developed institutions where CPA is often not disclosed or regulated and can take place through an illegal form. To safeguard ethics in corporate political activity, firm leaders may consider the following suggestions.

First, board directors need to carry out oversight of political spending. Oversight starts with directors' understanding of political spending and associated risks, and how political contributions can backfire. Directors need to enact clear policies that specify the corporate political activities that should or should not be pursued, outline the procedures that management needs to follow, and institute periodic checks to ensure compliance. In addition, board members should assess the impact of CPA on stakeholders, the firm's long-term interests, and the broader issues that affect the firm. Procter & Gamble has formalized its political spending decision procedure to ensure that the spending is backed by a strong business rationale and a downside assessment to avoid significant stakeholder conflict. For example, the company's public policy and legislative priorities are reviewed regularly with senior executives and annually with the governance and public responsibility committee of the board of directors and political activities are disclosed to shareholders in a timely manner.

Second, company leaders need to enhance the firm's internal control system—mechanisms, rules, and procedures implemented by companies to ensure the integrity of financial and accounting information, promote accountability, and prevent fraud. Internal control stands as a particularly important type of organizational control and is designed to assess risks, prevent fraud, and ensure the accuracy and completeness of accounting information in financial statements and disclosures. An ineffective internal control system makes it difficult for parent firms to monitor and supervise foreign operations, giving rise to a high probability of violations of antibribery provisions of the Foreign Corruption Practices Act (FCPA).

Third, firms need to create an ethical corporate culture. Although oversight by board members and an effective internal control system may reduce the likelihood of engaging in illegal CPA, directors are unable to provide oversight of all decisions and an internal control system may not address all the possible scenarios in actual decision-making. Therefore, the creation of an ethical culture, which needs to be shaped by the examples set by the organization's leadership, becomes crucial to ensuring integrity in political spending decisions. As noted by the chief ethics and compliance officer of Dell: "Dell has a political spending policy that is an integral part of our ethical culture, but we can't have policies for every kind of situation. Our culture guides our decisions and helps us make the right kind of judgments." Similarly, leaders at Microsoft have developed a leadership code of conduct and reporting that guides political activities and leaders at Dow Chemical worked to educate all employees about interactions with government officials. As in these cases, developing a code of conduct can facilitate the establishment of an ethical culture.

Sources: Liedong, T. A. (2020). Responsible firm behaviour in political markets: Judging the ethicality of corporate political activity in weak institutional environments. *Journal of Business Ethics*: 1–21. Mantere, S., Pajunen, K., & Lamberg, J.-A. (2009). Vices and virtues of corporate political activity: The challenge of international business. *Business & Society* 48(1):105–132.

Lastly, the reactive nature of anticipation and mending strategies can lead to negative perceptions by external stakeholders. A reactive approach suggests that executives constantly change their positions on specific issues, which could be perceived cynically by external stakeholders as actions driven only by political expedience rather than by principle, hurting executive relationships with stakeholders. Here, managers need to develop a holistic guideline of political spending, such as the policy developed by Procter & Gamble, so that they steer clear of supporting issues that conflict with one another.

Step 3. Leverage Governance Actors in Corporate Political Strategy

Governance actors may not only influence the choices of distinct political strategy but also facilitate the implementation of a successful chosen strategy. In particular, leveraging mass media and shareholders to manage a firm's political dependence helps create political advantage. A good public relations office and strategy allows firm executives to communicate their interests and views to policy makers and shape public perception,[75] as well as extend the reach of corporate advocacy in political debates.[76] In other words, the media provides a platform for managers to shape public opinion through their own framing of issues.[77] For instance, company leaders can advocate for a particular explanation and/or solution to a social problem through newspaper op-eds[78] and advocacy advertising,[79] helping them to persuade the public to support policy preferences and create pressure for policy makers. We would like to highlight that executives should express their views in a subtle manner that suggests their economic justification to avoid being perceived as if they are directly seeking to manipulate the media and thus triggering negative reactions from stakeholders.

Top managers may also leverage institutional investors under corporate political activity. In the United States, the securities and investment industry has been an important contributor to Washington in terms of campaign dollars sent to candidates and money spent on lobbying. As a matter of fact, since 2012, the industry has become the single largest source of political contributions. According to data from OpenSecrets, the industry accounted for at least $95.1 million in cash for political advocacy groups, with the bulk ($88.2 million) coming from individuals in the industry in 2012. In terms of lobbying, in 2013, the industry ranked eighth in overall spending on federal lobbying, funding a total of $98.3 million.

Activist institutional investors are particularly motivated to improve firm performance using their political connections. For example, investors' political ties can help firms attain government contracts and create legitimacy in the eyes of external stakeholders.[80] Yet, drawing mainly from activist institutional investors to build political connections can increase managers' dependence on these investors and strengthen their ability to influence firm strategic decisions. Therefore, managers need to develop their own political connections but at times seek help from activist institutional investors when their goals are aligned.

As firms face increasing political uncertainty, neglecting corporate political strategy can come to harm a firm's competitiveness in the marketplace. A key task for managers is to leverage governance actors in a way that allows them to design and implement effective corporate political strategy. Yet, corporate political activities involve high risks, including ethical issues and legal penalties when not conducted properly. Governance actors and managers alike must therefore remain highly attentive to corporate political activities and their impacts.

NOTES

1. Hillman, A. J., Keim., G. D., & Schuler, D. (2004). Corporate political activity: A review and research agenda. *Journal of Management* 30(6): 837–857.
2. Bach, D., & Allen, D. (2010). What every CEO needs to know about nonmarket strategy. *MIT Sloan Management Review* 51(3): 41.

3. Corkery, M., Yaffe-Bellany, D., & Swanson, A. (2020). Powerful meat industry holds more sway after Trump's order. *New York Times*. www.nytimes.com, April 29.

4. Bloomberg (2020). Unraveling the mysteries of China's multiple budgets. *Bloomberg*. 13 March.

5. Lux, S., Crook, T. R., & Woehr, D. J. (2011). Mixing business with politics: A meta-analysis of the antecedents and outcomes of corporate political activity. *Journal of Management* 37(1): 223–247.

6. Nownes, A. J. (2006). *Total lobbying: What lobbyists want(and how they try to get it)*. Cambridge., MA: Cambridge University Press.

7. Hillman, A. J., Zardkoohi, A., & Bierman, L. (1999). Corporate political strategies and firm performance: Indications of firm-specific benefits from personal service in the US government. *Strategic Management Journal* 20(1): 67–81.

8. Schuler, D. A., & Shi, W., Hoskisson, R. E., & Chen, T. (2017). Windfalls of emperors' sojourns: Stock market reactions to Chinese firms hosting high-ranking government officials. *Strategic Management Journal* 38(8): 1668–1687.

9. Milyo, J., Primo, D., & Groseclose, T. (2000). Corporate PAC campaign contributions in perspective. *Business and Politics* 2(1): 75–88.

10. Aggarwal, R. K., Meschke, F., & Wang, T. Y. (2012). Corporate political donations: Investment or agency. *Business & Politics* 14(1): 1–38.

11. Sun, P., Mellahi, K., & Wright, M. (2012). The contingent value of corporate political ties. *Academy of Management Perspectives* 26(3): 68–82.

12. Hillman, A. J., & Hitt, M. A. (1999). Corporate political strategy formulation: A model of approach, participation, and strategy decisions. *Academy of Management Review* 24(4): 825–842; Oliver, C., & Holzinger, I. (2008). The effectiveness of strategic political management: A dynamic capabilities framework. *Academy of Management Review* 33(2): 496–520.

13. Hillman & Hitt. Corporate political strategy formulation; Olson M. (2009). *The logic of collective action: Public goods and the theory of groups*. Boston, MA: Harvard University Press.

14. Hillman & Hitt. Corporate political strategy formulation.

15. Hillman, A. J., Keim, G. D., & Schuler, D. (2004). Corporate political activity: A review and research agenda. *Journal of Management* 30(6): 837–857.

16. Meznar, M. B., & Nigh, D. (1995). Buffer or bridge? Environmental and organizational determinants of public affairs activities in American firms. *Academy of Management Journal* 38(4): 975–996.

17. Dusso, A., Holyoke, T. T., & Schatzinger, H. (2019). The influence of corporate lobbying on federal contracting. *Social Science Quarterly* 100(5): 1793–1809.

18. O'Connell, J., & Lamothe, D. (2019). US and Boeing have long had a special relationship. *Washington Post*. 19 March.

19. McCabe, D. (2020). IBM, Marriott and Mickey Mouse take on tech's favorite law. *New York Times*. 4 February. www.nytimes.com.

20. Karbal, I. (2020). Tech giants named in Trump's executive order lobbied against similar laws for years. OpenSecrets. 1 June. https://www.opensecrets.org/news/2020/06/twitter-trump-eo-lobbied-against-similar-law.

21. Lin, H., Zeng, S., Ma, H., & Chen, H. (2015). How political connections affect corporate environmental performance: The mediating role of green subsidies. *Human and Ecological Risk Assessment: An International Journal* 21(8): 2192–2212.

22. Schuler, Shi, Hoskisson, & Chen. Windfalls of emperors' sojourns.

23. Lee, S-H., & Baik, Y-S. (2010). Corporate lobbying in antidumping cases: Looking into the continued dumping and subsidy offset act. *Journal of Business Ethics* 96(3): 467–478.

24. Pham, S. (2020). How Oracle ended up with TikTok. CNN. 14 September.

25. Lux, S., Crook, T. R., & Leap, T. (2012). Corporate political activity: The god, the bad., and the ugly. *Business Horizons* 55(3): 307–312.

26. Meznar & Nigh. Buffer or bridge?

27. Houston, J. F., Jiang, L., Lin, C., & Ma, Y. (2014). Political connections and the cost of bank loans. *Journal of Accounting Research* 52(1): 193–243.

28. Schuler, Shi, Hoskisson, & Chen. Windfalls of emperors' sojourns.

29. Kostova, T., & Zaheer, S. (1999). Organizational legitimacy under conditions of complexity: The case of the multinational enterprise. *Academy of Management Review* 24(1): 64–81.

30. Drutman, L. (2016). What we get wrong about lobbying and corruption. *Washington Post*. 16 April. https://www.washingtonpost.com/news/monkey-cage/wp/2015/04/16/what-we-get-wrong-about-lobbying-and-corruption/.

31. Lux & Crook., Leap. Corporate political activity.

32. Cummings, J. (2005). Cautiously, Starbucks puts lobbying on corporate menu. *Wall Street Journal*. www.wsj.com, April 2.

33. Hillman, A. J. (2005). Politicians on the board of directors: Do connections affect the bottom line? *Journal of Management* 31(3): 464–481.

34. Hillman. Politicians on the board of directors.

35. Goldman, E., Rocholl, J., & So, J. (2013). Politically connected boards of directors and the allocation of procurement contracts. *Review of Finance* 17(5): 1617–1648.

36. Goldstein, M., & Flitter, E. (2020). Goldman Sachs Malaysia arm pleads guilty in 1MDB fraud. *New York Times*, October 22. www.nytimes.com.

37. Aggarwal, Meschke, & Wang. Corporate political donations.

38. Hillman. Politicians on the board of directors.

39. Bagley C., Freed B., & Sandstrom K. (2015). A board member's guide to corporate political spending. *Harvard Business Review Digital Articles*, www.hbr.com, October 30, 2–7.

40. Hadani, M. (2012). Institutional ownership monitoring and corporate political activity: Governance implications. *Journal of Business Research* 65(7): 944–950.

41. Loftus, P. (2020). Drugmakers, worried about losing pricing power, are lobbying hard. *Wall Street Journal*, www.wsj.com, September 24.

42. Shi, W., Gao, C., & Aguilera, R. (2021). The liabilities of foreign institutional ownership: Managing political dependence through corporate political spending. *Strategic Management Journal* 42(1): 84–113.

43. Vormedal, I., & Skjærseth, J. B. (2020). The good, the bad, or the ugly? Corporate strategies, size, and environmental regulation in the fish-farming industry. *Business and Politics* 22(3): 510–538.

44. Dorn, S. (2019). Medical marijuana lobbyists donated over $150K to Cuomo's campaign. *New York Post*. 30 March. www.nypost.com.
45. Kersh, R. (2000). State autonomy & civil society: The lobbyist connection. *Critical Review* 14(2–3): 237–258.
46. Hadani, M. (2007). Family matters: Founding family firms and corporate political activity. *Business & Society* 46(4): 395–428.
47. Hadani. Family matters.
48. Dunn, A. (2020). Fact check: Chick-Fil-A has not resumed donations to groups that oppose LGBTQ rights. *USA Today*, June 30.
49 Dusso, A., Holyoke, T. T., & Schatzinger, H. (2019). The influence of corporate lobbying on federal contracting. *Social Science Quarterly* 100(5): 1793–1809.
50. Ibid.
51. Chen, C. J. P., Ding, Y., & Kim, C. (2010). High-level politically connected firms., corruption., and analyst forecast accuracy around the world. *Journal of International Business Studies* 41(9): 1505–1524.
52. Faccio, M. (2010). Differences between politically connected and nonconnected firms: A cross-country analysis. *Financial Management* 39(3): 905–928.
53. Pollock, T. G., & Rindova, V. P. (2003). Media legitimation effects in the market for initial public offerings. *Academy of Management Journal* 46(5): 631–642.
54. Lei, L., Li, Y., & Luo, Y. (2018). Social media and voluntary nonfinancial disclosure: Evidence from Twitter presence and corporate political disclosure. *Journal of Information Systems* 33(2): 99–128.
55. King, M. D., & Haveman, H. A. (2008). Antislavery in America: The press, the pulpit, and the rise of antislavery societies. *Administrative Science Quarterly* 53(3): 492–528.
56. McDonnell, M-H., & Werner, T. (2016). Blacklisted businesses: Social activists' challenges and the disruption of corporate political activity. *Administrative Science Quarterly* 61(4): 584–620.
57. Hadani, M., Doh, J. P., & Schneider, M. (2019). Social movements and corporate political activity: Managerial responses to socially oriented shareholder activism. *Journal of Business Research* 95: 156–170.
58. Hadani, Doh, & Schneider. Social movements and corporate political activity.
59. Hadani, M., Doh, J. P., & Schneider, M. A. (2018). Corporate political activity and regulatory capture: How some companies blunt the knife of socially oriented investor activism. *Journal of Management* 44(5): 2064–2093.
60. Gershman, J. (2015). Wal-Mart can block shareholder vote on gun sales., court rules. *Wall Street Journal*. July 7. www.wsj.com/articles/BL-LB-51674.
61. Nassauer, S. (2020). Walmart pulls guns, ammo displays in US stores, citing civil unrest. *Wall Street Journal*, October 29. www.wsj.com/articles/walmart-pulls-guns-ammo-displays-in-u-s-stores-citing-civil-unrest-11604002136.
62. The definition of FOCI is based on the National Industrial Security Program Operating Manual (NISPOM), which can be found at: http://acqnotes.com/wp-content/uploads/2014/09/DoD-522022M-National-Industrial-Security-Program-Operating-Manual-NISPOM-18-May-2016.pdf.

63. Shi, W., Gao, C., & Aguilera, R. (2021). The liabilities of foreign institutional ownership: Managing political dependence through corporate political spending. *Strategic Management Journal* 42(1): 84–113.

64. Calluzzo, P., Dong, G. N., & Godsell, D. (2017). Sovereign wealth fund investments and the US political process. *Journal of International Business Studies* 48(2): 222–243.

65. Baker, S. R., Bloom, N., & Davis, S. J. (2016). Measuring economic policy uncertainty. *Quarterly Journal of Economics* 131(4): 1593–1636.

66. Shepardson, D., Freifeld, K., & Alper, A. (2020). US moves to cut Huawei off from global chip suppliers as China eyes retaliation. Reuters, May 15. www.reuters.com/article/us-usa-huawei-tech-exclusive/u-s-moves-to-cut-huawei-off-from-global-chip-suppliers-as-china-eyes-retaliation-idUSKBN22R1KC.

67. Neretina, E. (2019). Lobbying externalities and competition. Available at SSRN 3297712.

68. Kong, X., Radhakrishnan, S., & Tsang, A. (2017). Corporate lobbying., visibility and accounting conservatism. *Journal of Business Finance & Accounting* 44(5–6): 527–557.

69. Goh, L., Liu, X., & Tsang, A. (2020). Voluntary disclosure of corporate political spending. *Journal of Corporate Finance* 61: 101403.

70. Croci, E., Pantzalis, C., Park, J. C., & Petmezas, D. (2017). The role of corporate political strategies in M&As. *Journal of Corporate Finance* 43: 260–287.

71. Sun, P., & Zhang, Y. (2006) Is there penalty for crime: Corporate scandal and management turnover in China. In Proceedings of the EFA 2006 Zurich Meetings Paper.

72. You, J. X., & Du, G. Q. (2012). Are political connections a blessing or a curse? Evidence from CEO turnover in China. *Corporate Governance—An: International Review* 20(2): 179–194.

73. Sun, Mellahi, & Wright. The contingent value of corporate political ties.

74. Yan, J. Z., & Chang, S. J. (2018). The contingent effects of political strategies on firm performance: A political network perspective. *Strategic Management Journal* 39(8): 2152–2177.

75. Kollman, K. (1998). Outside lobbying: Public opinion and interest group strategies. Pinceton, N.J.: Princeton University Press.

76. Murray, J., Nyberg, D., & Rogers, J. (2016). Corporate political activity through constituency stitching: Intertextually aligning a phantom community. *Organization* 23(6): 908–931.

77. Klein, J., & Amis, J. M. (2020). The dynamics of framing: Image, emotion and the European migration crisis. *Academy of Management Journal*.

78. Livesey, S. M. (2002). Global warming wars: Rhetorical and discourse analytic approaches to ExxonMobil's corporate public discourse. *Journal of Business Communication*(1973) 39(1): 117–146.

79. Brown, C., & Waltzer, H. (2005). Every Thursday: Advertorials by Mobil Oil on the op-ed page of The New York Times. *Public Relations Review* 31(2): 197–208.

80. Sojli, E., & Tham, W. W. (2017). Foreign political connections. *Journal of International Business Studies* 48(2): 244–266.

CHAPTER 9

Strategic Governance in a New Era

BOX 9.1   Strategic Governance Challenge: Managing Seemingly Incompatible Governance Trends

---

Strategic governance has become increasingly difficult because competing governance trends create complications for boards to manage. In this introductory strategic governance challenge, we highlight some of the potentially conflicting forces that board members and top executives confront.

Directors of company boards should be fully aware of international and political currents to develop viable strategies both domestically and internationally. In the United States, with tribal politics causing deep division in regard to governmental policies, firm leaders need to undertake corporate political strategy (see Chapter 8) to comply with regulatory changes, as well as to manage uncertainty arising from political transitions, such as the potential changes that might occur under the new Biden administration. Likewise, company leaders need to understand the current issues associated with competition with China and Europe and potential global strategy (see Chapter 6). For instance, the new agreement between the United Kingdom and the European Union over Brexit (the exit of the United Kingdom from the European Union) may carry important significance when conducting trade and foreign direct investment.

Board members also confront major societal trends, such as income inequality. Because CEO compensation has continued to increase in publicly traded firms (see Chapter 3), especially in the United States, more disparity exists relative to the average income of lower-level employees. Some countries have instituted requirements for firms to report the ratio of executive pay to average employee pay. In 2020, a new governance code in the United Kingdom instituted mandatory publication of company pay ratios, putting pressure on boards to keep CEO compensation within bounds to meet this societal concern. However, the market for human capital creates a push for higher compensation as competition increases for talented CEOs who face increased employment risk (see Chapter 3). At the same time, since boards undergo pressure to ensure that top managers do not expose the firms to excessive risks, board directors carry out risk assessments over management to restrict potentially jeopardizing moves.

Seemingly countervailing trends also occur among activist shareholders and environmental and social activists. Activist shareholders tend to create pressure for short-term financial performance as noted in Chapter 4 (innovation strategy) and Chapter 7 (stakeholder strategy) whereas environmental and social activists seek long-term investment to address climate change as well as increased diversity in the general work force. To achieve their goals, social activists take direct actions by seeking to get large owners (such as mutual, sovereign wealth, and university endowment funds) to divest assets of fossil fuel exploration and production companies. Likewise, employees can push an activism agenda on firms internally, as Amazon employees have pushed corporate leaders to "cut ties with big oil." As some governance advocates framed the issue: boards need to be agile enough to integrate "sustainability and corporate purpose with financial short-termism" (see Box 9.3 for an example of how Unilever sought to accomplish this dual goal). Although boards in the past have catered to shareholder demands, corporations today will need to evaluate how they will provide value to customers, communities, suppliers, and employees (see Chapter 7).

As disruptive innovation continues, boards must be aware of competitive threats, including how continuing digitalization will shape competition (Chapters 4 and 5). But directors must also pay attention to problems that might arise from technologies, such as artificial intelligence algorithms, which track an individual's purchases and even the media content that they are attracted to, in order to customize product and services advertising. However, the government and consumer advocates are scrutinizing these technologies as invasions of privacy (see Box 9.2 below). Boards can no longer seek to focus only on financial monitoring and disclosure compliance; they have to understand the competitive threats and social and government enforcement liabilities that may be associated with implementing these technological advances.

Sources: Mims, C. (2020). Joe Biden's 5 tech priorities. *Wall Street Journal*. www.wsj.com. December 19; O'Kelley, R., & Goodman, A. (2020). 2020 global and regional corporate governance trends. Harvard Law School Forum on Corporate Governance, January 18. https://corpgov. law.harvard.edu/2020/01/18/2020-global-and-regional-corporate-governance-trends; Peregrine, P. (2020). A 'twist' on top ten governance trends for 2020. *Forbes*, www.forbes.com. January 2; Swabey, P., Barker, R., Kakabadse, A., Hildyard, L., & Morrison, J. (2020), Key trends in corporate governance for 2020. *BoardAgenda*. January 2. https://boardagenda.com/2020/01/02/ key-trends-in-corporate-governance-for-2020; Weise, K. (2019). Over 4,200 Amazon workers push for climate change action, including cutting some ties to big oil. *New York Times*. www. nytimes.com. April 10.

As the Strategic Governance Challenge (Box 9.1) suggests, boards and top managers confront a complex set of often seemingly incompatible, competing strategic governance demands. The immense challenge requires a strategic mindset to meet the conflicting issues. We have taken a thorough and critical look at the influence of governance actors on a range of strategic decisions. We started with a look at internal and external governance actors and the mechanisms through which they shape managerial decisions and behaviors, and then elaborated on the heterogeneous influences of various governance actors on a myriad of strategic decisions, including corporate strategy, innovation strategy, competitive strategy, global strategy, stakeholder strategy, and corporate political strategy. Along the way, we have provided our recommendations on how company leaders can leverage the governance influencers to achieve effective strategic governance.

We conclude by turning our attention to the dominant global corporate governance trends, as sampled in the Strategic Governance Challenge (Box 9.1), and their ramifications on strategic decisions, including our recommendations for coping with them. But an understanding of strategic governance management must include an understanding of how executives themselves through their personal attributes influence the governance. After all, top executives, especially CEOs, carry the direct responsibility of making and implementing controlling decisions. Therefore, we introduce a model of governance-executive interactions to explain how governance actors and executive attributes jointly shape the firm's strategic direction.

CORPORATE GOVERNANCE TRENDS

Conceptions of good governance have changed over time as a result of interplay among social, political, and economic factors. Accompanying such a change is the shift in the purpose of businesses. In early periods of US business history, the primary goal of corporate governance lied in achieving growth instead of maximizing returns for shareholders.[1] To achieve growth goals, top executives adopted various strategies, such as creating cartels, trusts, and holding companies, engaging in vertical integration, and establishing conglomerate organizational firms. Although these strategies had been effective in spurring growth, they also led to negative consequences.[2] Namely, top executives had amassed significant power and discretion in influencing strategic decisions, which triggered the call for constraining managerial power and safeguarding shareholder power, known as the shareholder primacy model. In the modern era, the shareholder revolution has significantly increased the power of shareholders and pressured top executives to focus solely on maximizing shareholder value. Companies have been pushed to divest, spin off, and implement a stream of cost-cutting measures with the goal of creating shareholder value. Unfortunately, the effort to constrain managerial power and maximize shareholder value results in problematic managerial incentives, short-termism, and a neglect of other stakeholders.[3]

Recently, the pendulum of corporate governance focus has swung in another direction. The axiom of maximizing shareholder value faces increased criticism, as companies confront pressures to address the interests of non-shareholder stakeholders and to likewise focus on strategies that generate long-term societal value. Under this environment, stakeholders beyond shareholders gain influence and the following governance trends prove particularly relevant to understanding and managing strategic governance.

Increasing Focus on Stakeholders in Governance

The diffusion of the shareholder primacy model has markedly reduced managerial power in many countries, but with a byproduct that harms other stakeholder interests. For example, due to pressure from activist institutional investors, company leaders devote significant attention to operational efficiency and cost-cutting measures with the goal of boosting stock prices, but neglect investment in workplace safety, resulting in a higher rate of workplace injuries and illnesses.[4] The pressure to deliver shareholder value can also adversely affect consumer welfare. In an effort to boost sales and profits and be the first to hit the competitive market with new products and technologies, executives may allocate less attention to product quality or allow defective and unsafe products to reach the marketplace.[5] The shareholder primacy model also leads to social problems.[6] The disparity of wealth in the United States as well as other countries has significantly increased as an outcome of a governance focus on shareholder value maximization. The top 10 percent of the US population owns 81 percent of the stock while the bottom 90 percent own only 19 percent, giving rise to sharp wealth disparity.[7] To create shareholder value, company leaders in developed countries outsource jobs to low-wage countries or rely on subcontractors to fulfill needs. Oftentimes, subcontractors' employees suffer as a result of decreased wages and benefits. Mounting evidence suggests that the interests of stakeholders are left behind as a consequence of the shareholder primacy model, posing serious social and economic challenges.

Also, propelling the shift in focus toward a broader stakeholder orientation is shareholders' growing concern over ESG (environmental, social, and governance) issues. Larry Fink, CEO of BlackRock—the world's largest asset manager—noted that sustainability will be the firm's new standard for investing. As climate change and sustainability have turned into defining factors in companies' long-term prospects and become salient issues to many investors, asset managers integrate E&S (environmental and social) considerations into their investor decisions. Meanwhile, investors increasingly call for E&S-related disclosure, leading board members and top managers to define, integrate, and monitor E&S issues significant to their businesses.

Stakeholder considerations (see Chapter 7) have also led to a debate about corporate purpose. In August 2019, CEOs of the US Business Roundtable signed on to an amended statement on the Purpose of a Corporation, putting aside the traditional focus on shareholder value maximization and challenging company leaders to put stakeholders at the center of a company's purpose. Although a great deal of skepticism exists about the extent to which companies will compromise shareholders' interests for the sake of stakeholders, the latter's interests no longer occur as externalities for pundits, policymakers, and politicians to expound.

Investors' growing focus on E&S issues can profoundly influence strategic decisions, particularly corporate strategy (see Chapter 3), which pertains to what businesses a company should choose to operate in. Companies may divest or spin off businesses perceived negatively by investors in terms of environmental performance. For example, in 2015, DuPont spun off its specialty chemicals businesses into an independently traded company named Chemours as a way to mitigate potential environmental liabilities.[8] Meanwhile, companies with easy access to capital will compete to enter green or carbon-neutral businesses. Investors' attention to E&S issues can also shape competitive strategy (see Chapter 5). Executives can enhance their firms' competitive positions over their rivals by developing green technologies that result in less pollution. In this manner, competitive attacks during market entries can be replaced by rivals' attacks on each other for their poor E&S performance. In terms of global strategy (see Chapter 6), companies may refrain from expanding to countries with lax environmental protection.

Growing Shareholder and Stakeholder Activism

Shareholder activism (Chapter 2) will continue to evolve and diffuse around the world. After decades of being primarily a US-based phenomenon, the globalization of shareholder activism is increasing at an unprecedented speed. According to Activist Insight, shareholder activism campaigns took place in 45 countries, where non-US target firms reached 41 percent of all campaigns in 2019 (see Figure 9.1). Accordingly, boards around the globe need to maintain a certain degree of vigilance and prepare to respond to or assuage activist shareholder concerns (see Chapter 1). As the number of potential targets shrinks in North America, activist shareholders will continue to march into countries that are foreign to their activism. These shareholders will continue to focus on creating shareholder value through pushing executives to divest unrelated businesses, create value through divestitures, and implement cost-cutting measures.

The propagation of social media will continue to help stakeholder activism gain momentum. In the past, company leaders often dismissed protests, demonstrations, and boycotts by stakeholders, especially when they did not involve large numbers of people.[9] But in recent years, the changing landscape has strengthened the impact of stakeholder activism on managerial decision-making. In particular, employee activism has become a dominant force, as employees can individually or collectively stand up for or against their employers on controversial issues through staged walkouts, social media

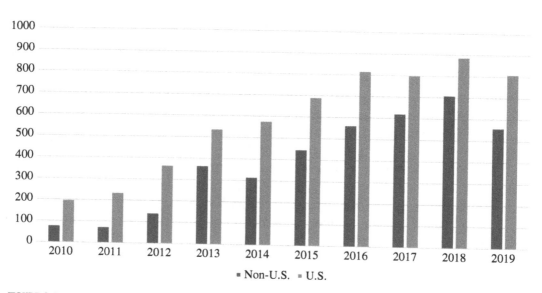

FIGURE 9.1 Number of shareholder activism campaigns targeting US and non-US companies. Data source: Activist Insight

campaigns, and protests. Oftentimes, employee activism centers on harmful or unjust employee experiences. Walkouts by Google employees in 2018, for example, were triggered by the company's lack of accountability regarding sexual harassment. In 2019, Walmart employees organized a 15-minute walk-out and moment of silence to show their stance on gun control, calling for their employer to cease selling firearms after 23 people were killed by a gun-man at a Walmart in Texas.[10]

Growing shareholder and stakeholder activism may have a profound influence on corporate governance and strategic decisions. Soon, boards may find it mandatory to take a proactive approach and develop an action plan to cope with both forms of activism. To protect companies from share-holder activism and to strengthen the board's negotiation power, boards may consider adopting a shareholder rights plan known as a *poison pill*. Poison pills gives existing shareholders the right to purchase additional shares at a discount, effectively diluting the ownership interest of activist shareholders. Yet, the adoption of poison pills may not always be an effective antidote to shareholder activism. For example, institutional shareholders often object to poison pills because they view these defenses as entrenching existing man-agement and denying shareholders the benefit of potentially valuable offers from a potential acquirer. To fend off stakeholder activism, managers need to cultivate relationships with internal and external stakeholders, listen to stake-holder activists, and provide a forum to share ideas and discuss concerns.[11]

Although shareholder and stakeholder activism have taken place indepen-dently so far, they may converge in the long run as shareholders pay increas-ing attention to ESG issues. A recent study examined the ESG credentials of around 1,300 companies in Europe and found that the worst perform-ers were more susceptible to activist shareholder intervention.[12] Shareholders are increasingly speaking up on ESG issues, partially because employees who hold shares in companies through workplace retirement plans are calling for more attention to such issues.[13]

Shareholder and stakeholder activism can shape managers' perceptions of risks and thus affect strategic decisions. To avoid being targeted by activ-ist shareholders, managers often eschew diversification into new businesses through acquisitions, instead choosing less visible corporate venture capi-tal investment. Whereas activist shareholders subject top executives to a high level of performance risks, activist stakeholders heighten their atten-tion to other sources of risks in managerial decision-making. Stakeholders' growing attention to environmental issues, for instance, may lead company executives to prioritize environmental risks, resulting in spinning off busi-nesses associated with high environmental liabilities, as illustrated in the DuPont example.

Changing Board Focus

The enactment of Sarbanes-Oxley Act in 2002 has profoundly changed board structures and roles (see Chapter 1). Boards intensify their monitoring role and take various measures to ensure that top executives serve the interests of shareholders. Also, as governance actors such as regulators believe executive directors to be beholden to CEOs and less effective in monitoring, outside directors constitute a majority of the board. But given the information gap between outside directors and top managers,[14] many boards rely on external auditors and compensation consultants to perform the audit function and the designing of executive compensations, and devote limited attention to companies' strategy and operations. Boards' dominant focus on monitoring and lack of attention to issues critical to sustainable competitiveness become insufficient as the landscape of business competition has changed.

As a result, large institutional investors such as BlackRock, Vanguard, and State Street Global Advisors are calling for directors to increase their oversight over corporate culture and human capital management, both of which pose financial risk to investors and are critical to firm long-term value. Culture enables strategy and is integral to effective strategy implementation. Meanwhile, as today's competition proceeds inherently as talent wars, human capital management oversight becomes crucial to preventing the mobility of human capital to rivals. Given the importance of talent management, in August 2020, the SEC adopted rule amendments to require a description of human capital resources to the extent such disclosures would be material to an understanding of a company's business. SEC Chairman Jay Clayton commented: "I am particularly supportive of the increased focus on human capital disclosures, which for various industries and companies can be an important driver of long-term value."[15]

As shareholders gradually become aware of the negative consequences of short-termism begotten by existing governance mechanisms, they place more pressure on boards to ensure that top executives prioritize long-term value creation and make corresponding strategic decisions. To achieve such a goal, directors should reduce their information gap with executives, as they face an urgent need to understand a company's strategy and engage more frequently with top executives. Directors also need to develop more collaborative relationships that allow the executives to focus on long-term value creation. In other words, boards must play a critical role in providing credibility with institutional investors when management is pursuing a strategy that can be significantly undervalued by the market.[16] To complement their individual expertise and engage successfully with management about strategic issues, board members are expected to acquire in-depth, firm-specific knowledge, a potentially difficult task for outside board members, many of whom lack a day-to-day working knowledge compared to insider managers.

The Governance Role of Platforms

Platform companies that operate Facebook, Shopify, YouTube, Amazon, and WeChat, among others, have become a serious force in today's economy. A survey by Accenture in 2016 suggests that 81 percent of executives find that platform-based business models will be core to their growth strategy within three years. As of 2016, over 170 platform companies were valued at US$1 billion or more.[17]

Two major types of platforms exist. Transaction platforms such as Amazon, Airbnb, and Uber help individuals and institutions find each other, facilitating their various interactions and commercial transactions. In contrast, innovation platforms provide a common technology framework on which others can build, including Apple's iOS and Google's Android. Platforms have spurred innovation and enhanced efficiency in sectors such as computers, videogames, automobiles, payment systems, and e-commerce.

Platform providers (i.e., parties providing platforms that connect platform producers and platform consumers), platform producers (i.e., parties who produce services or products for platform consumers), and platform consumers (i.e., parties who purchase services or products from platform producers) come together to form platform ecosystems. Although platform participants remain legally independent, they need to invest in co-specialized assets to create the platform or sign exclusivity agreements.[18] Unlike traditional organizations, platform providers such as Amazon and Alibaba do not have direct control over platform producers. In 2020, California voters sided with Uber by classifying Uber drivers as independent contractors rather than employees;[19] that the issue reached the ballot serves as an indication that platforms do not have direct control over their producers. Nevertheless, platform providers act as important governance actors for platform participants. For example, Apple screens apps designed for their platform for minimum quality and Facebook moderates posts for violations of their conditions such as fake news and copyright violations. Platform providers set the standards and establish transaction frameworks for their producers. In addition, platform providers offer indirect incentives for desirable quality or quantity of contributions by providing platform producers with information about what platform customers want, development kits, and performance awards.[20]

Although the number of large global platform-providing companies remains small, they generally enjoy a large assembly of producers and consumers. In fact, more than 30 percent of global economic activity will likely be mediated by digital platforms by 2025, according to a McKinsey research report.[21] The largest platforms have raised governance issues around the world, as described in the Strategic Governance Highlight Box 9.2. For example, platform providers face significant antitrust issues, and the outcomes of regulatory and court challenges will determine the future of platform ecosystems. Because platforms undergo significant governance challenges, and platform producers as well as platform consumers have lodged complaints, the governance actors confront increasing pressures. Board members of these platform providers need to design their internal governance in a way that creates balance between their own firms and platform producers and customers within the boundaries of platform ecosystems, but also meets the demands of regulators for fair competition.

MANAGING STRATEGIC GOVERNANCE IN A NEW ERA

The last section discusses several trends emerging in the corporate governance landscape that breed opportunities and pose threats to companies and can have profound ramifications on managing strategic governance. In terms of opportunities, as shareholders start to be wary of the adverse consequences of short-termism, they more willingly espouse strategic initiatives that may adversely affect short-term performance but give rise to long-term value creation. This shifting perspective can alleviate short-run performance pressures and enable top executives and boards to focus on long-term visions. In terms of challenges, executives and boards face an ever-more complex governance environment in which different stakeholders can impose competing or conflicting demands. In Figure 9.2, we enumerate a number of recommendations for managing strategic governance in a new governance era.

Build

The success of strategic governance hinges on selecting directors who are not only committed to corporate purpose but also possess experiences and knowledge that enable them to make effective strategic decisions. The importance of top executive selection is seemingly self-evident. Yet, directors that fail in their board deliberations are unlikely to select appropriate top executives. As board members are anticipated to engage more deeply in strategic decisions and consider the interests of stakeholders, they should rethink the function of the company more as a cooperative team to produce new wealth.[22] Accordingly, boards should represent those stakeholders that can add value, assume unique risk, and possess strategic information. The conception of boards only

BOX 9.2 Strategic Governance Highlight: Governance Challenges for Platform Firms

Platform technology firms face a number of governance challenges, especially from regulators. The first challenge involves net-neutrality, which relates to internet service providers (ISPs) as well as content providers who are owned by the ISPs. For example, AT&T, a large ISP, could offer its own HBO MAX service at a reduced rate while charging competitors Netflix and Disney Plus a fee to reach the same homes. On the one hand, net-neutrality provides a level playing field for all firms including internet startups who want to provide content. On the other hand, if there is bundling available (as in the AT&T example), some regulators project that overall broadband costs will be lower for those platforms that can bundle services, creating an advantage over other competitors, especially those that are not ISP providers. Net-neutrality is regulated by the Federal Communications Commission (FCC), but the FCC takes cues from the current administration as well as new legislation from the Congress. Under the Trump administration, net-neutrality regulation has been more lax than previously. What happens under the Biden administration is yet to be determined.

Another issue has to do with privacy. Large platform firms like Facebook use artificial intelligence to provide information based on individual posts and views, and sell advertising based on users' history in friendship networks. Facebook uses facial recognition technology to allow users to recognize themselves on someone else's post and thus extend its reach to others' networks. Facebook uses this type of intrusion into individual lives in order to fine-tune advertising based on users' observed preferences. Netflix and Amazon take similar actions in providing individualized movie selections as well as products that may meet individual tastes for content consumption. But what should be the limits on these firms in regard to an individual's privacy? We are likely to see more legislation on this topic in the future.

How much liability does a platform firm have in regard to the news and information that it provides to users through its platform? Section 230 of the Communication Decency Act enacted in 1996 provides protection for companies from liability for what their users post online. However, information providers like Twitter and Facebook have been doing more monitoring of online content and censoring articles that they believe encourage terrorism or foster public harm through fake news posts. Conservative politicians believe their censoring crosses the line, not only protecting users from harmful or dangerous content but also blocking access to conservative thought. In contrast, liberal politicians think that these platforms are not doing enough to supervise posts that they construe to be false or misleading. As a result, both sides are threatening to revoke section 230 or change it in a way that would increase these platform firms' liability exposure.

Finally, the market power of "trillion-dollar" firms such as Alphabet (parent of Google), Facebook, Amazon, and Apple presents another challenge. All of these firms are being referred to the Department of Justice for actual or potential antitrust prosecution. In October 2020, the Department of Justice accused Alphabet of using anticompetitive tactics to preserve its monopoly in the search engine business, especially with Apple and Samsung using Google as their default search engine. Furthermore, in December 2020, 38 state lawsuits were announced against Google. That the same month, the Federal Trade Commission (FTC) sued Facebook for buying startups and freezing small firms out of the social media business, thereby choking off competition from social media startups. As such, the FTC wants to unwind Facebook's acquisition of WhatsApp and Instagram. And Congress, through a lengthy investigation, has accused Amazon of holding monopoly power over its third-party sellers, as well as accused Apple of exerting monopoly power over application software providers through its App Store.

Interestingly, Chinese authorities are also seeking to rein in Alibaba and Tencent, large internet giants comparable to Amazon and Facebook, respectively. The authorities halted Alibaba's Ant IPO because Ant handles large amounts of online financial transactions and provides consumer loans that the Chinese banking system does not control, while also having data that is not currently available to the central government, especially for younger consumers. The Chinese government is unlikely to allow information that is not under its radar. But the government is also generally concerned about monopoly power and about these firms "colluding to share sensitive consumer data" and "forming agreements to block out smaller rivals."

Because of the powerful disruption that platform companies have caused in the advertising, media, and content production space, as well as in news distribution and retail sales, these issues and others will be salient governance topics that board members of platform firms will need to address. In fact, because of digitalization and the reach of large platform firms, all firms' strategic governance plans are already undergoing disruption to varying degrees. As such, board members need to watch what happens and seek to understand how the outcomes of these regulatory battles will shape competition and make sure that their firms are properly protected, including lobbying the government to shape policies (see Chapter 7) that allow them to compete in a fair and competitive environment.

Sources: Bartz, D., & Shepardson, D. (2020). U.S. says Google breakup may be needed to end violations of antitrust law. *Reuters*, www.reuters.com, October 20; Fenwick, M., McCahery, J. A., & Vermeulen, E. P. M. (2020). The end of 'corporate' governance: Hello 'platform' governance. *European Business Organization Law Review* 20, 171–199; McKinnon, J. D. (2020). These are the US antitrust cases facing Google, Facebook and others, *Wall Street Journal*, www.wsj.com, December 17; Mims, C. (2020). Joe Biden's 5 tech priorities. *Wall Street Journal*, www.wsj.com, December 19; Wei, J. (2020). Jack Ma makes Ant offer to placate Chinese regulators. *Wall Street Journal*, www.wsj.com, December 20; Schmeiss; J., Hoelzle, K., & Tech, R. P. G. (2019). Designing governance mechanisms in platform ecosystems: Addressing the paradox of openness through blockchain technology. *California Management Review* 62(1), 121–143.

as a monitoring body can no longer meet new governance challenges; in fact, boards can be a source of "inertia" in the face of environmental change and needed strategic adaptation if they only focus on monitoring or regulation compliance.[23]

The monitoring function of boards requires members to select independent directors who have no business ties with the company. This requirement

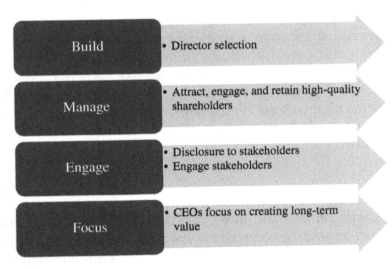

FIGURE 9.2 Managing strategic governance in a new era.

inevitably results in choosing directors who lack company knowhow and have to rely on information from managers and workers to make informed strategic decisions.[24] But in the absence of a solid understanding of the business, directors are unable to play an effective governance role, not to mention deeply engage in strategic decisions. Directors oftentimes rely on "board service providers" like external audit firms and compensation consultants to perform their board functions. As management selects service providers such as auditors, this may carry conflicts of interest and result in ineffective monitoring by these service providers whose revenues hinge on their relationships with management. In 2020, Ernst & Young, one of the big four auditors, verified three years of Wirecard's financial results even though the auditor had previously received a whistleblower's tip about fraudulent behaviors by Wirecard executives.[25] This case suggests that there are risks to relying exclusively on external auditors as a substitute for board and audit committee monitoring. Similarly, executive compensation consultants tend to make recommendations for higher CEO pay to "cross-sell" services and to secure "repeat business".[26] For these reasons, selecting directors based on their independence may not meet new governance challenges.

Instead, firms may prioritize the following attributes in director selection. First, director candidates need to espouse strategic goals. Directors who are not committed to a company's strategic objectives are unlikely to add long-term value to achieving those goals. Second, directors need to bring business savviness and strategic information to their board role. The savviness can occur in the form of knowledge about focal industries or vertically related industry or industries in which a company plans to enter. Third, directors should carry some firm-specific risks in the companies in which they serve. This condition may require directors to increase the level of wealth risks that cannot be diversified away to a moderate level. However, if a director has too much firm-specific wealth risk, he or she may refrain from strategic risk taking. As such, incentives need to be balanced to ensure that board members incur enough risk to meet the firm needs. Companies controlled by private equity (PE) firms tend to have high-performing boards because the directors often take a sufficiently large enough ownership stake, giving them credible "skin in the game."[27]

Manage

Shareholders will remain the most crucial stakeholder for most companies. Executives should hence actively manage their relationships with the owners. Shareholder management begins with shareholder segmentation. As discussed in Chapter 2, shareholders can be broadly classified as dedicated, quasi-indexer, or transient. Quasi-indexers are typically computer-run index funds or shareholders who use computer models to drive their trades. Given the mechanical rule used by these shareholders, it is difficult for firms to influence them. Transient shareholders seek short-term financial gain by betting on firm news announcements. Given their short-term focus, these shareholders do not have motivation to understand companies' businesses and long-term plans. Thus, leadership may not need to waste time on managing relationships with these shareholders. Dedicated shareholders typically take a long-term position in a company after rigorous due diligence and can be important allies for top managers. These shareholders should be the focus of shareholder management.

After performing shareholder segmentation, managers then need to deepen their understanding of the shareholders to be managed. Some of the questions to consider in shareholder analyses can be: (1) Have these shareholders accumulated rich industry experiences through portfolio holdings? (2) Have these shareholders targeted portfolio companies for activism? (3) Do these shareholders attend to ESG issues? (4) Do these shareholders make political campaign contributions? Do these shareholders have common ownership of rival firms in the focal firm's industry (see Chapter 5)? Addressing these questions can help executives make accurate predictions of the owners' behaviors and avoid scenarios in which their strategic decisions go against the shareholders' preferences.

The most critical component of shareholder management entails establishing a working group consisting of C-suite and board representation and engaging in frequent interactions. The communication between company leaders and dedicated shareholders should be two-way. Specifically, the leaders need to keep dedicated shareholders informed about the rationale behind their strategic decisions. Yet, they need to be cautious about what information can be communicated because the Regulation Fair Disclosure enacted in 2000 prohibits publicly traded firms from disclosing selective information to preferred analysts and institutional investors. But interactions with dedicated shareholders should also serve top executives as opportunities to learn from their expertise and understand their perspectives.

Engage

The debate about whether the primary purpose of a corporation is to serve shareholders or stakeholders has intensified, especially during the recent COVID-19 pandemic. Such a debate typically focuses on a zero-sum game in which shareholders' gains come at the expense of other stakeholders. However, the interests of shareholders and stakeholders are often aligned in the long run.[28] A case in point is that the majority of ESG funds outperformed the wider market over the last decade.[29] Alignment may also occur during social or economic crisis situations. During the pandemic, shareholders generally lend support to companies who have prioritized the health and safety of employees and customers and cease imposing pressure on companies to engage in share buybacks. Stakeholder engagement hence needs to start with acknowledging that conflicts of interest between shareholders and stakeholders are not irreconcilable.[30] Next, company leaders need to establish and actively maintain communication channels with various stakeholders. These channels enable stakeholders to convey their perspectives and opinions and facilitate building an inclusive culture. Since its establishment over 150 years ago, Cadbury has been known for its fair treatment of employees thanks to channels through which top managers communicate with employees directly. By consulting employees regularly and actively taking action to address their concerns, company leaders foster high morale and increase productivity.

For effective stakeholder management, executives need to identify core and peripheral stakeholders by analyzing each stakeholder's contributions to value-creating competitive advantages. This step requires top managers to combine their internal resource and capability analysis with stakeholder analysis. Specifically, managers need to identify to what extent each stakeholder can influence the firm's core competencies, and should maintain direct communication channels with those that prove integral to value-creation. However, managers may consider pursuing a less resource-consuming strategy by disclosing stakeholder engagement to peripheral stakeholders, such as communities and suppliers. Stakeholder engagement should not occur separately from shareholder engagement, since some shareholders such as pension funds may focus on how a company treats its employees.[31] Other shareholders are highly concerned about a company's investment in coping with climate change. Therefore, managers should understand whether shareholders are supportive of certain stakeholders. Otherwise, neglecting shareholders can lead executives to underestimate the power of a stakeholder group.

Platform companies constitute a new stakeholder group that platform producers as well as nonplatform producers need to cope with. As noted, platform business models have accelerated since the advent of digital technologies such as smartphones, which have greatly expanded the range of industries in which platform business models are feasible by making it easier to connect and coordinate different actors in real time.[32] In addition, platforms based on digital technologies face low transaction costs and few capacity constraints and can be scaled up rapidly, often with limited capital investments.[33] Platform companies like Amazon have the intrinsic advantage in a platform economy as they own the platforms and set the rules of engagement. Many platform companies are also replete with cash, enabling them to pursue unrelated diversification. Amazon is investing in server farms and drones, and

Jeff Bezos personally owns the *Washington Post*. Mark Zuckerberg's Facebook is investing in a number of platforms, including WhatsApp and Instagram, beyond Facebook itself, as well as in virtual-reality equipment. Elon Musk, head of Tesla, an electric-car maker, has separate companies that are investing in space travel and solar-energy systems. As technology continues to accelerate, all firms need to closely monitor platform companies and their strategic moves before disruption occurs and it is too late.

Focus

Effective CEOs allocate capital and human resources in ways that do not just enrich shareholders but also benefit all the important stakeholders. To allow these CEOs to do so, the board should establish long-term value creation as the company's governing objective. This focus requires CEOs to build productive relationships with their board members, since support from the board creates the bedrock for a long-term value creation emphasis. Meanwhile, although stakeholders are indispensable to long-term value creation, CEOs need to balance stakeholder preferences in the process. For instance, paying too much attention to employee relations can impede a company's competitiveness by reducing radical or disruptive innovation,[34] which may in turn adversely influence the viability of employees' interests. Yet, failing to pay employees adequately can result in a substandard workforce. Listening to shareholders and stakeholders is foundational to engagement strategies. However, CEOs are eventually responsible for companies' long-term value creation and succumbing to stakeholders' pressures without proper judgment can cause the risk of compromising strategic goals and the interests of all.

The Strategic Governance Highlight (Box 9.3) provides an example of how our model to build, manage, engage, and focus (see Figure 9.2) might be applied, using the case of Paul Polman, the former CEO of Unilever, a large European consumer products firm focused on food, soap, and cosmetics among other businesses. Polman was able to combine strong shareholder value creation while at the same time establishing strong stakeholder relations through its focal socially responsible actions to help alleviate poverty and improve environmental sustainability.

To ensure that CEOs focus on long-term value creation, directors may consider (1) developing forward-looking strategic metrics and deemphasizing short-term financial performance goals, (2) proactively communicating their long-term strategic metrics and goals to shareholders, (3) tying executive compensation with strategic metrics, and (4) granting CEOs a sufficient degree of flexibility and discretion that might be curtailed by an excessive focus on board monitoring.[35]

BOX 9.3   Strategic Governance Highlight: Unilever and Board Effectiveness in the New Era

In 2009, Paul Polman, a Dutch executive who previously worked for Procter & Gamble (P&G) as its European president, became the CEO of Unilever, a consumer product firm with iconic brands like Ben and Jerry's and Dove. During the 10 years of his tenure, which ended in early 2019, "the company implemented its ambitious Sustainable Living Plan aimed to double its growth, halve its environmental impact, and triple its social impact. The plan succeeded, with Unilever's annual sales rising from $38 billion to more than $60 billion, and the company becoming a beacon for those who wanted their work to matter" (Forbes).

We use Unilever, Polman, and his board of directors as an example of implementing our model to build, manage, engage, and focus. In 2008, shortly after being named the incoming CEO, he attended a meeting along with the Unilever board members at the Taj Mahal Hotel in Mumbai when terrorists attacked the hotel. Polman and the rest of the team apparently spent several anxious hours until rescued by police the next morning. The experience unified the company leaders and led them to form the Sustainable Living Plan, noted above, which established a strong purpose for the company and its employees.

With a strong purpose and a board committed to achieving it, executives need to manage and execute to fulfill the high-level goals, as those represented by the Sustainable Living Plan. Polman was able to deliver both top- and bottom-line performance, which enabled strong shareholder returns of 290 percent during his tenure. He also strengthened the firm's reputation for relieving poverty and improving its sustainability footprint, overall improving the firm's standing and increasing stakeholder commitment.

But Polman had to engage with financial analysts and fight off a takeover attempt by Kraft Heinz Co. that would have disrupted the strategic plan. Kraft had been managed by private equity owners and through these owners had established "a reputation for lifting earnings through cost-cutting." Polman nevertheless convinced his shareholders that the fit with Kraft would not build shareholder value in the long term. In particular, he pointed out that long-term brand investment was at the essence of Unilever's strategy. Furthermore, financial analysts had challenged him during earnings call question-and-answer periods about his commitment to reining in costs. But he was able to stick to his philosophy of increasing long-term shareholder value through brand investment while being socially responsible at the same time.

Focus on the Sustainable Living Plan allowed Polman and the board to fully meet the main goals outlined in the strategy. Although Polman once said that Unilever was "the world's biggest NGO" because of its global partnerships in alleviating poverty and goal of improving sustainability, on a comparative basis his approach worked in terms of shareholder value. By 2017 and early 2018, Unilever's share price had risen by 175 percent while Nestlé and P&G, comparable consumer product firms, had grown 100 and 50 percent, respectively.

Sources: Aziz, A. (2020). Paul Polman on courageous CEOs and how purpose is the growth story of the century (part 1). *Forbes*, www.forbes.com, May 25; Polman, P., Sisodia, R., & Tindell, K. (2020). What good business looks like. *Harvard Business Review Digital Articles*, www.hbs.com, May 13; Kalkowski, J. (2019). Unilever sets example of how to tackle sustainability. *Flexible Packaging*, August, 6; Buckley, T. (2018). Unilever's Polman mends fences after joust with Goldman analyst. *Bloomberg*, www.bloomberg.com, December 5; Grocer (2018). Paul Polman: fall guy, good guy, good bye. *Grocer*, December 1, 3.

GOVERNANCE-EXECUTIVE INTERACTION MODEL

Although governance actors can have a profound influence on strategic decisions, top managers, instead of the influencers, make the decisions. Our discussion of strategic governance would therefore be incomplete without considering executives' attributes. These top managers can differ from one another in personalities,[36] values,[37] and motives.[38] Such differences can help to explain distinct strategic decisions. CEO personality, for example, has been shown to influence the CEO's ability to adapt to environmental changes.[39] Those who exhibit a high level of overconfidence[40] tend to make large-scale acquisitions that destroy value. Similarly, narcissistic CEOs tend to prefer risky strategic decisions.[41]

Executive attributes pertain to "who executives are" and can shape their information processing and attention allocation, which will then affect their decisions. In terms of personality, the chief executives differ in character traits such as extraversion, openness, conscientiousness, agreeableness, and neuroticism.[42] For instance, extraversion, as a personality trait, signifies more or less positive affect, assertive behavior, decisive thinking, and desire for social engagement.[43] Different from personality traits, values pertain to "a broad tendency to prefer certain states of affairs over others."[44] Executives have been shown to differ in political values.[45] Research suggests that politically liberal CEOs are more sensitive to social issues in general and to such specific issues as diversity, social change, human rights, and the environment, as well as more willing to take risk than conservative CEOs.[46] Executives may also differ in terms of their motives,[47] which signify "wishes and desires."[48] The most influential set of motives has been termed as the "Big Three":[49] need for achievement, need for power, and need for affiliation. Executives motivated by achievement act in ways that will help them perform to a standard of excellence; executives driven by power seek to exert impact, control, and influence over others as well as limit others' influence over themselves; and executives motivated by affiliation highly value interpersonal relationships and distance themselves from those they dislike or who have conflicting viewpoints.[50]

Given the heterogeneity in executive personalities, values, and motives, executives may react differently to the intervention from governance actors. It is therefore critical for us to consider the interaction between top executive attributes and governance actors to gain a complete insight into strategic governance. We introduce a model of governance-executive interactions in Figure 9.3. Specifically, executives may respond to inducement and threat from governance actors in distinct ways, which in turn shapes strategic decisions.

Broadly speaking, governance actors impact managerial behaviors through inducement (e.g., incentives) and threat (e.g., loss of job). Top executives are rewarded if they meet firm financial and social performance—a type of inducement. Threat pertains to the ability of governance actors to discipline top executives if the latter fail to satisfy their expectations. For instance, CEOs can be fired by boards if found to have engaged in financial misconduct. The interaction between governance actors and executive attributes can have a "pull" or "push" effect on strategic decisions. Pull occurs when governance actors reinforce the influence of executive

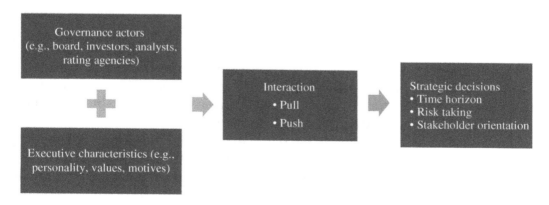

FIGURE 9.3   Model of governance-executive interactions.

attributes on strategic choices. CEOs with a strong need for achievement, for example, are anticipated to prefer risky strategic decisions. Providing these CEOs with high levels of incentive compensation may magnify the risk-taking propensity. Push occurs when governance actors weaken the influence of executive attributes on strategic choices. CEOs with a liberal political value may prefer business expansion, but board monitoring may weaken their investment tendencies, resulting in a push effect. However, for CEOs with a conservative political value orientation, boards may need to provide incentives and support—that is, pull—so that they will not forgo valuable expansion opportunities.

The interaction between executive attributes and governance actors can influence three dimensions of strategic decisions: time horizon, risk taking, and stakeholder orientation. In regard to time horizon, some strategic decisions can generate immediate payoffs whereas others focus on creating long-term value. Executive attributes can interact with governance actors to influence this time horizon. Take the conscientiousness personality trait. Individuals with high conscientiousness tend to exhibit a strong desire to do a task well, to take obligations to others seriously, and to display planned rather than spontaneous behavior. Thus, executives with high conscientiousness will focus on long-term strategic decisions. If the goal of governance actors is to incentivize conscientious CEOs to balance long-term and short-term strategic goals, the influencers should provide the chief executives a higher proportion of incentive pay tied to short-term performance because they are naturally oriented to the long term.

The second dimension, risk taking, reflects that strategic decisions are associated with varying levels of risk. Expansion to a new country through acquisitions generally proves riskier than through joint ventures. Entering an unrelated industry carries more uncertainty than entering a vertically related industry. Liberal and extraverted CEOs tend to opt for risky strategic decisions, which may not always serve the interests of stakeholders. In these cases, governance actors may need to closely monitor these CEOs' strategic decisions to ensure that they will not overinvest in high-risk projects.

The last dimension of strategic decisions pertains to stakeholder orientation. Strategic decisions often involve trade-offs among different stakeholders at least in the short run. Reorganizations and divestitures can increase operational efficiency and improve firm value, which is desired by shareholders, but can give rise to layoffs, adversely affecting the interests of employees. Corporate political activities used to protect a firm's market position and advance its business interests may harm the welfare of consumers. Meanwhile, executives may exhibit different propensity for safeguarding stakeholder interests. For example, CEOs with a strong liberal political value are anticipated to allocate more resources and attention to stakeholders than those with a strong conservative political value. To encourage CEOs with a strong conservative political value to consider stakeholders' interests in decision-making, board members may need to emphasize ESG performance in the executive compensation package.

In sum, the model of governance-executive interactions suggests that the influence of governance actors on strategic decisions hinges on executive attributes. To encourage top executives to make appropriate strategic decisions, governance actors need to understand their top leader's personality, values, and motives; otherwise, their intervention and attempts to influence strategic decisions can backfire and result in unintended consequences. Perhaps, if Kraft-Heinz had acquired Unilever (see Box 9.3 case), Unilever's long-term performance under CEO Polman would not have been as stellar as it turned out, given the possible mismatch between Polman's personal attributes emphasizing long-term brand investment and the governance orientation of Kraft-Heinz focused on cutting costs. If the merger had taken place and Polman had continued as CEO, there would have been need for adjustments to both the incentives provided and governance monitoring to make the arrangement work effectively.

Recommendations for Boards and Top Executives

Based on the model of governance-executive interactions, we have several recommendations for board members and top executives to implement strategic governance. Our recommendations are summarized in Figure 9.4.

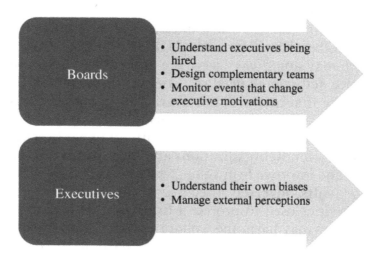

FIGURE 9.4 Recommendations for boards and executives.

Recommendations for Boards The first recommendation for directors of boards is to understand executive attributes prior to hiring. Boards need to evaluate the strategic needs of a company by first asking the following questions: Does the company need to actively pursue growth in the next few years? Does the company need to consolidate and streamline existing businesses? Does the company need a CEO who can quickly turn around the firm through effective implementation? Does the company need to increase its focus on stakeholders? Only if boards have a deep understanding of the firm's strategy as well as understand a potential CEO's strategic orientation can they hire executives with appropriately matched attributes.

The next step for directors consists of assessing potential candidates' personalities, values, and motives. Social psychologists have developed instruments to measure these traits. Yet, asking potential job candidates to complete surveys can be intrusive and oftentimes gives rise to biased responses. One unobtrusive way to measure individuals' personality, values, and motives can be based on their written language.[51] People's preferences, perceptions, and personalities are revealed in their written and spoken words.[52] Unobtrusive measures based on language can help eliminate much of the reactivity and researchers' expectations and provide reliable indicators of individual differences.[53]

Board members do not engage in and cannot feasibly monitor all strategic decisions. To counteract the limitation, directors may consider creating top management teams comprised of managers that complement each other and facilitate peer monitoring among themselves.[54] For instance, pairing an optimistic CEO with a pessimistic chief financial officer (CFO) may improve firm acquisition performance.[55] In this pairing, the more conservative CFO brings balance to the risk taking–oriented chief executive. In essence, designing a top management team with complementary values, personalities, and motives can improve the effectiveness of strategic decisions. However, a legitimate concern may be that the complementarity can give rise to a high level of diversity in character traits, which may harm cohesion among the top executives.

Finally, board members should monitor key events experienced by top executives for implications on their motives, as novel, disruptive, and critical events can change their motives.[56] Novelty captures the extent to which an event is distinct or at variation from current and past behaviors. Disruption reflects the amount or degree of change in usual activities. Criticality captures "the degree to which an event is important, essential, or a priority" to an organization.[57] CEOs may change their motives after they have experienced key events. For instance, CEOs who have experienced the death of a peer director are less motivated by wealth and social status and refrain from acquisitions,[58] but pay more attention to stakeholders.[59]

As noted in Chapter 3, CEOs who have lost prestigious performance awards to rival CEOs may engage in intensive acquisitions with the goal of enhancing their own external recognition.[60] Therefore, board members need to be aware of key personal and peer events experienced by executives and update governance mechanisms accordingly in response to changes triggered by such events.

Recommendations for Top Executives   First, top executives need to be aware of their own tendencies so that they can attend to potential decision biases arising from their own personality, values, and motives. Second, top executives need to manage the impressions that they leave on stakeholders, especially shareholders. Shareholders may create their assessment of CEOs and firms based on the executives' language patterns,[61] as spoken language represents an essential source of information for shareholders.[62] In particular, the way a CEO speaks may help shareholders form perceptions of her, thereby facilitating a better understanding of the motives underlying strategic decisions.

When shareholders perceive a CEO to have a strong agentic value—a value emphasizing self-advancement in social hierarchies, they may perceive that the chief executive engages in actions that commemorate a legacy for oneself and disregard interpersonal relations.[63] Focusing on oneself, agentic-oriented CEOs are more likely to be motivated by extrinsic rewards, such as money and power, and tend to speak more about the achievements that they have earned through their hard work.[64] This inclination can lead to negative reactions from shareholders. Thus, top executives should carefully manage their external perceptions in the eyes of stakeholders, including shareholders, so that they can align with them to garner input and support for their strategic decisions. With such input and support, their decisions have a greater chance of achieving strategic goals.[65]

The practice of strategic governance is not only a science but also an art. It requires constant updates, modifications, and intense board evaluation in response to changing internal and external environments. Making effective strategic decisions can have profound influences on the well-being of many stakeholders. We hope that this book helps governance practitioners better understand and exercise improved strategic governance.

NOTES

1. Chambers, J. W. (2000). *The tyranny of change: America in the Progressive Era, 1890–1920.* Rutgers University Press: New Brunswick, N.J.
2. Herman, E. S. 1981. *Corporate Control, Corporate Power.* Cambridge University Press: New York.

3. Dallas, L. L. (2017). Is there hope for change: The evolution of conceptions of good corporate governance. *San Diego Law Review* 54(3): 491–564.

4. Shi, W., Xia, C., & Meyer-Doyle, P. (2020). Who bleeds when activists attack? Activist institutional ownership and employee safety. Working paper, University of Miami.

5. Chen, Y., & Hua, X. (2017). Competition, product safety, and product liability. *Journal of Law, Economics, and Organization* 33(2): 237–267.

6. Cobb, J. A. (2016). How firms shape income inequality: Stakeholder power, executive decision making, and the structuring of employment relationships. *Academy of Management Review* 41(2): 324–348; Cobb, J. A. (2019). Managing the conflicting interests of workers and shareholders: Evidence from pension-assumption manipulations. *ILR Review* 72(3): 523–551.

7. Frank, R. (2014). The stock gap: American stock holdings at 18-year low. *CNBC.* www.cnbc.com, September 8.

8. Baker, A. C., Larcker, D. F., & Tayan, B. (2020). Environmental spinoffs: The attempt to dump liability through spin and bankruptcy. In *Stanford Closer Look Series*. Corporate Governance Research Initiative.

9. Vasi, I. B., & King, B. G. 2012. Social movements, risk perceptions, and economic outcomes: The effect of primary and secondary stakeholder activism on firms' perceived environmental risk and financial performance. *American Sociological Review* 77(4): 573–596.

10. Bhattarai, A., & Bensinger, G. (2019). Walmart employees stage a walkout to protest gun sales. *Washington Post.* www.washingtonpost.com, August 7.

11. Briscoe, F., & Gupta, A. (2021). Business disruption from the inside out: A playbook for employee activists and advice for leaders. *Stanford Social Innovation Review*: 48–54.

12. Saigol, L. (2019). Code green: Activist investors are coming for environmental offenders. *MarketWatch*, www.marketwatch.com, December 3.

13. Miller, M. (2020). Bit by bit, socially conscious investors are influencing 401(k)'s. *New York Times*, www.nytimes.com, September 27.

14. Boivie, S., Bednar, M. K., Aguilera, R. V., & Andrus, J. L. (2016). Are boards designed to fail? The implausibility of effective board monitoring. *Academy of Management Annals* 10(1): 319–407.

15. SEC (2020). SEC adopts rule amendments to modernize disclosures of business, legal proceedings, and risk factors under regulation S-K. US Securities and Exchange Commission. www.sec.gov.

16. Gilson, R. J., & Gordon, J. N. (2019). Board 3.0: An introduction symposium: outsourcing the board: how board service providers can improve corporate governance. *Business Lawyer* 74(2): 351–366.

17. Wladawsky-Berger, I. (2016). The rise of the platform economy. *Wall Street Journal.* www.wsj.com, February 12.

18. Kretschmer, T., Leiponen, A., Schilling, M., & Vasudeva, G. (2020). Platform ecosystems as meta-organizations: implications for platform strategies. *Strategic Management Journal.* https://onlinelibrary.wiley.com/doi/full/10.1002/smj.3250.

19. Siddiqui, F., & Tiku, N. (2020). California voters sided with Uber, denying drivers benefits by classifying them as contractors. *Washington Post*. www.washingtonpost.com, November 4.

20. Rietveld, J., Schilling, M. A., Bellavitis, C. (2019). Platform strategy: Managing ecosystem value through selective promotion of complements. *Organization Science* 30(6): 1232–1251.

21. Catlin, T., Lorenz, J.-T., Nandan, J., Sharma, S., & Waschto, A. (2018). *Insurance beyond Digital: The Rise of Ecosystems and Platforms*. McKinsey.

22. Blair, M. M., & Stout, L. A. (1999). A team production theory of corporate law. *Virginia Law Review* 85(2): 247–328.

23. Hoppmann, J., Naegele, F., & Girod, B. (2019). Boards as a source of inertia: Examining the internal challenges and dynamics of boards of directors in times of environmental discontinuities. *Academy of Management Journal* 62(2): 437–468.

24. Kaufman, A., & Englander, E. (2005). A team production model of corporate governance. *Academy of Management Executive* 19(3): 9–22.

25. Kowsmann, P., Davies, P. J., & Chung, J. (2020). Wirecard scandal puts spotlight on auditor Ernst & Young. *Wall Street Journal*. www.wsj.com, June 7.

26. Murphy, K. J., & Sandino, T. (2010). Executive pay and "independent" compensation consultants. *Journal of Accounting and Economics* 49(3): 247–262.

27. Gilson & Gordon. Board 3.0.

28. Amis, J., Barney, J., Mahoney, J. T., & Wang, H. (2020). From the editors — why we need a theory of stakeholder governance—and why this is a hard problem. *Academy of Management Review* 45(3): 499–503.

29. Riding, S. (2020). Majority of ESG funds outperform wider market over 10 years. *Financial Times*, www.ft.com, June 13.

30. Hoskisson, R., Gambeta, E., Green, C., & Li, T. (2018). Is my firm-specific investment protected? Overcoming the stakeholder investment dilemma in the resource based view. *Academy of Management Review* 43(2): 284–306.

31. Ibid.

32. Evans, D. S., & Schmalensee, R. (2016). *Matchmakers: The new economics of multisided platforms*. Boston, MA: Harvard Business Review Press.

33. Van Alstyne, M. W., Parker, G. G., & Choudary, S. P. (2016). Pipelines, platforms, and the new rules of strategy. *Harvard Business Review* 94(4): 54–62.

34. Gambeta, E., Koka, B. R., & Hoskisson, R. E. (2019). Being too good for your own good: A stakeholder perspective on the differential effect of firm–employee relationships on innovation search. *Strategic Management Journal* 40(1): 108–126.

35. Faleye, O., Hoitash, R., & Hoitash, U. (2011). The costs of intense board monitoring. *Journal of Financial Economics* 101(1): 160–181.

36. Harrison, J. S., Thurgood, G. R., Boivie, S., & Pfarrer, M. D. (2019). Measuring CEO personality: Developing, validating, and testing a linguistic tool. *Strategic Management Journal*. 40(8): 1316–1330.

37. Chin, M. K., Hambrick, D. C., & Trevino, L. K. (2013). Political ideologies of CEOs: The influence of executives' values on corporate social responsibility. *Administrative Science Quarterly* 58(2): 197–232.

38. Veenstra, K. (2020). CEO implicit motives: their impact on firm performance. *Behavioral Research in Accounting*, 32(2): 57–89.
39. Nadkarni, S., & Herrmann, P. (2010). CEO personality, strategic flexibility, and firm performance: The case of the Indian business process outsourcing industry. *Academy of Management Journal* 53(5): 1050–1073.
40. Malmendier, U., & Tate, G. (2008). Who makes acquisitions? CEO overconfidence and the market's reaction. *Journal of Financial Economics* 89(1): 20–43.
41. Li, J. T., & Tang, Y. (2010). CEO hubris and firm risk taking in China: The moderating role of managerial discretion. *Academy of Management Journal* 53(1): 45–68.
42. Harrison, Thurgood, Boivie, & Pfarrer. Measuring CEO personality.
43. Malhotra, S., Reus, T. H., Zhu, P., & Roelofsen, E.M. (2018). The acquisitive nature of extroverted CEOs. *Administrative Science Quarterly* 63(2): 370–408.
44. Hofstede, G. (1980). *Culture's Consequences: International Differences in Work-Related Values*. Sage: Thousand Oaks, p.19.
45. Chin, Hambrick, & Trevino. Political ideologies of CEOs.
46. Graffin, S. D., Hubbard, T. D., Christensen, D. M., & Lee, E. Y. (2020). The influence of CEO risk tolerance on initial pay packages. *Strategic Management Journal* 41(4): 788–811.
47. Schultheiss, O. C. (2008). Implicit motives. In John, O. P., Robins, R. W., & Pervin, L. A. (eds.) *Handbook of Personality Psychology: Theory and Research*. New York: Guilford Press.
48. Winter, D. G., John, O. P., Stewart, A. J., Klohnen, E. C., & Duncan, L. E. (1998). Traits and motives: Toward an integration of two traditions in personality research. *Psychological Review* 105(2): 230–250.
49. Kehr, H. M. (2004). Integrating implicit motives, explicit motives, and perceived abilities: The compensatory model of work motivation and volition. *Academy of Management Review* 29(3): 479–499.
50. Shi, W., DesJardine, M. (in press). Under attack! CEO implicit motives and firm competitive responses following short seller activism. *Organization Science*.
51. Daly, J. P., Pouder, R. W., Kabanoff, B. (2004). The effects of initial differences in firms' espoused values on their postmerger performance. *Journal of Applied Behavioral Science* 40(3): 323–343.
52. Webb, E. J., Campbell, D. T., Schwartz, R. D., Sechrest, L. (1999). *Unobtrusive Measures*. Newbury Park, CA: Sage Publications.
53. Pennebaker, J. W., & King, L. A. (1999). Linguistic styles: Language use as an individual difference. *Journal of Personality and Social Psychology* 77(6): 1296–1312.
54. Shi, W., Zhang, Y., & Hoskisson, R. (2019). Examination of CEO–CFO social interaction through language style matching: Outcomes for the CFO and the organization. *Academy of Management Journal* 62(2): 383–414.
55. Shi, W., & Chen, G. (2019). CEO-CFO relative optimism and firm mergers. Available at SSRN 3428760.
56. Liu, D., Fisher, G., & Chen, G. (2018). CEO attributes and firm performance: a sequential mediation process model. *Academy of Management Annals* 12(2):

789–816; Morgeson, F. P., Mitchell, T. R., & Liu, D. (2015). Event system theory: An event-oriented approach to the organizational sciences. *Academy of Management Review* 40(4): 515–537.

57. Morgeson, F. P., & DeRue, D. S. (2006). Event criticality, urgency, and duration: Understanding how events disrupt teams and influence team leader intervention. *Leadership Quarterly* 17(3): 273.

58. Shi, W., Hoskisson, R. E., & Zhang, Y. A. (2017). Independent director death and CEO acquisitiveness: Build an empire or pursue a quiet life? *Strategic Management Journal* 38(3): 780–792.

59. Chen, G., Crossland, C., & Huang, S. (2020). That could have been me: Director deaths, CEO mortality salience, and corporate prosocial behavior. *Management Science* 66(7): 3142–3161.

60. Shi, W., Zhang, Y., & Hoskisson, R. (2017). Ripple effects of CEO awards: Investigating the acquisition activities of superstar CEOs' competitors. *Strategic Management Journal* 38(10): 2080–2102.

61. Hollander, S., Pronk, M., & Roelofsen, E. (2010). Does silence speak? An empirical analysis of disclosure choices during conference calls. *Journal of Accounting Research* 48(3): 531–563; Pan, L., McNamara, G., Lee, J. J., Haleblian J., & Devers, C. E. (2018). Give it to us straight (most of the time): Top managers' use of concrete language and its effect on investor reactions. *Strategic Management Journal* 39(8): 2204–2225; Tetlock, P. C. (2007). Giving content to investor sentiment: The role of media in the stock market. *Journal of Finance* 62(3): 1139–1168; Tetlock, P. C., Saar–Tsechansky, M., & Macskassy, S. (2008). More than words: Quantifying language to measure firms' fundamentals. *Journal of Finance* 63(3): 1437–1467.

62. Matsumoto, D., Pronk, M., & Roelofsen, E. (2011). What makes conference calls useful? The information content of managers' presentations and analysts' discussion sessions. *Accounting Review* 86(4): 1383–1414.

63. Markus, H. R., & Kitayama, S. (1991). Culture and the self: Implications for cognition, emotion, and motivation. *Psychological Review* 98(2): 224.

64. Decter-Frain, A., & Frimer, J. A. (2016). Impressive words: Linguistic predictors of public approval of the US Congress. *Frontiers in Psychology* 7: 240; Pietraszkiewicz, A., Formanowicz, M., Gustafsson Sendén, M., Boyd, R. L., Sikström, S., & Sczesny, S. (2019). The big two dictionaries: Capturing agency and communion in natural language. *European Journal of Social Psychology* 49(5): 871–887.

65. Henisz, W. J., Dorobantu, S., & Nartey, L. J. (2014). Spinning gold: The financial returns to stakeholder engagement. *Strategic Management Journal* 35(12): 1727–1748.

Index